Contemporary Issues in Heterodox Economics

Heterodox economics can provide a more complete and robust explanation of economic realities than orthodox (or mainstream) economics. *Contemporary Issues in Heterodox Economics: Implications for Theory and Policy Action* argues that this greater explanatory power gives heterodox economics the ability to illuminate appropriate policy for the major crises of our time, as well as proffer the basis for a more rounded, pluralist approach to economic theory.

The chapters in this wide-ranging volume address some of the key issues facing the global economy, including the growing disparity of income/wealth between persons and economic areas, environmental degradation, issues associated with employment, and the regularity of economic/financial crises. The authors examine potential policy responses such as modern monetary theory, models of public ownership, and the need to move beyond standard concepts of growth. They also explore the deficiencies of orthodox economics, and contend that a more pluralist approach to economics is required in the public sphere, in academia, and in the classroom in order to help face the challenges of the twenty-first century.

This book is invaluable reading for students and scholars across the social sciences who are interested in alternatives to mainstream economic thinking.

Arturo Hermann is *Primo Ricercatore* at the Italian National Institute of Statistics (ISTAT), Italy.

Simon Mouatt is Emeritus Associate Professor in Economics at Solent University, UK.

Routledge Advances in Heterodox Economics

Series Editors: Mark Setterfield, *The New School for Social Research, USA* and **Peter Kriesler,** *University of New South Wales, Australia*

Over the past two decades, the intellectual agendas of heterodox economists have taken a decidedly pluralist turn. Leading thinkers have begun to move beyond the established paradigms of Austrian, feminist, Institutional-evolutionary, Marxian, Post Keynesian, radical, social, and Sraffian economics—opening up new lines of analysis, criticism, and dialogue among dissenting schools of thought. This cross-fertilization of ideas is creating a new generation of scholarship in which novel combinations of heterodox ideas are being brought to bear on important contemporary and historical problems.

Routledge Advances in Heterodox Economics aims to promote this new scholarship by publishing innovative books in heterodox economic theory, policy, philosophy, intellectual history, institutional history, and pedagogy. Syntheses or critical engagement of two or more heterodox traditions are especially encouraged.

Advancing Pluralism in Teaching Economics
International Perspectives on a Textbook Science
Edited by Samuel Decker, Wolfram Elsner and Svenja Flechtner

What is Heterodox Economics?
Conversations with Leading Economists
Andrew Mearman, Sebastian Berger and Danielle Guizzo

Principles and Pluralist Approaches in Teaching Economics
Towards a Transformative Science
Edited by Samuel Decker, Wolfram Elsner and Svenja Flechtner

Contemporary Issues in Heterodox Economics
Implications for Theory and Policy Action
Edited by Arturo Hermann and Simon Mouatt

For more information about this series, please visit: www.routledge.com/series/RAHE

Contemporary Issues in Heterodox Economics

Implications for Theory and Policy Action

Edited by
Arturo Hermann and Simon Mouatt

Routledge
Taylor & Francis Group
LONDON AND NEW YORK

First published 2021
by Routledge
2 Park Square, Milton Park, Abingdon, Oxon OX14 4RN

and by Routledge
52 Vanderbilt Avenue, New York, NY 10017

Routledge is an imprint of the Taylor & Francis Group, an informa business

British Library Cataloguing-in-Publication Data
A catalogue record for this book is available from the British Library

Library of Congress Cataloging-in-Publication Data
Names: Hermann, Arturo, editor. | Mouatt, Simon, editor.
Title: Contemporary issues in heterodox economics : implications for theory and policy action / edited by Arturo Hermann and Simon Mouatt.
Description: 1 Edition. | New York : Routledge, 2020. |
Series: Routledge advances in heterodox economics |
Includes bibliographical references and index.
Identifiers: LCCN 2020019645 (print) | LCCN 2020019646 (ebook)
Subjects: LCSH: Economics. | Economic policy–21st century.
Classification: LCC HB171.5 .C8655 2020 (print) |
LCC HB171.5 (ebook) | DDC 330–dc23
LC record available at https://lccn.loc.gov/2020019645
LC ebook record available at https://lccn.loc.gov/2020019646

ISBN: 978-0-367-36504-2 (hbk)
ISBN: 978-0-429-34641-5 (ebk)

Typeset in Times New Roman
by Newgen Publishing UK

MIX
Paper from responsible sources
FSC™ C013985

Printed in the United Kingdom
by Henry Ling Limited

Contents

List of contributors viii
Foreword by Alan Freeman xiv

Introduction 1
ARTURO HERMANN AND SIMON MOUATT

PART I
Pluralism, ethics and economic method 11

1 Dynamics versus statics: On the nature of heterodox and orthodox economics 13
ANDERS EKELAND

2 The past and the future: The philosophy and history of economics, and the emerging Risk Society 34
JON MULBERG

3 Hegel, Marx and the economics of inclusion: Towards an economic philosophy for a post-(non-)truth political class 48
SIMON MOUATT

4 What Marx and Kalecki/Post-Keynesians do not share, and why this is not a barrier to their learning from each other to their mutual advantage 63
NICK POTTS AND PHIL ARMSTRONG

PART II
Sustainable macroeconomy and structural policies 85

5 Green economics insights for economists: Diversity leads us out of our silos 87
MIRIAM KENNET

6 Value within the resource-based view of the firm: An approach drawing on the temporal single system interpretation of Marx 100
THORALF DASSLER

7 The economic imbalances of our days and the heterodox economics alternative 116
ARTURO HERMANN

PART III
Money and monetary regimes 139

8 Central banking and income inequality: The impact of monetary policy on income distribution 141
JALAL QANAS

9 Getting the Financial Crisis wrong: The dead end that is Neoclassical macro modeling 160
JOHN T. HARVEY

PART IV
Development issues and the role of public action 169

10 Center and periphery in global value chains: An interpretation based on the pioneers of development 171
CRISTINA FRÓES DE BORJA REIS AND FERNANDA GRAZIELLA CARDOSO

11 Models of fair public ownership: Lessons from Singapore and Hong Kong 191
ANDREW PURVES

12 The other side of paradise: The cost of tourism in the Caribbean 209
WENDY SEALY AND SIMON MOUATT

PART V
Improving pluralism in economics education 229

13 Heterodox Economic Journal Rankings revisited 231
BRUCE CRONIN

14 Institutional practice and the inadequacy of orthodox macroeconomics: A challenge for pluralism? 259
JAMES JUNIPER, ANDREW NADOLNY, GEORGE PANTELOPOULOS, AND MARTIN WATTS

15 Pluralism and heterodox economics 275
SHEILA DOW

16 Improving pluralism in economics education 282
JACK REARDON

Postscript by Victoria Chick 299
Index 302

Contributors

Phil Armstrong recently retired from full-time economics teaching. He now works part-time in the Engineering Division at York College, UK and is a final year, DPhil Economics student at the Solent University, under the supervision of Professor Nick Potts. He is a strong advocate of Modern Monetary Theory (MMT) and has recently written several articles, which have been published in peer-reviewed journals. He is an associate at the Gower Initiative for Modern Money Studies and a member of the Association for Heterodox Economics.

Fernanda Graziella Cardoso obtained a PhD in Economic Development at the University of Sao Paulo. She is Professor at Federal University of ABC (UFABC), coordinates the Bachelor of Economics course, and co-coordinates the Global Value Chains Research Group and the Center for Strategic Studies in Democracy, Development and Sustainability of UFABC. Her research interests include Socioeconomic Development, History of Economic Thought and Economic History.

Victoria Chick is Emeritus Professor of Economics at University College London, which has been her base throughout her career. She has written *The Theory of Monetary Policy* (Basil Blackwell, 1973; 2nd edn 1977) and *Macroeconomics After Keynes: A Reconsideration of The General Theory* (MIT Press, 1983) and numerous articles on money, macroeconomics (especially the economics of Keynes) and methodology. She has been Bundesbank Visiting Professor at the Free University in Berlin and held other visiting posts at the University of California at Berkeley, Santa Cruz, McGill University, Universities of Aarhus and Dijon, the Reserve Bank of Australia and the Federal Reserve Bank of New York, and served on the Council of the Royal Economic Society and several editorial boards. She is an adviser to Rethinking Economics.

Bruce Cronin is Professor of Economic Sociology at the University of Greenwich in London, UK. He is Director of Research for the Business School and Director of the Centre for Business Network Analysis, having previously been Head of the Department of International Business and Economics (2006–2014). He researches the ways in which social networks contribute to the formation and reproduction of epistemic communities within and among businesses and social elites. With Frederic Lee he was co-author of the influential *Research Quality Rankings of Heterodox Economic Journals* (Wiley Blackwell, 2010) and co-editor of the *Handbook of Research Methods in Heterodox Economics* (Edward Elgar, 2016). His work has appeared in the *Review of Political Economy*, *Critical Perspectives on Accounting*, *On the Horizon*, *American Journal of Economics and Sociology*, *European Journal of Management*, *Global Networks*, *International Journal of Knowledge, Culture and Change Management*, *Emergence: Complexity and Organization*, *International Journal of Decision Sciences*, *Risk and Management* and *Social Networks*. He serves as Treasurer of the Association of Heterodox Economics.

Thoralf Dassler obtained a Masters degree from the Technical University of Ilmenau, and has worked in Project Management at a leading car manufacturer in Germany. He then obtained an MSc in Business Research for Birmingham University and proceeded with PhD research at Aston University. Before joining Westminster Business School, he has worked as a research fellow at the Cranfield School of Management and at Queen Margaret University in Edinburgh, following which he took up a Lecturer position at Salford Business School. His research has the common underlying theme of economic value, currently focusing on value creation within the resource-based view of the firm.

Sheila Dow is Emeritus Professor of Economics at the University of Stirling, Scotland, and Adjunct Professor of Economics at the University of Victoria, Canada. Her main academic focus is on raising methodological awareness in the fields of macroeconomics, money and banking, and the history of economic thought (especially Hume, Smith and Keynes). While her career has primarily been in academia, she has held positions with the Bank of England and the Government of Manitoba, and as special adviser on monetary policy to the UK Treasury Select Committee. She has held positions such as Chair of INEM and is currently a member of the Academic Council of INET and of the Academic Advisory Board of the ISRF. Recent books include *Economic Methodology: An Inquiry* (OUP, 2002), *A History of Scottish Economic Thought*, co-edited with Alexander Dow (Routledge, 2006), and *Foundations for New Economic Thinking* (Palgrave Macmillan, 2012).

Anders Ekeland is senior advisor at Statistics Norway and a member of the Management Committee of the Association for Heterodox Economics since 2011. Anders has been working on economic theory, innovation, and environmental policies from Marxian and Schumpeterian perspectives.

Alan Freeman is co-director, with Radhika Desai, of the Geopolitical Economy Research Group (GERG) at the University of Manitoba. He was an economist at the Greater London Authority between 2000 and 2011, where he held the brief for the Creative Industries and the Living Wage.

He was a founder member of the Association for Heterodox Economics, is a special adviser to the *World Cities Cultural Forum*, and currently serves on the Board of Manitobans for the Arts, and Winnipeg Video Pool. He is a former Board member of the Winnipeg Symphony Orchestra. He wrote *The Benn Heresy* (Blackwells, 1982), a biography of British politician Tony Benn, and co-edited three books on value theory: *Ricardo, Marx, Sraffa* (Verso, 1984, with Ernest Mandel), *Marx and Non-equilibrium Economics* (Edward Elgar, 1996, with Guglielmo Carchedi), and *The New Value Controversy* (Edward Elgar, 2004, with Andrew Kliman). With Radhika Desai he edits GERG's news and analysis website www.newcoldwar.org. He is active in community affairs in Winnipeg having contributed to many debates on culture and creativity, and is a member of the Winnipeg Venezuela Peace Committee. His main works are on his website at www.geopoliticaleconomy.academia.edu/AlanFreeman.

Cristina Fróes de Borja Reis obtained her PhD in Economics at the Federal University of Rio de Janeiro (Brazil). She is Professor of Economics and International Relations at the Federal University of ABC (UFABC, Brazil), and currently a post-doctoral fellow at the International PosDoc Initiative (IPODI), Technische Universität Berlin (Germany). She co-coordinates the Global Value Chains Research Group of UFABC. Her research interests include Economic Development, Political Economy, International Economics, Industrial Organization and Macroeconomics.

John Harvey is Professor of Economics at Texas Christian University in Fort Worth, Texas, where he has been on the faculty for over 30 years. His main areas of research interest are exchange rates and business cycles and his teaching responsibilities include Intermediate Macroeconomics, International Monetary Economics, and Contending Perspectives in Economics. He has published over 40 refereed articles, two edited volumes, and two books. He served as the director of the International Confederation of Associations for Pluralism in Economics for six years.

Arturo Hermann is an economist working as *Primo Ricercatore* at the Italian National Institute of Statistics (ISTAT), Rome, Italy. His research interests include Institutional and Keynesian Economics, Sustainable and Equitable Development, Political Economy also considered in their relations with Psychology and Psychoanalysis. He has authored several books and book chapters with qualified publishers, and numerous articles in scholarly journals. With Routledge he has published *The Systemic Nature of the Economic Crisis: The Perspectives of Heterodox Economics and Psychoanalysis* in 2015. He is a member of the Advisory Board of the *International Journal of Pluralism and Economics Education* and scientific director of the journal *Il Pensiero Economico Moderno*. He is also on the Management Committee of the Association for Heterodox Economics and regularly participates in the Conferences and activities of various economics associations.

James Juniper is an economist and a conjoint academic in the Newcastle School of Business. Before entering academic life in 1990, he worked as a researcher and project officer in both the Commonwealth and State Public Services as well as for the United Trades and Labor Council in South Australia. His research interests include Post-Keynesian Macroeconomics, Continental Philosophy, Environmental and Economic Modelling, and the Digital Economy. In 2018 he published a Routledge Research Monograph on *The Economic Philosophy of the Internet of Things*. He is an Associate of the Centre for Full Employment and Equity (CofFEE) at the University of Newcastle and has supervised PhD research on Modern Monetary Theory and Stock-Flow-Consistent Macroeconomic Modelling.

Miriam Kennet is a member of Mansfield College at Oxford University, and the Environmental Change Institute, Oxford. Her research at South Bank University, and at Templeton College, Oxford focused on green issues and the strategic management of international firms. She was co-editor of *Green Economics, beyond Supply and Demand to Meeting People's Needs* (Green Audit, 1999) and has authored articles on green economics, stakeholder theory, corporate social responsibility, green jobs, geo-engineering, women's pay, climate change, poverty and biodiversity economics. She is CEO, director and co-founder of the Green Economics Institute, a member of the Chartered Institute of Purchasing and Supply (MCIPS) and the founder and editor of the *International Journal of Green Economics*. She is a regular trainer, speaker and adviser to governments and universities as well as running a very lively international intern college and international green economics conferences.

Simon Mouatt is Emeritus Associate Professor in Economics at Solent University, UK. He has taught at City University and currently teaches at Chichester University. His main research interests are in Monetary Economics, Economic Development, International Political Economy and Economic Philosophy from Marxian and Keynesian perspectives. He has authored/edited two books, has various chapters in qualified books and several articles in scholarly journals. He is also the current coordinator for the Association for Heterodox Economics and regularly participates in heterodox/pluralist economics conferences and related activities.

Jon Mulberg is currently an Honorary Associate in Economics at the Open University, where he teaches Social Sciences as an Associate Lecturer. Previously he has lectured in a number of universities throughout the UK in a range of disciplines. He has also worked for the UK Data Archive. Publications include *Social Limits to Economic Theory* (Routledge, 2013), an introductory statistics textbook *Figuring Figures* (Pearson, 2001), and a range of journal articles. At present he is the membership secretary of the Association of Heterodox Economics.

Andrew Nadolny is a lecturer in Economics at Newcastle Business School, Australia. He has a PhD from the University of Melbourne. His has 15 years' experience of teaching foundation Microeconomics and Macroeconomics. His research interests include Pedagogies of Economics, Labour markets and Environmental Economic Challenges.

George Pantelopoulos is currently a PhD Economics candidate at the University of Newcastle, Australia. His research interests include international macroeconomic theory and policy. He has presented papers at conferences in both Europe and Australia.

Andrew Purves was brought up in Hong Kong, Tokyo, New York and Edinburgh, and is now settled in London. He obtained a degree in Modern History and Politics and has worked in the retail of high-end contemporary furniture for the last 30 years, establishing his own business: Purves & Purves, in 1992. He has a special interest in the concept of Economic Rent, how it arises and is captured by landowners. He teaches Economics at the School of Philosophy and Economic Science in London. He has published a book that explores Hong Kong's Economic Miracle, *No Debt, High Growth, Low Tax* (Shepheard-Walwyn, 2015) and completed a Masters in Spatial Planning in 2018. He is currently completing a PhD at UCL in London, focusing on Singapore's use of land rent for public revenue.

Nick Potts is an Associate Professor of Economics at Solent University. He serves on the editorial board of *Capital and Class*. His research applies Marx's value theory and analysis of capitalism to the economic issues of today, including the 2008 crisis, globalisation, the environment, the Euro, knowledge-based production/the creative industries, and how banks, monetary policy and government finances really work.

Jalal Qanas is Assistant Professor in the College of Business and Economics at Qatar University. He obtained his PhD in Economics from Leeds University Business School in 2018. He has been Teaching Assistant in Economics for Undergraduate and Postgraduate students at the University of Leeds from 2013 to 2017. He has also taught a summer course in the Economics of Brexit at Oxford University. Before joining Qatar University, he was Visiting Lecturer at the University of West London. He has teaching experience in Macroeconomics, Microeconomics, Monetary Economics, Economics Controversies, International Political Economy, Economics of Brexit, International Finance and Trade, Economics for Management, Business Economics, Statistics and Mathematics for Economics and Business. His research interests are mainly in Macroeconomic Policies, Monetary Economics, Central Banking, Money and Banks, International Finance and Economics, Political Economy.

Jack Reardon earned his PhD in Economics from the University of Notre Dame. He is a research fellow at Cusanus University (Bernkastel-Kues, Germany), and a visiting lecturer at the Narsee Monjee Institute of

Management Studies (NMIMS) (Hyderabad, India). He currently teaches economics at the University of Wisconsin-Eau Claire. He is founding editor of *The International Journal of Pluralism and Economics Education*, and author of *The Handbook for Pluralist Economics Education* (Routledge, 2014), and *The Economics Curriculum: Towards a Radical Reformulation* (WEA Books, 2014, with Maria Madi). His latest book, *Introducing a New Economics* (Pluto Press, 2017), comports economics education with the 17 UN Sustainable Goals. He has just finished a novel and is currently working on a book exploring the intersection of physics, art, economics, psychology, and management with Graham Boyd, based in Brussels.

Wendy Sealy has a professional background that spans over 20 years in luxury resorts. She is currently a Senior Lecturer in Event Management at the University of Chichester in the United Kingdom. She has lectured at universities in Barbados, the United Kingdom, Nepal and Greece. Her research covers areas in pedagogy, tourism, hospitality, events management and health, safety and crisis management. She has researched and published several journal papers and books that address the impacts of transnational ownership of tourism businesses and distribution channels on tourist destinations. Other publications include stakeholder management in event management and more recently a book on event risk and crisis management, which was designated by the publishers as a thought-provoking discourse, making it a pinnacle publication from our full collection of 5,300+ reference books. She is regularly requested to be a keynote speaker at international conferences and has presented her work on heterodox economics at the Green Economics Conference and at the Sustainable Tourism Conference in Nepal. She was recently a keynote speaker on the impacts of COVID-19 on tourism, a webinar series called Impacts & Challenges on UN Sustainable Development Goals hosted by the *Journal of Sustainable Tourism*. She is also pioneering the use of more qualitative research methods including ethnography and mystery shopping in business research. She is Associate Editor of the *Journal on Tourism and Sustainability* and is on the editorial board of the *Journal of Adventure Tourism*.

Martin Watts is Emeritus Professor of Economics at the University of Newcastle, NSW, Australia and Research Associate of the Centre of Full Employment and Equity (CofFEE). He has published over 60 peer-reviewed articles in a broad range of leading international and domestic academic journals, and co-authored 16 book chapters. His areas of research expertise include contemporary macroeconomic theory and policy analysis, the conceptualisation and measurement of segregation and spatial modelling. He has secured funding for Australia Research Council Discovery Projects with colleagues and also participated in an ARC Linkage grant. He recently co-authored a textbook with William F. Mitchell and L. Randall Wray, entitled *Macroeconomics* (Palgrave Macmillan, 2019). He holds a BA from Essex University, an MA from Manchester University and a PhD from the University of British Columbia.

Foreword

Alan Freeman
VICE-PRESIDENT, ASSOCIATION OF HETERODOX ECONOMISTS

Pluralism: Scientific, emancipatory, and here to stay

Twenty-two years ago, a small fringe conference outside the UK's Royal Economic Society (RES) drew together researchers from approaches as diverse as Feminist, Post-Keynesian, Marxist, Institutionalist, Behavioural, and Austrian economics,[1] in the common endeavour of preventing the RES from excluding them. I am pleased and proud to introduce a collection of work demonstrating the maturity, creativity, and relevance of the results.

To be precise, the conference, proposed by Fred Lee, sought to end the RES's practice of assigning orthodox reviewers to judge heterodox papers, which generally resulted in their rejection. Making the excluded papers available to RES conference participants, in a kind of *Salle des Refusées*, offered an exhibition of what they were missing. In one sense, we did not succeed; the RES did not change its practice. Indeed, the fringe's impact worried it so much that it refused to countenance any repetition, on the memorable grounds that if it tolerated fringe events, it would appear to be excluding people.

Notwithstanding the Queen's concern at the results (Pettifor 2009; Pierce 2008; Stewart 2009), her Society remained steadfastly impervious to dissent. Yet, that small band achieved something unintended: it created something better. This is a strong statement; supported by the Association of Heterodox Economist's (AHE's) record, I propose to prove it.

What is 'good' economics? Pluralism and the problem of doctrine

Why should the public, and its economists, pay attention to the chapters in this volume? My response, which may surprise, is not that these chapters provide the 'right answer' to the huge and obvious problems of the modern world and national economy. This is impossible, since the authors are informed by a diverse range of approaches and theories, which are in conflict not just with the mainstream, but with one another. They cannot all be right; if they are, something serious has gone wrong.

The strength of the heterodox movement is not that it produces right answers, but that it produces economists who know how to get to them. This strength does not flow from any particular approach but from the method of enquiry. Put simply, if you have an economic problem, you are more likely to get a better solution by engaging economists who have read, grasped, and understood the multiple approaches that these articles present, and in consequence know how to tell a better theory apart from a worse one, than economists who understand only one approach which they simply repeat in new forms in response to every setback. The former, to define terms, are *pluralist* economists and the latter are *doctrinaire* economists.[2]

The reasons pluralists succeed where doctrinaires fail have been copiously documented.[3] The fundamental such reason, now widely recognised, is that scientific knowledge is attained only through controversy, by testing alternative theories and explanations against observed facts. A discipline that rules out the study of alternatives, on the grounds that it has already produced a single correct explanation of events, is doomed from the get-go.

To present a grossly oversimplified illustration, suppose on the basis of its current theory, the Treasury tells us a tax cut of 2 per cent will release funds for investment, raising output by 3 per cent and so reduce poverty by 5 per cent, and upon applying the tax cut, poverty really does fall by 5 per cent. Any charitable person would say the policy worked. But if the tax cut leads to profligate spending among the rich, and a rise in indigence among the poor, causing a 10 per cent increase in inequality with no rise in output, any critical person would say the policy failed. What policy, then, will actually reduce poverty? More significantly, what *theory* should such a policy be based on?

Clearly, since the policy did not work, we should find out which assumptions and theories produced it and cast around for others. The need to systematically question our beliefs and assumptions on the basis of events, especially (though not only) the outcome of policies based upon them, applies to complex real-world issues: reducing inequality, cutting carbon emissions, increasing life expectancy, increasing Jigme Singye Wangchuck's 'Gross National Happiness', developing national economies, or preventing bank crashes.

Orthodoxy, simply put, fails, not because any particular orthodox theory is wrong or right, but because it rejects the need for any systematic mechanism to replace failed theories with better ones. It reacts to failure not by questioning the theory that led to it, but by supposing the theory was badly applied, or overwhelmed by 'external' circumstances. When its policies result in huge and harmful outcomes, like the crash of 2008 or the immense rise in inequality and poverty produced by the IMF's structural adjustment policies, it resorts to minor tweaks, preserving the core theory as intact as possible without total embarrassment. Morgan et al. (2015) study this phenomenon exhaustively, citing Bernanke's (2010) instructive remarks:

> Some observers have suggested the need for an overhaul of economics as a discipline, arguing that much of the research in macroeconomics

> and finance in recent decades has been of little value or even counterproductive. Although economists have much to learn from this crisis, as I will discuss, I think that calls for a radical reworking of the field go too far.

This same Bernanke testified to the US Senate that the crash contradicted everything he ever believed in.[4] Yet here he is, two years later, telling us a radical reworking is uncalled for. Even this is not the most fundamental problem. The issue is not whether the field should be 'overhauled'—though it probably should be—but whether other alternatives should be, and should have been, explored. The orthodox research of 'past decades' may or may not be treated as valuable; the point is that the clearly valuable research of these same decades, which warned that the crash was coming, was suppressed and ignored. Bernanke can retain the whole of his discredited theory intact, provided only that he lets his colleagues examine the alternatives. This, he will not do, for fear that the alternatives may prevail. His priority is the preservation of doctrine. This has nothing to do with genuine science. The author Carl Sagan, who has probably reflected more on the nature of scientific enquiry than any contemporary, presciently noted in 1995:

> Science is more than a body of knowledge; it is a way of thinking. I have a foreboding of an America in my children's or grandchildren's time—when the United States is a service and information economy; when nearly all the key manufacturing industries have slipped away to other countries; when awesome technological powers are in the hands of a very few, and no one representing the public interest can even grasp the issues; when the people have lost the ability to set their own agendas or knowledgeably question those in authority; when, clutching our crystals and nervously consulting our horoscopes, our critical faculties in decline, unable to distinguish between what feels good and what's true, we slide, almost without noticing, back into superstition and darkness.
>
> (Sagan and Druyan 1995)

Sagan, in the same book, proposed a 'baloney detection kit', which could stand as a model of everything wrong with the current methods of economics and everything that must be done to correct it:

1. Wherever possible there must be independent confirmation of the 'facts'.
2. Encourage substantive debate on the evidence by knowledgeable proponents of all points of view.
3. Arguments from authority carry little weight—'authorities' have made mistakes in the past. They will do so again in the future. Perhaps a better way to say it is that in science there are no authorities; at most, there are experts.
4. Spin more than one hypothesis. If there's something to be explained, think of all the different ways in which it could be explained. Then think of tests

by which you might systematically disprove each of the alternatives. What survives, the hypothesis that resists disproof in this Darwinian selection among 'multiple working hypotheses', has a much better chance of being the right answer than if you had simply run with the first idea that caught your fancy.

5. Try not to get overly attached to a hypothesis just because it's yours. It's only a waystation in the pursuit of knowledge. Ask yourself why you like the idea. Compare it fairly with the alternatives. See if you can find reasons for rejecting it. If you don't, others will.
6. Quantify. If whatever it is you are explaining has some measure, some numerical quantity attached to it, you'll be much better able to discriminate among competing hypotheses. What is vague and qualitative is open to many explanations. Of course, there are truths to be sought in the many qualitative issues we are obliged to confront, but finding them is more challenging.
7. If there's a chain of argument, every link in the chain must work (including the premise)—not just most of them.
8. Occam's Razor. This convenient rule-of-thumb urges us, when faced with two hypotheses that explain the data equally well, to choose the simpler.
9. Always ask whether the hypothesis can be, at least in principle, falsified. Propositions that are untestable, unfalsifiable, are not worth much. Consider the grand idea that our Universe and everything in it is just an elementary particle—an electron, say—in a much bigger Cosmos. But if we can never acquire information from outside our Universe, is not the idea incapable of disproof? You must be able to check assertions out. Inveterate sceptics must be given the chance to follow your reasoning, to duplicate your experiments and see if they get the same result.

Genuinely scientific communities contain institutional mechanisms that force them to develop and consider alternatives. True, as Kuhn (1966) notes, even in the natural sciences, defenders of old ideas tend to preserve them beyond their useful shelf life. This is, however, an observation of behaviour, not a recommendation of best practice. When such resistance dominates, theory ossifies. The most relevant example is clerical resistance to heliocentrism, first formulated in 200 BC by Aristarchus of Samos (Heath 1913) but suppressed by the church until well after its famous persecution of Galileo.

Some bluntness is called for. An ossified practice is not a science: this is the situation of economics today, and this is why the pluralist movement is superior. The regulatory principle of orthodoxy is the reproduction of doctrine. Economics, organised around the defence of doctrine, is hence more accurately understood as a religion (Freeman 2007a; Nelson 2014 [2001]). Its criterion for endorsing or promoting theories (Freeman 2010) is conformity. Far from suppressing wrong theories, this propagates them, by the mechanism of 'adverse selection'—a preference for economists who conform to the dominant theory above those who explore alternatives to it.

This is cemented in place by 'regulatory capture'; the discipline promotes persons, publications and institutions whose explanations find favour with those who fund them and weeds out those which find disfavour. The banks being the principal source of economic funding, and national states being the second, both with vested interests in the results, theory simply tracks their interplay. This is exacerbated by the employment of economists, a kind of revolving door between banks, governments, and academia. This is why its results are so poor, and this is why pluralism is required.

Economics in its own words

The above are not wild, conspiratorial, or unsupported assertions. They are well-documented and indeed, proudly proclaimed, perhaps most notoriously by Richard Portes, Secretary-General of the RES from 1992–2008, who was paid £58,000 in 2007 by the Icelandic Chamber of Commerce to co-author a report giving a clean bill of health to Iceland's banks only a few months before they collapsed (Wade and Sigurgeirsdóttir 2012; Black 2014). Might Iceland have usefully considered a second opinion? Clearly not: when their judgement was questioned by economist Robert Wade, Portes and co-author Fridrik Baldursson used their *Financial Times* column of 4 July 2008, and several subsequent letters, to defend the soundness of Icelandic banks and question Wade's professional competence:

> By end-2007, their [the Icelandic Banks'—AF] funding structure was similar to their peers in other Nordic countries, in many cases with better deposit-loan ratios and maturity structures. They have had higher returns on equity and higher capital ratios than their Nordic peers. And the Icelandic banks had virtually no exposure to the toxic securities that almost all other banks did buy. These facts do not square with aspersions about people with 'scant experience in modern banking' ... The rest of Prof Wade's comments are political, including rumour mongering. This and his carelessness with the data are regrettable in the fragile conditions of today's international financial markets.

Portes's (2008) distaste for second opinions was forcefully expressed in his valedictory address on retiring from the RES, in which he laid out his objections to European referees who rejected a grant application because '[D]espite the excellence of the partners' record within mainly economic science, they fail to include alternative, complementary or even competing approaches', in the following terms:

> The proposal failed. Referees like these have regrettably been taken seriously. Mediocrity is rationalised on the grounds that it it [sic] is hard for the 'heterodox' to publish in top journals...

The words deserve careful attention. First, the referees did not request a 'heterodox' view but simply a *different* view, which could be 'alternative, complementary or even competing'. Portes studiously elides this with 'heterodox', which can only be interpreted to mean that *any* dissenting view is mediocre. Second, he does not even consider that the reason 'heterodox' papers are unpublished may be faults in the top journals, rather than the papers. If the criterion for publication is that the author must agree with Richard Portes, publication would indeed be difficult—but not because the contributions are mediocre. In fact, economic journals have a long record of rejecting papers, since recognised as stellar and seminal. Gans and Shepherd (1994) contacted over 140 leading economists to enquire into their experience of rejection:

> More than 60 per cent responded, many with several blistering pages ... Paul Samuelson states 'Yes, journals have rejected papers of mine, some of them later regarded as "classics." I used to say, with only moderate exaggeration, that the quality of papers of mine at first rejected is not less than the quality of papers accepted at once.' Our survey indicates that many papers that have become classics were rejected initially by at least one journal—and often by more than one.

These facts, and Shepherd's (1994) landmark book *Rejected!* cast a different light on the notion that journal publication is a criterion of merit. Of course, it should be, however, when the journals are themselves simply a cog in a machine for producing doctrine by means of doctrine, it is not the writers whose conduct needs attention. The adverse consequences of the doctrinal system were fully documented by the leaders and official institutions of economics themselves—after the 2008 crash made them impossible to ignore any longer. The IMF's independent evaluation office, in its investigation into the conduct of the IMF in the run-up to the crisis (IEO 2011), found that:

> The IMF's ability to correctly identify the mounting risks was hindered by a high degree of groupthink, intellectual capture, a general mind-set that a major financial crisis in large advanced economies was unlikely, and incomplete analytical approaches.

Is not 'groupthink' just another word for the domination of conformity over the unprejudiced study of the facts? Which economists were 'intellectually captured', and is it not reasonable to count Portes and his colleagues among them? Who, exactly, were they 'captured' by and shouldn't the Icelandic Chamber of Commerce, and its like, be numbered among the captors? Was the 'general mindset' informed by a theory, and did that theory not predict that a crisis was 'unlikely', and does this not call for a search for alternative theories? Finally, if analytical approaches were 'incomplete' then why is the economics profession a closed door to those alternative approaches that might complete them?

In 2009 (Stewart 2009) the Queen summoned Mervyn King, Bank of England Governor, to a private audience in the wake of the crash to ask what he was doing about it. She received a letter signed by London School of Economics professor Tim Besley, a member of the Bank of England monetary policy committee, and the historian of government Peter Hennessy, following a seminar at the British Academy attended by Treasury permanent secretary Nick MacPherson, Goldman Sachs chief economist Jim O'Neill, *Observer* economics columnist William Keegan, Paul Tucker, deputy governor of the Bank of England, Vernon Bogdanor, a constitutional expert from Oxford University, and HSBC's chief economist, Stephen King.

> '[F]inancial wizards', says the letter, managed to convince themselves and the world's politicians that they had found clever ways to spread risk throughout financial markets. 'it is difficult', they concluded, 'to recall a greater example of wishful thinking combined with hubris … Everyone seemed to be doing their own job properly on its own merit. And according to standard measures of success, they were often doing it well.' 'The failure', they continue, 'was to see how collectively this added up to a series of interconnected imbalances over which no single authority had jurisdiction.'

Was not the RES, arrogating to itself the right to regulate everything deemed legitimate economics in the UK, such a 'single authority'? Is it not time to question the 'standard measures' that its secretary energetically and gainfully promoted, and which led to such collective folly?

Robin Jackson, chief executive and secretary of the British Academy, noted: 'The global recession is a huge development, and it is reasonable to ask to what extent it could have been foreseen. What's more, we can't say "never again" if we don't fully understand what occurred'.

But how can this be achieved by asking the very same experts who produced the crisis, to identify their mistakes by applying the very same theoretical framework that they used to produce it? When the ill-fated Challenger space mission crashed, causing the tragic death of seven astronauts, NASA and the White House established an independent commission of enquiry (Rogers 1986) whose mission was to 'prevent any recurrence of the failure related to this accident' and to 'reduce the risks in future flights'. The reason for an independent enquiry was, precisely, that the people who produce failures cannot be expected to explain it; it was necessary to bring in independent expertise employing fresh thinking to get to the bottom of its causes. Were the British monarch's economists' response to her reasonable question subjected to the mildest judicial enquiry, it would not stand up for a second. Culpability oozes from every pore.

'What we need', said Besley, 'is a forum where people can come together on a very open basis, to provide challenges and have a debate'. But, dear Professor

Besley, such a forum exists; it is exactly what the AHE proposed in 1998 and has systematically fought for, ever since, as has a growing body of pluralist economists whose numbers, according to the World Economics Association, now exceed 13,000 worldwide. We humbly await your exalted presence.

The most telling comment comes from Luis Garicano, to whom the Queen directed her initial question:

> She seemed very interested, and she asked me: 'How come nobody could foresee it?' I think the main answer is that people were doing what they were paid to do, and behaved according to their incentives, but, in many cases, they were being paid to do the wrong things from society's perspective.

If they were being paid to do the wrong thing, then any normal enquiry would conclude that society should stop paying them, or at least, pay them to do something else. But second, a definite group of people *did* foresee it—a fact that is not mentioned in any of the above responses to the Queen. These were the very people on whom the RES has closed its door since well before 1998. The problem is not that the economics profession is blind: it is that it refuses to see.

Pluralism vs heterodoxy: The fallacy of the wise doctrinaire

An incontrovertible conclusion from the above is that 'good economic practice' is not reducible to 'technical competence'. Somebody who applies a wrong method, no matter how diligently, will get wrong answers. This may seem obvious—but it tells us that the benchmark of the UK's Quality Assurance Agency (QAA), on which basis British Universities have trained a half-generation of economists (Freeman 2007b, 2009), is wrong, precisely because it reduces economic competence to the technical capacity to reproduce the conclusions of others. No: economic competence consists in discovering what is absent from the conclusions of others.

A second conclusion is that pluralism is *scientific*; it constitutes the scientific method in the field of economics. The 'good' economist is one who can select, from a variety of possible theories, those that best explain the observed facts. The doctrinaire cannot do this, because he only ever tests one theory.[5] If this leads to mistakes, he leaves himself no option but to repeat it—Albert Einstein's definition of insanity. The pluralist, even if she starts out wrong, will make her way to better answers because she has been trained to learn from error.

This leads to my most controversial conclusion, which the AHE reached slowly through respectful engagement: the scientific quality of good economics does not depend on an economist's convictions but on the determination with which she seeks out, and recognises, error. It is, unfortunately, as easy to be a bad Keynesian or a bad Marxist as a bad neoliberal. All you have to do is ignore uncomfortable facts and close your mind to the alternatives. Indeed, it would be a misunderstanding to see heterodoxy as the idea that neoclassicals contribute nothing to economic understanding. In establishing the UK statistical standard for measuring employment and output in the Creative Industries (Bakhshi et al. 2011, 2013) I, and other economists, worked perfectly effectively together, bringing our different persuasions to bear on the practical study of this new but rapidly growing economic sector. The CJE special edition on Samuelson's 'Whiggish History' project (Freeman, Chick, and Kayatekin 2014) was a spirited collaboration between Keynesians, Marxists, Austrians and others in which contributors respected both the facts and each other.

The central issue is pluralism itself. Any economist who sets out to solve an economic problem by supposing he already knows how to do it is bound, sooner or later, to get it wrong. Therefore, good economics cannot be arrived at by substituting one doctrine for another, an idea I term the 'fallacy of the wise doctrinaire'. It took the AHE a while to arrive at this point, and not all heterodoxy agrees with it.

Fred's original idea, which he later gracefully abandoned, was that the AHE could express some kind of united, vaguely left-wing, alternative to neoclassical economics. But first, we were not united on anything much except our opposition to the behaviour of the RES, and second, the Austrians, an important component of the AHE, are politically several degrees to the right of the neoclassicals. The AHE overcame these difficulties by organising consciously to foster *engagement*. Instead of segmenting its conferences into siloed 'schools', it constructed panels around *issues*—finance, development, pricing, or whatever—deliberately placing speakers from different 'schools' in each panel.

The pluralist movement is hence a larger break than is generally recognised with predecessors that explored or promoted particular theoretical frameworks. The AHE is not a simple extension of Post-Keynesianism, Marxism, Institutionalism, or Evolutionary Economics, least of all is it the inheritor of the Radical Economics movement in the US, or the UK's Conference of Socialist Economists, born of the radicalisation of the 1960s.

The difference arises because of the history of neoliberalism, which effectively dethroned the (orthodox) Keynesians early in the 1980s, starting with the 'neoclassical counter-revolution' (Todaro and Smith 2009) in the international financial institutions, which, by degrees, became a new orthodoxy. Typified by blind faith in markets, neoliberalism has undoubtedly contributed to harmful economic disasters, which has driven its opponents to band together to defend the alternatives. This gave rise to the idea that heterodox economics consists of 'schools'—people of like mind. The AHE brought together economists of *unlike* mind. Its purpose was not to reach agreement but to promote controversy. It proposed no special alternative to the mainstream; its aim was to ensure that *all* viable alternatives were available to students, clients and researchers in economics.

These represent two very different notions of how to confront current orthodoxy; more often than not, they turned out to be two conflicting notions, a difficulty at the heart of the problem of reforming economics. This arose because 'schools' such as Keynesians, Marxists, Behaviourists, or Institutionalists are divided within, but seek to make a common cause to replace the reigning orthodox doctrine with theories they see as superior. This leads in short order to an urge to replace the reigning doctrine with an alternative doctrine. Schools then easily become policemen; 'breaking ranks' is seen as a danger to an endangered cause, and dissent becomes a threat. When a 'school', conceived of in this way, captures a University department, or secures funding for a Thinktank, unless structured as pluralist from the get-go, practices every bit as intolerant as in the neoliberal bastions can easily emerge.

The 'any schools' concept of heterodox economics then mutates into a kind of Westphalian doctrinal system, in which *cui regio eius religio* reigns supreme. In order to present a unified view, a 'school' must define which of the conflicting views within its own ranks should be presented to the outside world. A mainstream Keynesian will differ from a New Keynesian and both will differ from a Post-Keynesian. New Institutionalists differ profoundly from Old Institutionalists.[6] Sraffian Marxists differ equally profoundly from Temporal Single System Interpretation Marxists and indeed from Marx himself, as they readily acknowledge; each will differ from Value Form Marxists, New Interpretation Marxists, Political Marxists, and so on.

Any notion, therefore, that the reigning orthodoxy can be defeated by substituting 'good' theories for the 'bad' theories in current favour, immediately runs into the problem that nobody agrees on what a 'good' theory is.

As Andrew Kliman and I (Freeman and Kliman 2008 [1996]) pointed out, beneath the surface of every heterodoxy lies an orthodoxy in waiting. Suppressive tendencies are as manifest within the schools as in the mainstream. I vividly recall, not long after the 2008 crash, a high-level UK meeting chaired by a prominent Keynesian to present a prominent Behaviouralist, both of whom shall be nameless. Radhika Desai pointed out, when discussion turned to practical matters, that Keynes called for the Euthanasia of the Rentier and the Socialisation of Investment. The alacrity with which the chair assured listeners that Keynes said no such thing, or that if he did, it was a mere aside, was a performative rival to the Denial of the Apostle Peter.

The doctrinal method in economics is *systemic*. It is not reducible to the triumph of neoliberalism. If neoliberalism were tomorrow pronounced anathema, if Paul Krugman were put in charge of the IMF and David Harvey of the World Bank, economics would be no less doctrinaire than today.[7] Doctrinaire tendencies are embedded in the entire institution of economics; they are constitutive of what an economist *is*. Why?

Diagnosis

The practices described above, if we are honest, do not just occur at the top levels but throughout the institution that is 'economics'. The material forces that underlie these systemic problems (Colander et al. 2009) go well beyond the triumph of neoliberalism, which is where most criticism stops, and arise from the nature of economics as an institution.

We live in a world of money. It is impossible to live without it. The language of money—economics—is therefore universal. When Margaret Thatcher said a government must manage its money like a household, this assertion may have been wrong, but everyone understood it. Money is mysterious. As Marx and Keynes noted, it stands between producers and consumers. In most cases we don't even know who the producers are, and even when we do, we have no idea of what life is like in their countries, factories, or families. Nor, conversely, do they know anything about us. We both know only the price. Naturally, we want a better price, so we both take part in the market, which is even more mysterious. We then erect, in our imaginations, the market into a deity, an entity above us all to which we pay obeisance, in preference to simply talking to each other or getting to know each other. Yet nobody really understands the market. The most revered economists in the world failed to predict it would produce the crash of 2008. In news reports, the market acquires a personality. We are told that the markets 'do not like' what some president just said, or 'tell us' we should sell our public assets. The market becomes a new kid on the Olympian block, seeing off the gods of fire, love and war in short order. Even those who pray to the old gods pay homage to the new; whether they seek love, victory, or merely life, the god of money is on hand to intercede.

This is just another way of saying that the market conceals what goes on. Its appearance is different from its essence, from what it really is. Economic *theory* becomes a necessary part of life, whether or not economists as such are surplus to requirements. People need to understand the market but cannot do so without some systematic way of thinking, even if this goes no further than balancing budgets and shopping wisely. This may make for a poor theory, but a theory it is. In an emancipated society, economic knowledge would be a universal right. Just as everyone is entitled to read and write, they would be entitled to know which economic measures can abolish poverty or stop the planet roasting.

This, however, is not what has happened. Early in the twentieth century (Desai 2016) economics became the monopoly of a select group of people, of 'experts' who run the banks and dictate policies to governments. These experts command awesome and unwarranted respect: in 2002 the Argentine peso collapsed because of neoliberal policies of pegging it to the US dollar, selling off Argentina's productive assets, and lading the country, a poster child for structural adjustment, with unrepayable debt. Rudiger Dornbusch then proposed that the country should be run by a committee of economists. This Dictatorship of the Econocracy amounted to handing the fire brigade to the arsonists; nevertheless, opinion polls showed, 50 to 60 per cent of the very same people who had violently turfed out three successive presidents, supported it.

From this arises the peculiar and unique relation between economics, government, and banking. Economics is, essentially, the language that money speaks to power. As such, it has a price. Economic theory is not produced: it is purchased. When governments want to take unpopular measures like cutting welfare, or indeed popular ones with adverse consequences, like reducing taxes on the wealthy, they hardly ever state what they actually intend. They do not say that they want poor people to die early in pain and rich people to dance on their graves, but explain their actions as *economic* decisions, designed to balance the budget, unleash trickle-down, stimulate the economy, and all these other wonderful yet counter-intuitive achievements which 'our economists tell us will work'.

Economists also exercise direct political power. 'Structural adjustment' was not just a take-it-or-leave-it suggestion: it was imposed, by 'conditionalities' which the IMF attached to its loans. Within governments, budgetary control dominates all other considerations: The Treasury is the only UK Ministry that scrutinises other Ministers' policies *before* they are released for Cabinet discussion.

Naturally, therefore, politicians have a vested interest in obtaining economic advice that endorses what they intend to do. They may even believe their own rhetoric: that starving the poor will foster self-improvement, or rewarding the greedy will convert them into philanthropists. It makes no difference: they then seek out economists who 'sound sensible'—that is, confirm their prejudices.

It is well-known that monetarism, when Thatcher came to office, was an obscure theoretical backwater, politely ridiculed by the mainstream of the time. So, she sought out economists whose theories corresponded to her political prejudices and saw to it that their ideas became Treasury doctrine. Friedman was a heterodox economist, on the fringes of the Samuelsonian Chicago mainstream, until Western governments found it expedient to reverse the entrenched 'Keynesian' wisdom that accompanied the post-war boom, and found, in the ideas of the Mont Pellerin circle, a ready-made justification for what they had already set their hearts on.[8] Therefore, when Keynes wrote: 'Practical men who believe themselves to be quite exempt from any intellectual influence, are usually the slaves of some defunct economist. Madmen in authority, who hear voices in the air, are distilling their frenzy from some academic scribbler of a few years back', he could not have been more wrong.

The scribblers do not provoke the madness; the madness seeks out scribblers. The madmen do not 'hear' voices; they listen for them. Their frenzy is not distilled from the ideas of scribblers; it is commandeered from the feeders of habits. To pursue the analogy to its dismal end, power and money join hands to turn economists into pushers. They kindle, in the hearts of our brightest researchers, a thirst for patronage nourished by the belief that supplying what madmen desire will propel them to heights of fame and recognition. They pervert the thirst for enlightenment into a brute concern to satisfy superiors. They reduce our centres of learning to manufactories for economic catechisms, purveyors of indulgences, and prisons for the confinement of reason. It is time for society to claim back, from its economists, what every citizen should be entitled to: the right to understand, scrutinise, and choose between rival economic theories that actually determine whether she attains life, liberty, or happiness.

Prognosis

Having outlined the malady, let us consider the cure. Three developments point to ways forward. The first is the growth of pluralism itself. The second is growing concern with the *ethical* responsibilities of economists. The third is the *assertive pluralism* movement, which seeks to develop codified, and peer-reviewed accreditation systems that offer the public some guarantee of pluralist teaching and practice.

The pluralist movement has grown from early beginnings to a worldwide movement with a mass following, in which the AHE was only a catalyst. It had responded to important precedents. A seminal 1992 call for pluralism (Hodgson et al. 1992) was signed by forty-three leading economists, whose four winners of the 'Sveriges Riksbank Prize in Economic Sciences in Memory of Alfred Nobel'[9] included Paul Samuelson. This responded to growing concerns within economics with *La Pensée Unique*—a single, unified and doctrinaire view of how economies work, leading to the[10] systematic exclusion of alternative paradigms from publication, from appointment, from curricula and funding. They called for:

> [A] new spirit of pluralism in economics, involving critical conversation and tolerant communication between different approaches. Such pluralism should not undermine the standards of rigor; an economics that requires itself to face all the arguments will be a more, not a less, rigorous science.

The year 1993 saw the foundation of the International Confederation of Associations for Pluralism in Economics (ICAPE)—still going strong. It called for:

> greater diversity in theory and method in economic science. A new spirit of pluralism will foster a more critical and constructive conversation among practitioners of different approaches. Such pluralism will strengthen standards of scientific inquiry in the crucible of competitive exchange.

These initiatives laid the foundation for ever-broader movements of dissent, especially among students, the seminal initiative being the French 'Post-autistic economics' (PAE), launched in 2000 with a petition calling for 'a pluralism of approaches, adapted to the complexity of the objects and to the uncertainty surrounding most of the big questions in economics', and supported by a teachers' petition arguing that:

> [p]luralism must be part of the basic culture of the economist. People in their research should be free to develop the type and direction of thinking to which their convictions and field of interest lead them. In a rapidly evolving and evermore complex world, it is impossible to avoid and dangerous to discourage alternative representations.

PAE, assisted by pioneers ably led by Edward Fullbrook, grew into the World Economics Association (WEA),[11] founded in 2011, now with over 13,000 members worldwide. It pioneered Open Peer Review, publishes three journals and has hosted 15 online conferences since 2012.

The French student initiative was followed by another from Cambridge students calling for an 'opening up' of economics. 'We are not arguing against mainstream methods', they explained,

> but believe in a pluralism of methods and approaches justified by debate. Pluralism as a default implies that alternative economic work is not simply tolerated, but that the material and social conditions for its flourishing are met, to the same extent as is currently the case for mainstream economics. That is what we mean when we refer to an 'opening up' of economics.

The 2008 crash ignited a swathe of student initiatives in the country's premier Universities: *Rethinking Economics* started in the LSE and has morphed into a worldwide network animated by a permanent thinktank:[12] its work includes Earle et al.'s (2016) excellent *Econocracy*. The 'Post-Crash Economics' movement, initiated by Manchester students,[13] hit national headlines when the economics department dismissed a lecturer it had hired explicitly to meet student requests for a broader and more diverse curriculum. An international call from Glasgow students (ISIP 2016), signed by 65 student associations from 30 countries, declared:

> It is not only the world economy that is in crisis. The teaching of economics is in crisis too, and this crisis has consequences far beyond the university walls. What is taught shapes the minds of the next generation of policymakers, and therefore shapes the societies we live in … The real world should be brought back into the classroom, as well as debate and a pluralism of theories and methods. Such change will help renew the discipline and ultimately create a space in which solutions to society's problems can be generated.

The strength of pluralism in Europe was already clear from the size of the European Association for Evolutionary Political Economy (EAEPE), an umbrella heterodox organisation with more members than its neoclassical counterpart. It was confirmed at the 2012 founding conference of the Association Française pour l'Économie Politique (AFEP), jointly organised with AHE and the SOAS-based International Initiative for Promoting Political Economy (IIPPE) and attracting over 500 participants. The French hosts explained that nothing since PAE had improved—not a single heterodox Professor had been appointed in 25 years.

Space does not allow a proper assessment of the significant developments in China and the Global South. Two things are, however, clear. First, pluralism, as a movement *within* economics, has reached critical mass. As a method of teaching, researching, practicing and publishing, it is completely practical for employers, citizens, journals, and institutions of learning to reorganise on pluralist principles. Second, the chief obstacle is neither lack of means nor lack of will, but conscious obstruction; that is to say, it is a question of governance.

Treatment

An old lightbulb joke runs: 'How many psychoanalysts does it take to change a lightbulb?' The answer is 'Only one—but the bulb must really want to change'. Economics will change if society demands that it change. The root cause of its dysfunctionality is not the way economists behave—it is what society asks them to do.

George DeMartino's (2011) enquiry into the ethical outlook of working economists sheds significant light on this. He was motivated by the reasonable question 'should economists have a code of ethics?' He found, surprisingly, that a significant majority are ethically troubled at what they are asked to do. Indeed, some kind of ethical standard would *protect* economists who feel that, unless they give 'the answer the boss wants' they risk their jobs and reputations. The idea that society should find ways to require ethical responsibility of its economists is hence kicking at an open door (Freeman 2015).

The stock economics response is unique: the economist practices 'positive' economics. He merely tells society what its options are, and society then decides what to do. The economist bears no responsibility for what happens. Among the many errors in this myth, one stands out: what happens if the economist gets it wrong? The very idea that if an economist does his job, he cannot get the answers wrong, exposes the doctrinal presumptions behind the separation. He is 'merely a technician' as IMF representative Anoop Singh said, after the peso crash, in explaining why ordinary Argentinians must not only suffer the personal ruin brought on by the crash, but also pay off the huge debts run up under the IMF's insanely corrupt protégé, ex-president Menem. But as we have seen, first, he is not a mere technician but a hired agent and, second, even with the best will in the world, economists *do* get things wrong.

When this happens, they cause harm. As we have seen, even the economics profession recognises it caused a few difficulties in the run-up to the 2008 crash; there is also a strong case, which we have not examined in detail, that structural adjustment was a very harmful policy causing millions, if not hundreds of millions, of deaths; and at least one of the architects of 'shock therapy' admits the damage it caused.

DeMartino carefully dissects the issues via the concept of 'econogenic harm' or harm done by economists, in an analogy with the concept 'iatrogenic harm' coined by the medical profession to describe harm done by doctors. It arises, simply, when the advice given by the economists makes things worse.

Here is where pluralism comes in. If an economist is asked 'what policy do you recommend?' of course, she has a duty to make some kind of recommendation. *She also has a duty to explain that there are other possible answers.* What is missing from the positive-normative separation, at least in its doctrinal form, is the *right of the client to choose*. The Argentines did not have to take Singh's advice, and wisely decided to pay off the IMF and have done with it, but not to pay off the 'odious debt' owing to the vulture funds. Argentina went through a significant recovery before the New York Courts ruled that they had to pay the vultures and a new president—roundly defeated in the October 2019 elections—re-imposed the IMF formula. Now, we can make whatever judgement we like on whether the Kirchners, Macri, or the new president Fernandez, are best for Argentina. What we cannot claim is that there was no economic choice. The decision to resume debt repayments on odious terms was a *political and legal* decision, not an economic decision.

Pluralism, in short, suggests that the ethical economist has a duty to offer the public a real choice—to emancipate it economically. The significance of the lightbulb joke now becomes clear. The systemic problems of economics will only begin to erode once the public starts to demand pluralism—as a political and legal right. Indeed, if an economist could be sued in law, or stripped of the right to practice, for failing to disclose alternatives, or for presenting untried and risky solutions as sure-fire fixes, the climate in the profession would change overnight. Yet that is exactly the way the medical and legal professions, which abound with checks, scrutiny, and client rights, understand their ethical responsibility. These may not always work—but at least they are acknowledged to be necessary.

Society can, therefore, not only improve the economics that is, so to speak, delivered to its door, but also provide much-needed support for economists who desire to act ethically, by starting to insist on pluralist practice, pluralist teaching, and pluralist research—exactly as did the unfortunate European targets of Richard Portes' ire, but on a scale sufficient to affect matters. Pluralism should be written into the *contracts* that govern any disbursement of money to economists—whether for teaching, for research, for publication, for employment, or for consultancy.

This is practical. It imposes what Andy Denis (2009) terms 'assertive pluralism', converting it from a mere right to a social duty. It opens the way for two closely related UK developments: 'Promoting Economic Pluralism' (PEP)[14] and the 'Reteaching Economics' initiative.[15] The PEP project seeks to codify criteria for pluralist teaching and practice, leading to accreditation—credentials agreed on and scrutinised by accepted peer review processes. This may seem like a small step, but its implications are large. Through initiatives like 'Reteaching', economists can demonstrate, using accreditation systems, the practicality of a pluralist institutional relation between society and its economists.

From there to a proper transformation of the system is a huge step, and the lightbulb joke retains its full relevance. Unless society asks for change, it will not get it. However, 22 years ago, a small group of dissidents took a small step towards establishing an alternative to the doctrinal system that then produced the disasters of recent years. In that short time, the numbers of committed pluralists have swelled to tens of thousands. If public support grows as fast, the door to economic emancipation will be open; once open, we are confident it will not close.

Notes

1 The ecologists arrived not long after.
2 In this chapter 'doctrinaire' is interchangeable with 'monotheoretic', which pluralists commonly speak of.
3 It is difficult to do justice to the now massive literature on pluralism, and I apologise to those not cited. Sent (2006), Denis (2009), Morgan et al. (2015), Freeman et al. (2014), Jo and Todorova (2015), and Earle et al. (2016) all treat the issue in detail and contain extensive bibliographies. The *International Journal of Pluralism and Economics Education*, edited by Jack Reardon, is also an important source.
4 Sanders (2009), arguing against Bernanke's reappointment, supplies an instructive list of his words and actions prior to the crash. Comparing these with his 2010 evaluation, the remarkable thing is how few of his wrong judgements he has retracted.
5 For literary simplicity, I use male gender pronouns to refer to individuals who practice doctrinaire methods, and the female gender for those who don't.
6 As an editor responsible for an article criticising the New Institutionalism, I had the enlightening experience of receiving two reviews, both from institutionalists, one of which encouraged immediate publication, whilst the other proposed outright rejection.
7 Both Paul Stiglitz and Justin Yifu Lin expressed considerable frustration with their own staff's unwillingness, during their term of office at the World Bank, to contemplate anything except the Washington Consensus.
8 Which may account for Samuelson's conversion, in the 1992 declaration, to the pluralism he scorned elsewhere.
9 There is no Economics 'Nobel Prize'. The award, which both the economics profession and the press wrongly refer to by this name, was established in 1968 and is based, as the site archly records, 'on a donation received by the Nobel Foundation in 1968 from Sveriges Riksbank on the occasion of the Bank's 300th anniversary'.
10 See https://icape.org/
11 See www.worldeconomicsassociation.org.
12 See www.rethinkeconomics.org.
13 See www.post-crasheconomics.com.
14 See https://economicpluralism.org.
15 See http://reteacheconomics.org/; see also the heterodox pages of the TRUE network at www.economicsnetwork.ac.uk/heterodox.

References

Bakhshi, H., A. Freeman, and P. Higgs. 2013. A Dynamic Mapping of the UK's Creative Industries, NESTA, January.

Bakhshi, H., A. Freeman, and J. Potts. 2011. *State of Uncertainty: Innovation through Experimentation*. NESTA provocation 14. London: NESTA.

Baldursson, F. M. and R. Portes. 2008. 'Criticism of Icelandic Economy Does Not Square with the Facts', *Financial Times*, 4 July.

Bernanke, B. 2010. 'Implications of the Financial Crisis for Economics', lecture, Princeton, NJ, 24 September. Available at: www.federalreserve.gov/newsevents/speech/bernanke20100924a.htm.

Black, W. K. 2014. 'The Icelandic Chutzpah Prize is Retired: Portes and Baldursson Win by Losing', New Economic Perspectives website. Available at: http://neweconomicperspectives.org/2014/01/icelandic-chutzpah-prize-retired-portes-baldursson-win-losing.html.

Colander, D., H. Foellmer, A. Haas, M. Goldberg, K. Juselius, and A. Kirman. 2009. *The Financial Crisis and the Systemic Failure of Academic Economics*. Available at: www.debtdeflation.com/blogs/wpcontent/uploads/papers/Dahlem_Report_EconCrisis021809.pdf.

DeMartino, G. F. 2011. *The Economist's Oath*. Oxford: Oxford University Press.

Denis, A. 2009. Special Issue of the *International Review of Economics Education on Pluralism in Education*, 8 (2).

Desai, R. 2016. 'The Value of History and the History of Value', in T. Subasat (ed.), *The Great Meltdown of 2008: Systemic, Conjunctural or Policy-created?* Cheltenham: Edward Elgar.

Earle, J., C. Moran, and Z. Ward-Perkins. 2016. *The Econocracy: The Perils of Leaving Economics to the Experts*. London: Penguin.

Freeman, A. 2007a. 'Heavens Above: What Equilibrium Means for Economics', in V. Mosini (ed.), *Equilibrium in Economics: Scope and Limits*. London: Routledge.

Freeman, A. 2007b. 'Catechism versus Pluralism: The Heterodox Response to the National Undergraduate Curriculum Proposed by the UK Quality Assurance Authority', MPRA Paper, 2 June. Available at: http://mpra.ub.uni-muenchen.de/6832/.

Freeman, A. 2009. 'The Economists of Tomorrow: The Case for a Pluralist Subject Benchmark Statement for Economics', *International Review of Economics Education*, 8 (2) (December): 23–40.

Freeman, A. 2010. 'The Economists of Tomorrow: The Case for Assertive Pluralism in Economics Education', *American Journal of Economics and Sociology*, 69 (5) (1 November): 1591–1613.

Freeman, A. 2015. 'First Tell No Untruth', in G. DeMartino and D. McCloskey (eds.), *Handbook on Professional Economic Ethics*. Oxford: Oxford University Press.

Freeman, A. and A. Kliman. 2008 [1996]. 'Beyond Talking the Talk: Towards a Critical Pluralist Practice', in E. Fullbrook (ed.), *Pluralist Economics*. London: Zed Press.

Freeman, A., V. Chick, and S. Kayatekin. (eds.) 2014. 'Whig History and the Reinterpretation of Economic History', Special Edition. *Cambridge Journal of Economics*, 38 (3), May.

Gans, J. S. and G. B. Shepherd. 1994. 'How are the Mighty Fallen: Rejected Classic Articles by Leading Economists', *Journal of Economic Perspectives*, 8 (1) (Winter): 165–179.

Heath, T. L. 1913. *Aristarchus of Samos, the Ancient Copernicus; a History of Greek Astronomy to Aristarchus.* Oxford: Clarendon Press.

Hodgson, G., U. Mäki, and D. McCloskey (originators). 1992. 'A Plea for a Pluralistic and Rigorous Economics', *The American Economic Review*, 82 (2): xxv. The plea was published as an advertisement. Ironically it is not accessible in the AER archives.

IEO [Independent Evaluation Office of the International Monetary Fund]. 2011. 'IMF Performance in the Run-up to the Financial and Economic Crisis: IMF Surveillance in 2004–07', 10 January.

ISIP (International Student Initiative for Pluralist Economics). 2016. 'An International Student Call for Pluralism in Economics'. Available at: www.isipe.net/open-letter/.

Jo, Tae-Hee and Z. Todorova. 2015. *Advancing the Frontiers of Heterodox Economics: Essays in Honor of Frederic S. Lee.* Abingdon: Routledge.

Kuhn, T. S. 1966. *The Structure of Scientific Revolutions*, 1st Edition. Chicago, IL: University of Chicago Press.

Morgan, J. (coordinator), B. Philp, B. Cronin, V. Bigo, V. Chick, R. Desai, A. Ekeland, A. Freeman, A. Hermann, F. Lee, A. Mearman, I. Negru, W. Olsen, J. Reardon, and J. Wells. 2015. *Pluralism, Heterodoxy, and the Prospects for a New Economics Curriculum: Assessing the Potential of INET, What's the Use of Economics, and the CORE Project.* London: AHE.

Nelson, R. H. 2014 [2001], *Economics as Religion: From Samuelson to Chicago and Beyond.* University Park, PA: Pennsylvania State University Press.

Pettifor, A. 2009. 'I blame the Queen for this crisis', *The Guardian*, 26 February.

Pierce, A. 2008. 'The Queen Asks Why No One Saw the Credit Crunch Coming', *Daily Telegraph*, 5 November.

Portes, R. 2008. Valedictory Report to the Royal Economic Society. *RES Newsletter*, April.

Rogers, W. P. 1986. *Report to the President*. Presidential Commission on the Space Shuttle Challenger Accident. Washington, DC: NASA.

Sagan, C. and A. Druyan. 1995. *The Demon-Haunted World: Science as a Candle in the Dark*. London: Penguin, Random House.

Sanders, B. 2009. 'Bernanke in his own words'. Available at: www.sanders.senate.gov/newsroom/recent-business/bernanke-in-his-own-words.

Sent, E-M. J. 2006. 'Pluralisms in Economics', in S. Kellert, H. Longino, and K. Waters (eds.), *Scientific Pluralism*, Minnesota Studies in the Philosophy of Science, Minnesota, MN: Minnesota University Press, pp. 80–101.

Shepherd, G. B. (ed.). 1994. *Rejected: Leading Economists Ponder the Publication Process*, Reprint Edition. Sun Lakes, AZ: Thomas Horton & Daughters.

Stewart, H. 2009. 'This is How We Let the Credit Crunch Happen, Ma'am', *The Guardian*, 26 July. Available at: www.theguardian.com/uk/2009/jul/26/monarchy-credit-crunch.

Todaro, M. P. and S. C. Smith (2009) *Economic Development*, 10th edition. Harlow: Addison Wesley.

Wade, R. and S. Sigurgeirsdóttir. 2012. 'How to Discredit a Financial Regulator: The Strange Case of Iceland', Triple Crisis Website. Available at: http://triplecrisis.com/the-strange-case-of-iceland.

Introduction

Arturo Hermann and Simon Mouatt

Main themes and objectives

This book was first inspired by the desire to mark the twentieth anniversary of the *Association for Heterodox Economics* (AHE), with an edited volume of current papers that showcases some of the pluralist methodology and policy implications of AHE associates' work. In this regard, one of the main purposes of the book is to illustrate how heterodox economics can provide a more complete and robust explanation of economic realities than orthodox economics, and thus provide appropriate policies for the major imbalances of our time. The particular imbalances we address include: (i) the growing disparity of income/wealth between persons and economic areas; (ii) environmental degradation; (iii) employment issues; and, finally (iv) the regularity of economic/financial crises. It is our contention that these economic imbalances exert a significant negative impact on the well-being of society and further lead to worsened instability in international relations, resurgent nationalism, unsustainable ecological systems, climate change and armed conflict.

Since it is increasingly evident that the orthodox economic analysis, and the policies derived from it, are inadequate at addressing these problems, our hope is for heterodox economics to assume a stronger role in proposing an alternative course of policy action. One of the reasons for the historic sidelining of heterodox thought is that the genre has been borne out of critical thinking. In other words, in opposition to accepted paradigms, with the consequence that it has defined itself as an 'outsider'. This situation has been galvanized by its exclusion from orthodox economic science and policymaking circles. Once this kind of identity has been established it can be a very difficult label to transcend. In such conditions, our objective is to show that heterodox economists can make great strides in reversing this image by presenting themselves and their work in such a way that legitimately asserts the need for an alternative paradigm. In this way, the likelihood of gaining attention amongst the political class is enhanced.

Another aim of the book is to illustrate the importance of fully adopting pluralism in economics, given that economic study involves examining human behaviour in its collective expression. It is nonsensical to imagine a rigorous study of human behaviour without the inclusion of ideas derived from, inter alia, the subjects of psychology, sociology and political theory. It is our view that this approach constitutes a full adoption of a broader conception of scientific method, also embodying a qualitative assessment of economic and social phenomena. In this regard, when economists display a willingness to adopt alternative models or synthesize ideas, in order to obtain a better grasp of economic realities, this, we suggest, reveals a predisposition to solution-seeking rather than simply supporting academic career progression. Their economic research is therefore likely to be of greater value to the design of public policy.

Orthodox analysis chiefly rests on the postulates of neoclassical economics. There are various versions of this theory, such as partial or general equilibrium models, for instance, but the basic postulates remain the same and can be so summarized: (i) economic agents are (or can easily become) 'rational' and hence tend to maximize their utility function; and (ii) markets are (or can easily become) perfect and self-equilibrating mechanisms.

It is clear that, if things stand like this, the best policy is to not overly interfere with this wonderful mechanism, especially by the state that is deemed to be unskilled in this activity. However, as underscored by many studies, these postulates are not only far from reality but are also intrinsically unattainable or unsustainable. This comes about because the notion of a rational agent acting in a perfect market can only exist in an imagined world based on static markets and static (and exogenously conceived) motivations of economic agents. Hence, in the real economy, characterized by a growing complexity of actual human motivations and economic action, these neoclassical postulates then become increasingly unrealistic and of limited public policy use.

In addressing these issues, we do not deny the progress that has been realized in some provinces of the neoclassical domain and even the circumstances where assuming simplified hypotheses can be usefully applied in certain cases. But we wish to underscore that progress so realized is one-sided, and incomplete, and generally takes the form of the discovery of new exceptions to the neoclassical model of perfect competition or random exogenous factors. In this sense, our view is that the weak aspects of neoclassical economics relate not so much to its simplistic hypotheses, but to the circumstance that these hypotheses do not allow for pluralism (and its associated critical thinking), since they do not leave room for any real (or comprehensive) verification.

As an example, if available data shows that consumers buy an item at its lowest price, then the hypothesis of the 'rational consumer' is confirmed. If, however, the data reveals a different story, this would not put in doubt the theory, because the phenomenon would simply be ascribed to exceptional or exogenous factors. In other words, the prime postulates of orthodox analysis are not subject to methodological challenge and remain the same in the light of new data.

This also partly explains why orthodox economics – perhaps to present itself with a mantle of 'scientificity' – is usually based on the construction of mathematical models accompanied by an unwarranted employ of quantitative econometric analysis for their 'validation'. What makes this methodological approach unconvincing is the scant consideration of alternative explanatory frameworks (i.e. pluralism) based on the qualitative interpretation of complex phenomena. A neoclassical general equilibrium model based on a perfect flexibility of prices (including labour remuneration), for example, would ascribe unemployment to the 'rigidity' of these factors. These aspects can play a role of course (and more flexibility can help in some cases). But, at the same time, it could also be considered that, as extensively analysed by many post-Keynesian's and institutional economics' contributions, prices embody complex social relations and, therefore, some kind of stickiness is necessary for ensuring the stability of the system. In fact, if every price were wildly flexible, no social life would be possible. Relatedly, the reasons for unemployment can be mainly found in other structural factors, for instance (i) the structural tendency of effective demand to lag behind the supply of full employment; (ii) the complex role of technological progress; or (iii) the phenomenon of satiation for many products.

For these reasons – and in order to avoid the well-known dangers of simplification and reductionism – quantitative analysis should always be coupled with case studies and other methods for acquiring more 'direct and qualitative' data on the phenomena under investigation. In fact, it is only through a more comprehensive approach that both the common and distinctive aspects of the various contexts can be thoroughly investigated.

We can illustrate the differences between orthodox and heterodox approaches in a number of relevant issues.

Explaining economic imbalances from a heterodox perspective

Microeconomic imperfections

In the orthodox domain there are scores of models dealing with various forms of imperfect competition, such as monopolistic competition, oligopoly or monopoly. These models highlight that in such situations the likely outcomes are higher prices and lower supply, with a corresponding loss of total welfare.

In this respect, we have tried to convey a more comprehensive and interdisciplinary explanation of these phenomena, by underscoring the following aspects: (i) the multiplicity of factors explaining scale economies – technological, organizational, financial (with the market power associated with them); (ii) the endogenous nature of consumers' preferences and firms' strategies, which implies that these actions are determined by the complexity of human motivations in their collective and context-specific interaction, rather than by an abstract principle of utility or profit maximization; (iii) the circumstance that market imperfections (for instance in the form of the slow reaction of prices to changes in demand) are also related to the need to provide a relative stability to key social relations underlying economic action relations; if prices were always wildly flexible, no meaningful social life would be possible; (iv) the circumstance that markets (and the related notion of competition) are not exogenous mechanisms but institutions created, maintained and defined by laws and institutions.

The analysis of these aspects is not only interesting *per se*, but it is also pertinent for policy implications. One other relevant field where heterodox economics can help to attain more effective policies is the trade-off between static and dynamic efficiency. For instance, in many sectors it can be more convenient, in terms of scale economies and hence lower cost for units of product, to have one or few large firms than a multitude of small firms. In this respect, the concepts of natural monopoly and optimal firm size do exist in mainstream economics, however we argue that heterodox perspectives allow a more complete and realistic interpretation of these types of phenomena.

In these instances, there arises the issue of reducing the monopolistic power of these firms and giving adequate voice to their stakeholders. A heterodox-oriented approach, by a better identification of the various sources of market power and scale economies, can help to frame industrial and competition policies better and thus facilitate efficiency and sustainability at a sectoral and firm level.

These aspects also relate to investment policy and the role of interdisciplinary orientation – typical of heterodox economics – in illuminating these aspects. In this regard, issues related to the motivation of economic agents can, in our opinion, be better understood by a more far-reaching perspective. Does, for instance, the *homo economicus* seek to maximize money solely for material reasons? Or does the quest for money also cover the partly unconscious need to be accepted, by following a socially approved behaviour? This kind of analysis would shift attention from the all-important role attributed to profits to the ways to enliven 'animal spirits' namely, a tendency to make initiatives not strictly related to the 'economic motive'.

A more general implication for policy action is that, in order to promote positive behaviour in economic and social spheres, measures aimed at improving motivation and participation will play a relevant role. These measures, besides their intrinsic worthiness, would foster a virtuous circle. As a matter of fact, a better participation, by improving the process of social valuing – namely, a better understanding of the motivations pertaining to the various policy options – would also help to overcome its most conflicting aspects.

Macroeconomic imperfections

In this field there are marked differences between orthodox and heterodox economics. First, in the framework of the general equilibrium model, no macroeconomics would exist at all since markets are supposed to easily reach maximizing equilibrium. Of course, in order to address the complexity or real world, orthodox analysis has developed various models to take account of the 'rigidities' of real markets.

In this respect, also various 'neo-Keynesian' models are in effect neoclassical models with 'rigidities'. The underlying idea informing these models is that if markets (for goods and for labour) were perfect and flexible, involuntary unemployment would disappear (neoclassicals do not accept the concept of involuntary unemployment that Keynes elaborated). This kind of analysis, however, whilst contributing to explain some relevant phenomena, remains highly simplified and unrealistic in its premises. In this regard, the various strands of heterodox economics – in particular, institutionalism, post-Keynesianism, neo-Marxism and environmentalism – point out a number of structural factors that render economic imbalances endemic. In fact, given the microeconomic imperfections illustrated before, it is wildly unrealistic to suppose a perfect flexibility of markets at full employment level. One central reason for this is that the phenomenon of satiation for a large category of products, which, by lowering the price elasticity of demand, makes it unprofitable for firms to reduce prices. For instance, if we need one smart phone, four t-shirts and five kilos of tomatoes for a given period, it is rather unlikely that we will buy the double amount if the prices halve. For the same reason, it becomes even more unlikely that a reduction of prices of, say, 90 per cent, would induce to buy nine times more the initial quantity demanded.

Second, another relevant field of difference between orthodox and heterodox analysis pertains to the appraisal of public spending. In orthodox analysis, such spending is conceived of as rigorously residual and sub-optimal in respect to the private sector. Hence, the related prescription is one of *laissez-faire*, namely, to reduce such spending to the strictly unavoidable public goods (such as contracts enforcement). Any public spending in excess of that level is believed 'to crowd out' private spending. The crowding-out thesis implies that there is a fixed level of loanable funds in a system 'naturally' converging towards an equilibrium of full employment. If things stand like this, increased state spending leads to higher interest rates for state and market. This account, however, is unrealistic. In particular, the orthodox hypothesis of 'crowding out' does not hold true in real economies. In fact, a reduction of public spending (even if deemed useful) is rarely replaced by a corresponding increase of private spending in practice. The analysis of real economies instead shows that it is not full employment, but a structural underemployment of economic resources (in particular of labour) that is the standard for capitalist economies.

Heterodox contributions, whilst pinpointing the possible inefficiencies of public (and also private) spending, also focus attention on its paramount role in fostering economic development. As a matter of fact, public spending not only provides public goods like useful research and knowledge, and material and immaterial infrastructures – strategic for the development of the economy – but it also constitutes a relevant (and most often irreplaceable) means for maintaining effective demand.

A difference of approach of the same magnitude can be found in another central issue, the analysis of money and credit creation. Here, the orthodox tenet focuses on the notion of the 'neutrality of money'. This means that money is thought of only as a way to facilitate economic transactions through the adoption of a common measure of market values, and hence with no effects on the real economy (except via some kind of an exogenously conceived 'natural' interest rate). This conclusion goes in tandem with the conception of a banking system that only exists as an intermediary between saving and investment. Conversely, heterodox analysis highlights that the distinctive character of a money economy lies in its non-neutrality. This implies that in the latter case the continual accrual of monetary values becomes the means and the goal of economic process (and the start and finish of a continual monetary circuit, M-C-C'-M', elaborated by Marx and other authors). For this reason, money function is far from neutral, since it plays a central role in creating effective demand.

In this connection, the heterodox post-Keynesian concept of 'endogenous money' suggests that there is virtually unlimited credit available for the private sector at a given interest rate. Such availability does not warrant, however, as Keynes put it, that 'the horse will drink' (e.g. that firms would increase productive investments), especially when the effective demand and expectations are low. For these reasons, we believe that these heterodox perspectives provide a much better explanation of the functioning of state and private sector spending in a modern capitalist economy.

Another significant implication of this analysis is that, whilst saving can play a role in financing investment, it is by no means the central one. Credit creation, actually, generates new demand and then new income, and thus contributes to form saving rather than the other way around. In the dynamics of modern economies, therefore, the role of monetary policy in influencing the real interest rate and the orientation of the banking system towards credit creation can hardly be exaggerated. This is also on account of the fact that these aspects heavily impinge on the Keynesian notion of the 'marginal efficiency of capital' – the difference between expected rate of profit and real interest rate – which plays a relevant role in real decision-making towards investments.

The foregoing examples of micro and macroeconomic imperfections, although by no means exhaustive of the differences between the orthodox and heterodox analysis, point out some important domains where heterodox perspectives can clearly provide a more comprehensive analysis – in theory and in policy action – of the major economic imbalances of our time.

Pluralism, economics education and the effectiveness of policy action

As noted, the heterodox approach summarized has implications for policy issues. This aspect, and in particular the capacity of heterodox economists to bring out specific policy implications of their analyses, is also paramount for the full development of their perspectives. As a matter of fact, if we present our activities as a forum for pluralism, this looks fine, but risks being perceived both by the more informed audience and by laypeople as an interesting intellectual venture but with no tangible results in terms of better policies. And this in a period where there is a high, explicit demand for new policy solutions for the problems of our time. But why is the heterodox approach likely to lead to a more effective policy action? There can be two reasons for this:

(I) One refers to the capacity of most heterodox theories to more realistically address the characteristics of economic systems. As a consequence, many argue that these theories are more able than mainstream ones to analyse the imbalances and propose adequate policy solutions.
(II) The other reason is the pluralist practice of heterodox economics. Most heterodox theories, by being based on more realistic premises, can be considered as 'open systems'. This implies that the theories are more open to critical analysis of their premises, and to comparison with other theories, leading to much more robust policy. Hitherto, however, this potential has perhaps remained underexplored. True, there is a growing collaboration between various strands of heterodox economics, but in the main, at least in our view, fragmentation remains relevant.

One reason for this is that the main heterodox fields of economics embody different and competing perspectives. In this respect, these economists tend to perceive themselves more as exponents of a particular strand – for instance, institutionalism, post-Keynesianism, Marxism, environmentalism and their related sub-fields – rather than as 'heterodox economists'. The same applies in public discourse and in the wider media coverage where the notion of an alternative or heterodox economics is rarely heard of. As a consequence, we posit that it is of paramount importance to overcome the limited collaboration often present in heterodox economics (and other social sciences). In this respect, we can ask what is the utility of promoting a better collaboration within heterodox economics?

One reason is that these theories deal with the same phenomenon, the study of the economic system, especially in its evolutionary dimension. Whilst such theories are different in many respects, they also present notable complementarities, in the sense that the aspects more overlooked by some are more completely considered by the others. This suggests the camps will benefit from greater pluralist work.

Heterodox strands are, therefore, not 'closed systems' but, in full respect of their respective identities, represent theoretical perspectives 'open' to comparison with other ideas/theories in a pluralist spirit. This contributes to building a stronger common foundation for the analysis of economic imbalances. As observed by the sociologist Karl Mannheim, a landscape can only be seen from a determined ontological perspective, and without perspective there is no landscape. In this sense, observing a landscape (or phenomenon) from different angles (or disciplines) helps to attain a much clearer insight into the features of each considered perspective. In fact, rather than pluralist economic science exhibiting less rigorous research the opposite is true.

In all of these issues mentioned, economics education can play a paramount role in promoting such a pluralistic approach, by clarifying that a better collaboration within heterodox economics can have two beneficial effects: (a) bringing out the distinctive aspects of various heterodox strands; and (b) helping to build a wider economics paradigm for interpreting and finding solutions to the most pressing problems of our time.

The organization of the book

The book is organized in five Parts: (I) Pluralism, ethics and economic method; (II) Sustainable macroeconomy and structural policies; (III) Money and monetary regimes; (IV) Development issues and the role of public action; and (V) Improving pluralism in economics education.

Part I: Pluralism, ethics and economic method

In Chapter 1, Anders Ekeland distinguishes the mainstream from heterodoxy by its use of static models rather than dynamic ones. He then explores marginalist founders, for example, Walras and Pareto, and notes they sought to emulate natural science, especially physics, but were not regarded by the natural scientists as good practitioners. He argues these economists did not first envisage static modelling to last but instead aspired to formulating dynamic models. He concludes it is orthodox ideology that has mitigated the likelihood of this occurring. In Chapter 2, Jon Mulberg posits that current protest is aimed at challenging the political neutrality of economic science, alongside traditional protest aims. Jon suggests the ideas of Foucault help us to understand the current power discourse and advocates an 'archaeological dig' into the historical economic narrative to facilitate counter-discourse to debunk non-pluralist orthodoxy. In Chapter 3, Simon Mouatt discusses economic philosophy by exploring the Hegel/Marx dialectic as a basis for pluralism, and Hegel's master/slave concept as a basis for inclusive policy outcome criteria for critical economic science.

In Chapter 4, authors Nick Potts and Phil Armstrong give an interesting account of pluralism, critical thinking and Kuhn's paradigm shifts and then provide insight into the reality of synthesis in interdisciplinary work with a case study of the Temporal Single System Interpretation of Marx (TSSI) and Modern Monetary Theory (MMT).

Part II: Sustainable macroeconomy and structural policies

In Chapter 5, Miriam Kennet, from the Green Economics Institute, presents a case for adopting a deeper form of pluralism, informed by green issues, which has been partly absent from heterodoxy. She further argues that diversity is a prerequisite for a meaningful pluralism. In Chapter 6, the TSSI is synthesized with the resource-based view of the firm, to provide an explanation of how value translates into price, a question that orthodox economics is unable to answer. Thoralf Dassler thus illustrates how pluralism provides a foundation for better science and, hence, policy. Arturo Hermann, in Chapter 7, provides a defence of democratic planning for a sustainable economy by examining effective demand from evolutionary/institutionalist perspectives and the myths of Keynesian policy failure from the past.

Part III: Money and monetary regimes

In Chapter 8, Jalal Qanas explores inequality and income distribution from a central banking perspective, by considering debates on their cause and effect from both mainstream and Keynesian perspectives. In Chapter 9, John Harvey provides the reader with an explanation of how the orthodox profession failed to predict the financial crisis by leaving financial markets and debt out of their neoclassical models. John argues that the post-Keynesian approach, instead, takes account of the monetary sector and exhibits strong pluralist credentials.

Part IV: Development issues and the role of public action

In Chapter 10, authors Fernanda Graziella Cardoso and Cristina Fróes de Borja Reis examine how the ideas of the pioneers of development theory during the 1950s relate to the current reality of global value chains, with a focus on the mechanisms of trade specialization. The authors conclude that the centre/periphery division continues, albeit in a remodelled form. In Chapter 11, Andrew Purves considers state versus private ownership of assets and asks whether certain assets should remain in the public realm since their revenue arises from economic rent. Using case studies from Hong Kong and Singapore, the author illustrates how state revenue can be raised without deterring the use of the public good. In Chapter 12, authors Wendy Sealy and Simon Mouatt explore the tourism sector in the Caribbean and illustrate how the economic relations that existed prior to decolonialization still exist in their essential nature. The authors then present some policy options for Caribbean leaders in order to combat transnational tourism and economic dependency.

Part V: Improving pluralism in economics education

In Chapter 13, Bruce Cronin builds on his 2010 Heterodox journal-ranking work, conducted with Fred Lee, and concludes that, whilst the rankings have not changed much, heterodoxy has become more distinguished as an academic field distinct from orthodox economics. In addition, the reliability of traditional citation impact factors has been subject to recent critique and there are developments in subject-normalized journal impact factors.

In Chapter 14, James Juniper et al. provide the reader with an interesting account of the inadequacy of orthodox macroeconomic textbooks for undergraduate reading lists. In response, the authors give a review of some key texts that have sought to rectify the erroneous teaching about the monetary sector prior to the 2008 crisis. In Chapter 15, Sheila Dow builds on her oft-cited previous work on economic pluralism and posits that some heterodox academics can also advocate monism. She argues for a clear definition of the nature of pluralism, outlines her perspective and then considers the future of heterodoxy. In the final contribution, Chapter 16, Jack Reardon considers how to make pluralism more effective and argues for a reorientation of economics education as an issue for immediate attention by policymakers. He also argues that diversity should be a key part of this process.

Part I

Pluralism, ethics and economic method

1 Dynamics versus statics

On the nature of heterodox and orthodox economics

Anders Ekeland

Introduction

This chapter is a contribution to the discussion of the question: what are the fundamental characteristics of heterodox economics? My answer is very simple: dynamics. Heterodox economics has real, causal time; orthodox economics has not. Of all economics systems we have seen, capitalism is clearly the most dynamic. The chapter argues that the motivation to use a static model to understand such a dynamic phenomenon was, and is, politically and ideologically motivated. The goal of all founding fathers and high priests of neoclassical economics, Walras, Pareto, Hicks, Samuelson, was of course to have a *dynamic model*, proving that free, perfect markets gave the optimal use of resources and maximal utility. As it turned out – at every stage of the ever-more sophisticated mathematical version of Walras's initial model, it became more and more obvious that it was impossible to prove the *dynamic stability* of the model; and without proof of stability – the *static* Walras model was scientifically irrelevant. It could not say anything about a *dynamic* phenomenon, but as we know by now, scientific irrelevance of the model did not matter much, because of its enormous political relevance. This means that static versus dynamic models is the fundamental dividing line between heterodox and orthodox economics. When you have real time, real causation and real feedback loops in your model, you have a model suited to the object of study, the economic aspect of human society, and in particular such a highly dynamic system as capitalism. That is science; a static model is fundamentally ideological.

The chapter primarily relates to two recent contributions to the debate about the essence of heterodox economics, Tony Lawson's 'Economics and Ideology' (Lawson 2016) and Geoffrey Hodgson's 'Is there a Future for Heterodox Economics?' (Hodgson 2019). Both Lawson and Hodgson discuss whether orthodox economics is an ideology, but while having somewhat different definitions, they both have too narrow a concept of ideology, thus rejecting the view that orthodoxy is an ideology. Lawson argues that orthodoxy is a special kind of ideology, an 'obsession' with mathematics. Hodgson is mostly concerned to argue against the view that neoclassical theory is a pro-market ideology since it has been used to prove that socialist, centralised planning can work (2019, p. vi–viii). Whatever the case, as Hodgson argues, heterodox economists should perhaps take the view that 'if you can't beat it, join it'. Being aware that the dividing line is *methodological*, that the dividing line has fundamentally nothing to do with politics, could give heterodox economics a common paradigmatic–theoretic fundament, which Hodgson correctly points out it lacks. In my opinion, Shaik's (2016) concept of 'real competition' and 'turbulent regulation' is an example of a way to model the dynamics of capitalism that could be a common theoretical basis for heterodox economics in the future. Shaik has an analysis of competition that is fundamentally common to Marx, Schumpeter and Hayek who all agree that what really characterises capitalism is a specific type of (dynamic) order emerging out of (dynamic) disorder.

Scientific and vulgar economics: The case of Walras and Pareto

The debate on the nature, that is the scientific relevance of the various utility value theories, is of course not new. Marx put quite some effort into studying and elaborating upon a critique of 'vulgar economics'. It is far beyond the scope of this chapter to deal with that transition of economics as science into what Marx called 'vulgar' economics. I will be more specific and look at the way modern, orthodox economics emerged (which, in my opinion, clearly indicates that it was an ideology from the start), by quoting extensively from Philip Mirowski's book, 'More Heat Than Light: Economics as Social Physics, Physics as Nature's Economics' (Mirowski 1989).

Mirowski's book is a study of the aspirations of the early marginalists in an endeavour to create a 'social physics'. A social theory mathematically formulated has the enormous advantage that, if one accepts the axioms, if the deductions are correct, then you must just accept the results. Deduction is logic, and you 'can't argue with logic'. In Mirowski's opinion, economics suffers from a century-long physics envy. Mirowski's problem is that neoclassical theory, as he himself is the first to point out, did not and does not slavishly imitate, or creatively apply, either the conceptual or the mathematical developments of physics. This is obvious from the very beginning in the last decades of the nineteenth century, but the split is becoming more and more obvious as relativity theory, entropy, path dependency, chaos theory become important in modern physics, as Mirowski points out with admirable detail and clarity. The key point is that, when challenged by contemporary pro-capitalist physicists and mathematicians about the lack of dynamics in their economic theory, both Walras and Pareto flatly refused to seriously engage with the challenges. That is always a very good indicator that we are dealing with a fact-denying, ideological project. From the very beginning Mirowski points to the real motivation of Walras, Pareto and the Marginalist school, making very clear who they saw as their adversaries:

> The Marginalists appropriated the mathematical formalisms of mid-nineteenth-century energy physics, which for convenience we shall refer to as 'proto-energetics', made them their own by changing the labels on the variables, and then trumpeted the triumph of a truly 'scientific economics'. Utility became the analogue of potential energy; the budget constraint became the slightly altered analogue of kinetic energy; and the Marginalists Revolutionaries marched off to do battle with classical, Historicist and Marxian economics.
>
> (p. 9)[1]

Mirowski's first conclusion is that,

> to put it bluntly, economics finally attained its objective to become a science through a wholesale appropriation of the mid-nineteenth-century physics of energy ... The seemingly simultaneous discovery [of neoclassical theory] was the direct result of the preceding watershed in nineteenth-century physical theory, and the fact that all of the progenitors of neoclassicism were trained in engineering level physics and subject to particular philosophical trends of the time.
>
> (pp. 196–197)

This conclusion would be easy to accept, if it were not for the fact that this 'appropriation' was of a very peculiar kind, or as Mirowski puts it:

> this increased dependence on science had a number of perverse side effects. The first was that the more fervent the invocation of science (physics) by political economists, the correspondingly lesser were their efforts in delineating precisely what those methods consisted of, or in finding out what it was that contemporary scientists actually did.
>
> (p. 198)

But this 'invocation of science' without really caring about it – is that not just the same as using physics as mere rhetoric, just to give scientific credibility to an ideology? What real scientists do is no mystery, they create theories to explain observations, and – as Mirowski describes in his book at length – change those theories when new facts obviously are not explained well by their original theories. But this is precisely what neoclassical economists *do not do* – and have never done. The Great Depression, or the last financial crisis, are both outside the theoretical framework of static equilibrium theory. Crisis is not a concept in a theory where equilibrium and harmony are the only things that really exist. Twenty per cent unemployment is also outside this paradigm, since there is no concept of involuntary unemployment. The static core of the neoclassical paradigm has shown itself to be practically immune from even the most dramatic economic events. Is that science – or ideology?

This, in my opinion, ideologically based hostility to using the dynamic methods of natural and social sciences is well documented by Mirowski. He describes how Walras, in an article, boasts that his new

> physico-mathematical science of the *Elements* uses *precisely* the identical mathematical formulas [as physics]. Walras then proceeded to scold physicists who had expressed scepticism about the application of mathematics to utilitarian social theories on the ground that utility is not a measurable quantum …
>
> (p. 220, original emphasis)

Already here we meet the problem with the way the early neoclassicals 'imitate' physics. They are 'scolding' the leading natural scientists who have some comments/objections to that imitation.

As Mirowski points out, the ambitions of Pareto were, if possible, even greater. Pareto argued that

> thanks to the use of mathematics, this entire theory … rests on no more than a fact of experience, that is on the determination of the quantities of goods which constitute combinations between which the individual is indifferent. The theory of economic science thus acquires the rigor of rational mechanics.
>
> (p. 221)

As we will see below, Mirowski is not impressed by Pareto's grasp of physics, be it rational mechanics or more modern theories.

But let us first look at the one person who clearly had all the mathematical training needed to get things right, Irving Fisher. Mirowski goes in detail through the efforts of Fisher to make a close analogy between mechanics and economics, where space in mechanics is the commodity in economics, force is a 'marginal utility or disutility', etc. (p. 224). After describing what Fisher tried to do, Mirowski is neither impressed nor amused: 'Fisher, the most sophisticated scientist among the nineteenth-century neoclassical economists, still displayed an inadequate comprehension of the formalism of the energy concept and, as a corollary, lack of appreciation of the metaphorical dissonances involved' (p. 228). Mirowski then goes through all of Fisher's mistakes, which to a modern reader seem rather obvious: 'At the top of the list, the identification of a particle with an individual is incorrect … Fisher's next mistake is the conflation of two incompatible meanings of the term "work"' (p. 229). But it is not only what Fisher wrote that fails to impress Mirowski, 'the gaps in his lexicon of correspondences are more serious than that' (p. 230). Again, we see this extraordinarily 'amateurish' imitation, even by people with superb mathematical skills. Is there really any other explanation than that the neoclassical school wanted their 'results' to be accepted as natural laws, that is, not to be opposed by anyone at all? Mirowski's description of the reaction of Walras, Pareto and Fischer to the critique from the physicists and mathematicians clearly supports that hypothesis.

> It would have been extraordinary for so many economists to mangle and misrepresent the energy model so frequently without eventually calling down the wrath of physicists upon their labours. Indeed, one of the skeletons in the neoclassical closet is that around the turn of the century, quite a number of physicists turned their attention to this species of upstart proto-energetics and pronounced it wanting.
>
> (p. 241)

The reader probably already can guess what the reaction of the neoclassical core cadre was:

> Time and again they [the neoclassicals] met these inquisitions with hurt, incomprehension, bluster, farrago, protests, the physics was irrelevant, and finally, a feeling of betrayal: How did it come to pass that those in the forefront of trying to make economics a science should be so abused by those whom they were trying to emulate?
>
> (p. 241)

The last question is rather easily answered – the physicists were serious scientists, not ideologists, so they cared about conceptual consistency, mathematical rigour, empirical relevance as is amply demonstrated by Mirowski. The first man out is Joseph Bertrand, specialist in the mathematics of rational mechanics and the editor of the third edition of Lagrange's *Mecanique Analytique.* Bertrand reviewed Cournot's *Recherches* and Walras's *Théorie Mathématique de la Richesse Sociale*. Mirowski sums up Bertrand's view:

> Most of his review centred on the thesis that the neglect of mathematical political economy in the French academy had been deserved, because the existing attempts had been devoid of *any serious empirical content, not to mention their numerous mathematical and conceptual errors.* ... Bertrand observed that in general there would exist what in the modern literature is called false trading – namely, some exchanges are conducted at non-equilibrium prices in the process of trying to discover the market-clearing price. Bertrand pointed out, quite correctly, that the mere existence of false trading, or indeed any mercantile speculation, would obviate the determinacy of Walras' general equilibrium.
>
> (p. 242, my emphasis)

What would a real scientist do, faced with such criticisms? The answer is, of course, respond seriously to them. What would an ideological warrior do? Mirowski gives the clear answer: 'Walras never directly answered the criticism'

(p. 242). The next scientist out is Willard Gibbs, Irving Fisher's thesis advisor. He asked

> why Fisher's indifference lines should be able to be integrated into utility surfaces. Far from being a minor technical point, Gibbs probably tried to make Fisher aware that the absence of integrability would necessarily mean that there could exist no such quantity as total utility, *and path-independence of equilibrium* would be compromised. ... Fisher's stock reaction to the problem of conservative entities within his economic theories was *simply to deny the possibility of any serious dynamic theory* ... We can date the collective neoclassical neurosis with regard to the physics metaphor from this point.
>
> (p. 243, my emphasis)

The mathematical jargon around integrability etc. is not important to understand in this context. The key point is that, when challenged about statics versus dynamics Fisher does not respond in any meaningful way.

So here we are at the start orthodoxy of with the much admired Walras and Pareto, who refused to engage in serious debate as soon as real scientists challenged their static model. Mirowski is no less critical of Samuelson. According to Mirowski, it was first and foremost Samuelson 'who by word and deed was responsible for the twentieth century self-image of the neoclassical economist as a scientist' (p. 378). Would the neoclassical school have been able to establish the false Nobel prize in economics without posing as physicists of the economy? Mirowski writes that one aspect of Samuelson's work that had not 'drawn any comment in the numerous *Festschriften* and evaluative volumes dealing with Samuelson's career' was 'Samuelson's habit of making reference to modern physics in superficial and rhetorical ways while persistently misrepresenting both its content and its relationship to neoclassical theory' (p. 379). One example being Samuelson's 'correspondence principle'. The term was taken from Bohr where the principle said that in some contexts one could use predictions from pre-quantum mechanics as a fairly good approximation. The stated purpose of Samuelson's correspondence principle was to 'suggest that dynamic stability analysis in a neoclassical context could lend some structure to the comparatively static results in neoclassical price theory' (p. 379). But as Mirowski correctly points out:

> At the most prosaic level, Samuelson's mathematical model had no connection with those of Bohr, either in the old or the post-1925 quantum mechanics ... Even from the most Olympian heights there is no plausible analogy between Bohr's and Samuelson's Correspondence Principles.
>
> (p. 379)

Another example is the Le Châtelier principle – which I shall not try to explain, but Mirowski's conclusion is clear enough: 'Again the reference to a physical principle was *not* being seriously used as a heuristic research device' (p. 382).

Mirowski's global view of Samuelson's track record is quite harsh: 'Throughout his career, Samuelson has been the master of scientific rhetoric, continuously and consciously hinting at parallels between neoclassical theory and twentieth-century physics, and just as consciously denying them, usually in the very same article' (p. 382). Mirowski goes on to quote Samuelson's 'Nobel Prize' lecture where Samuelson said:

> There is really nothing more pathetic than to have an economist or a retired engineer try to force analogies between the concepts of physics and the concepts of economics. How many dreary papers have I had to referee in which the author is looking for something that corresponds to entropy or to one or another form of energy.
>
> (p. 382)

Mirowski's comments:

> Nevertheless, Samuelson's *Collected Scientific Papers* are chock-full of titles such as 'A Quantum Theory Model of Economics', 'The Law of the Conservation of the Capital-Output Ratio', 'Two Conservation Laws in Theoretical Economics' and 'A Biological Least-Action Principle'. Papers with less misleading titles such as 'Causality and Teleology in Economics' and 'Maximum Principles in Analytical Economics' contain at least as many explicit references to physics as they do to economics. Nevertheless, the single most salient aspect of those papers is that their scientific rethoric is entirely decoupled from their paltry substantive physics content. The 'Quantum Theory' paper has nothing whatsoever to do with quantum mechanics; the 'Conservation Laws' paper never actually comes to grips with the problem of what neoclassical theory actually assumes to be conserved in its proto-energetics model …
>
> (p. 382)[2]

A cool distance indeed – from anything dynamic, which would have been the only appropriate tools for modelling a dynamic market economy.

Debreu – a mathematical exercise – or a value theory?

Why was Debreu's final mathematical proof of the existence of a general equilibrium entitled 'The Theory of Value: An Axiomatic Analysis'? Although Debreu describes the subject matter of his book as 'the explanation of the price of commodities resulting from the interaction of the agents of a private ownership economy', it is clear that the term 'explanation' is not used in the ordinary everyday sense of the term, that is, that the model explains observed reality. 'Explaining' here means purely a mathematical-logical exercise, that given a set of neatly defined axioms/equations Debreu has shown that the system has a solution, but as Debreu reminds the reader, the theory is 'logically entirely disconnected from its interpretation' (Debreu 1959, p. x). Which is Debreu's way of saying that the model does not say anything about a real economy.

The totally static – and thus unrealistic – nature of Debreu's 'solution', whereby neither prices, technology nor 'initial endowments', are allowed to change as much as one iota, was not intended. On the contrary – as shown in Currie and Steedman's (1990) excellent discussion of how the orthodoxy have always 'wrestled with time', Walras, Lindahl and Hicks all saw the static model as just the first step towards a dynamic model. The same 'wrestling' story is told by Ingrao and Israel (1990), emphasising that Walras 'did not fail to point out, however, the need to proceed from static to dynamic analysis as the next stage of study' (p. 103). Ingrao and Israel conclude that 'none of the three analytical problems raised by general economic equilibrium theory – existence, uniqueness and stability – received either solution or clear definition in the *Élements*' (p. 112). More than six decades after Debreu, uniqueness and stability is still not proved. So, the key question remains, why should we call Debreu's mathematical exercise a theory of value? A theory of value that has no connection to reality?

The role of general equilibrium in shaping economic policy

What is important in this context is that the static equilibrium concepts have strong implications for policymaking. Take the concept of 'market failure'. In real life, as is known, markets work in both creative and destructive ways. All markets have to fail, compared to an ideal fixed-point equilibrium, proved on an unbelievably high level of abstraction, requiring totally unrealistic preconditions like perfect information, no trading outside equilibrium, no increasing returns to scale etc. That does not mean that most policymakers have not seen the 'first best' as the best of all worlds. Everybody is of course realising that we will never reach this equilibrium nirvana because of the various types of market imperfections and failures. Still, the first best remains the uncontested 'guiding star' for the economic policies of the IMF, World Bank, European Commission, OECD and most governments. Since 'perfect competition' gives the (Pareto) optimal solutions, you are irrational if you do not deregulate the financial sector, privatise health care, railroads, schools – in fact there should be markets for everything. The theory says that you should create markets in all spheres of society and when not directly possible, try to mimic 'competition' as best you can.

The fact that everybody realises that we live in a second-, third- or fourth-best world does not diminish the normative power of orthodoxy – quite the contrary. The concept of second best has no meaning without a first best, without 'believing' in the welfare theorems of orthodoxy. That the Lipsey-Lancaster theorem proves that once we are not in equilibrium – with 'imperfections' all over the place – we have no scientific basis for saying what policy will bring us closest, does not matter much. It just means that all interest groups (to use a neutral term) can tell their story about what to do to correct these 'market failures'. Those who have the greatest 'storytelling power' will win the game, because the model is 'logically disconnected from its interpretation', that is, from reality.

The false identification of 'perfect competition' with real-life competition

One of the reasons why orthodoxy is so hard to get rid of is precisely because most people – including most economists – do not grasp that the Debreu model has absolutely nothing to say about a real market economy. Most people know that it is highly abstract, but that is also the theory of an ideal gas, so they see the static theory as an extreme, but still useful and fundamentally correct model of real, existing capitalism. 'It must be a good theory since capitalism is such a success'. This false identification is, in my opinion, too often not combated clearly enough by heterodox critics. Regrettably, many heterodox critics attack secondary aspects of the model, like atomism, perfect rationality and/or information. These are clearly closely related to the static nature of the model but can – seen in isolation and given a more common sense, broader interpretation – be seen as 'real' abstractions. As Guerrien (2004) correctly notes regarding Lawson's critique of one of the standard assumptions:

> The problem with this objection is that a neoclassical theorist would agree with it. He would argue that he is considering only a special aspect of human behaviour: the fact that people try to pay less (rather than more) for a given good or try to get more satisfaction (rather than less) from given resources. They then try to derive or to 'deduce' (to use a word that Lawson doesn't like) certain *ceteris paribus* consequences from this assumption.
>
> (Guerrien 2004)

The point here is that it is the ceteris paribus (static) nature of the argument that has to be attacked, not that the orthodox models have completely unrealistic assumptions like 'infinite lives'. As Guerrien (2004) points out: 'This is an approximation that can be accepted: in general, when we take a decision concerning present and future, we do not think about death'. Regarding selfishness, Guerrien points out that 'who can deny that self-love exists? Even Marx supposes that the capitalist's motive is profit and that workers try to get a better life. This is all that is meant when neoclassical theorists assume that people are rational'.

I will return to this topic when discussing Hodgson's insistence that utility maximisation is an absolute key component of orthodox economics, which is correct, and that it cannot be falsified in its static orthodox formulation, but as soon as there is real time in the model, as soon as there is a specified time horizon, then it can be falsified. You buy a good that you thought would maximise your utility, and then it turned out that it did not. You married a person you thought would be the best choice for a life-long partnership and it turned out to be 'hell'. With real time, utility maximisation is what we try to achieve, we try to learn, to change preferences and thus increase our utility. Since the only thing we perfectly know is that we do not have perfect information and there is no way of getting perfect information, it is entirely rational sticking to 'sub-optimal' routines (satisficing) since we cannot know what is 'absolutely' optimal in an only partially known and ever-changing world.

Another way to illustrate the fundamental difference between static and dynamic utility maximisation is to say that a lot of the heterodox critique of the Debreu model is unfair, because it does not start from the fact that there is no time in a Debreu model. One way to try to imagine the utter static character of these models, is to imagine you are in a shop with 100 GBP and you have two nanoseconds before the end of the world. In the first nanosecond you make your choices, the next nanosecond you 'enjoy' what you bought. In that case the information you have is, for all practical purposes, 'perfect', because even if it is wrong, there is no time to learn. There is no time/possibility to do differently next time, since there is no 'next time'. In such a nanosecond world other people can (must?) be treated as 'facts'. Morals, social relations, empathy, altruism do not have any real meaning in a nanosecond world. Neither do such concepts as 'regularities', since there are no events regularly occurring. Every economics student learns that the decision about 'future consumption' is taken in the same split nanosecond as existing goods. The 'period 2 good' is just a subscript. Maybe heterodox economics should start to call this strange 'rationality' for nanosecond rationality, or 'end-of-the-world rationality', or 'no-learning rationality', if one should be so generous as to use the word 'rationality' in connection with this theory at all.

Perfect stagnation vs. dynamic competition

One important way of illustrating the utterly static nature of orthodoxy is to look closer (something Lawson does not do), to the core mechanism of capitalism – competition. As pointed out by, for example Hayek (1948) and Morgenstern (1972), what in orthodox jargon is called (perfect) competition has in fact nothing to do with (real life) competition. This is because neither prices, technology nor preferences change – in fact nothing at all changes. One of the founding fathers of modern game theory, Oscar Morgenstern, wrote very critically about the concept of competition:

> Consider 'competition': the common sense meaning is one of struggle with others, of fight, of attempting to get ahead, or at least to hold one's place. It suffices to consult any dictionary of *any* language to find that it describes rivalry, fight, struggle, etc. Why this word should be used in

> economic theory in a way that contradicts ordinary language is difficult to see. No reasonable case can be made for this absurd usage …
>
> (p. 1164)

No reasonable case from a scientific point of view, but politically there are very good reasons. What orthodoxy calls the perfect competition state should be called *perfect stagnation*. If you are a referee, or at a conference, as a heterodox economist you should always demand that the term 'perfect stagnation' should be used instead of perfect competition. That is one way of pointing out the false identification of real dynamic capitalist innovation-based competition where prices, preferences and production technology change all the time. Frank Hahn, an author who Lawson knows well, always insisted on the fundamental importance of 'price-taking':

> For instance, the competitive equilibrium gains its interest from the postulate that prices must change in all other states of the economy. But there are many other plausible dynamics and the competitive [the Debreu model] one suffers from having *no theory of agents who change prices*.
>
> (Hahn 1984, p. 3)

Another way to illustrate this is to take the common myth that there must be many actors for firms to be price-takers, '*to a market in which no firm or consumer is large enough to affect the market price*' (Samuelson and Nordhaus 2010, p. 35, my emphasis). But this is again just a small-talk story without any scientific value. If the prices are given, one firm – a monopoly – will also have to be a price-taker.[3] What is more, if the price is given, that is, if a firm can sell all it produces at that *given* price (even unit costs only fall marginally due to 'learning by doing'), then the amount supplied would be infinite at constant or increasing returns to scale. That means that the model has no mathematical solution, as pointed out by Hahn:

> But when there are increasing returns it may not be possible to show that there are any logical economic states which qualify as either Arrow-Debreu equilibria or as members of the core. It may also be wrong to think of a very large number of firms.
>
> (Hahn 1984, p. 50)

Franklin M. Fisher – the admirable attempt at dynamics

It took 59 years after Walras's death to prove rigorously the existence of a static equilibrium fixed point (Debreu 1959). After Debreu the obvious challenge was to show the same optimal result in a dynamic model, that is, proving stability.

In 1983, Franklin M. Fisher published his *Disequilibrium Foundations of Equilibrium Economics*. In the introduction, Fisher is critical to the habit among orthodox economists of regarding the system's dynamic motion as no more than an appendix to the static model, but as Fisher points out – 'If stability theory is unsatisfactory, then that foundation [of orthodoxy] is lacking' (Fisher 1983, p. 2). One of the reasons for this is that:

> Much of what economists have to say about the results of competition, the usefulness or lack thereof of governmental intervention and the role of the price system is based on propositions about general equilibrium. These are the propositions rigorously formulated in modern times as the central theorems of welfare economics concerning the relations between Pareto optima and competitive equilibria. These propositions, which may be the single most important set of ideas that economists have to convey to lay people, *implicitly assume that general competitive equilibrium is stable and, indeed, that convergence takes place relatively quickly.* If this were not so, welfare comparisons of equilibria would be largely irrelevant since what would matter would be comparison of the relatively 'transient' behaviour of alternative systems including alternative forms of market organization.
>
> (Fisher 1983, p. 9, my emphasis)

After an impressive analysis of how 'far' it is possible to introduce dynamics, Fisher comes to the conclusion: 'The lesson is clear. Following Schumpeter, we cannot suppose it to be true that an economy in which new opportunities constantly arise will converge to equilibrium …' (Fisher 1983, p. 90).

In 2006, a collection of articles with the title *Samuelsonian Economics and the Twenty-First Century* was published. Of special interest is a brief, four-page article by Franklin M. Fisher entitled *Paul Samuelson and the Stability of General Equilibrium*. Fisher starts by stating:

> The study of the stability of general equilibrium is not a popular indoor sport among present-day economists. Yet, the lack of a fully satisfactory stability analysis is a gaping hole in microeconomic theory. … Samuelson pointed out that the modelling of disequilibrium behaviour over time was essential, but also suggested an adjustment equation[12] that has little or nothing to do with such behaviour.
>
> (Fisher 2009, pp. 142, 144)

We note that Fisher – like Mirowski – points out that Samuelson tries to look like he is dealing with the problem of stability, that is, dynamics, without doing so at all.

Hodgson and many others repeatedly urge heterodox economists to engage seriously with orthodoxy. I fully agree, but one must clearly start with discussing the fundamental axioms of orthodoxy and Fisher shows that there is a 'gaping hole' in orthodox theory. Debreu proved the existence of an equilibrium fix-point, but not uniqueness and no stability – even when you rule out capitalism's most important characteristic, relentless innovation. Hodgson wants heterodox economists to publish in more prestigious journals – and it might be a wise tactic – to write 'around censorship' to get into more prestigious journals and get more prestige and resources to fight orthodoxy more efficiently. Such a 'smart' tactic must not mean that we have any kind of scientific respect for orthodoxy.

Every orthodox economist should be forced to admit – when they use a price-taking model – that they have a *deus ex machina* auctioneer setting the prices. If Lawson had directed his fire against these fundamental weaknesses of the static paradigm, and not at maths in general, that would in my opinion have promoted heterodox, that is, real-world economics, much more efficiently, because many – even the 'core cadre' of heterodox economics – are, in my experience, not sufficiently aware of how utterly weak the scientific basis of orthodoxy actually is.

Hodgson and Cambridge as the heterodox citadel

Hodgson devotes much space and attention to Cambridge as a 'citadel' of heterodox economics. The title of the first chapter is 'Space Exists to stop Everything Happening in Cambridge'. In the introduction, Hodgson writes: 'This book considers the future of heterodox economics. But it is not principally a dissection of ideas' (Hodgson 2019, p. 2). Even if the book is not primarily a dissection of ideas, I still hold that it would be interesting to discuss the theoretic heritage of Keynes and the Cambridge 'circus'. Was Keynes really heterodox? In what sense were Robinson and Kaldor Keynesians? Hodgson quotes several economists who were in Cambridge after the Second World War and experienced a non-pluralistic atmosphere. What I find strange is that although he refers to Luigi Pasinetti's book, Pasinetti (2007), in a footnote, he does not discuss it. The title of Pasinetti's book is '*Keynes and the Cambridge Keynesians: A "Revolution in Economics" to be accomplished*', which seems to me to demand more attention than a mere sentence saying that Pasinetti was in Cambridge, 1960–1976 and that 'he tried to combine Kaldorian and Sraffian approaches'.

Especially since Pasinetti's main theses is that Keynes and the Cambridge Keynesians started a revolution in economics that 'succeeded halfway – it did from an economic policy point of view, but it did not succeed on the theoretical level'. Pasinetti's book 'deals mainly with the half that did not succeed – at least not yet' (2007, p. xiii). Pasinetti raises many important questions, but he does not pose clearly and sharply enough the key question: how radical was Keynes' *theoretical* break with neoclassical Economics? In my opinion, it is clear that Keynes' theoretical heritage is very contradictory and consequently has given legitimacy to both 'bastard' and 'true' Keynesians. Evidence shows that Robinson, Kaldor and Goodwin were critical of Keynes' 'Marshallian luggage', however Pasinetti is not very willing to admit that.

Sraffa is given a prominent role in Pasinetti's book, but is Sraffa really a Keynesian-inspired economist? Pasinetti argues for the need for dynamics, but

Sraffa is entirely static – and it is obvious that Sraffa cannot be 'dynamised' any more than general equilibrium theory can. Is Pasinetti really proposing a Keynesian research agenda or a more general, dynamic heterodox one, which neither takes Keynes nor Sraffa as its starting point? What kind of value theory did Keynes have? Are wages really the marginal productivity of labour? What is the relation between profits and the marginal efficiency of capital? Are profits a result of exploitation? Do the Cambridge Keynesians have a value theory? Pasinetti – like most heterodox economists – does not discuss whether static general equilibrium theory (SGET) is an ideology or a scientific theory, despite the fact that the description he gives of when and how the SGET emerged – as a reaction to Marx's theory of value – is clearly making 'ideology' a candidate in Pasinetti's book.

Pasinetti's starting point – Keynes' unaccomplished revolution

Pasinetti quotes – as many have done before him – a letter from Keynes to George Bernard Shaw from 1 January 1935, where Keynes writes: 'I believe myself to be writing a book on economic theory which will largely revolutionise ... the way the world thinks about economic problems' (2007, p. 6). Pasinetti is, of course, aware that there are very many alternative interpretations. Pasinetti writes that it is possible to

> ... assemble (perfectly orthodox) arguments that Keynes had used earlier in similar contexts. In this way, one may even conclude that, essentially, there is essentially nothing new, in spite of the claims to the contrary. In a nutshell, 'it was all in Marshall', whose orthodoxy was, after all, on many points ambiguous.
>
> (2007, p. 6)

Pasinetti disagrees with this way of understanding Keynes. Pasinetti wants to 'claim that a genuine effort was made to break with tradition. The effort was real and radical. It was strongly aimed at "scientific revolution"' (2007, p. 6). Like Pasinetti, I think there is enough evidence to conclude that Keynes intended to make a paradigm shift. But intentions are one thing, another is how these intentions were realised in the 'General Theory' (GT).

An overview of the enormous literature on the genesis and interpretation of the GT is way beyond the scope of this chapter, but I think that by now there is almost a consensus – as Pasinetti himself indicates – that there are elements of both continuity and a break with orthodoxy. The question then becomes, what theoretical shortcomings made the 'revolution' not only unfinished, but so easy to incorporate into orthodoxy in the form of 'bastard Keynesianism', to use Joan Robinson's concept? The short answer is that there is no real time, no real dynamics in the formulas that Keynes used in the 'General Theory'. The Norwegian, Nobel "memorial" prize laurate, T. Haavelmo wrote in 'The Keynesian Revolution' from 1977 that the attacks by the Keynesians on orthodoxy:

> ...paradoxically showed that to a large degree Keynes and his followers were attached to the old theoretical system. Instead of starting directly with the problem, how the high unemployment level of around 30% should be explained, Keynes had a tendency to start with how such an underemployment should be explained in a neo-classical model. [...] The most important error that was committed was the one to try to explain the world of the thirties by means of a Walras-model. That model was irrelevant. Especially it was misleading to analyse saving-investment processes with the aid of an ordinary supply-demand scheme. [...] Keynes looked at a dynamic-demanding phenomenon, which one could not shed light on by static exchange-market models of the classical variety.[4]

Haavelmo concludes his discussion of the Keynesian revolution by stating that since Keynes 'did not build an explicit dynamic theory, he was always in a logical danger-zone, and that created a lot of confusion'.[5] Hodgson points out, referring to Lawson, that confusion has in no way ended (Hodgson 2019, p. 51).

Dynamics, Goodwin and Schumpeter

I agree with Hodgson that the neo-Schumpeterian evolutionary theory is an important heterodox current. It would have been very interesting if Hodgson had discussed Pasinetti's chapter on Goodwin, because Pasinetti clearly indicated that Goodwin did not blossom in the Cambridge atmosphere. After 30 years in Cambridge, Goodwin went to Sienna and 'the effects were astonishing. Goodwin's scientific productivity literally exploded' (2007, p. 211). Pasinetti's chapter on Goodwin is entitled: 'the missed Keynes–Schumpeter connection' and Pasinetti mentions the fact that Goodwin, of the three original patrons of the *Cambridge Journal of Economics*, 'most of all, regretted the absence of Schumpeter among the authors explicitly mentioned for inspiration' (2007, p. 205).

I think Pasinetti underestimates the theoretical differences that Goodwin probably had with Keynesianism. As Pasinetti points out, Schumpeter's review of the 'General Theory' was 'significant – extraordinarily caustic and sarcastic' (2007, p. 27). Goodwin was so close to Schumpeter that he was asked by Schumpeter's widow to edit for publication the last and unfinished part of Schumpeter's *History of Economic Analysis*, so it's reasonable to think that Goodwin shared most of Schumpeter's critique of 'General Theory'. Schumpeter does not agree with Keynes' connection between employment and output:

> ... reasoning on the assumption that variations in output are uniquely related to variations in employment imposes the further assumption that all production functions remain invariant. Now the outstanding feature of capitalism is that they do not but that, on the contrary, they are

> constantly revolutionized. The capitalist process is essentially a process of change of the type which is being assumed away in this book, and all of its characteristic phenomena and problems arise from the fact that it is such a process.
>
> (Schumpeter 1936, p. 794)

The point I want to make is that if one is to re-establish the Keynes–Schumpeter connection, one must dare to go into the real differences between them. Keynes has a concept of competition that is very Marshallian. Keynes does not have any fundamental critique of the concept of perfect 'competition' (= perfect *stagnation*). This means that his model is a static equilibrium, one with a dynamic story artificially attached to it. One consequence – pointed out by Schumpeter and implemented by the 'bastard Keynesians' – is that we are down to friction, stickiness etc., that is, 'imperfections' and the only rational, rigorous answer is to try to get rid of the imperfections, getting wages and interest rates as flexible as theory assumes that they are etc. etc.

Another point that needs to be sorted out is Keynes' use of 'psychological laws'. Schumpeter is also very critical of Keynes' use of concepts like liquidity preference, 'which is another *"deus ex machina"*, there is a whole Olympus of them' (Schumpeter 1936).

Robinson and Kaldor on Keynes

There are at least three articles by Robinson that give an overall evaluation of the 'Keynesian revolution'. There is a series of lectures delivered at the Delhi School of Economics entitled 'Marx, Marshall and Keynes' from 1955, there is 'Kalecki and Keynes' from 1964, articles on aspects of Keynes' theory, but first and foremost the article entitled 'The Keynesian revolution' from her 'Economic Philosophy' published in 1962 that goes directly to the heart of the matter. One is tempted to cite it in its entirety since it is really very much to the point from start to end. Robinson starts out by countering those who do not like the term 'Keynesian revolution' and say that there was nothing so very new in the GT. Robinson points out that the Marshallians in the Treasury, by impeccable Marshallian logic, proved that public works would be to no advantage for the economy as a whole – and Robinson comments: 'Nowadays this seems merely laughable'.

Robinson then singles out some points that were really new in the 'General Theory'. First, Keynes thought that 'capitalism wisely managed, can probably be made more efficient for attaining economic ends than any system yet in sight'. That is, farewell to self-regulating capitalism and Soviet-style planning. As a follow-up she credits Keynes for bringing back 'the moral problem that *laissez-faire* had abolished [...] Pigou set out the argument of his *Economics of Welfare* in terms of exceptions to the rule that *laissez-faire* ensures the maximum satisfaction; he did not question the rule' (Robinson 1962, p. 74). The conclusion is: 'What made the *General Theory* so hard to accept was not its intellectual content, which in a calm mood can easily be mastered, but its shocking implications' (1962, p. 75). On the political level:

> By making it impossible to believe any longer in an automatic reconciliation of conflicting interest into a harmonious whole, the *General Theory* brought out into the open the problem of choice and judgment that the neoclassicals had managed to smother. The ideology to end ideologies broke down. Economics once more became Political Economy.
>
> (1962, p. 76)

She acknowledges that Keynes:

> brought history and theory together again. But for theorists the descent into time has not been easy. After twenty years, the awakened Prince is still dazed and groggy. Keynes himself was not quite steady on his feet. His remark about the time-less multiplier [GT, first edition, p. 122] is highly suspicious. And the hard core of analysis, round which his flashing controversy wheels, is based upon comparisons of static short-period equilibrium positions each with a given rate of investment going on, though it purports to trace the effect of a change in the rate of investment taking place at a moment of time.
>
> (1962, p. 78)

This is very close to agreeing with Haavelmo, that Keynes was constantly in a logical danger zone, with his dynamic reasoning, but static models. Robinson follows up the above with another important observation:

> We have broken out of static equilibrium at least in connection with the accumulation of capital. ... In other branches of economics, the replacement of timeless equilibrium by historical development has still a long struggle before it. Keynes himself was not interested in the theory of relative prices. Gerald Shove used to say that Maynard had never spent the twenty minutes necessary to understand the theory of value. On these topics he was content to leave orthodoxy alone. He carried a good deal of Marshallian luggage with him and never thoroughly unpacked it to throw out the clothes he could not wear. The Keynesian revolution is only now slowly fighting its way into this terrain.
>
> (1962, p. 79)

Hodgson and Lawson on economics and ideology

There are some interesting differences between Lawson and Hodgson when it comes to the question of ideology. If one goes through all the pages where the index in Hodgson's book says that he discusses ideology, it is very clear that Hodgson does not have a concept of ideology as a mindset, thought habits and framework, that can contain very different, even totally opposed political projects. Take Catholicism: it is an ideology because, for almost a thousand years, that is, before the slow and gradual secularisation of society beginning with the Enlightenment, it forced practically everybody to formulate their political programme in religious terms. An ideology is important because it offers a world view that has a certain grip on people's mind. But not a total grip. The Catholic Church is against contraception, but of course millions of Catholics do not obey the 'ban'. The Catholic Church does not expel them since they still have power over other aspects of people's lives, in particular their political and moral views etc. Hodgson sees that there is not a one-to-one relation between being orthodox and being a Chicago-style pro-market neoliberal; a few orthodox economists are social-democrats. From this he draws the conclusion that the orthodox theory does not function as an ideology. But a few catholic Liberation theologians do not disprove the fact that, for centuries, the Church used its ideological power to protect elite interests from critique.

Lawson really deserves credit for having started and continued an interesting debate about the nature of heterodox and orthodox economics, not least the debate about in what sense orthodoxy is an ideology. In a recent book chapter 'Economics and Ideology', he puts forward two possible definitions of ideology, Ideology 1 and 2, in the following way:

> **Ideology 1**: A relatively unchallenged set of (possibly distorted or misleading) background ideas that every society or community possesses which forms the basis of, or significantly informs, general opinion or 'common sense …'.
>
> **Ideology 2**: A set of ideas designed, or anyway intentionally employed, in order to justify, preserve, reinforce, develop or transform some existing state of affairs, where the intended outcome is preferred for any of a number of reasons, perhaps because it facilitates or legitimates various advantages for some dominant or privileged or even some disadvantaged group, and where these ideas mostly work in the manner described by way of intentionally masking or misrepresenting the nature of reality or what is actually taking place.

But what immediately strikes me is that there is no contradiction between these two definitions. On the contrary, in most cases there is a strong will and an organisation behind spreading an ideology, but a particular set of ideas would not be useful for that 'organisation' if it was not internalised by parts of society as their own ideas.

Lawson argues against both versions of ideology and proposes an alternative definition of ideology that is 'a set of beliefs that bears *not* directly upon the nature of the underlying economic system at all. Rather it *is precisely the doctrine that all serious economics must take the form of mathematical modelling*'. But, as Hodgson points out, Coase, for example, who Lawson himself describes as a 'mainstream' contributor, did not use mathematics and even ridiculed the excessive use of mathematics (Hodgson 2019, p. 68). Marshall did not use much mathematics; does that make him a heterodox economist? Or does the content of verbal economic thinking count? If the use of mathematics is just a rough criterion, what is then, the decisive criteria for being heterodox? Lawson seems to have a substantial criterion because he also asks himself 'What is wrong with economics?' and replies 'The clear answer is that it is mostly simply irrelevant'. An answer that resonates with Kaldor's 'The irrelevance of equilibrium economics' (Kaldor 1972). The problem is that an ideology might be completely irrelevant as a way to understand the world, to make roughly correct predictions, but at the same time it can be very *politically* relevant. The ideology of 'non-historic' peoples was of course wrong, but very politically relevant. When the command economies after the fall of the Berlin Wall were treated with shock therapy, that is yet another instance of an irrelevant static theory being used on a highly dynamic transition. The static theory was, of course, scientifically irrelevant but politically it was very relevant for those who correctly knew that they would benefit from the shock therapy. Since economic theory always operates in society, one must always discuss both a theory's scientific and political relevance.

Is there a future for heterodox economics?

Hodgson gives several reasons why it is necessary to raise that question. First of all, 'As several prominent exponents of heterodoxy have noted, there is little consensus on the meaning of the term' (Hodgson 2019, p. 49). Second, while heterodoxy 'can legitimately and beneficially be diverse ... it is unlikely to make substantial progress unless the criteria of inclusion and the *raison d'être* are agreed, at least in some rough outline' (2019, p. 49). One consequence of this lack of a common understanding is that it has the danger that excessive pluralism means endless debates over everything, which greatly inhibits cumulative, collective progress (2019, p. 155). At the end of the book Hodgson launches eight different survival strategies. They all contain 'food for thought' for those of us regarding themselves as heterodox economists.

My reason for discussing the basis of orthodox general equilibrium theory, was to try to show that from the very beginning it was an ideological project and not a scientific one. Only mental or mathematical models with real time can be scientific economics, given the dynamic character of its core object of study – markets. Can perfect, static equilibrium models be used in meteorology? No, meteorology would cease to be a science. Consequently, when Hodgson poses most of his eight strategical choices of working inside or outside of 'economics', that frames the choices in a wrong way. How one should relate tactically to the institutions that are based on GET is important, but what is most important now is to agree that the static equilibrium model was chosen for politico-ideological, and not scientific reasons. There obviously is a need for a common 'rough' consensus on how capitalism works, and as we know from history, Schumpeter and Marx had a very similar analysis of the dynamics of capitalist competition, despite being politically worlds apart. In my opinion, Anwar Shaik's magnum opus, 'Capitalism. Competition, Conflict, Crises' is a good basis for further scientific progress. His key concepts of 'real competition' and 'turbulent regulation' are constantly confronted with, and developed from, facts, what Marx called 'Realabstraktionen'. There is also a need, as Robinson and Kaldor (Kaldor 1983) pointed out, to get rid of the Marshallian luggage and the 'psychological laws' in Keynes. If it still makes sense to define oneself as 'post-Keynesian' after that – time will show. That is a revolution to be finished.

One aspect of economics that is lacking in Shaik is the ecological one. No economic theory is relevant for all epochs; a theory of such generality is more a philosophy, like historical materialism. The success of Keynesianism was, as Pasinetti points out, mostly political. It broke the taboo of state intervention. In this century, humanity must get onto a sustainable path, both regarding global warming and our use of finite resources, so therefore insights from the heterodox currents in ecological economics must be part of the heterodox paradigm.

My answer to Hodgson's challenges is yes, there is a future for dynamic (heterodox) economics, because only dynamic economics is economics as science and not an ideology.

Notes

1 All page numbers refer to 'More Heat than Light', Mirowski (1990), if not otherwise stated.
2 References to Samuelson's papers left out for reasons of readability.
3 For a more detailed discussion of this point see Guerrien (2002).
4 These 'Memorandums' are edited notes from Haavelmo's lectures in the Spring semester 1977 by J. C. Andvig, but the real author is Haavelmo. Regrettably the Memorandum has not been translated into any foreign language. All translations are mine.
5 My translation from Norwegian.

References

Currie, M. and Steedman, I., 1990. *Wrestling with Time, 1990 Problems in Economic Theory*, Manchester: Manchester University Press.

Debreu, G., 1959. *The Theory of Value: An Axiomatic Analysis of Economic Equilibrium*, New York: Wiley.

Fisher, F. M., 1983. *Disequilibrium Foundations of Equilibrium Economics*, Cambridge: Cambridge University Press.

Fisher, F. M., 2009. Disequilibrium and Stability, in M. Szenberg, L. Ramrattan and E. Fullbrook (eds.), *Ontology and Economics: Tony Lawson and His Critics*, Abingdon: Routledge.

Guerrien, B., 2002. *Dictionnaire d'Analyse Economique*, 3rd edition, Paris: La Decouverte.

Guerrien, B., 2004. Irrelevance and Ideology, *Post-Autistic Economics Review*, 6 December, no. 29, article 3.

Hahn, F., 1984. *Equilibrium and Macroeconomics*, Cambridge: MIT Press.

Hayek, F. A., 1948. The Meaning of Competition, in F. A. Hayek (ed.), *Individualism and Economic Order*, Chicago, IL: University of Chicago Press.

Hodgson, G., 2019. *Is there a Future for Heterodox Economics? Institutions, Ideology and a Scientific Community*, Cheltenham: Edward Elgar.

Ingrao, B. and Israel, G., 1990. *The Invisible Hand: Economic Equilibrium in the History of Science*, Cambridge, MA: MIT Press.

Kaldor, N., 1972. The Irrelevance of Equilibrium Economics, *Economic Journal*, 82 (328): 1237–1235.

Kaldor, N., 1983. Keynesian Economics after Fifty Years, in G. D. N. Worswick and J. Trevithick (eds.), *Keynes and the Modern World: Proceedings of the Keynes Centenary Conference*, King's College, Cambridge: Cambridge University Press.

Lawson, T., 2016. Economics and Ideology, in P. Ness and L. Price (eds.), *Crisis System: A Critical Realist and Environmental Critique of Economics and the Economy*, London and New York: Routledge.

Mirowski, P., 1989. *More Heat than Light: Economics as Social Physics. Physics as Nature's Economics*, Cambridge: Cambridge University Press.

Morgenstern, O., 1972. Thirteen Critical Points in Contemporary Economic Theory: An Interpretation, *Journal of Economic Literature*, 10 (4): 1163–1189.

Pasinetti, L. L., 2007. *Keynes and the Cambridge Keynesians: A Revolution in Economics to be Accomplished*, Cambridge and New York: Cambridge University Press.

Robinson, J., 1962. *Economic Philosophy*, Bungay: Penguin.

Samuelson, P. and Nordhaus, W., 2010. *Economics*, 19th edition, Boston, MA: McGraw-Hill Irwin.

Schumpeter, J. 1936. The General Theory of Employment, Interest and Money by John Maynard Keynes, *Journal of the American Statistical Association*, 31 (196): 791–795.

Shaik, A., 2016. *Capitalism: Competition, Conflict, Crises*, Oxford: Oxford University Press.

2 The past and the future

The philosophy and history of economics, and the emerging Risk Society

Jon Mulberg

Introduction

While the Extinction Rebellion protests, alongside the school student environmental protests, have marked out 2019, heterodox economists may have missed the significance of an earlier protest because it is so familiar to them – the protests of students of Economics. These began with the 'Post-Autistic' group in France, and later spread worldwide, including renowned centres of economics such as Cambridge.

Student protests are not new, but these protests are somewhat unique in that the protest is not about politics (such as peace or poverty), or the use that the 'science' is being put to (as nuclear research or animal experimentation might be). The protest is about the *content* of the discipline and the syllabus being taught. The complaint is that economics is vacuous and that knowledge of alternative schools and other disciplines, and even the history of their own discipline, is needed.

The neutrality of economic 'science' was also challenged during the 'Brexit' debate, where most publicly funded economics bureaus (including the Bank of England and the IMF to name but two) lined up to denounce an EU exit. This advice was dismissed by the majority of UK voters.

These challenges to scientific authority signify a new departure, and can be viewed as part of an emerging, self-confrontational society, where the old certainties of the past no longer apply. This chapter outlines this new society and what a new economics of this emerging society might look like, using the ideas of Foucault to suggest that the new economics will be about politics and power. Also, following Foucault, the chapter traces the political debates behind the development of economic thought, which have been airbrushed out of most histories. This process lays bare the political basis of economic 'science'.

The politics of these past debates will also help an understanding of the inadequacies of contemporary economics of the environment. The chapter will conclude by looking at alternative, heterodox schools to show how an alternative ecological economics, and a Green New Deal, could be constructed.

The Risk Society and the idea of science

The protests that we are now witnessing are therefore different in character to those of the past. They represent a challenge to expertise as much as a protest about outcomes. Beck viewed this form of protest as part of a new form of society, in which science, expertise and knowledge, as well as authority, are challenged. He termed this form 'reflexive modernity'. 'Reflexivity' is used to describe a 'self-confrontational', questioning society, where certainty and trust no longer exist (Beck, 1994). Beck believes this is due to the 'side effects' of industrial society (Beck, Bonss and Lau, 2003) – the growing level of environmental degradation, which is creating unprecedented risks. Risk is not new, but Beck maintains that the risks we now face are different in character. These are now massive risks that transcend time and space – they cut across national boundaries and can affect future generations. The risks are also *manufactured* rather than natural. They are the by-product of the normal functioning of the industrial society. The risks are also increasingly invisible – they can only be investigated and understood using scientific equipment and knowledge (Beck, 1992). This new society, characterized by massive manufactured risks and reflexivity, Beck called the *Risk Society*. He viewed it as the next phase of the modernization of industrial society (Beck, Bonss and Lau, 2003). While the old industrial society was focused on the production of goods, the new emerging Risk Society will be focused on the avoidance of 'bads'.

The new Risk Society will require a new approach to knowledge and understanding (a new ontology and epistemology), and also a new approach to the study of scientific method (a new methodology). The sort of knowledge required for the production of goods will not suffice for the avoidance of 'bads'. Modern risks show up starkly the limitations of modern conceptions of science.

The usual conception of science, the idea of science most people would hold, would be some notion of what is known as *positivism*. Smith outlines six main features of positivism:

1. *Naturalism*: There is one scientific method, and both social sciences and physical sciences should use the same methods.
2. *Phenomenalism*: Knowledge is gained empirically.
3. *Nominalism*: Concepts are rooted in experience and have no independent existence.
4. *Atomism*: The objects of study are discrete and cannot be broken down into smaller units.
5. *Universal Laws*: Science involves the investigation of empirical regularities.
6. *Objectivity*: Facts and values are distinct, and science is value free.

(Adapted from Smith, 1998, p. 76)

There has been much debate over the adequacy of this approach for economics (see Mulberg, 1995 and the writings of Tony Lawson), but the point being made by Beck is that many of the risks in contemporary society have gone beyond the boundaries of the methodology. It is, for example, hard to apply universal laws for the long-term effects of risks – we cannot know if the regularities found in laboratory testing will apply in the world outside or in the long term. Similarly, it is impossible to isolate discrete units of analysis in a world characterized by interconnectivity and complexity.

Furthermore, conducting science in the Risk Society purely on the basis of empirical knowledge and without unobservable concepts will be impossible. Indeed 'Risk', itself, cannot be seen until it becomes manifest and damage is done. As Beck puts it 'threats are not things' (Beck, 2009, p. 9). Beck suggests that many risks are either incalculable, or the calculation is subjective. In addition, 'safety' is not a scientific concept, and often the safety of other people is being decided. These factors mean that facts and values cannot be separated. Beck believes physical and social science need to converge, and rather than social science (including economics) becoming like physical science, the two need to overlap: 'scientific rationality without social rationality remains empty, but social rationality without scientific rationality remains blind' (Beck, 1992, p. 30).[1]

It should be noted that avoiding *all* risks is simply impossible – we would go nowhere and do nothing. In fact, we can say that decisions on risks are also decisions on how we live our lives. They are economic, social and political decisions as much as technical measurements of probabilities (Beck, 1992).

Given this, perhaps instead of asking what the 'scientific' method consists of, we should ask what we want scientific knowledge to do – scientific knowledge for what? Why would a scientific economics be valuable? Fay suggests that our discussion of knowledge is always linked to an understanding of the world (Fay, 1987). Knowledge is instrumental, and there is always an implied political theory in accounts of social life. This applies to positivism also, in spite of its claim to separate facts and values. Positivism is justified by Comte's conception of 'prediction and control' – we can use scientific knowledge to predict the future and control or react to it. Fay points to the congruence of explanation and prediction in positivism – a positivist 'explanation' could equally have been a prediction, and the explanation is tested by its predictive ability (Fay, 1975). This leads to an idea of 'policy science', that technocrats decide the best policy for a given objective.

This has implications for both economics and for the conception of the Risk Society. Fay (1975) believes that positivism is linked to the development of the very industrial society that Beck claimed is in decline. As Beck points out, presently we neither predict nor control. As he dramatically puts it: 'The idea that we are masters of the universe has totally collapsed and turned into its opposite' (2015, p. 75). Indeed, we should not be attempting mastery of the social world: 'social science can no longer take a god's eye point of view, and the control that goes with it, but it can find another way to know' (Beck, Bonss and Lau, 2003, p. 3).

This other way Fay calls 'Critical Social Science'. Fay regards humans as 'self-interpreting' and can change themselves through self-reflection (Fay, 1987). The project of critical social science is to change how people think of themselves by offering alternative conceptions both of the self and of society. Critical social science can change people and alter the social order by revealing to social actors that their own conception of their 'capacities and interests', and their conception of the social order, is false. Critical social theory uncovers patterns hidden from social actors. It can change people and the society they live in by making manifest how our lives are impoverished because they are ordered around falsehoods (Fay, 1987).

For critical social science, the test of explanations of social actors and the social order is that they should be ratified by those who they are attempting to emancipate (Fay, 1987). This is not dissimilar to the conclusion Beck reaches concerning risk, when he suggests decisions need to be made in the 'public sphere'. He suggests we need a 'communicative logic' of risks, which are after all decisions about how we live our lives (Beck, 1992). At present there is only a facade of pluralism, but in actual fact the discourse is dominated by a technocracy (Lash and Wynne, 1992).

An emancipatory and transformative social theory is likely to be fraught, though. As Fay points out, abandoning self-(mis)conceptions and relinquishing known social orders virtually involves acquiring a new identity (Fay, 1987). One of the ways of overcoming this resistance to emancipation is to show up exactly how our lives have been ordered around falsehoods, and to make manifest the social patterns that are hidden. The next section discusses one way to attempt this.

Social power and the history of economic thought

One of the social sciences that has come under fire precisely for taking both 'a god's eye point of view' and also for 'the control that goes with it' is the so-called science of economics. If nothing else, the 2008 crash has prompted questions of legitimation for the economics discipline. After all, if economics claims to be a positive science, with an attendant congruence of explanation and prediction, a spectacular failure to predict does not leave this 'science' with much to say.

Curiously, there appears to be little change within the economics discipline (Hodgson, 2009). While we might understand there being resistance to change within the discipline, what is less clear is why economics continues to be held in high esteem, why it continues to inform policy, and indeed why economists continue to be employed.

To understand this, we can apply the ideas of Foucault. He maintained that human sciences, including economics, are not politically neutral. They serve a political function of maintenance of the social and political order. Economics is part of a system of *governance* (Foucault, 1979). It acts as a legitimator for political decisions, and indeed serves to alter our beliefs, which Foucault calls *governmentality* (Foucault, 1979; Gordon, 1991).

Foucault explains how it is that, almost regardless of the activities of its practitioners, a human science is held in regard. This is precisely because the strictures of positive science are ignored. For Foucault, what is accepted as scientific knowledge is historically specific, and will vary in different places at different times. It is governed by rules that determine all aspects of enquiry – what is to count as false or true, what evidence is acceptable, what subjects investigated and what questions asked, even what is thought (Kologlugil, 2010). These he called 'discursive rules', and the collective practices 'discourses'.[2] For Foucault, the content of knowledge is political – he refers to a 'Politics of Truth'.

This political dimension of knowledge links it to power. When Foucault says, 'knowledge is power', he means that power determines what is to count as legitimate knowledge. For Foucault the discourse is now the main source of power, replacing the coercion of the past. The discourse creates processes of self-modification (Lemke, 2002); Foucault calls this the 'conduct of conduct' – social conduct is orchestrated as part of a social structure. However, power is everywhere and cannot be avoided – we cannot be emancipated from power; indeed, power can itself be emancipatory. Foucault views power as a network flowing along interconnecting pathways. Social actors constantly use power or have power used on them; power is never one-way (de Lima, 2010).

Power is different to domination, where those subordinated have no real choices (Foucault, 1988, cited in Lemke, 2002, p. 5). Power involves manipulating the decisions and choices of others. This is similar to Lukes' 'third face' of power, whereby power is used to manipulate how we think (Lukes, 2004). Governmentality denotes governance through the manipulation (deliberate or otherwise) of our beliefs. Economics, and the explanations it proffers in the name of science, are a major constituent of modern society and the way it is governed.

To achieve this governmentality, each scientific discipline maintains discipline over its practitioners. It does this by enforcing discursive rules and disciplining those who challenge them – perhaps by asking awkward questions or challenging evidence. Economics (and the other human sciences) is not a value-free objective science, but part of a political order. Economic decisions are an example of what Habermas called the 'scientization of politics', whereby political decisions are removed from the political forum and instead taken by policy scientists (Habermas, 1969).

To create a 'counter-discourse' we need to debunk the current regime of truth. One of the ways to do this is by studying the discipline's past. This is not simply a history of who said what but is instead a critical examination of application of the discursive rules – what questions were asked, what counted as evidence, which theories flourished, and which were subjugated. This Foucault called an 'archaeology' – the study of the archives of the discipline. Kuhn (1962) pointed out how sciences re-wrote their history so as to make it appear a smooth path leading to the current paradigm. Foucault suggests that, instead of the authorized histories, we should look for discontinuities, schisms and debates (de Lima, 2010). These show how claims to truth were contested (Kologlugil, 2010) and show up the political character of the 'science'.

This approach to the study of the past has two elements. The deconstruction of the discipline – bringing to light the hidden assumptions, history and doctrine – is the 'negative' aspect. There is also a 'positive' construction of alternative approaches, generating new discursive rules. To begin this, Foucault suggests we combine 'erudite knowledge' of heterodox approaches with 'naive knowledge' from social movements. Foucault refers to this as a *genealogy*. However, he does not regard the creation of discipline-specific archaeologies and genealogies as his task. It is instead the task of those creating the historically situated counter-discourses; this is in fact our job. Foucault described his writings as a 'toolbox' to attack power systems (Foucault, 1975, cited in McLaren, 2009), and said pointedly that 'I write for users, not readers' (Foucault, 1974, cited in O'Farrell, 2005).

A Foucauldian archaeology of economics will bring out its hidden history – the hidden assumptions, debates and fissures within the discipline, and show up the political basis of so-called economic 'science'. By looking at the archaeology of economics and focusing on the ruptures and trajectory of economic thought, we can expose the ideological basis of economic 'science' and give the lie to the notion that the science has progressed. We can show how the past debates are political, and that they are still relevant. We can also search for 'subjugated knowledge' from heterodox schools to provide an alternative.

The hidden history of Economics

An archaeology of Economics reveals that there is a fundamental dilemma at the heart of an economic 'science'. In order for economics to fulfil its function as a legitimator of existing social order, it needs be accepted as scientific. The modern notion of science – positivism – has, as we noted above, an inbuilt political programme, not of *laissez-faire* but of policy planning. Positive science is justifiable by reference to prediction and control, which actually suggest state intervention rather than individualism and a minimal state. The need for a modernist economic science does not square with the contemporary political programme. As Myrdal pointed out, while this does not mean *laissez-faire* cannot be defended, this would require a demonstration of why intervention is not optimal (Myrdal, 1958 [1933]). This dilemma was never resolved (Robinson, 1962).

This is a throwback to classical economics. The 'true neoclassical' theory of Marshall and Pigou could be said to be a continuation of the classical economics. While the received view is that the break with the classical economics of Ricardo[3] began with the neoclassics, Foucault (justifiably) believes this came later (Foucault, 1979); actually, the term 'neoclassical' (implying a revision of the classics) was applied to economics by the institutional economist Thorstein Veblen. The socialist aspect of Ricardian theory was brought out by Marx's critique of the labour theory of value and, given that neoclassical economics was a development of classical economics, it is unsurprising that the socialist corollaries of value theory persisted in the neoclassical reformulation. Diminishing marginal utility could be applied to income, so that the maximum overall utility would obtain when income was equally distributed. As Joan Robinson pointed out, this suggests a raft of egalitarian interventions, not a policy of *laissez-faire* (Robinson, 1962).

This fundamental predicament was behind the development of economic thought (Robinson, 1962). The marginalists (and it is worth reiterating that contemporary orthodox economics is *not* neoclassical – see Mulberg, 1995 and Colander, 2000), had a clear political programme involving the avoidance of socialist conclusions. Jevons simply denied utility could be compared between people, Edgeworth developed his indifference curve approach to price, Pareto developed his 'efficiency' criteria, and Samuelson developed a 'revealed preference' approach. The success of these theories can be explained because they avoid the egalitarian conclusions of the classics and neoclassics.

These developments in economic theory are often couched in terms of scientific development and the rejection of non-observable concepts such as measurable utility, but this was not even the aim of the early marginalists. Jevons and Edgeworth were utilitarians, the latter even proposed an ethical calculus alongside an economic calculus. Pareto realized that any 'pure' economic theory would be limited, and the condition of 'Pareto optimum' was simply a statement of the limits of such a pure economics and was never meant to be a decision rule (Mulberg, 1995).

Later authors tried to avoid the issues raised by marginal utility by dispensing with it. Hicks and Allen proposed an ordinal measure of utility which cannot be directly compared between people. They plugged this into indifference analysis. Samuelson proposed dispensing with utility altogether and looked at observed behaviour in his 'revealed preference' theory. These were justified as scientific advances that did not use unobservable concepts. Of course, they were nothing of the sort – ordinal utility is no more observable than cardinal utility, indifference is unobservable, and revealed preference theory has identical axioms and is de facto an identical theory to that of Hicks and Allen. Furthermore, these theories have no maximand – we have *price* theory but no *value* theory. As Arrow and Sen subsequently showed, we also cannot get a social optimum from ordinalism (see Mulberg, 1995, ch. 2).

The underlying dilemma of squaring a need for a positivist science based on prediction and control with a political programme based on *laissez-faire* was never solved, either by the neoclassics or the marginalists. One approach that took the idea of prediction and control seriously was market socialism. These economists pointed out that if economic data is objective, or even if a market feedback mechanism obtains, then there was no reason why goods and services could not be provided by state enterprises. If pricing was wrong then shortages or surpluses would signal this, and prices could be adjusted.

This was a major debate in the 1920s to 1930s; it was first promoted by Fred Taylor as president of the American Economic Association. The main response did not come from orthodox economics but from the Austrian School; indeed, it was this debate that helped the school realize its distinctive character (Mulberg, 1995). It was the Austrian School that furnished Robbins' 'choice' definition of economics that is now ubiquitous. This definition was expressly contradictory to that of Marshall, and Robbins employed an expressly different theory (1932, p. 1). The Austrian School approach was expressly political and not scientific; Hayek railed against 'scientism'. *Homo oeconomicus* was an ideal type to be used as a heuristic device, this was not a real person who can be observed. Choice and evaluation are not observable. Furthermore, economic commodities are never fully specified, and have an infinite range of different qualities. The entrepreneur must constantly alter commodities to meet constantly changing demands (Mulberg, 1995). Hayek's concern was really with factor markets, and there is evidence from Soviet-bloc command economies that his fears on this were not unjustified. However, his approach marked a complete break with neoclassical and marginalist economics, the consequences of which are profound, and we shall investigate these shortly.

The orthodox response is to simply incorporate Austrian School concepts alongside orthodox economics concepts and ignore their incompatibilities. Other embarrassing theories were treated in a similar manner. Imperfect competition was a critique of market equilibrium; marginal-cost pricing was part of the market socialist approach. We have already mentioned the work of Arrow and Sen, but the theory of second best was also (unwittingly) a critique of general equilibrium. The development of macroeconomics by Keynes and Kalecki (including the latter's mark-up price theory), were all critiques of orthodox economics that have been appropriated into the theory, as was Mitchell's discovery of trade cycles and the behavioural economics of Thayler.

Towards a green new deal

The idea of the Risk Society and the issue of environment highlights the shortcomings of both orthodox economics and the Austrian School. Their approach involves the commodification of environmental resources (Jacobs, 1994), and environmental problems are regarded as market failures. The solutions usually put forward 'resemble the solutions to any market failure' (Perry and Primrose, 2015, p. 134), and either incorporate environmental resources into markets through cap and trade schemes or through taxation (see Rosewarne, 2010; Stilwell, 2011). In fact, these policies are simply disguised politics. Levels of tax, compensation and the detailed application of the environmental tax regime are invariably part of political debates (Stilwell,

2011). The same political decisions are taken as before, but these now have a numerical guise. The key decisions – the level and the allocation of trading permits to entities that have no previous ownership claims, or the level of environmental taxation and the way it is levied – remain political decisions. The fact that the decisions are about numerical levels does not alter the political content. Environmental economics is simply politics with numbers.

They are also policies that are now politically impossible. If environmental protection is taken seriously, the levels of cap or tax rate would be ruinous to many and would result in unsurmountable governance problems unless a vast array of egalitarian remedies are also enacted. This was known by the neoclassics; although taxation is sometimes called Pigouvian tax, Pigou's system was actually quite limited (more a community compensation scheme similar to the Fairtrade premium), since he was writing after the First World War and was well aware that taxation – and market allocation in general – was likely to be inappropriate under conditions of insufficient supply. We will return to this later.

The issue of environment also shows the consequences of adopting the individualism of the Austrian School. In particular, they explicitly eschew the use of the economic aggregates that preoccupies economic policy worldwide. Using economic aggregates as a measure of value has no validity and yields bizarre results – expenditure on environmental clean-up raises GDP, whereas using less fuel lowers it. There is no real measure of economic efficiency. Behind this is the inability to distinguish ends and means – ends can be intermediate and may themselves be means to a further end (cars are driven for another purpose – to travel to work or leisure for example – and not as an end in themselves). Costs and benefits cannot easily be separated out, and so GDP does not 'add up' (Hirsch, 1977).

It might also be noted how the use of tax to encourage technical efficiencies may backfire. This is the 'Jevons Paradox'. Jevons noted how the increased efficiency of coal-powered machines in the steam era increased the use of coal rather than lowered it. He hypothesized this was due to the relative price of coal inputs falling as a result of the technological change (Jevons, 1865). Similarly, cars becoming more fuel efficient in the present day may simply result in more miles being driven in bigger cars. There can also be indirect effects, with money saved through efficiencies redirected elsewhere – cash not spent on driving may be spent flying. Without demand management, changes will not fix environmental problems. Market incentives alone are insufficient.

Indeed, as we saw earlier, markets are often viewed as inadequate when resources are depleted, which is why we have rationing, price controls and planning during wartime (Stilwell, 2011). Under conditions of resource depletion, the Robbins definition is inapplicable. To the extent the choices can be said to exist at all under these conditions, the choices will be zero-sum; my consumption will be at the expense of others. Markets will clearly not lead to a social optimum in these circumstances.

Given the inadequacy of the choice definition under conditions of resource depletion, we may wish to suggest alternatives. I propose the following definition:

> *Economics concerns the selection and implementation of allocation mechanisms for depleted or for scarce resources.*

This creates a focus on economic *process* rather than an end state, and also emphasizes the political nature of economics. The issues for the new political economy will be the appropriateness of the respective methods of allocation for particular circumstances, the specific *modus operandi* of these allocation mechanisms and the objectives and constraints on the process. Allocation will require an allocating agency, using an allocating mechanism that follows an allocating principle.

There are four allocation mechanisms that come to mind (although analysis may unspring others). They are allocation by:

- Ration (including equal-chance lotteries).
- Need or right (including social norms and custom).
- Price.
- There can also be maladministration (including diktat, supplier convenience, and artificial exclusion), and we need to guard against this.

Examples of these are familiar: rationing is common during wartime or other shortage situations (and is sometimes used by retailers to combat hoarding or reselling), and lotteries have been used to ration non-divisible resources, such as secondary school places in desirable schools (it was also used in the London Olympics). Allocation by need is used in many welfare state policies and health care services, and the social norm of queuing is commonplace. Pensions are often allocated by right. On the negative side, exclusion through unfair selection processes is rife in education and employment. Analysis will be required for guidance as to the circumstances under which the prospective forms of allocation are appropriate. Note that price will still play a major role in the political economy; a command economy is not being suggested here.

The overarching allocation principle would no longer be to maximize consumption but, rather, following K.W. Kapp (1976), to maximize economic security.[4] This could then form the basis of an attractive green new deal, where we agree to forgo maximum consumption, but in return replace risk and insecurity with guarantees of economic security.

How this objective is put into operation is a matter for further discussion. Barry suggests using the ILO criteria as objective data (Barry, 2012), and this might be a good starting-point. Alternatively, security might be viewed as a more subjective issue requiring the sort of public or political forum Beck envisaged, with more emphasis on participatory democracy.

I suggest two main principles for a new ecological economics – *demand management* and *market management*.

Demand management has been a perennial issue within the Green movement, and has a long tradition in the institutional economics school of Veblen and Galbraith. Veblen outlines how our wants are manipulated by the 'vested interests', and how this was a vital part of capitalism (Mulberg, 1995), while Galbraith discussed how the production of goods precedes demand creation through advertising and marketing – he described the notion of consumer sovereignty as being like applauding a squirrel on a wheel (Galbraith, 1958).

Market management: The idea of a legal basis for market activity goes back to John Commons (1924). Market exchange actually involves exchanges of legal rights. This suggests the possibility of legal control over market operations.

Deakin and colleagues have more recently called this *legal institutionalism*. Law, which underpins markets, involves both state and community. Law is a relationship of power, and part of a power structure (Deakin et al., 2017). In this sense the 'free market' is a misnomer – markets require law, which involves both governments and communities.

Deakin suggests a focus on corporate law, which he regards as another form of commons. He suggests altering limited liability law to limit corporation size – a long-standing issue in the Green movement – and also employs the work of Ostrom (see e.g. Ostrom, 1990), who investigated how commons are actually managed to suggest how corporations could be administered, which includes giving stakeholders management rights (Deakin, 2012). Corporation size and ownership have also been issues within the Green movement (e.g. Schumacher, 1973).

However, underlying all discussion of law is international trade law. If the economy is larger than the polity it is not clear any real governance is occurring. Daly and Cobb suggest international trade could usefully be state controlled (Daly and Cobb, 1990). Again, a long-standing clarion call of the Green movement has been to think globally and act locally and calls for local and international governance (governance up and down) have been frequent.

Conclusion

One of the issues surrounding Beck's analysis of the emerging Risk Society is his belief that the massive hazards we all face will cut across class lines, and cause the class system to crumble; as risks become global they also become promoted in importance and 'democratized' and the 'escape routes' for the rich eventually disappear, which gives an impetus for everyone to change the present iniquitous social institutions (Beck, 1992). However, there is little evidence of this happening at present – individual hazards remain high on the personal agenda for most people (see Curran, 2013; Ekberg, 2007). The full emergence of the Risk Society may come too late.

Given this, we may need to confront the power of the present *episteme* now. The argument in this chapter is that a vital part of this confrontation is to use the history of economics to debunk the present theories and show up their ideological basis. This is also vital tactically, because it pits the present theory against the famous founders of the discipline, which will have far more impact than arguments from a few recalcitrant economists. However, this history of economics needs to be guided by Foucault's concept of an 'archaeology' of economics, which accepts that human sciences are part of a power structure and directs us to the arguments and discontinuities of the past.

By doing this it manifests the political decisions behind what is touted as an economic science. Environment is one of the areas at the sharp end of these issues.[5] The environment is viewed by orthodox economics simply as a commodity, but a commodity subject to market failures. Because this conception is inadequate, orthodox economics is unable to correct these failures, indeed the issue of environment challenges the very definition of economics.

A counter-discourse could redefine economics, and the trajectory of consumption it follows, and study an 'economics of enough'. It could examine the generation and management of market demand, as well as the roots and management of markets themselves. I believe any new orthodoxy will not resemble the theory of the present, but a new political economy will certainly be influenced by the past.

Notes

1 This is a reference to Einstein: 'science without religion is lame, religion without science is blind'.
2 Note this concept is also used by postmodern writers, but Foucault uses it in a different way; it is not concerned with conversation or the use of language.
3 Foucault believed modern economics began with Ricardo, as did Keynes (2010 [1933]).
4 This phrase is chosen to distinguish from national or military security.
5 Others include development economics and feminist economics.

References

Ball, T. (ed.), 1977. *Political Theory and Praxis: New Perspectives*, Minneapolis, MN: University of Minnesota Press.

Barry, J., 2012. *The Politics of Actually Existing Unsustainability*, Oxford: Oxford University Press.

Beck, U., 1992. *Risk Society: Towards a New Modernity*, London: Sage.

Beck, U., 1994. *Reflexive Modernization: Politics, Tradition and Aesthetics in the Modern Social Order*, Cambridge: Polity.

Beck, U., 2009. Critical theory of world risk society: A cosmopolitan vision, *Constellations*, 16(1), pp. 3–22.

Beck, U., 2015. Emancipatory catastrophism: What does it mean to climate change and risk society? *Current Sociology*, 63(1), pp. 75–88.

Beck, U., Bonss, W. and Lau, C., 2003. The theory of reflexive modernization: Problematic, hypotheses and research programme. *Theory, Culture & Society*, 20(2), 1–33.

Colander, D., 2000. The death of neoclassical economics, *Journal of the History of Economic Thought*, 22(2).

Commons, J.R., 1924. *Legal Foundations of Capitalism*, New York: Macmillan.

Curran, D., 2013. Risk society and the distribution of bads: Theorizing class in the risk society, *British Journal of Sociology*, 64(1), 44–62.

Daly, H.E. and Cobb, J.B., 1990. *For the Common Good*, London: Green Print.

Deakin, S., 2012. The corporation as commons: Rethinking property rights, governance and sustainability in the business enterprise, *Queen's Law Journal* 37, 339–381.

Deakin, S., Gindis, D., Hodgson, G.M., Huang, K., and Pistor , K., 2017. Legal institutionalism: Capitalism and the constitutive role of law, *Journal of Comparative Economics*, 45, 188–200.

de Lima, I.V., 2010. *Foucault's Archaeology of Political Economy*, London: Macmillan.

Ekberg, M., 2007. The parameters of the risk society: A review and exploration, *Current Sociology*, 55(3), 343–366.

Fay, B., 1975. *Social Theory and Political Practice*, London: Allen & Unwin.

Fay, B., 1987. *Critical Social Science: Liberation and its Limits*, Ithaca, NY: Cornell University Press.

Foucault, M., 1979. *The Birth of Biopolitics* (Michel Foucault: Lectures at the College De France 1978–1979), translated from the French by G. Burchell, London: Palgrave 2008.

Galbraith, J.K., 1958. *The Affluent Society*, Harmondsworth: Penguin.

Gordon, C., 1991. Governmental rationality, in G. Burchell, C. Gordon and P. Miller (eds.), *The Foucault Effect*, Chicago, IL: University of Chicago Press.

Habermas, J., 1969. *Towards a Rational Society*, trans. J. Shapiro, 1971, London: Heinemann.

Hirsch, F., 1977. *Social Limits to Growth*, London: Routledge and Kegan Paul.

Hodgson, G.M., 2009. The great crash of 2008 and the reform of economics, *Cambridge Journal of Economics*, 33(6), 1205–1221.

Jacobs, M., 1994. The limits to neo-classicism, in M. Redclift and T. Benton (eds.), *Social Theory and the Global Environment*, London: Routledge.

Jevons, W.S., 1865. *The Coal Question: An Inquiry Concerning the Progress of the Nation, and the Probable Exhaustion of Our Coal Mines*, London: Macmillan.

Kapp, K.W., 1976. The nature and significance of institutional economics, *Kyklos*, XXIX(2), 209–232.

Keynes, J.M., 2010 [1933]. *Essays in Biography*, Springer.

Kologlugil, S., 2010. Michel Foucault's archaeology of knowledge and economic discourse, *Erasmus Journal for Philosophy and Economics*, 3(ii), 1–25.

Kuhn, T.S., 1962. *The Structure of Scientific Revolutions*, Chicago, IL: University of Chicago Press.

Lash, L. and Wynne, B., 1992. Introduction, in U. Beck (ed.), *Risk Society: Towards a New Modernity*, London: Sage.

Lemke, T., 2002. Foucault, governmentality, and critique, *Rethinking Marxism*, 14(3), 49–64.

Lukes, S., 2004. *Power: A Radical View*, London: Macmillan.

McLaren, H., 2009. Using 'Foucault's toolbox': The challenge with feminist poststructural discourse analysis, in I. Goodwin-Smith (ed.), *Foucault: 25 Years On*

Conference, Adelaide: Hawke Research Institute. Available at: http://w3.unisa.edu.au/hawkeinstitute/publications/foucault-25-years/mclaren.pdf (accessed 12 November 2016).

Mulberg, J. 1995. *Social Limits to Economic Theory*, London: Routledge.

Myrdal, G., 1958 [1933]. Ends and means, in G. Myrdal (ed.), *Value in Social Theory*, London: Routledge and Kegan Paul.

O'Farrell, C., 2005. *Michel Foucault*, London: Sage.

Ostrom, E., 1990. *Governing the Commons: The Evolution of Institutions for Collective Action*, Cambridge: Cambridge University Press.

Perry, N. and Primrose, D., 2015. Heterodox economics and the biodiversity crisis, *Journal of Australian Political Economy*, 75, 11–31.

Robbins, L., 1932. *An Essay on the Nature and Significance of Economic Science*, London: Macmillan.

Robinson, J., 1962. *Economic Philosophy*, Harmondsworth: Penguin.

Rosewarne, S., 2002. Towards an ecological political economy, *Journal of Australian Political Economy*, 50, 179–199.

Schumacher, E.F., 1973. *Small is Beautiful*, London: Blond & Briggs.

Smith, M.J., 1998. *Social Science in Question: Towards a Postdisciplinary Framework*, London: Sage/The Open University.

Stilwell, F., 2011. Marketising the environment, *Journal of Australian Political Economy*, 68, 108–127.

3 Hegel, Marx and the economics of inclusion

Towards an economic philosophy for a post-(non-)truth political class

Simon Mouatt

Introduction

During the latter stages of modernity, critical thinking remains subjugated by power narratives that serve to perpetuate the use of neoclassical economics and obfuscate some of the undesired realities of capitalist mechanics. Marx had argued that this undermined the scientific value of the Enlightenment project. If we want to reverse the bad science of our time and restore the confidence of a distrustful post-truth public, critical thinking must be valued and popularized. If normative economics formed the public policy discourse, for instance, rather than the usual neoclassical pseudo-science, the likelihood of desired outcomes is enhanced. Criteria could be devised that set out aims for economic activity and then pluralist critical thinking and synthesis could deliver the theory-driven policy most likely to deliver the desired outcomes. The opposite of an optimal self-regulating market. Any outcome and implementation success would in turn serve to evaluate the theoretical approaches adopted. In this chapter, I posit that the Marxian and Hegelian dialectic provides us with a suitable philosophy to undergird the evolution of such hypothetical economic criteria, since they visualize a totalized system and are both rooted in a trajectory towards universal emancipation.

The combination of critical thinking with unbiased research, however, may prove difficult to achieve and/or use to convince others of its scientific value. After the 2008 crash, Trump's election and the UK Brexit vote, the Anglo-Saxon world is different. In particular, objective truths are less likely to shape public opinion than appeal to emotion and personal belief – a phenomenon defined by the Oxford Dictionary as *post-truth* (Oxford Dictionary 2017). This assumes, of course, that it is meaningful truth being rejected. Many are currently dissatisfied with capitalism, and feel lied to by political, academic and technocratic narratives which support it and belie the realities of their daily lives. In this sense, they are actually rejecting what they believe to have been a falsehood. But, if a systemic imperative requires the capitalist class to lie, or obfuscate certain realities, it is not disingenuous behavior that is at fault but rather the lying constitutes a necessary condition for capitalism's function and survival. In this sense, populist views are actually rejecting historic *non-truth* rather than truth, and express desire for more reality. Yet, ironically, if any newer narratives also obfuscate realities, there is likely to be further disappointment. Bullshit thrives, as Ball notes, when there is a market for it, that is, producers of bullshit gain political office or influence and the consumers get an alternative to the (perceived or otherwise) falsehood of the previous narrative (Ball 2017, p. 199). Meanwhile, the narrative of power that supports capitalism remains unchallenged in many hearts and minds.

It is consciousness of the false narrative of capitalism, facilitated by critical thinking, that Marx regarded as a crucial prerequisite for the emancipation of humanity. In this conception, the proletarians, determined by material relations of production, become aware of the 'rational kernel inside the mystical shell' and then, driven by their 'revolutionary praxis', the historical dialectical process occurs (Marx 1976 [1867], p. 103; Lowy 2003, p. 98). I argue in this chapter that these ideas formed in Marx in the 1840s and constituted the philosophical underpinning of his entire mature work. In Hegel's system (of ideas), on the other hand, the 'notion' drives our behavior and is subject to critique, that is, contradictions contained in the idea itself lead to critical thinking/discourse, and the idea develops. For Hegel, ideas are the starting point (for Marx, the material reality), and he argued it was the real matter that informs our consciousness on a trajectory towards emancipation.

The chapter is set out in two sections. The first considers the philosophical roots of the capitalist narrative, from the Enlightenment to its modern manifestation, and considers the causes and impact of the scarcity of pluralist/critical thinking. The second section explores the Marx/Hegel dialectic as a basis for pluralist thinking, and Hegel's master/slave concept as an inspiration for the formulation of specific economic criteria based on the principle of inclusion. It is concluded that these, with pluralist economic thinking, could offer a preferable alternative to the current use of neoclassical science to inform government policy.

The capitalist narrative from Enlightenment to today

To claim capitalism has had a disingenuous narrative from the outset is not to suggest there are no qualities of the system, but rather it suggests certain realities have been downplayed, lied about or ignored. Also, since all economic systems require order, which presupposes an ethical code, capitalism also has its own rules. The use of property must be protected, for instance, for labor to be productive, and capitalism depends on this being privately owned. John Locke, usually cited as providing the rationale for this, claimed there was plenty to provide for all needs and the political class should therefore protect property rights (Locke 1988 [1689], chap. 5). Yet, the limitless accumulation of assets, and formation of intellectual, legal or physical monopolies, mean large parts of society are *de facto* excluded from capital altogether. In addition, it is not necessary for property to be privately owned in order to protect it, the state or commune can do this, but the capitalist narrative has not presented this as a viable option for society. The questioning of private property remains taboo. Other key capitalist features, namely the competitive pursuit of profit and free markets, have also been traditionally presented as beneficial to the operation of the economic system whereby incentives lead to growth, increased productivity and the efficient allocation of resources. But by emphasizing benefits and downplaying the detrimental impact of competitive pressure and/or manipulated markets, the capitalist narrative fails to provide people with sufficient illumination of the real-life impacts on their lives.

In the early days of mercantilist capitalism newer entrepreneurial wealth was in the ascendance, and the land-owning feudal class faced fresh challenges to the political order. Since feudalism relied on duties and obligations to the pope and king with consequences for non-compliance, early Enlightenment thinkers were reserved in the content and promulgation of their ideas. Religious belief was still pervasive, with those in public office expected to uphold its ethics. Mandeville, for example, was castigated for inferring that vices enabled the economy to function better, commenting 'prodigality, that noble sin; whilst luxury employed a million of the poor, and odious pride a million more' (Mandeville 1989 [1714]). Adam Smith later balked at Mandeville's implication even though, as Robinson noted, Smith conceded that he had some points (Robinson 1962, p. 23). Yet, the establishment of Smith, as a capitalist narrator, is itself subject to suspicion since Smith provides a sanitized version of the enclosures that wrought misery on huge numbers of the rural poor in Britain, from Tudor times onwards. At the time of writing, as Perelman noted, there were other commentators with more realistic accounts of the suffering (including famines) that took place but were ignored by elites (Perelman 2000). The enclosures are seen by some as part of the political project of the ascendant capitalist class, to create a needy proletariat ready and eager to work in the emerging factory system (Orwell 1944; Polanyi 1944; Perelman 2000). The capitalist narrative has emphasized the increase in agricultural yields that enclosures facilitated, preparing conditions for the industrial revolution since the new proletariat could be adequately fed. This stylized version of history downplays the disregard of ethics by an aspirational capitalist class, whether the enclosures were an unintended consequence of their activity or a premeditated plan to dispossess the rural poor of their sustenance. Factory workers were later persuaded by the 'protestant work-ethic', or 'American dream', to believe for a better future, only to discover that harder (more efficient) work cheapened the value of their wage rate (in abstract labor terms).[1] The agrarian revolution prior to industrialization was thus subject to a dubious narrative that still remains the mainstream historical record.

Finance has also been the subject of an inaccurate narrative. The rise of endogenous credit, facilitated by Calvin's justification of usury, was crucial for the growth of mercantilist capital, reversing the ideas of the scholastics.

Rothbard notes that this was a courageous edict by Calvin, based on theological reasoning and support from the likes of devout banker, Jacob Fugger (Rothbard 1995, p. 141). At first, capitalist banking, such as the discounting of bills of exchange, did not involve the levying of excessive interest (Calvin had posited a 5 percent cap). But banking has been an exploitative activity after Calvin, leading to great fortunes for investors. Calvin's narrative did not conceal the nature of usury, but the failure of the political class to accurately reflect the increased level of exploitation since then, does represent a disingenuous capitalist apologetic. In the pursuit of 'life, liberty and happiness', capitalist firms have pursued profits and thus paid a proportion of their surplus value to the financial rentiers in the process. In the later industrial revolution, Smith also ignored excessive usury to focus on technical and allocative efficiencies to be derived from competitive markets and the profit incentive (Smith 2003 [1776]). Smith's 'real bills doctrine', emphasized the significance of finance being productively applied, rather than spent on conspicuous consumption, and was less concerned with the size of private bank profits per se (Itoh and Lapavitsas 1999, p. 18). Later, Ricardo wanted more political control of banking to better meet the needs of the economy, via a public national bank, but met with stiff opposition (Ricardo 1824; Itoh and Lapavitsas 1999, p. 23). In addition to the usual *currency school* concern with excessive credit creation, this also implied that Ricardo had wanted to mitigate the exploitation of private banks as well.

Critics of the ethics of private finance exist today. Prior to the global financial crisis of 2008, decades of financialization led to clear increases in bank profits in comparison to non-financial corporations, leading to many calls for less exploitative banking and reform of the sector that would better serve the general economy (Mouatt 2015, p. 203).

The decline of Enlightenment critical thinking in economic science

Marx praised Smith and Ricardo for adhering to versions of the labor theory of value, despite their minimal focus on labor exploitation, and also commended them for their holistic and scientific commentary (Ormazabal 2004). Critical thinking clearly existed to some extent. Marx had noted, however, by the mid-1800s that the language of the subject of economics changed, and the presentation of economic concepts by the political class demonstrated a lack of integrity:

> It was thenceforth no longer a question whether this theorem or that was true, but whether it was useful to capital or harmful, expedient or inexpedient, politically dangerous or not. In place of disinterested inquirers, there were hired prizefighters, in place of genuine research, the bad conscience and the evil intent of apologetics.
>
> (Marx 1976 [1867], afterword to the 2nd German Edition)

As a consequence, Robinson comically stated, it became the task of the economists to justify the contradictions of capitalism, since no one wanted to live with a bad conscience (Robinson 1962, p. 25). At the end of the 1800s, with Marshall et al., the modern formation of economics (as a distinct discipline) was established. Complete with its own new language and marginalist mathematics, meaningful political economy discourse was rendered inaccessible to the common person (Marshall 1890; Walras 1926 [1874]). Since then, the professional economists have inhabited the policymaking, academic and media circles defining the science parameters to such an extent that even forms of critical economics have been unable to extricate themselves from equilibrium models. This practice was viewed as psychopathological when applied to Marx (Freeman 1996) and was also criticized by Keynes when his contemporaries poorly described his model of interest-rate determination (Keynes 1937; Cencini 2003).[2] The bad science continues as new students are still taught the so-called 'economic problem', that is, a resource scarcity combined with unlimited wants and needs, as the key basis for the subject; the possibility of a manipulated scarcity, or even workable alternative economic systems which can (at least theoretically) eliminate scarcity, are barely explored. Alas, since early career researchers are eager to establish their credentials, they are oft-disincentivized from any critical thinking until a 'Kuhn' scientific paradigm[3] shift occurs, and subsequent new ideas gain some professional academic kudos (Kuhn 2012 [1962]). These paradigms form part of what Michel Foucault referred to as 'modes of domination' since they set out parameters for discourse, disable critical thinking and are dispersed through society (Poster 1984, p. 80; Mills 2003, p. 34). Foucault remarked that 'we must perceive of discourse as violence which we do to things', preventing the formation of critical ideas, and hence policy, that has the latent ability to transform our economies and our environment for the better (Mills 2003, p. 55).

Another key consequence of nearly 500 years of a flawed economic science is that if narratives fail to resonate with perceived realities, they engender fear in the listeners. Wrenn has identified that the move towards populist belief, religion and traditional thinking is enhanced if fearful, and this is a factor in the current post-truth mood (Wrenn 2014). It can also be argued there is specific manipulation of fear by the political class, in order to foster uncertainty, enhancing the susceptibility of the narrative's audience to accept implausibility (Curtis 2016). For elites in the globalization era, the integration of production, finance and trade has enhanced their fear of change and so, Curtis argues, they simply regurgitate the capitalist narrative, and manage any proximate threats to the system. Human thinking is diminished in the context of fear, or uncertainty-driven stress, as research has clarified. Military training, for example, known as hostile environment awareness training (HEAT), drills an automatic-response procedure into combat servicemen so they act instinctively in moments of fear, since their brain processing efficacy is diminished (Bond 2017). So, when people feel safe, they experience better thinking, whereas uncertainty and fear lead to poorer mental health and, by implication, a diminished ability to engage in effective critical/pluralist thought that can provide explanation of economic realities (Fletcher 2017). If people experience cognitive dissonance, an emotional attachment to the narrative can be considered pathological and lead to schizophrenic conditions. A false narrative is analogous to an excess of dopamine which can cause the brain to process stimuli in distorted ways. In the normal mind, new stimuli are processed, threats/rewards are placed in priority order and objective/subjective perceptions are differentiated, categorized and stored. Dopamine excess can cause these processes to skew– threats are placed in incorrect order and impressions from the imagination can be perceived as objective facts and mixed with thinking that is known to be objective. Fear, as psychologists have noted, exacerbates the condition (Fletcher 2017). If there is an underestimation of realities, as the *Dark Mountain Project* has identified, there may be consequences for humanity when it is unaware of its vulnerability to capitalist or environmental crises (Kingsnorth and Hine 2009).[4]

I argue in this chapter that critical thinking, which inevitably leads to heterodox/pluralist ideas in economics, is imperative to dispel the unrealities of mainstream economics, so capitalist contradictions can be first seen and then transcended. Marx pointed us towards a culpable ruling class and its adherence to 'vulgar' economics, which is 'nothing more than a didactic and more or less doctrinaire translation of the everyday notions of the actual agents of production' (Marx 1981 [1894], p. 969). This is not to say that the best ideas/policies for our economy are Marx's, but rather his analysis helps us appreciate how the capitalist elite rules and how 'false consciousness' (Engel's term), via bad science, maintains this status quo (Eyerman 1981).[5]

Although it is difficult to pursue critical discourse when people are fearful, as stated above, if the prevailing culture were to attribute a high value to critical thinking, as well as agency and pluralism, it is more likely to engender it. As Tali Sharot has noted, people are more likely to be emboldened in their autonomous thinking in environments where large numbers of people hold alternative views, since their primeval instinctual need for 'safety in numbers' is satisfied (Sharot 2017). It is fair to assert that whilst people desire agency they also possess a strong emotive need to belong, and tend to be aware of the consensual mood(s) of people-groups they wish to be included in, thus relinquishing (at least in part) their agency.[6] Veblen noticed that 'leisure classes', as economic agents, made purchases driven by desire for recognition in their particular group, rather than by their own evaluation of utility in relation to price (Veblen 1922 [1899], p. 75). Veblen figured that their need for acceptance took preference over their choices. Transaction analysis also reveals that the need to belong often leads people to adopt dependent child-to-adult behaviors with others, rather than an autonomous adult-to-adult relation (Berne 1964). Critical thinking needs to be popularized and valued in an environment where it is safe to be free thinking, and also defer to the views of other free thinkers. Keynes noted that market investors could be incentivized to follow the views of others, in his beauty contest analogy, where competitive judges pick the six prettiest faces from a hundred entrants and the winner is the judge closest to the average preferences of others (Keynes 1936, p. 156). I argue that the general principles of the Hegel/Marx dialectic provide a theoretical approach that is suited for such as task.

The Hegel/Marx dialectic and pluralism

The grand theorists of historical transition, Hegel and Marx, are attractive for pluralists since their idea of the dialectical process allows for the fullest possible range of thought.[7] There are differences between their positions, of course, but a full discussion of these nuances is beyond the scope of this chapter for two key reasons.[8] First, the task would be better undertaken by someone with a background in academic philosophy, and, second, this would detract focus from the key chapter proposition–that the formation of a critical pluralist culture for economic science is served by the Hegel/Marx conception of dialectics and is likely to contribute towards improved policy that provides solutions (or partial solutions) to some of the intractable problems facing humanity. In order to set out the method, the section begins with an introductory account of Hegel's philosophy, followed by an outline of Marx's contribution to the dialectical process.

Hegel's dialectic dominated German philosophy whilst Marx was at university, and Marx was an avid student. Hegel's system developed partly in response to philosophical dualism, which maintained Descartes' concept of a separation between mind and matter, where Hegel argued instead that matter (including language) was crafted by thought (Blunden 2012, p. 9).

In the Hegelian dialectic the central focus is the idea, constituted by reasoned, intuitive, imaginative, sensual and mystical thought, which goes through a time process of reasoning. The idea is first posited and then, via its internal reasoning, is subjected to negation. According to Hegel, the idea negation transcends the initial presentation of the idea, but also preserves the idea's essential nature in the negation's existence. Next, new negation of the negation then transcends both, but yet preserves the initial idea and the negation in the new system of thought. Mental labor, therefore, is the basis for human action, and explains historical transformation. Rather than being conceived as the 'final *outcome* of a never-ending historical process, the idea is a *process*' (Blunden 2012, p. 16). In this sense, the historical trajectory towards emancipation, for Hegel, is not a linear one but evolves according to a dialectical process firmly located in human thinking. This may mean the process takes a step backwards before progress is made.

An example of the dialectical process could be the idea of a social contract between people and the state. In the Hobbes state of nature, where life is 'solitary, poor, nasty, brutish and short', the individual first has a notion of their freedom (Hobbes 1968 [1651], chap. 13). Next, the negation of the idea, through reasoning, suggests that if they deferred to a 'Leviathan' they will transcend the inadequacy of this freedom, since the concept of freedom is nonsensical if life is too dangerous and short. Later, during the process of reasoning with the idea, deference to the Leviathan is theorized as giving a much-improved freedom in the order created –the negation of the negation. The idea has thus now developed into a higher stage, by transcending and yet preserving the initial stages (Hegel called this process sublation). In contrast to the existential Kant, Hegel had also conceived of an idea being present in groups, which he termed spirit, manifested in the collective mental activity of a people (Blunden 2012, p. 6). This occurs because, as Hegel writes (quoted by Blunden), 'the world is continually at odds with how it should be', and so the historical dialectical process becomes the story of the resolution of these conflicts in the arena of thought (ibid., p. 15). Since the individual ideas also sit within an overall 'system of ideas' in Hegel, part of the idea's internal reasoning process is driven by the internal reasoning process of the other ideas until such a time is reached when the idea (or, theoretically, all of the ideas together) becomes 'absolute spirit', that is, is then no longer subject to a latent negation.[9] Historical transition has then reached its zenith.

Marx had been in agreement with the Hegelian system after the philosopher's death, and joined the so-called 'left Hegelians', but following Feuerbach's critique of Hegel, Marx's views began to change. Feuerbach pointed out that Hegel's system started with an initial positing of an idea as a philosophy, rather than an idea derived from the sensual experience of the material (Marx 2017c [1845], p. 1). In this sense, Hegel outlined what Marx had called only 'the abstract, logical, speculative expression for the movement of history, which is not the actual history of man as a given subject, but only the act of creation' (Marx 2017a [1844], p. 64). Marx, on the other hand, had argued that the idea did not follow from what 'men say, imagine, conceive, nor from men as narrated', but rather starts with the 'real, active men' with their 'ideological reflexes' (Marx 2017b [1845]). Marx presupposed matter as reality and argued for analyzing the actual social processes of man's response to these material realities experienced, rather than simply attributing a theoretical logic to the process.

Marx also criticized the materialism of Feuerbach, for not taking into consideration any subjective thinking in the dialectical process. Feuerbach had dismissed religious thinking, for instance, as 'the dream of the human mind' (Feuerbach 2008 [1841], p. xii). Marx had wanted to include subjective with objective thinking in 'human sensuous activity', rather than one-sided objectivity (Marx 2017c [1845], p. 1). In other words, rather than Marx rigidly holding to a crude materialist dialectic, Marx posited a dialectical process where both subjective and objective reasoning, combined in ideological activity, manifest in the critical thinking activity itself. Marx saw transformation deriving from a dialectical process that was first derived from realities, and human responses to it. Hegel, on the other hand, first posits an independence of thought, with the idealist dialectic process driving behavior, and then the thinking changes in reaction to realities. Both Marx and Hegel unify the material and the ideal and also include objective and subjective thinking. Marx had theorized revolutionary practice, and Hegel a thinking process defined by an objective reality. It is implicit in both men's views of the dialectic that removing false consciousness is crucial to meaningful change; as Lenin noted 'there is no revolutionary practice without revolutionary theory' (Lowy 2003, p. 108). Marx also contended that an allegiance to pope and king falsified the consciousness of agents in the way Feuerbach reasoned man was alienated by religion, since people deferred to a defined behavior/belief/priest rather than seeking an enlightened consciousness of their actual ability to change the material conditions of existence. It can be extrapolated from this that Foucault's 'narratives of power' actually function in a similar way to religion and mitigate the existence of effective critical thinking.

It was in the 1840s, writing in the Paris (Economic and Philosophic) manuscripts, that Marx first explored his dialectic and changed his focus from a philosophic reasoning process to one focused on 'sensuous' proletariat activities. Instead of the intelligentsia providing theory to the revolutionary movement, Marx argued that the theory should emerge from the practice (praxis) of the revolutionaries themselves. Marx criticizes the case of the Lyon silk workers protest in 1834, where the political understanding that was provided to the workers 'falsified their ability to find their own consciousness' (Lowy 2003, p. 93). Marx mused that the likes of Bauer and Kautsky were unhelpful to the cause of revolution, since ideas needed to derive from the proletariat's mind itself. Marx writes that 'a philosophical people can find its corresponding practice only in socialism; hence it is only in the proletariat that it can find the dynamic element of its emancipation' (ibid., p. 94). Marx's argument rested on the view that the proletariat had 'nothing to lose' and their shared condition enabled them to more easily identify the principles of their collective emancipation. Marx, unlike many of his contemporaries, was particularly excited by the Silesian Weavers uprising of 1844, which he viewed as surpassing the prior uprisings in France and England as a consequence of their 'consciousness of the nature of the proletariat' (ibid., p. 92). It was this *real* animated consciousness, containing elements of both objective and subjective thoughts, which Marx argued was the key ingredient for revolution. Indeed, since the consciousness derives directly from responses to experiences, the critical thinking would be more likely to overcome any prior emotional attachments.

It is not necessary, of course, for policy outcomes derived from critical thinking to seek, like Marx, the common ownership of the means of production. Indeed, there are many theorists who argue this would lead to a centralized autocracy. The poignant point is that critical thinking in economic science is likely to be vacuous if its conclusions ignore the animated sensuous experiences of those directly affected by the topic considered. The critical thinking is not the exclusive preserve of the intelligentsia. It is for this reason, I argue, that Marx's notion of the dialectic can be useful in the post-truth world of today.

Towards the formation of inclusive economic criteria

In the neoliberal era, the consequences of leaving economic decision-making to the collective agents in the market is causing concern for growing numbers of interested parties. In order to break the ideological impasse, namely a bias against increased state regulatory capacity or ownership, populist faith in any state planning is required.[10]

An entrenched wariness of big government is common in the Anglo-Saxon world. Hayek pointed out that any new political class with an economic plan is often soon subject to opposition. The planners then face a dilemma, they first seek to persuade the specific recalcitrant individuals to change their views and comply; if the strategy fails, the planners must subjugate those concerned or abandon their plans altogether (Hayek 1994 [1944]). This implies that a consensus based on an animated sensuous response to economic realities, facilitated by a Hegel/Marx approach towards critical thinking, has more chance of success through mitigating opposition. Simply becoming aware of any non-truth in the capitalist narrative, via experts, is unlikely to be a sufficient condition to create a necessary populist mood, for reasons stated above. In addition, if economic outcome criteria are formulated in order to create policy objectives, guide their implementation and provide for their later evaluation, pluralist economic science could continually evolve until all criteria are fulfilled. Furthermore, if the society designs an economic system that works for all, humanity and environs need no longer be subject to the vagaries of the market. This constitutes, of course, utopian goal setting but has clear advantages over alternatives. In order to design such economic criteria, I argue that the concept of inclusion is extrapolated from the philosophical ideas of Hegel and Marx. Simply put, these notions posit that emancipation is not possible until all are free and, therefore, economic benchmarks are required that can deliver a policy trajectory towards the standards, and tools of analysis can be calibrated for measuring progress. These benchmarks can also be subject to evaluation and reformulation.

Marx held that the essence of man was communal and was not able to find expression in the capitalist mode of production. In contrast to theorists like Rousseau and Kant et al., who argued for a social contract between people and the state through the law (the general will or categorical imperative), enabling society to transcend the (selfish) state of nature, Marx posited that if the social relations that derived from capitalist production were changed, our human nature would also change (Rousseau 1968 [1762]; Sullivan 1994, p. 10). In other words, Marx claimed the economic system drives agent behavior, and man's inner nature is not inherently selfish, despite its capability to be so. It is our alienation (or estrangement) from this essence, and the non-consciousness of it, that Marx viewed as problematic and its transcendence constituted an essential condition of his concept of emancipation. Marx describes how the 'estrangement of man to man', which was inherent in commodity production, caused separation from his 'specie-being' (Marx 2017a [1844], p. 32).

Marx's idea of historical transition, outlines contradictions between classes, determined by material relation to production, leading man (via their communal, sensuous and perceptual engagement with their condition) to engage in the transformation of the economic system through the class struggle. As Marx noted 'we call communism the real movement which abolishes the present state of things' (Marx 2017b [1845]). For Marx, the historical process continues until all the class contradictions have been transcended and history is complete, and a classless society is created.

Hegel's concept of the master/slave had clearly inspired Marx's materialist dialectic, and points towards a similar utopian society, and the establishment of 'absolute spirit', at the culmination of the dialectical process. Notwithstanding Hegel's known propensity towards misogyny and racism (partly excusable given the cultural context of nineteenth-century Prussia), Hegel provides us with the notion of critical discourse driving humanity towards a society with an emancipated systemic ideology that works for everyone (Blunden 2012, p. 1). Hegel's example begins by describing the formation of a master and slave relationship, a social phenomenon occurring many times throughout history. At first sight, it appears that the master has created a rewarding relationship of personal benefit to himself, but if the issue of the master's self-consciousness of their identity is explored (better received via an [autonomous] other person), contradictions arise in the 'idea' of the master/slave relation itself. The reason is that the master does not value the validity of the (deferential) slave's view, and so is unable to receive the appropriate recognition of his/her own identity. The slave, on the other hand, does receive real recognition of their identity (albeit with the absent existence of freedom) from an autonomous thinking master. As Hegel puts it, the 'servitude has the lord for its essential reality; hence the *truth* for it is the independent consciousness that is *for itself*' (Hegel 1977 [1807], p. 117). In addition, whilst the slave's own labor is now objectified, as the slave awaits their emancipation, the slave becomes conscious of the master's alienation from the slave's produce consumed. Meanwhile, the slave is not subject to the same alienation and becomes aware of their master's need and vulnerability. Hegel's essential point is that neither master nor the slave can experience mental emancipation until both are free, and the process of the master/slave idea undertakes its internal reasoning process of negation until this emerges. The newly formed idea, which defines the new social relation, has not discarded the notions associated with the old relationship concept, but rather the current idea *preserves* all the notions so that they can define the reality of the newer free-men relationship more appropriately. If the master/slave concept of emancipation is applied to economic criteria established, for purposes of policy, the state objectives will aim to facilitate transformation of the current economic system for the benefit of all, and the earth. It is not necessary for the dialectical process, and critical thinking, to lead to radical changes to our economies, of course, but the approach offers the ability for humanity to take charge of its own affairs rather than be passive recipients of the current market rulers.

Conclusion

The capitalist narrative presented by the prevailing political classes, has been a disingenuous one since the onset of the mercantilist era. Yet, the narrative's existence, and sustenance, reveals a systemic need to obfuscate many core realities, rather than expose the poor ethics of political elites. The narrative has covered such topics as the enclosures, the existence and limits of private property, efficiency, competition, usury etc. and has transferred power to elites to effectively set the parameters of economic science. Yet, in the current post-truth era, it appears there is fresh dissatisfaction with the political class, as a direct consequence of feeling lied to, and this has led to much more populist responses driven by emotive factors. In this new context, any substantial transformation of our current economic system will therefore require an improved understanding of psychological drivers, and economic policies that take account of any emotional attachments. I have argued in the chapter that a generalized Marx/Hegelian dialectic is an appropriate method of analysis for a consideration of these subjective factors, since Marx's 'sensual activity' and Hegel's 'idea as a process', both suggest a more holistic evaluation of human-centered ideological drivers. These also work towards an emancipation for everyone. However, though the existence of 'false consciousness' implies that an objective reasoning, derived from revealing 'non-truth', is a necessary condition to alter the emotional attachments, this is not likely to be a sufficient one. The chapter concludes, therefore, that if a more realistic capitalist narrative is presented, combined with a critical thinking commune, the prospects for a meaningful transition towards a desirable economic system are much more likely to occur. This can be achieved by the establishment of clear economic criteria for government policy, combined with an economics profession committed to pluralist and critical discourse.

Notes

1 The workers may still consume the same basket of commodities, which enable the reproduction of their labor power, but, as Potts notes, Marx illustrated that increased labor exploitation can occur through the production of relative surplus value being extracted by the capitalist (Potts 2011, p.65).

2 Cencini noted that Hicks first formed the ISLM model with the specific intention of 'reducing Keynes's contribution to a particular case of Walras's approach' for his audience of simultaneous neoclassical economists (Cencini 2003, p.299).

3 Thomas Kuhn's scientific paradigms suggest that discourse generally takes place within the current accepted paradigm and, therefore, the paradigm needs to change as a precursor to effective critical discourse (Kuhn 2012 [1962]).

4 The *Dark Mountain Project* initiative has cast light on historic human hubris evident in its conception of invincibility during times of disaster (Kingsnorth and Hine 2009).
5 In his notion of false consciousness, Engels, with Marx, had reasoned that people were subjugated by accepting the false narratives of the ruling class (Eyerman 1981).
6 Research reveals that emotion is a key part of consciousness (Holmes 2017, p.29). The heart is also involved in cognitive function as a self-organizing processing system that communicates with the brain via the nervous system. Neural messages are first received and then acted on (McCraty 2001, p.3). New stimuli affect emotions that then influence the brain processing in terms of its selection and prioritization of information.
7 This is notwithstanding the critique of Marx's historical materialism from the likes of Sartre, Foucault or Nietzsche (Poster 1984, pp.44–69).
8 This is not to suggest that the conclusions of a particular bit of historical materialist analysis, or any Hegelian inspired analysis, will necessarily contain full thoughtful discourse but rather that the Hegel/Marx method allows for it to occur.
9 This idea of Hegel is his equivalent of Kant's 'categorical imperative', whereby maxims achieve universality since they are no longer particularist (Sullivan 1994).
10 This remains true whether people are on the left or right of the political spectrum or in favour of big or small states.

References

Ball, J., 2017. *Post-Truth: How Bullshit Conquered the World.* Croydon: Biteback.

Berne, E., 1964. *Games People Play: The Basic Handbook of Transactional Analysis.* New York: Ballantine Books.

Blunden, A., 2012. *Foreword to Hegel's Logic* [viewed August 21, 2017]. Available from: www.marxists.org/reference/archive/hegel/help/foreword.pdf.

Bond, M., 2017. In the Face of Danger. *New Scientist*, May 13.

Cencini, A., 2003. IS-LM: A Final Rejection. In: P. Rochon and S. Rossi, eds. *Modern Theories of Money: The Nature and Role of Money in Capitalist Economies.* Bodmin: Edward Elgar.

Curtis, A., 2016. *Hypernormalisation.* BBC Documentary.

Eyerman, R., 1981. False Consciousness and Ideology in Marxist Theory. *Acta Sociologica*, 24(1–2), 43–56.

Feuerbach, L., 2008 [1841]. *The Essence of Christianity.* New York: Dover Publications.

Fletcher, P., 2017. Why Did I go Mad? *BBC Horizon.*

Freeman, A., 1996. The Psychopathology of Walrasian Marxism. In: A. Freeman and G. Carchedi, eds. *Marx and Non-Equilibrium Economics.* Cheltenham: Edward Elgar, pp. 1–29.

Hayek, F.V., 1994 [1944]. *The Road to Serfdom.* Chicago, IL: University of Chicago Press.

Hegel, G.W.F., 1977 [1807]. *Phenomenology of Spirit.* New York: Oxford University Press.

Hobbes, T., 1968 [1651]. *Leviathan.* Aylesbury: Penguin.

Holmes, B., 2017. Why be Conscious? *New Scientist*, May 13.

Itoh, M. and Lapavitsas, C., 1999. *The Political Economy of Money and Finance.* Chippenham: Macmillan.

Keynes, J.M., 1936. *The General Theory of Employment, Interest and Money.* London: Macmillan.

Keynes, J.M., 1937. Alternative Theories of the Rate of Interest. *Economic Journal,* 47, 241–252.

Kingsnorth, P. and Hine, D., 2009. *Uncivilisation: The Dark Mountain Manifesto.* Available from: www.dark-mountain.net.

Kuhn, T., 2012 [1962]. *The Structure of Scientific Revolutions: 50th Anniversary Edition.* Chicago, IL: University of Chicago.

Locke, J., 1988 [1689]. *Two Treatises of Government,* ed. P. Laslett. New York: Cambridge University Press.

Lowy, M., 2003. *The Theory of Revolution in the Young Marx.* Canada: Haymarket Books.

Mandeville, B., 1989 [1714]. *Fable of the Bees: Or, Private Vices, Publick Benefits.* Indianapolis, IN: Hackett.

Marshall, A., 1890. *Principles of Economics.* New York: Macmillan.

Marx, K., 1976 [1867]. *Capital: Volume One.* St Ives: Penguin.

Marx, K., 1981 [1894]. *Capital: Volume Three.* Bungay: Penguin.

Marx, K., 2017a [1844]. *The Economic and Philosophic Manuscripts.* [viewed August 21, 2017]. Available from: www.marxists.org/archive/marx/works/download/pdf/Economic-Philosophic-Manuscripts-1844.pdf.

Marx, K., 2017b [1845]. *The German Ideology.* [viewed August 21, 2017]. Available from: www.marxists.org/archive/marx/works/1845/german-ideology/ch01a.htm.

Marx, K., 2017c [1845]. *Thesis on Feuerbach.* August 21. Available from: www.marxists.org/archive/marx/works/1845/theses/index.htm.

McCraty, R., 2001. *Science of the Heart: Exploring the Role of the Heart in Human Performance.* Volume One. Boulder Creek, CA: Heartmath Institute.

Mills, S., 2003. *Michel Foucault.* London, New York: Routledge.

Mouatt, S., 2015. *The Dissolution of the Financial State: A Marxian Examination of the Political Economy of Money since the 1930s.* Lanham, MD: Lexington.

Ormazabal, K.M., 2004. Adam Smith on Labour and Value: Challenging the Standard Interpretation. *Department of Foundations of Economic Analysis.* University of the Basque Country, Bilbao, Spain.

Orwell, G., 1944. As I Please, *Tribune,* August 18.

Oxford Dictionary, 2017. [viewed July 21]. Available from: https://en.oxforddictionaries.com/definition/post-truth.

Perelman, M., 2000. *The Invention of Capitalism: Classical Political Economy and the Secret History of Primitive Accumulation.* Durham, NC: Duke University Press.

Polanyi, K., 1944. *The Great Transformation.* New York: Octagon Books.

Poster, M., 1984. *Foucault, Marxism and History: Mode of Production versus Mode of Information.* Cambridge: Polity.

Potts, N., 2011. Marx's Big Idea. In: S. Mouatt and C. Adams, eds. *Corporate and Social Transformation of Money and Banking: Breaking the Serfdom.* Chippenham and Eastbourne: Palgrave Macmillan, pp. 56–70.

Ricardo, D., 1824. *Plan for the Establishment of a National Bank.* London: John Murray.

Robinson, J., 1962. *Economic Philosophy.* Bungay: Penguin.

Rothbard, M., 1995. *Economics before Adam Smith: An Austrian Perspective on the History of Economic Thought, Volume One.* Aldershot: Edward Elgar.

Rousseau, J., 1968 [1762]. *The Social Contract.* London: Penguin.

Sharot, T., 2017. *An Influential Mind: What the Brain Reveals about our Power to Change Others.* London: Little, Brown.

Smith, A., 2003 [1776]. *The Wealth of Nations.* New York: Bantam Dell.

Sullivan, R., 1994. *An Introduction to Kant's Ethics.* Cambridge, MA: Cambridge University Press.

Veblen, T., 1922 [1899]. *The Theory of the Leisure Class: An Economic Study in the Evolution of Institutions.* New York: B.W. Huebsch.

Walras, L., 1926 [1874]. *Elements of Pure Economics.* Paris: Pichon.

Wrenn, M., 2014. Fear, Envy and Neoliberalism. *John Pheby Memorial Conference, Mount Pleasant Hotel*, Malvern, United Kingdom.

4 What Marx and Kalecki/Post-Keynesians do not share, and why this is not a barrier to their learning from each other to their mutual advantage

Nick Potts and Phil Armstrong

Introduction

In this chapter, we look at the examples of Marx and Keynes, focusing on their 'big pictures' to identify where they may co-exist. We contend that, in some cases, the *apparent compatibility* of much Marxist and Post-Keynesian economics – leading to the identification of a group of Keynesian-sympathising Marxists (Howard and King 1992) (and the denial of its existence by anti-Keynesian Marxists) – is, in fact, due to their mutual closeness to the mainstream's method or, in Lee's metaphorical terminology, their 'heretical' status and, perhaps implicit, desire to 'stay in the economics department'.[1] We do not deny the possibility of compatibility between Post-Keynesianism and Marxism but we contend that such commonality exists at a deeper level that is consistent with this dichotomy. The next section of this chapter explores the deficient methodology of orthodox economics and explores methodology from the standpoint of heterodox economics. The following two sections consider the contribution of Marx and the contributions of Keynes, Post-Keynesians and Modern Monetary Theory (MMT), respectively. Further sections consider some potential sources of false compatibility between Marx, Kalecki and Keynes. The final section concludes.

The methodology of orthodoxy and heterodoxy contrasted

Neoclassical economists generally pay little explicit attention to methodology, other than modelling themselves upon *their perceptions of the behaviour of natural scientists*. When they do discuss their approach they describe it as essentially deductivist. Methodological individualism forms the basis of neoclassical theory; models are built up from axioms (or 'self-evident' truths) notably the fundamental idea that 'rational' actors (utility maximising individuals and firms) interact in a universal market form to produce equilibrium outcomes. Starting from these axioms, logical development allows models to be developed, facilitating the generation of predictions which, in turn, are then (at least allegedly) compared with reality in an attempt at corroboration – or falsification.

Popper (1965 [1959]) considers that the appraisal of scientific theory depends on the accuracy of its predictions. He rejects the idea that corroboration is enough since many (even absurd) theories might be expected to generate predictions in line with experience. Popper contends that testing the validity of a theory relies on it passing a much tougher test, that is, that events specified in advance as potential falsifiers have not been observed (Blaug 1992: 23).

Popper's methodology is normative and consists of providing a guide to 'best practice' in science. It is this approach to methodology which appeals to neoclassical economists with their aspiration of matching what they consider to be this superior scientific activity. However, from a heterodox perspective, formal mathematical modelling and simple falsificationism will severely hamper the profession's ability to establish valuable economic knowledge; having assumed away any real-world social and political factors in the derivation of their models, neoclassical economists then use the very same narrowly based deductivist theories to analyse the actual world, including situations they had deliberately excluded when constructing their theories. The ontological presupposition of a world made up of atomistic agents in neoclassical economics precludes consideration of the key issues of power, class and conflict, meaning that neoclassical theory is unable to provide a rich and full analysis of how a market economy actually functions (Fine 2016).

In contrast to neoclassical economists, heterodox economists have generally been much more inclined to discuss methodology and have moved beyond Popper (and a desire to emulate an imagined 'best practice'). The work of Thomas Kuhn[2] has been a major focus of heterodoxy; his analysis is *positive* and provides a description of the actual practice of science. Kuhn considers the forces at work in the behaviour of scientific communities and rejects the notion that science progresses in an essentially cumulative process (Hands 2001).

Kuhn contends that most scientific activity is puzzle-solving within a given paradigm ('normal science' for Kuhn). Basic questions – such as: What are the fundamental entities involved? How do they interact? and What techniques could be legitimately employed to discover their nature? – would need to be answered in order to construct the paradigm and this, in turn, would act as a precursor to the research process (Kuhn 2012 [1962]: 4–5).

'Theory-ladenness'[3] is critical; in other words, the question to be answered presupposes the existence of the paradigm and the theories it contains. Discrepancies are commonplace and may well generate discussions within the profession. Failure to resolve stubborn problems may well frustrate scientists but they are quite likely to be patient and usually content themselves with other aspects of normal science in the meantime (Kuhn 2012 [1962]). An 'anomaly' is usually seen as the fault of the scientist rather than of the paradigm itself (Hands 2001: 101–2).

Revolutions in science are possible but they require a significant accumulation of contradictory empirical findings, often requiring an extended period of time. Kuhn notes the significance of 'crisis'; a period characterised by the existence of just such a body of evidence contrary to the predictions of the established theory. It is this crisis that might lead to the overthrow of the paradigm and its replacement with an alternative. However, Kuhn notes that this is no simple process and is at pains to stress that the simple falsification of a theory is not enough (Kuhn 2012 [1962]: 77). A weight of evidence might cause a paradigm to be relinquished but this only occurs when a superior alternative is available and the body of support for new theory is great enough to counteract scientists' inclinations to rely on *ad hoc* modifications to protect the status quo provided by the original paradigm (Kuhn 2012 [1962]).

We might reasonably highlight a clear inconsistency between the methodology neoclassical economists claim they employ – namely, checking theoretical predictions against reality and being open to the possibility that their theories might be falsified – and the method they actually employ when faced with contradictory evidence – namely, making use of a *ceteris paribus* clause to immunise their theory and adding *ad hoc* modifications to make their theory more 'robust' in the future. It is also important to recognise how the ability of orthodox economics to protect itself from criticism from the public is built upon its nature as a highly technical, formal and mathematically based discipline. Replacement of neoclassicism as the mainstream hegemonic approach thus appears to be a very difficult task.

We would argue that building a heterodox alternative to neoclassicism begins with its philosophical basis, and we would suggest that such a foundation is provided by transcendental realism, in particular the work of Roy Bhaskar and (in the case, of economics) Tony Lawson. Bhaskar (2008 [1975]) commends the progress made by Kuhn, Lakatos (1970) and others in developing understanding of the community-based nature of the practice of science but he notes that more is required; additional work with an *explicit focus on ontology* is essential, both to provide deeper insights into science as a social activity and to act as a bulwark against positivism. He goes on to suggest that the activity of social science presupposes the existence of this 'revised ontology' (Bhaskar 2008 [1975]: 9). Bhaskar then argues in favour of transcendental realism – an approach based upon such a revised and explicit ontology.

For Bhaskar, real structures and mechanisms – which he describes as the *objects* of knowledge – exist independently of the events they cause. Bhaskar also contends that, in turn, the occurrence of events is distinct from the empirical experience of scientists themselves as they interpret the results of these events (Bhaskar 2008 [1975]: 56). Transcendental realism supports the contention that the social activity of science is necessary for the production of knowledge of the structures and the mechanisms present in nature, and this natural order, although it is not dependent upon human cognisance, necessarily finds its expression in human apprehension (Bhaskar 2008 [1975]: 2).

From the perspective of critical realism (CR),[4] the economic structures, mechanisms and emergent powers that constitute the real domain manifest themselves in economic 'events'. Economists then study these events or phenomena in the domain of the empirical in an attempt to develop meaningful knowledge of these real structures, mechanisms and powers. For Lawson, the phenomena thus observed take the form of partial regularities or *demi-regularities* ('demi-regs') which require explanation by economists. These demi-regs stand out in the flux of experience and naturally demand explanation (Lawson 1997: 204).

Despite the open nature of social systems,[5] for Lawson, the preponderance of these demi-regs provides the basis for meaningful social science (Lawson 2003). He goes on to consider the importance of 'contrastive demi-regs'. He notes that a contrast is only surprising or significant if our theories or current understanding lead us to conclude that the contrasted phenomena stand *a posteriori* in a different relation than might reasonably have been expected (Lawson 2003: 107). Lawson stresses the idea that the 'surprise element' can be the trigger for study, leading to the use of retroductive reasoning or the attempt to postulate a mechanism that may provide an explanation for observed phenomena (Lawson 1997: 209). For Lawson, it is impossible to provide a complete and certain causal explanation of any social event but the identification of one mechanism or set of mechanisms in a particular period in time and space is nevertheless possible (Lawson 1997: 209).

Having acknowledged the importance of an explicit recognition of ontology, we also believe that importance of pluralism in all its forms[6] cannot be overestimated. The hegemony of New Consensus Macroeconomics (NCM) has been accompanied by restricted academic freedom (Bilgrami 2015), the sidelining of heterodox economics as a whole and the embedding of a monist deductivist methodology, eschewing pluralism. Dow notes how there are two separate aspects of the argument in favour of pluralism. First, a range of analyses from different perspectives will assist economists to develop a deeper understanding of a complex dynamic reality and second, an acceptance of pluralism brings with it a necessity for economists to be aware of the limitations of their own method if they are to engage in scholarly debate with colleagues who favour different approaches (Dow 2017: 2).

Heterodox economists have traditionally been much more inclined to embrace pluralism and accepting of its possible benefits than their neoclassical counterparts. Lee (2009: 6–7) explains the nature of heterodox economics using an analogy –the contrasting relationship of an established church with those it deems to be heretics as opposed to those it deems to be blasphemers. Lee (2009: 6) asserts that mainstream economists have generally accepted 'heresy' in the form of new theories and models –provided those who are responsible for their introduction use the technical apparatus (Fine 2016) as they do – since heretical theories can usually be absorbed into the existing approach. This process serves to enrich the approach and give at least the appearance of progress (Lee 2009: 6). In contrast, Lee contends that mainstream economists have rejected their heterodox counterparts as potential rivals, contending that they are not even 'doing economics'. Heterodox economists are viewed as 'blasphemous' outliers, their exclusion from influence is entirely justified since they have nothing valuable to offer. Indeed they may face extensive social penalties including being ostracised and discriminated against (Lee 2009: 6) and, given the extent of disenfranchisement faced by heterodox economists, Lee considers that their actual survival as a viable working community might legitimately be regarded as surprising.

Lee contends that the different groups that collectively form the heterodox community have each produced meaningful and telling criticisms of mainstream economics. More than that, the separate criticisms form complementary elements of an overall critique of both the methodology and technical apparatus of mainstream economics (Lee 2009: 7–8). Together these groups provide the core of the heterodox community's collective approach: 'there have emerged a number of elements that have come to constitute the provisional and methodological core of heterodox theory' (Lee 2009: 9).

We would argue that this 'methodological core' provides a basis for complementarity, especially when combined with a desire to associate and share ideas. From this perspective, different heterodox schools might be considered as distinct but complementary elements, capable of operating within the same paradigm or 'disciplinary matrix'. Pratten (2013) looks at Post-Keynesianism and stresses that Post-Keynesians need to recognise the foundational importance of social ontology to avoid the mistaken assumption that the weakness of orthodox economics merely lies in their theories (implying that simple theory replacement is all that is required). He argues that Post-Keynesians need to adopt an explicit ontological position in order to fulfil the potential for fruitful complementarity with those other heterodox groups which can be 'under-laboured' by CR, such as Marxists.[7]

We would argue that those heterodox groups – such as Post-Keynesians, Marxists and Modern Monetary Theorists – that accept the importance of a philosophical unpinning of their theorising (or the need for an 'ontological turn' [Lawson 1997, 2003]), explicitly utilise a layered ontology (as in CR) and embrace pluralism, might successfully co-exist within one community studying economics and, importantly, interact in such a way as to encourage progress by fostering the advancement of knowledge of real economic mechanisms and structures.

What might Marx be doing?

In *Capital* Marx uses abstraction to identify the key universal features of capitalism, with his theory of value representing the consistent thread of his argument. He is trying to definitively identify the source of profit and how capitalists tend to behave in their competitive search for this profit. When he puts it all together in *Capital* volume I, chapter 25 he is focusing on capitalism's inevitable, periodically reoccurring, instability, its phoenix-like nature, with boom setting the scene for slump and slump setting the scene for boom, with workers being damned all the way. Marx does all this at an abstract aggregate level, without the need for any grand formal mathematical model, that is, he is not being, in our terms, an 'economist'.

In *Capital* volume II, part 3, Marx does explore the circuit/reproduction of capital through employing a stylised model of simple reproduction (constant output) and expanded reproduction (growing output). He also illustrates, in *Capital* volume III, chapter 9, how different compositions of productive capital, between living and dead labour, for different sectors of the economy will require the commodities produced by these different sectors to deviate in appropriated value (price) from their produced value, to tend to equalise the profit rate across sectors. In *Capital* volume III part 3, Marx explores the tendency for capitalist competition to reduce the overall profit rate, restressing that the produced value of a commodity is the average over all its producers, leaders, average and laggards, explaining how it will benefit the leader to introduce labour-saving technology, despite it reducing the overall profit rate.

Clearly Marx does have an 'economic theory', but to say that he is acting how an economist would conventionally behave from the twentieth century onwards is nonsense; he does not build a grand economic model in equations to make his point. However, as Kliman (2007) explains, it is precisely this lack of 'proper' economic behaviour that leads economists to force Marx's ideas into an 'economic' approach. Concerning the superiority of a simultaneous approach,

> Alfred Marshall said once of Ricardo: 'He does not state clearly, and in some cases he perhaps did not fully and clearly perceive how, in the problem of normal value, the various elements govern one another *mutually*, not *successively*, in a long chain of causation'. This description applies even more to Marx … (*who*) held firmly to the view that the elements concerned must be regarded as a kind of causal chain, in which each link is determined, in its composition and its magnitude, only by the preceding links … Modern economics is beginning to free itself gradually from the successivist prejudice, the chief merit being due to the mathematical school led by Leon Walras.
>
> (Bortkiewicz 1952: 22–3, quoted in Freeman 1996a: 15; Freeman's emphasis and bracketed comment)

The consequence of this 'adjustment' of Marx's approach to reflect conventional simultaneous equilibrium economics thinking is, as Steedman (1977) proves, the redundancy of the (now) dual system's concept of labour values; labour values are now perfectly proxied by 'physical' relations between commodities.[8] The tendency for boom to reduce the rate of profit disappears (Okishio 1961), with the focus now falling on labour being the sole source of profit,[9] which now defines you as 'Marxist' (Morishima 1973). If you set your models to explore the generation and smooth reproduction of a physical surplus, as

Sraffa (1960) did, and his Marxist followers still continue to do today, you arrive at a model that, although very different to mainstream models in terms of how it treats 'agents' and their 'rational' behaviour, is still a model organised by the principle of equilibrium (the dominance of centres of gravity).

As with conventional macroeconomic models, once you have based the 'real' economy on the direct exchange relations between commodities, with those relations depending on equilibrium conditions such as equalised profitability, you have thus determined where the 'real' economy 'should' gravitate to, so money can, consequently, only be an addition, which has either no effect on real variables, or, at most, has a temporary disruptive effect on the real economy. Moseley's (2016) simultaneous single system macro model is a good example. If money is a commodity, it definitively sets prices, or if it is 'value-less', its quantity will set nominal prices in a strict way, as explained by the quantity theory of money. So, Marxist economists, like all the macroeconomists in the department, struggle to make money central to anything in their grand mathematical models. Furthermore, Marx's simplifying assumption of a fixed in value gold commodity money in much of his analysis is simply taken by many as Marx's definitive view of money, providing another argument why his theory is redundant and needs to be updated to fit modern times and economic practice.

But we started with Marx's complex theory, not a strict grand mathematical economic model. In fact, Marx does have lots to say about money, not least how in capitalism it is essential to allow commodities' appropriated values to deviate from their produced values, with money being the very form of expression of abstract social labour. *Capital* volume III, part 5 extensively concretely analyses the financial system.

In summary, if you want to be part of the economics department with your crazy radical ideas, like non-identical, non-perfectly maximising rational agents, then please, at least, construct a stylised equilibrium mathematical model to express (but, in fact, limit) your crazy ideas.

What are Keynes and the Post-Keynesians (including Modern Monetary Theorists) doing?

Keynes (1936) focuses upon a demand-driven world by ignoring some (and only some) of the features of conventional analysis[10] in order to develop a theoretical approach that is able to deal with the nature of a real-world monetary production economy with an explicit consideration of historic time (not merely the logical time of conventional economics).

For Post-Keynesians, investment determines saving. In a simple model (with no government or foreign trade sector, and with firms' investment the only source of borrowing) savings are merely the accounting record of investment. Demand is injection-led and investment generates and equal amount of saving at all points in time (explained by the 'conservation of saving' principle [Dalziel 2001: 77]) as the multiplier process[11] generates income.[12]

A development of this logic provides a means to analyse the accounts of an open economy with a government sector; the 'sectoral balances' approach.[13] There are three sectoral balances: the budget deficit (G – T), current account balance (X – M) and private domestic balance (S – I). The sectoral balances equation, (S – I) = (G – T) + (X – M), says that total private savings (S) minus private investment (I) [private sector net saving] has to equal the public deficit [spending, (G) minus taxes, (T)] plus net exports [exports (X) minus imports (M)], where net exports represent the net savings of non-residents (Mitchell 2009). If the public deficit is too small the private sector will not be able to realise its net saving desires at full employment income and, assuming no change in the current account deficit, income will fall until desired saving is equal to actual investment through a dynamic process which might be best regarded as a *tendency*.[14]

Post-Keynesians generally agree that the government's fiscal policy should be designed to achieve the goal of full employment but the advocates of MMT go further by providing a key insight; the explicit recognition that the state must issue money before it can collect it. Spending precedes taxation; the currency is a public monopoly. Thus, for advocates of MMT, when the state issues its own non-convertible currency under floating exchange rates, there is never an 'affordability' question in a monetary sense for the government. It never 'has' or 'doesn't have' money. It issues money *ex-nihilo* and can purchase anything available within its own sovereign monetary space. In such a situation the limits of production and consumption of goods and services are real, not monetary. The quantity and quality of factors of production determine what can be produced and consumed domestically. The state must ensure the economy performs so as to ensure that the nation lives up to its means. It must use its position as a monopoly issuer of the currency to ensure full employment (Armstrong 2015).

Such a view is shared by Lerner in his advocacy of functional finance (1943, 1944, 1947);[15] a deficit would only be too large if it increased private sector net saving beyond desired levels at the full employment level of income. In this case, inflation would be the result. Neither the public sector deficit, nor the public sector debt, would be of any consequence in of themselves, only the macroeconomic outcomes matter. The existence of significant unemployment or underemployment would be *de facto* evidence that the deficit was too small no matter its absolute size or its magnitude in relation to national income.

Although Keynes was prepared to treat the quantity of money as a 'given' in order to concentrate attention upon the paramount importance of effective demand in his approach (Robinson 1971: 81–2; Wray 1990: 122–3), Post-Keynesians embrace the non-neutrality and endogenous nature of money. The importance of the endogenous money approach associated with Post-Keynesianism and MMT cannot be overestimated. It underpins MMT economists' explanations of the nature of the financial system and their analysis of core or operational reality as a whole. Within Post-Keynesianism, a debate between 'accommodationists' and 'structuralists' (Pollin 1991) exists but an acceptance of the accommodationist view characterises MMT (Mosler 2012); from this viewpoint, central banks *necessarily* supply the volume of reserves required by the banking system – at the same time as the loan creates the deposit – by accounting for a reserve requirement as an overdraft or loan. Failure to do so would be an error of accounting. The volume of loans *per se* will not affect interest rates and banks will advance credit in response to increased demand at current rates, acquiring reserves, as required, at a price determined by the central bank (Wray 1990, 1998). This 'accommodative' view contends that the central bank acts in a *passive* manner; banks can always access the *quantity* of reserves they require but it is the central bank that chooses the *price*.[16]

Post-Keynesians stress the importance of real-world institutions and market power when they study the financial system, and advocates of MMT argue that their analysis is both consistent with the core principles of Post-Keynesian economics, and provides a rigorous and compelling explanation of how the real-world monetary system works.

False Compatibility I – Kalecki and Marx: The period

Let us summarise the nature of the period that Post-Keynesians and Circuit Theorists employ (typically, see Lavoie 2009). It is a self-contained period, running from the advance or creation of bank credit to its repayment or destruction. It is within this sequential period that Kaleckian macroeconomic criteria are thought to apply:

> profits cannot exist prior to a spending decision. Clearly if no profits are consumed by capitalists, this is tantamount to saying that Savings cannot precede Investment. Hence the Kalecki accounting relation
>
> $$P = I + C - W,$$
>
> where P is the level of profits, I is gross investment, C total consumption and W is the wage bill (total costs) with a zero propensity to save. Total profits are thus equal to capitalists' investment decisions plus their consumption expenditures. ... Assume that all profits are saved, with a positive propensity to save out of wages we have the Kaleckian equality
>
> $$S = P + S_w = (C + I - W) + (W - C),$$
> $$S = I,$$
>
> where S are savings and S_w the level of savings out of wages. Savings emerge as a result of a monetary evaluation of output; therefore they cannot but appear after investment and production have taken place. ... . The equalisation between savings and investment does not depend on the existence of a prior amount of loanable funds, being rather the outcome of the Kaleckian principle where, in order for profits to arise, prior spending is required.
>
> (Halevi and Taouil 2002: 93)

> Now it is clear that capitalists can decide to consume and invest more in a given period than in the preceding one, but they cannot decide to earn more. It is therefore their investment and consumption decisions that determine profits and not vice versa.
>
> (Kalecki 1971: 78–9)

So, Post-Keynesians and Circuit Theorists are trying to escape mainstream notions of savings determining investment, but within a self-contained period, where what happens at the start of the period determines what happens at the end of the period. Demand must be just 'right', or profit will be reduced. Furthermore, within the Kaleckian macroeconomic system, acts of prior spending (incurring debt), through both the state's budget deficit and possible net household indebtedness, increase firms' returns, acting as a positive influence on aggregate profit (Parguez 2002), all within the same self-contained period.

An abstract illustration of Marx's theory would also abide by the Kaleckian accounting relation, but in a different way, due to its different concept of the time period or sequentiality. Following the Temporal Single System Interpretation (TSSI) of Marx, we focus on how periods of production are separated sequentially by periods of circulation.[17] In circulation, firms realise profits, extracted from labour in the *previous* production period, by acts of spending prior to the *next* production period, not by a prior act of spending in the *same self-contained period.* Abstracting from any worker saving or budget deficit, firms must collectively in circulation clear the market, through their own consumption and purchase of constant capital and labour inputs for the following production period, to successfully realise their profits *in money* from the preceding production period. The Kaleckian accounting relation thus holds in circulation *between* production periods.

Furthermore, even if all output is not sold or realised in money, profit is still accrued by capitalists equal to the surplus-value extracted from labour. As long as price is established at the end of production, the appropriated value of commodities is determined with, in aggregate, the total value of newly produced commodities exceeding the total value of constant capital consumed in producing those commodities, plus total wages paid to variable capital (workers), by the surplus-value extracted from labour. Any accountant will tell you unsold stock is valued at its price; value does not come into existence through circulation, but in production (Freeman 1996b). Clearly if stock continues to build up, production will be cut back sometime, and old stock will lose value if price falls (Potts 2016).

But demand is not balanced on a knife-edge. Output will rise next period if total inputs rise, so even if the capitalists consume, or just destroy, a proportion of their profits, as long as they invest some of their profits in expanding production, and as long as they extract more surplus-value *next period*, profit will rise next period.

If demand from capitalists (worker indebtedness or government budget deficit) is more than sufficient at the prices established at the end of production to buy all the newly produced commodities, then stocks can be sold to satisfy this demand, but this does not increase profit for that period. The stocks were carried into the period as part of the capitalists' total capital, which can only grow by the total surplus-value extracted from labour. The value in the stocks simply changes form to money, creating a release of capital, not an increase in that period's profit. Also, if productive capitalists invested more this period and if this investment just involved expanding constant capital input, with living labour input and the surplus-value extracted from this living labour remaining constant, then total profit would remain unchanged, as total profit is determined by total surplus-value and does not simply come into existence as 'demanded'.

In summary, for Marx, profit is not simply a demand-led monetary phenomenon. Periods are thus more definitely linked if we follow the TSSI of Marx, with a sequence of periods representing a dynamic 'spiral flow', and not, as for Post-Keynesians and Circuit Theorists, a connected sequence of self-contained circuits. This does not rule out investigating the role of creation of credit in the process, or mean we have to assume, like the mainstream, that the interest rate adjusts total investment to total saving. Neither does capitalism's potential for growth through extracting surplus-value mean that growth is inevitable or the market must clear (Say's Law). In response to low profitability, or indeed anything that causes pessimism amongst capitalists, production can be cut back, creating falling demand and output. TSSI models are not balanced on a demand management or price adjustment knife-edge to achieve equilibrium, because they are not simultaneous/equilibrium constructs, like 'economics' *must* be.

False Compatibility II – Kalecki and Marx: The mark-up

Cooper (2016) examines the possible links between Marx, Kalecki and MMT. He suggests three elements of compatibility. First, in Marx macroeconomics dominates microeconomics. But for Marx it is hard to think of a macro/micro split at all. The overall situation is the sum of the individual capitalists' actions, but Marx has no Macro 'model'. It is misleading to say the macro dog is wagging the micro tail. For Marx, the overall 'macro' rate of profit falls precisely because at the 'micro' level capitalists tend to invest in constant capital more than they increase input of living labour.

Second, Cooper contends, in common with Keynes, Kalecki and the Post-Keynesians, that Marx rejects the classical dichotomy as his work *applies to a monetary production economy*; and third, Marx's analysis of the private monetary circuit is consistent with the endogenous money approach which characterises the work of the Post-Keynesians, Kalecki, Circuit theorists and MMT. As explained above, Marx's theory definitely does not follow the classical dichotomy, yet money is neutral in 'Marxist' models, like that described by Moseley (2016), while, as we have explained, at least for the TSSI of Marx, the nature of the period is very different to that used by Post-Keynesians, Kalecki and Circuit Theorists.

Cooper sets out to demonstrate the close relationship between Marx's concept of surplus-value and Kalecki's idea of the mark-up. Cooper links Kalecki's concept of the 'degree of monopoly' (which takes account of the cost of raw materials) to Marx's concepts of surplus-value and the rate of profit:

$$Degree\,of\ Monopoly = \frac{Proceeds}{Money\,Wage\ Bill + Materials\,Cost}$$

Cooper states for Marx that total price is the equivalent of proceeds. Materials costs are taken to represent constant capital (c) through abstracting from any fixed capital, ensuring the following equation applies:

$$Degree\,of\ Monopoly = \frac{\$c + \$v + \$s}{\$c + \$v} = 1 + \frac{s}{c + v} = 1 + r$$

Cooper concludes that Kalecki's degree of monopoly is equivalent to one plus the rate of profit (r). He then suggests that Marx's value analysis might be used to explain the Kaleckian concepts of the mark-up and the degree of monopoly.

> For instance, Kalecki argues that the degree of monopoly reflects various institutional factors. These factors include the concentration of industry, the development of marketing and advertising strategies, the strength of trade unions and the ratio of overheads to prime cost (also known as variable cost). These institutional factors can just as easily be regarded as influencing the rate of surplus value (s/v) and the organic composition of capital (c/v).
>
> (Cooper 2016)

He shows Marx's definition of the rate of profit as,

$$Rate\,of\ Profit = r = \frac{s}{c + v} = \frac{\frac{s}{v}}{\frac{c}{v} + 1}$$

He is then able to derive an equation for the degree of monopoly in Marxian terms,

$$Degree\,of\ Monopoly = 1 + r = 1 + \frac{\frac{s}{v}}{\frac{c}{v} + 1}$$

In this way, Cooper is able to show how an argument might be made to suggest that, viewed through Marxian eyes, the rate of surplus-value and the organic composition of capital underlie the so-called 'institutional factors' which affect the degree of monopoly.

So, does this analysis really fit Marx? At an aggregate level, in a pure circulating capital model, the equations do hold, but does Cooper's interpretation hide the essential difference between Marx and Kalecki?

The reason that, at an aggregate level, the mark-up and the degree of monopoly power relate to the aggregate rate of profit is because, at the aggregate level, according to Marx's theory, total produced value equals total appropriated value/price, and total surplus-value equals total profit. But this is in no way dependent on the 'level' of competition; total profit will equal total surplus-value whether we assume firms to be in 'perfect' competition or that they are all monopolies. In a model, for simplicity, we may assume that all firms are identical, so are equally monopolies or are equally competitive, but in Marx's work he imagines both monopolies and competitive firms and considers how they affect each other. Monopolies (Marx 1981: 1001) are outside the tendency to profit rate equalisation operating across the sectors in the competitive economy. They are likely to appropriate more profit than they produce, thus reducing the profit that can be appropriated in the competitive sectors, because total profit is already determined in production by the total extraction of surplus-value.

Cooper's equations cannot hold for an individual sector or an individual firm. For a monopoly, their mark-up or degree of monopoly power will determine how much value they can appropriate, not the value they produce ($c + v + s$). Firms in competitive sectors with below than the average organic composition of capital will tend to appropriate less value than they produce, while firms in competitive sectors with above average organic composition of capital will tend to appropriate more value than they produce, to tend to equalise the profit rate across sectors. In addition, we need to remember that within each competitive sector, individual firms are highly unlikely to appropriate the value that they produce for another reason; they are not all the same! Assuming no monopolies, in a sector with average organic composition of capital (and assuming the profit rate is equalised between sectors), the average firm would appropriate the same value as it produces, so would earn the overall average rate of profit. But, within this sector, all firms ahead of the social average level of productivity, the leaders, would appropriate more value than they produce and have a higher profit rate, while laggard firms, behind the social average, would appropriate less value than they produce and have a lower profit rate than the average. So, the aggregate equalities cannot be translated into what happens to individual firms, as no firm is at all likely to appropriate the same value as they produce.

The factors Cooper thinks may change the aggregate mark-up must change the aggregate rate of profit by changing the rate of exploitation (ratio of s to v) or the organic composition of capital.[18] Firms cannot all become more 'monopolistic' and thus magically increase the rate of profit, unless somehow this action successfully changes the rate of exploitation or the organic composition of capital. Marx does explain how relative surplus-value can be produced, through technological change cheapening workers' means of subsistence, allowing v to fall and s to rise. But this is likely to be accompanied by a rising organic composition of capital, the very cause of the technological change, ensuring an overall tendency for the profit rate to fall. If the rate of exploitation is changed by simply changing workers' standard of living (Marx does consider wages to depend on moral/social considerations), then this change in absolute surplus-value will change total profit. But the macro dog is not simply wagging the micro tail, it is not Cooper's 'The distribution of value between workers and capitalists depends on the rate of profit', rather for Marx it is clearly the rate of profit that depends on the distribution of value between workers and capitalists (and the organic composition of capital).

In summary, from Marx's perspective, it makes as little sense to imagine that the degree of competition somehow alters total profit, if total surplus-value is unchanged, as it does to imagine that a change in total investment changes total profit, if total surplus-value is unchanged. Yet these are the macro dogs, which are wagging the micro tails in the Kalecki, Post-Keynesian and MMT models that Cooper is imagining represent a 'compatibility' with Marx.

False Compatibility III: The value of money

Marx's theory of value tells us that technological change reduces the value of commodities. This 'natural' rate of deflation can be seen as the base from which to at least define what inflation is, or rather what unit is being inflated, and that is, according to Marx's value theory, the Monetary Expression of Labour-Time (MELT), (Ramos-Martínez 2004). The TSSI concept of MELT does not, in itself, explain price determination (Potts 2017b), but it does allow us to adjust from nominal to Marx's concept of value. MELT does not rely on assuming equilibrium or balanced growth; rather, it just relies on the concept that commodities have an aggregate appropriated value expressible in money and an aggregate produced value expressible in labour-time. In TSSI models MELT is reestablished at the end of each production period when prices are formed, with this MELT holding through the next production period until at its end prices, and thus MELT, are reestablished again.

Cooper (2016) considers the possible complementarity between the 'Marxist' notion of the MELT and MMT's concept of the value of the currency. Wray notes that,

> once the government realizes that its spending decision determines the quantity of fiat money available to meet tax obligations it imposes it can exogenously set the prices of those goods and services [including labour] it buys from the private sector. This determines the value of the currency.
>
> (Wray 1998: 159)

Cooper thinks that it is possible to define the value of the currency in terms of labour-time. Cooper (2010) provides equations for the MELT (m) and the value of the currency (z).

$$m = \frac{Net\ Product}{Total\ Employment} = \frac{PY}{L}$$

$$z = \frac{Total\ Employment}{Wage\ Bill} = \frac{L}{W}$$

He shows how both the MELT and the value of the currency can be expressed to illustrate their complementarity,

$$m = \frac{1}{z} \times \frac{PY}{W} \quad z = \frac{1}{m} \times \frac{PY}{W}$$

Where: W = the wage bill (assumed to be equal to variable capital), L = total employment, P = the general level of prices and Y = 'real' output.

So has Cooper really found compatibility here? First, he is only considering the net product MELT. Foley (1986) pioneered the Marxist net product approach, terming it the New Interpretation. Essentially, constant capital is ignored, as output of constant capital cancels out input of constant capital, with any increase in output of constant capital representing net investment which, in turn, is part of 'real' output/the net product. But the TSSI of Marx does not just focus on the net product, as Marx did not employ this approach. Crucially, the cancelling out of constant capital stands in the way of understanding how inputs can vary in unit-value to outputs. This key insight underpins Marx's tendency for the profit rate to fall. If we calculate input and output values simultaneously, or use replacement cost valuation, we miss Marx's 'most important law' (Marx 1973: 748), and miscalculate the monetary expression of *his* unit of value.

Wray's value of currency, as presented by Cooper, is just the average wage. It is very similar to Keynes's idea of the wage unit for a standard hour of labour (Keynes 1936, chapter 4), which he introduces to take analysis away from conventional real terms, that is, a physical concept of value. However, Wray's value of currency and Keynes' wage unit are both very imperfect measures of value, as they are not invariant to the distribution of new value between capitalists and workers (Potts 2013). If wages fell relative to the price of inputs and profit (just profit for net product), total output measured in wage units would rise, because inputs and profits would represent more labour-time as the 'price' of labour-time has fallen. However, all that has really changed is the distribution of value, not value itself. So, how can we see this as any improvement on total output, or profit, being dependent, as it is, on relative prices (that aggregate heterogeneous physical commodities) in mainstream macroeconomic models?

In contrast, Marx's unit of measurement, also an hour of simple labour, is not the monetary expression of the wage, which is, of course, variable (variable capital), but is the monetary expression of an hour of newly created value. In addition this value is not calculated just for the net product; it is the monetary expression of an hour of value, whether it is new value produced by living labour or transferred value from constant capital. MELT does not depend on the distribution of value, the value of total output simply equals the value transferred in production by constant capital and the total living labour worked in production. So, if wages were higher, then profit would be lower, with total value remaining the same.

Again the compatibility that Cooper suggests is skin deep; dependent on particular assumptions in particular restricted models.

To Wray, the value of currency is 'set-able' by the government, whereas for the TSSI of Marx, MELT is the result of price determination; it is the right tool to find a reliable unit of value, that is, Marx's unit of value.

Some Post-Keynesian economists see Marx's value theory as a barrier to the integration of Marxist economics with other heterodox schools. Steve Keen is highly critical of the 'labour' theory of value and considers it to have had a detrimental effect, even within Marxism itself (Keen 2004: 298). So, what does Keen really mean? If he is referring to simultaneous and dualistic Marxists with their redundant concept of value, we should keep away. But if Keen is really rejecting Marx's concept of value, and all Marx's understanding of capitalism that comes from it, including his 'most important law' and an explanation of where profit really comes from, then Keen is rejecting Marx, full-stop, and hoping that by acting more like economists Marxist economics can be more like his economics and leave Marx behind as nothing but a creation myth.

Conclusion – So what can Marxists and Post-Keynesians/Modern Monetary Theorists learn from each other?

We would argue that commonality exists between the work of Marx and Keynes and, although complex to establish, nevertheless exists at a philosophical level and has the potential to generate fruitful knowledge; importantly, CR provides the 'under-labouring' (Lawson 1997) for both Marxism and Post-Keynesianism (and MMT). Both approaches reject methodical individualism and favour a richer social ontology (Collier 1994: 139), eschew deductivism in favour of retroduction, and posit causal mechanisms that explain observed economic events. Both concentrate on explanation rather than prediction, reject spuriously precise forecasts and instead propound tendencies, which, although not quantitatively precise, are nevertheless deeply significant (Fleetwood 2013).

We would caution that nothing profound can be gleaned from a comparison of neat narrow equilibrium models but much can potentially be gained by combining the concepts of how value is created (in Marx) and how the financial system works (in Keynes), with an analysis of how the government chooses to influence both in MMT (see especially, Mosler 2012).

We would stress the significance of pluralism, which should involve mutual respect and understanding of ideas (Dow 2017), not the sharing of 'scraps of method' from the economics department. We think the advocates of MMT would seriously benefit from considering Marx's prediction of the inevitable periodic self-defeat of capitalism and that those who take Marx seriously would gain from exploring how the state's action, with respect to the operation of the financial system, can effect, or distort, the pattern of accumulation, particularly given how the state's status as a monopoly issuer of the currency enables it to reduce unemployment to zero by the use of a Job Guarantee or Employer of Last Resort Policy (Wray 1998: 122–54; Mitchell 2013; Mosler and Silipo 2016).

Marx's analysis is set in a world with a relatively small state sector where the capitalist economy is characterised by booms and slumps, recurring crises and, crucially, a tendency for the profit rate to decline. For Marx, it is the decline in capital values in a slump that allows capitalists to escape the decline in their profit rate. However, in a modern context with a much larger state sector and a government Employer of Last Resort (ELR) policy, unemployment would be eliminated, and the effects of slumps may be significantly ameliorated. Thus, the slump required to drive the reduction in the price of capital may be absent (or at the very least reduced in impact) decreasing the potential for the profit rate to rebound. If the profit rate remains depressed we might expect that a progressive socialisation of investment (Keynes 1936) and a general tendency for the size of the public sector to expand to be the result. On the other hand, if policy was constructed so as to allow significant recession in the private sector, with the state sector growing temporarily to absorb the increased unemployment, capital values could still significantly adjust, recreating the conditions for strong growth. When growth is strong again state sector employment could quickly fall. Understanding when a crisis is *inevitable*, and *who* needs to be sheltered from its effects, would thus radically redefine our notion of effective economic policy (supporting people not particular businesses or asset values).

Further, we might suggest that Marxists should take the actual history of money and, importantly, anthropology seriously. Marx's support for the Banking School vis-à-vis the Currency School in *Capital* volume III (in particular, chapter 27; also see Lapavitsas 1994) shows that Marx understood the idea of endogenous money. Thus, it would be possible for Marxists to embrace MMT's analysis of the monetary system and the 'taxes drive money' approach (Wray 1998: 155–75). In turn, MMT advocates might embrace value theory within the framework of the TSSI of Marx, in recognition of how this approach is able to provide an explanation of the ultimate source of profit lying at a deeper level of abstraction than the Circuitist/Kaleckian approach, which only deals with financial flows within a self-contained period.

Notes

1 The tie is the dominance of the model as the end in itself (equilibrium based, with self-contained periods, that are usually simultaneously calculated), over any concept and resulting logical development of real mechanisms.

2 Kuhn (1962) analyses the progress of scientific knowledge and contends that its nature is non-continuous, 'paradigm-based', and community consensus determines the key problems to consider and the methods used to solve them.

3

> For Kuhn, scientists do not just 'see,' they 'see as,' and it is their shared conceptual framework, that determines what is seen as what. The paradigm provides the lens, or interpretative framework, by which various aspects of the world are observed … there are no 'out-of-theory experiences' [Kitcher 1993: 133].
>
> (Hands 2001: 103)

4 The term critical realism is a hybrid of 'critical naturalism' and 'transcendental realism' (Bhaskar 1989: 190).

5 Bhaskar defines open systems,

> supposing that at some time 't' an event of type 'a' was not followed by an event of type 'b' we would have to say that the system was 'open', our criteria of openness just being the fact that events of type 'a' had not been invariably followed by events of type 'b' *under their given descriptions*; i.e. the instability in space or over time, of actually recorded empirical relationships.
>
> (Bhaskar 2008 [1975]: 73; emphasis in the original)

6 In addition to methodological pluralism, Dow (2017: 8) goes on to distinguish between three further forms of pluralism: pluralist methodology, ontological pluralism and theoretical pluralism.

7 See Westra (2018).

8 Kliman (2007) discusses fully the rise of simultaneous and dualistic Marxism in the twentieth century. Commodities prices and values at both the start and the end of the period are simultaneously calculated, with price being one system and labour-values being another separate system (to link by the equality of total price to total labour-value, or, but not and, total profit to total surplus-value). In contrast, the TSSI of Marx imagines sequential periods, with the unit-value of commodities as inputs not necessarily equalling their unit-value as outputs through, for example, technological change. A single system of value is imagined, with value being expressible in either hours or money, with the monetary expression of labour-time (MELT) being established at the end of each period by the total appropriated value/price of commodities in money divided by the total produced value of those commodities in labour-time (Potts 2016). Following this method there is no mistake in Marx's transformation 'problem' to correct; surplus-value is the sole source of profit, value is not perfectly proxied by physical quantities and Marx's tendency for the profit rate to fall in times of accumulation is 'rediscovered' (Kliman 2007). However new knowledge is not embraced by 'Marxist' economists, rather every attempt is made to dismiss it (Potts 2014).

9 Potts and Kliman (2015) collect and summarise the debate around 'when' total profit equals total surplus-value extracted from labour.

10 Robinson (1971: 81–2) argues that Keynes had to retain some aspects of conventional analysis 'in order to get a hearing'. From this perspective, he was able take the money supply as a 'given' (Robinson 1971: 81–2; Wray 1990: 123), and accept the assumptions of flexible wages and perfect competition and show that, *even with these conditions applying*, the economy could still settle down at an under-full employment equilibrium (Keynes 1936: 267). In reality, Keynes understood the endogenous nature of money (Keynes 1930; Wray 1990) and accepted the existence of imperfect competition and the inflexibility of wages in practice (Keynes 1936) but wished to show that they were not the essential cause of under-full employment equilibrium; which was, in his view, lack of effective demand.

11 Richard Kahn (1931) is credited with developing the 'multiplier' concept, which became a key concept in Keynesian economics. Dalziel (2001: 77) shows how the multiplier concept and the conservation of saving principle (Meade 1993) are linked. An initial investment initiates a multiplier effect and at the end of every round of spending, the increase in saving always equals the increase in investment

> made up by the accumulated increases in voluntary saving in each round so far, plus the income generated by the current round's induced consumption expenditure (which is involuntarily held until an opportunity to spend or voluntarily to save it the following round. Thus any act of consumption during the process does not reduce aggregate savings but simply redistributes savings in the form of new income to the supplier of the purchased consumption goods.
>
> (Dalziel 2001: 77)

12 The Circuit Theorists' sequential application of the Kaleckian macroeconomic criteria over the circuit leads to the conclusion that the multiplier must equal one (Deleplace and Nell 1996), that is, savings are not brought up to an increased level of investment by a process of income adjustment. Over the circulation period increased investment will automatically generate matching saving.

13 As associated with Wynne Godley (Mitchell 2015).

14 Collier (1994: 61–5) notes that, from the perspective of critical realism, 'explanation in open systems is in terms of tendencies' (Collier 1994:63).

15 Keynes' views on functional finance are complex to unravel; perhaps he meant it to be that way (Colander 1984; Aspromourgos 2014; Armstrong 2018).

16 For Post-Keynesians, the short-term interest rate is an administered variable. Advocates of MMT also recognise that the central bank, by virtue of its role as monopoly issuer of state money, has the power to control the full spectrum of interest rates (Armstrong 2015).

17 Circulation is usually assumed to occur instantaneously between production periods; see Potts (2017a) for an exploration of circulation occurring alongside production periods.

18 We should note, given Cooper's mentioning of advertising increasing the mark-up/the rate of profit, Marx's (mainly see, Marx 1978) notion of productive labour, of value and surplus-value, and unproductive labour that produces no value and consumes surplus-value produced by productive workers. Increasing the unproductive labour of advertising reduces total profit. It may cause individual firms to be able to appropriate more, but at the cost of leaving other firms to appropriate far less (to bear the cost of advertising, and any rise in profit for those who

advertise). Increased advertising cannot in aggregate increase the mark-up/the rate of profit; it will reduce it. Potts (2007) explains how, for Marx, research and development works in exactly the same way, to devastating effect for the laggards, in practice the vast majority of the world's population who live in developing countries.

References

Armstrong, P. (2015), 'Heterodox Views of Money and Modern Monetary Theory'. Available at: https://moslereconomics.com/wp-content/uploads/2007/12/Money-and-MMT.pdf.

Armstrong, P. (2018), 'Keynes's View of Deficits and Functional Finance: A Modern Monetary Theory Perspective', *The International Review of Applied Economics,* 32 (6), 713–31.

Aspromourgos, T. (2014), 'Keynes, Lerner and the Question of Public Debt', *History of Political Economy,* 46 (3), 408–33.

Bhaskar, R. (1989), *Reclaiming Reality*, London: Verso.

Bhaskar, R. (2008 [1975]), *A Realist View of Science*, London: Routledge.

Bilgrami, A. (2015), *Who's Afraid of Academic Freedom?* New York: Columbia University Press.

Blaug, M. (1992), *The Methodology of Economics: Or How Economists Explain*, Cambridge: Cambridge University Press.

Colander, D. (1984), 'Was Keynes a Keynesian or a Lernerian?', *Journal of Economic Literature,* 22 (December, 4), 1572–5.

Collier, A. (1994), *CR: An Introduction to Roy Bhaskar's Philosophy*, London: Verso.

Cooper, P. (2010), 'Value of the Currency'. Available at: http://heteconomist.com/value-of-the-currency-2/.

Cooper, P. (2016), 'The Monetary Circuit & Compatibility of Marx, Kalecki and Keynesian Macro'. Available at: http://heteconomist.com/the-monetary-circuit-compatibility-of-marx-kalecki-and-keynesian-macro/.

Dalziel, P. (2001), 'A Note on Mr. Meade's Relation and International Capital Movements', in G. C. Harcourt (ed.), *50 Years a Keynesian and Other Essays*, London: Palgrave.

Deleplace, G. and Nell, E. (1996), 'Introduction: Monetary Circulation and Effective Demand', in G. Deleplace and E. Nell (eds.), *Money in Motion: The Post Keynesian and Circulation Approaches*, London and Basingstoke: Macmillan, pp. 3–41.

Dow, S (2017), 'Pluralist Economics: Is it Scientific?', in S. Decker, W. Elsner and S. Flectner (eds.), *Teaching Economics in the 21st Century: A State of the Art Compilation*, London: Routledge.

Fine, B. (2016), *Microeconomics: A Critical Companion*, London: Pluto Press.

Fleetwood, S. (2013), 'What is (and what isn't) CR?'. Available at: www2.uwe.ac.uk/faculties/BBS/BUS/.../What%20CR%20is%20and%20is%20not.pdf.

Foley, D. (1986), *Understanding Capital: Marx's Economic Theory*, Cambridge, MA: Harvard University Press.

Freeman, A. (1996a), 'The Psychopathology of Walrasian Marxism', in A. Freeman and G. Carchedi (eds.), *Marx and Non-Equilibrium Economics*, Cheltenham: Edward Elgar, pp. 1–28.

Freeman, A. (1996b), 'Price, Value and Profit – A Continuous, General, Treatment', in A. Freeman and G. Carchedi (eds.), *Marx and Non-Equilibrium Economics*, Cheltenham: Edward Elgar, pp. 225–79.

Halevi, J. and Taouil, R. (2002), 'On a Post-Keynesian Stream from France and Italy: The Circuit Approach', in P. Arestis, M. Desai and S. Dow (eds.), *Money, Macroeconomics and Keynes: Essays in Honour of Victoria Chick, Volume One*, London: Routledge, pp. 91–102.

Hands, D. W. (2001), *Reflection Without Rules: Economic Methodology and Contemporary Science Theory*, Cambridge: Cambridge University Press.

Howard, M. and King, J. (1992), *A History of Marxian Economics, Volume 2, 1929–1990*, Princeton, NJ: Princeton University Press.

Kahn, R. F. (1931), 'The Relation of Home Investment to Unemployment', *Economic Journal*, 41, 173–98.

Kalecki, M. (1971), 'Class Struggle and the Distribution of National Income', *Kyklos*, 24 (1), 1–9.

Keen, S. (2004), *Debunking Economics*, London: Zed Books.

Keynes, J. M. (1930), *A Treatise on Money*, 2 vols, New York: Harcourt and Brace.

Keynes, J. M. (1936), *The General Theory of Money, Interest and Employment*, New York: Harcourt and Brace.

Kitcher, P. (1993), *The Advancement of Science*, New York: Oxford University Press.

Kliman, A. (2007), *Reclaiming Marx's 'Capital'*, Lanham, MD: Lexington Books.

Kuhn, T. (2012 [1962]), *The Structure of Scientific Revolutions*, Chicago, IL: University of Chicago Press.

Lakatos, I. (1970), *The Methodology of Scientific Research Programmes*, Cambridge: Cambridge University Press.

Lapavitsas, C. (1994), 'The Banking School and the Monetary Thought of Karl Marx', *Cambridge Journal of Economics*, 18 (5), 447–61.

Lavoie, M. (2009), *Introduction to Post-Keynesian Economics*, Basingstoke: Palgrave Macmillan

Lawson, T. (1997), *Economics and Reality*, London: Routledge

Lawson, T. (2003), *Reorienting Economics*, London: Routledge

Lee, F. (2009), *A History of Heterodox Economics*, Abingdon: Routledge

Lerner, A. P. (1943), 'Functional Finance and the Federal Debt', *Social Research*, 10, 38–51.

Lerner, A. P. (1944), *The Economics of Control*, New York: Macmillan.

Lerner, A. P. (1947), 'Money as a Creature of the State', *American Economic Review*, 37, 312–17.

Marx, K. (1973), *Grundrisse: Foundations of the Critique of Political Economy*, London: Penguin.

Marx, K. (1976), *Capital: A Critique of Political Economy, Volume I*, London and New York: Penguin/Vintage Publishers edition.

Marx, K. (1978), *Capital: A Critique of Political Economy, Volume II*, London and New York: Penguin/Vintage Publishers edition.

Marx, K. (1981), *Capital: A Critique of Political Economy, Volume III*, London and New York: Penguin/Vintage Publishers edition.

Meade, J. (1993), 'The Relation of Mr. Meade's Relation to Khan's Multiplier', *Economic Journal*, 103, 664–5.

Mitchell, W. (2009), 'Norway and the Sectoral Balances', May 19. Available at:
http://bilbo.economicoutlook.net/blog/?p=2418.

Mitchell, W. (2013), 'What is a Job Guarantee?'. Available at: http://bilbo.economicoutlook.net/blog/?p=23719.

Mitchell, W. (2015), 'Flow of Funds and Sectoral Balances'. Available at: http://bilbo.economicoutlook.net/blog/?p=32396.

Morishima, M. (1973), *Marx's Economics: A Dual Theory of Value and Growth*, Cambridge: Cambridge University Press.

Moseley, F. (2016), 'The MELT and Circular Reasoning in the New Interpretation and the Temporal Single System Interpretation', *Marxism 21,* 13 (2), 123–46.

Mosler, W. (2012), *Soft Currency Economics II*, US Virgin Islands: Valance.

Mosler, W. and Silipo, D. (2016), 'Maximising Price Stability in a Monetary Economy', *Journal of Policy Modelling,* 39 (2), 272–89. Available at: www.sciencedirect.com/journal/journal-of-policy-modeling/.

Okishio, N. (1961), 'Technical Changes and the Rate of Profit', *Kobe University Economic Review,* 7, 86–99.

Parguez, A. (2002), 'Victoria Chick and the Theory of the Monetary Circuit: An Enlightening Debate', in P. Arestis, M. Desai and S. Dow (eds.), *Money, Macroeconomics and Keynes: Essays in Honour of Victoria Chick, Volume One*, London: Routledge, pp. 45–55.

Pollin, R. (1991), 'Two Theories of Money Supply Endogeneity: Some Empirical Evidence', *Journal of Post Keynesian Economics,* 13 (Spring, 3), 366–96.

Popper, K. (1965 [1959]), *The Logic of Scientific Discovery*, New York: Harper Torchbooks.

Potts, N. (2007), 'Some Preliminary Thoughts on Knowledge-based Production: 49 Seconds on Mustafar', *Critique: Journal of Socialist Theory,* 35 (3), 357–73.

Potts, N. (2013), 'Keynesian Economics: In Search of Unnatural Stability', *Critique: Journal of Socialist Theory,* 41 (2), 183–97.

Potts, N. (2014), 'An Unacceptable Misrepresentation: Dismissing Marx's Value Theory by Deliberately Distorting the Temporal Single System Interpretation of Marx', *World Review Of Political Economy,* 5 (1), 66–116.

Potts, N. (2016), 'Two Temporal Single System Interpretation of Marx Calculations of the MELT', *Marxism 21,* 13 (2), 94–122.

Potts, N. (2017a), 'TSSI Experiments in Circulation', International Working Group on Value Theory Working Paper, posted 8 November. Available at: http://copejournal.com/tssi-experiments-in-circulation-by-nick-potts/.

Potts, N. (2017b), 'Exploring Marx's Value Theory in our Inflationary World: Why it is not Moseley's Way or the Highway!', *Marxism 21,* 14 (Summer, 2), 198–232.

Potts, N. and Kliman, A. (2015), *Is Marx's Theory of Profit Right: The Simultaneist-Temporalist Debate*, Lanham, MD: Lexington Books.

Pratten, S. (2013), 'Post-Keynesian Economics, CR and Social Ontology', in G. C. Harcourt and P. Kriesler (eds.), *The Oxford Handbook of Post-Keynesian Economics*, 2 vols, Oxford: Oxford University Press.

Ramos-Martínez, A. (2004), 'Labour, Money, Labour-Saving Innovation, and the Falling Rate of Profit', in A. Freeman, A. Kliman and J. Wells (eds.), *The New Value Controversy and the Foundations of Economics*, Cheltenham: Edward Elgar.

Robinson, J. (1971), *Economic Heresies*, New York: Basic Books

Sraffa, P. (1960), *Production of Commodities By Means of Commodities: Prelude to a Critique of Economic Theory*, Cambridge: Cambridge University Press.

Steedman, I. (1977), *Marx after Sraffa*, London: New Left Books.

Westra, R. (2018), 'Roy Bhaskar's CR and the Social Science of Marxian Economics', *Review of Radical Political Economics*, 1–18.

Wray, L. R. (1990), *Money and Credit in Capitalist Economies*, Aldershot: Edward Elgar

Wray, L. R. (1998), *Understanding Modern Money*, Cheltenham: Edward Elgar.

Part II

Sustainable macroeconomy and structural policies

5 Green economics insights for economists

Diversity leads us out of our silos

Miriam Kennet

Introduction

Today, we are probably the richest, most comfortable set of humans who have ever walked the earth, yet we are facing a set of crises as big as any that have ever struck humans in the last 73,000 years – since the Tolba Eruption wiped out half of humanity (Prothero 2018) – and which have the capacity to wipe us out completely, unless we can act together as one humanity in time. The fragility of our survival and well-being, our economy and security is becoming much more evident (Pachauri 2007 in Kennet 2007). The very survival of our species is at risk (Lean 2005 in Kennet 2007). Our economy, the online-knowledge economy, may be the least resilient of any that has gone before, and we are creating health problems for ourselves and other species (IPBES 2019; Wainer, Kennet and Grabauskaite 2015) of unimaginable proportions (Kennet et al. 2012: 33; Watts et al. 2019). NASA (Reddy 2019) has just announced that the arctic soil, which for tens of thousands of years was a carbon sink, has now shifted to becoming a carbon emitter, which will further accelerate the heating of the planet and the rising of sea levels. Patricia Espinosa, Executive Secretary of the United Nations Framework Convention on Climate Change (UNFCCC), recently remarked that our house is on fire. 'If the house is on fire, you don't go back and start negotiating, you do everything possible to put the fire out' (Espinosa 2019). This book argues that Heterodox Economics can help, but only if economic policymakers reorientate immediately towards a more realistic, pluralist and holistic interdisciplinary model.

A major part of the problem is our subject of economics, at least the orthodox version, which has been used to justify some of humanity's most destructive acts ever; its ignorance of science, of heterodoxy and of other disciplines has been instrumental in some of economics' most barbaric and short-sighted policy recommendations and conclusions. The subject is simply not fit for purpose and must undergo transformation and improvement now! This chapter argues that the present climate emergency and coming hostile climate changes, human induced ecological fragility, resource depletion and mass extinction require a specific pluralist, economic science that will offer real and effective change immediately. The mainstream structures are predicated on a 'silo mentality', which has been termed 'monocultures of the mind' (Shiva 1993). An illustration of this point is the theory and practice of monoculture agriculture from the West – a model foisted on the South – that has impoverished farmers. The same can be said of much of mainstream economics. We know that in nature diversity, at all levels, makes a species far more resilient and so a monocultural education, economic discipline and industry, make the world much less resilient and far less able to adapt to the changing dynamic conditions of today. Therefore, in order to achieve a transformation to a stronger economics discipline, mainstream academics must engage with their heterodox counterparts and all groups of economists need to 'climb out of their silos' and engage, where appropriate and beneficial, in pluralist method/theory for the purposes of consensual and meaningful policymaking. The market can no longer be relied on to deliver or self-regulate, and so crises will continue until it is too late for humanity.

Ban Ki Moon, the previous General Secretary of the United Nations, famously declared, 'We are living in an age of Green Economics' (Moon 2008). The current General Secretary António Guterres (*UN News* 2019) has also said 'the Green Economy is the future' (Hermann 2018) and he repeated this in Katowice at COP24 UNFCCC, stating that Green Economics is the 'most important way we can combat climate change' (Guterres 2018). Kennet has always aimed to include natural science data and observations, combined with social science data and narratives, in order to reflect the real world. We build on diverse ideas of ecologism, conservation, socialism, feminism, political economy, counter hegemonism, as well as all aspects of natural science. The ideas are indivisible (not one of them can be simply a social or positivist science), and must now be explored in a holistic manner (Kennet and Heinemann 2006: 3). Kennet and Heinemann argued from the beginning, 'We would fundamentally disagree with departmentalising economics. We argue for a radical reform of Economics' (Kennet and Heinemann 2006). Harrison (1992) put it well:

> it means creating the framework for a more interdisciplinary approach to research and first degrees. The demands of the environment will break down the compartmentalism of knowledge. We desperately need an overarching science of human interactions with the environment combining socio-economic and technical studies with dynamic analysis of the physical environment.
>
> (Harrison 1992 in Kennet and Heinemann 2006: 3)

It is imperative to create such a discipline in Green Economics, and it is becoming ever clearer that this methodology is now required by mainstream and heterodox economics in policy and practice. UK Research assessments seemed to move in the other direction, splitting economics into a science concerned solely with mathematics and statistics, removing all other narratives and distancing it from knowledge of geography and the environment from which it receives all its inputs. In our view this policy did untold damage and now needs urgent reversal.

Destructive economic theory, education and policies

The problem has been that economists' graphs with unlabelled axes were allowed to override common sense. It is only when the climate scientists sounded the alarm that the world woke up from their deeply held core belief that the market, and Adam Smith's Invisible Hand, would solve everything and would take care of everyone, that they finally saw what this 'economics plague' had done – the destruction of almost the entire natural world. Today, the race is on to try and stop this process before it is too late, but the toolbox of mainstream economics is not suitable for, or capable of, stopping this destruction. A more holistic set of tools must be brought into use, to reflect the complexity and holism of nature. Green Economics and the Green New Deal, and even the Citizen's Income (Lord 2012), are ideas that have been building support around the world (Kamaruddin and Kennet 2012), and are now taking centre stage. These ideas offer holistic goals based on an economics incorporating much of science, climate science physics, earth science and much more. There are no silos and there are no boundaries, only reality and relevance. This a very different construction of economics based on flourishing, abundance, resilience, survivability and sharing a beautiful world with each other, nature, other species and the planet and its systems (Kennet 2006). Green Economics accepts that human domination is probably not a given and probably won't last. Green Economics is the economics of caring, sharing and supporting each other (Kennet 2019).

Neoclassical economics has always considered the market economy to be able to somehow ensure, as if by magic, that humans make the right decisions, and somehow it will all come out right in the end. But as Stern (2007) stated: 'climate change is the biggest market failure the world has ever seen' and to that failure we could add plastics and dead zones in the sea, air pollution and the sixth largest ever mass extinction of species (Wainer, Kennet and Grabauskaite 2015). Whole seas and lakes are drying up (Marks 2019) whole cities and countries will fall beneath the waves and whole ice sheets are melting (NASA 2019). The North Pole was 35 degrees centigrade warmer in winter 2017 than the average (Watts 2019), and much of the UK and the Netherlands may be underwater in the mid-century. In spite of the existing environmental stresses, earthquakes are deliberately induced simply by fracking fossil fuels out of the ground. It doesn't take a genius to work out that we are in deep trouble but somehow it seems to have escaped the economists. Their work is almost entirely narrative and qualitative free, future scenario free, long-term free and impact blind. It resides in a silo devoid of human feeling or sensitivity or any kind of ethical enquiry. Its sole aim is to destroy the state to create 'perfect competition' (Friedman 2018) in a world of unspeakable cruelty, combined with a world of deliberate lack of empathy or integrity. The key externality is likely to be simply the destruction of humanity and the entire natural world. To make matters worse, orthodox research has inevitably led to bad education that reproduces the same type of economics and policy for the future. Similarly, a common mainstream tool is to discount the future because (up to now) technology, resources, knowledge and wealth have always increased for humans in historic times. But this is quite possibly about to change. Future generations will be harmed by the economics of this generation and will have fewer resources of all kinds. So, discounting the future when it comes to the economy or the effects of climate change are now being heavily criticised.

In 2008, Queen Elizabeth II famously asked the economists how they managed to entirely fail to predict the Global Financial Crisis (Pierce 2009) – on their own patch – and it may not be surprising that they are not noticing what is going on around them outside of their spreadsheets. It is time to call a halt to this charade. It is time to change what the profession does and how it sees its role. It is time for economists to notice the utter mess they have justified and made. When they have seen the mess, they then need to understand the dynamics and change their methodology and philosophy to lead investment and economies into a more relevant and beneficial outcome. Silo economics has later led to silo education and 'perverse policy incentives' that leave whole economies depending on fossil fuels– this must be reversed. Heterodox economics has some tools available to end this threat to life – but heterodoxy needs to transform and become more pluralist – aided by holistic insights derived from green economics (Kennet 2014).

The eruption of protest

Many of us involved with heterodox economics are aware of the student-led movements that have emerged since the 2008 financial crash, such as the *Manchester Post-Crash Society*, or the international *Rethinking Economics* (also inclusive of lecturers) group. In addition, new institutions like the *Institute for New Economic Thinking* (INET) and *Young Scholars Initiative* (YSI) have also emerged and provide support for the academic economists considering a more pluralist approach. Grassroots protest is also erupting everywhere. Young people, in particular, have had enough and are taking to the streets in utter frustration all over the world in a wave of protests reminiscent of 1848, or even the French Revolution, and they are risking their lives in their thousands from Chile to Hong Kong. At the time of writing this chapter, Hong Kong, Chile, Sweden and many other countries have experienced protests, and this time the young will not be placated or bought off – their very future is what they are trying to defend – and economics appears to have no clear answers. Our Green Economics Institute Television Station, GEIClimateTV, has interviews with young people protesting, showing how they feel disenfranchised and excluded from the economy, and its mainstream actors and institutions (GEITV 2019).

Meanwhile, education today is largely designed to keep people quiet and pacify bystanders, that is, create compliant citizens. In China today, the 'social security system' is tantamount to a citizen subservience points system, and the young people can consume social media but not initiate or even propose anything controversial online – reminiscent of Orwell's 1984. One of the main requests of the climate strikers is that they receive an education fit for their future lives whilst education today is based on a mid-twentieth century discourse where profit and growth were the end game. Today the very same policies, rooted in the mechanics of a failing orthodox mainstream global economic system, are the foundation of the problems we have. Young people need new knowledge, skills and expertise, which is not being provided in schools or universities. And that set of skills and expertise has to reflect the world's physical complexity and so it must be pluralist at every level.

The idea that climate change futures can be bought or traded is complete and utter nonsense. Yet, that was the orthodox economist's solution without even mentioning the actual science or physicality of the issues. What we need is for economists to take the lead in showing how an economy will really work in new scenarios, and how people can run their lives today. Given the devastation that Internet shopping causes to the environment or the suicide rates in Amazon or Apple warehouses and factories, the impact of business as usual economics, and the destruction it is causing, needs to be clearly explained to everyone so that they can make much better choices.

So, in order to understand and address these issues, we need to include climate science data on air, water and much more. We need to understand the true impact of economic decision-making, not just as a financial cost–benefit analysis that considers environmental externalities, but one that provides much wider understanding of the impact of our economic system. This naturally involves an interdisciplinary and intradisciplinary work practice, delivering professional and workable policies. We have failed as a species and we must reverse the mess.

I lead a delegation to the United Nations Climate Change Convention, the UNFCCC, and as such, the role of economists is to lead, facilitate and enable the response and preparation for stopping climate change and reversing it to ensure the survival of humans, eco-systems and other species. However, economists today appear to be stuck in a time warp of post-Second World War profit, consumption (Rostow 1953) and growth maximisation, massaging income and GDP figures whilst also destroying clean air, water, the sea level, soil and biodiversity and, of course, the climate. It is bizarre, but true, that the short-term rewards are mostly for trashing the planet and other species. Interestingly this week, in the USA, new evidence has emerged that Exon scientists knew about climate change with chilling accuracy 50 years ago and funded and ran a deliberate campaign to deceive the world and to carry on ruining the climate (Hall 2015). They predicted that if they continued their business as usual the climate would warm by about 1 degree centigrade and CO_2 parts per million equivalents would reach 415 – which it has. A video from the Oversight Committee of Congress recorded the evidence and confessions and the actual methods used to deliberately and accurately ruin the world's climate, surely one of the greatest, most far-reaching and damaging crimes humanity has ever committed (Oversight Committee of Congress 2019). The scientists who implemented this campaign of misinformation have confessed and shown everyone the documentary evidence. Thus, they led the precision trashing of the planet in the name of profit and economics. Meanwhile, many people still invest their pension savings in these companies. This means that government regulatory power (including strong sanctions) needs to be enhanced to combat the behaviour of such firms. This requires a stronger political will than has existed hitherto.

The precondition of diversity

If the economics profession is going to be able to achieve a meaningful pluralist approach to its science, then it is helpful for it to be exposed to different voices. I argue in this chapter that, to achieve inter- and/or intradisciplinary work, diversity is a prerequisite. Women's views, for instance, have been absent for much of historic economic thought. In ancient Greece, Aristotle believed that women (half the human species) were too stupid to take part in the economy (Russell 1946: 197). Yet, even today there is a strong chance that if you pick up an economics book, there will be white men on the cover and no women, for example *Modern Macroeconomics* (Snowdon and Vane 2005). Women and their voices are suppressed in a huge number of countries, a veritable war against women. But do we hear much about this in mainstream economics? Scarcely a peep. It is time to sort this out; both the mainstream and heterodoxy need to become more diverse and inclusive. Different kinds of people inevitably hold 'other' perspectives and the world, the economics and science will be richer for the discourse. In addition, as Plato believed, those who engage more in broader debates are more able to arrive at better decisions and, therefore, make better rulers – or 'philosopher kings', in Plato's terminology (Russell 1946: 129). However, a key hindrance to the establishment of economic pluralism is that the researchers who engage in broader considerations are perceived by some to be weaker in their rigour. So, how does the economic profession broaden its discourse, and sources of influence, whilst combatting an economic orthodoxy with a (misguided) superiority complex? Young scholars, for instance, who are keen to establish careers, cannot be expected to be easily incentivised to pursue research programmes deemed to be of limited value and, therefore, non-pluralist practice remains stuck in its own confirmation loop. So, what can be done?

Simply put, economists need to read the newspapers, look at the Internet, link their own work and outcomes to the real world and proactively engage in broader narratives of all descriptions without shame. But, at the same time, also seek to maintain and enhance their academic rigour. Economic policies that directly address the urgent issues of today, and subsequently deliver a measure of beneficial outcomes, will later provide kudos for the economic research on which they are founded. In time truth will emerge into the daylight, so contemporary academics are wise to exert more courage. Today we see gangs of people trafficking goods, services and people around the world and the largest migration and slave trade in history (Fielgar and Kennet 2016). The trafficking of women for sweatshops, prostitution or pea-picking in the Mediterranean (for the likes of Tesco) rarely appears in economic models (Tezza and Tezza 2019; Tondo and Kelly 2017). Yet, this is the reality of today. To add to this list of research omissions we can add corrupt regimes, corrupt laws and organised crime spreading on an unimaginable scale. Meanwhile, the general public is losing confidence in government, leaders and experts. Economics must change now. Heterodox economics has certainly led the profession in the correct direction, but it needs to do more and also provide the tools to deliver this complex change. This chapter argues that a start has been made with green economics, and its sister disciplines and daughters, that is, the green economy, decarbonisation, the green new deal, deep ecology, eco-socialism, the circular economy, and environmental and ecological economics. This Green Economics active commitment to reality, holism and diversity provides a beacon for the heterodox community to follow a sustainable future.

The knowledge economy

Some of the new tools of economic efficiency, and economies of scale, are automation, artificial intelligence and Internet technology. The knowledge economy is predicted to form one-third of the future economy by 2025 – so we ignore it at our peril. Sticking to ordinary graphs and 'business as usual' in economics means to entirely miss the opportunity to devise economic models that account for the forthcoming smart cities and pervasive use of 5G broadband. Is there any meaningful global regulation of it? Absolutely not, so it is no wonder the thieves and criminals are moving in fast and before anyone else. We need a new (knowledge economy) codex and an economic structure which is highly regulated yet still creative and diverse and on a smaller scale (Schumacher 1974), or a medium and regional scale, or global but with appropriately high standards.

The problem with global scale, however, is that, more than ever, IT purchases mean that if we buy parcels from large Internet providers, they rely on larger lorry loads of deliveries using fossil fuels from oppressive regimes, mostly in the Middle East. They destroy whole economies, are subsidised by consumers, and in many countries with huge oil deposits the general populace is deprived of normal income and is far poorer than they should be, for example Albania and Nigeria. But there are alternatives, including locally created renewables, which mitigate the need for global scale, and free up economies to work with less pressure. The future belongs to where large numbers of young people will actually live, especially those with the fastest growing populations, such as Africa or South America. We need to green our purchasing and supply chains

(Nutburn 2019), supported properly by mainstream economists. However, Jeremy Rifkin's powerful vision of an ultra-clean energy renaissance, which some see as the foundation of the German Energiewende Transformation, has already begun a locally derived, interlinked energy democratisation, which offers hope for the sustainability of life on the planet.

> Crucially, it depends on the development of a smart supergrid that can provide a 'mega-platform' for what Rifkin calls 'the democratisation of energy', a transformation of energy users into producers through the micro-generation of renewable electricity that can be sold back to the grid.
>
> (Nelsen 2013)

Suggestions for economists, politicians and individuals

A pluralist economics, in my view, needs to look at new ways of being physical and practical as it matures more fully, which means spending far more time looking at:

- The long-term considerations – not five- or ten-year business cycle impacts.
- The pre-historic economic conditions prior to the introduction and spread of sedentary lifestyles, agriculture, farming and domestication.
- Temporal and spatial contexts.
- Ancient wisdoms deriving from indigenous peoples.
- How to include everyone, even leaders, in a diverse and inclusive economic model.
- The ecological significance of biodiversity in terms of sustainability.
- The latest scientific predictions of climate change and sea-level rise.
- The multitude of factors impacting global migration.
- Modern supply chain issues, for example, slavery and trafficking.
- The implication of automation, IT and artificial intelligence.
- Women, gender, inclusion, access and other diversity issues.
- The awareness of changing demographics, for example, the youth of Africa and South America.
- Renewables versus finite resources.
- The development of appropriate economic tools to do all of the above.
- Ensure a global atmosphere of decoloniality and start decolonizing economics and ending the enduring inequalities and lack of economic access caused by casual or violent everyday, state or institutional racism.

In tandem with this pluralist economics research, and its derived policy, we must also transform the legal system with an inclusive new codex (as far-reaching and different as the Hammurabi or Justinian codex, or the Bible) to create a holistic sustainable development. This will serve to regulate the economy in order to make it the servant rather than the master of the people. Here are my recommendations for the political class to pursue in the future:

a) We need everyone to monitor their own carbon footprints and cut consumption down.
b) We need to end red meat farming and reduce all barbaric livestock management.
c) We need to stop using pesticides, fertilisers and hazardous chemicals of all kinds.
d) We need to start to value water and ensure we provide free access to it for all the peoples of the earth.
e) We need to listen to our human instinct to survive and flourish then build our economics of abundance (Hoeshele 2010) for all species and nature (Kennet 2014; Wainer, Kennet and Grabauskaite 2015).
f) We need an end to human trafficking and the arms trade.
g) We need to free people from the dependencies of the past, such as oil, debt or slavery.
h) We need to outlaw all ethnic cleansing whilst promoting self-determination for peoples.
i) We need to support global, national, regional and also local economies, and many other diverse economies such as those of indigenous peoples.
j) We need to end the cult of personality and adopt a different kind of leader who has the benefit of all at heart, rather than being drawn to those with more selfish ambitions.

States also need to continue to engage in meaningful and substantive international agreement. The Paris COP21 climate conference was enhanced by the fact that all francophone countries carried out the diplomacy. It was they, most importantly, who enabled that historic agreement to happen, as they, and the small island states, are in the frontline of climate change impacts already being felt today and already affecting their economies. I would also advise that everyone becomes familiar with the NASA website that presents us with earth's daily vital signs, such as the number of parts per million CO_2 in the atmosphere, which, at the time of writing, is 412 parts per million, the highest it has been for 600,000 years and an accurate indicator of contemporary warming. Additionally, I would recommend using a carbon checker to reduce our own individual carbon footprint – moving towards 2 tonnes of carbon equivalent consumption per person per year by 2022 and reducing to zero by 2025 (Kennet 2019). To this end, I would suggest the following actions for readers to think about:

Switch your power source to renewables and switch your transport to work to buses or trains.

Stop taking cheap short flights for weekend breaks.

Stop eating too much meat.
Stop creating all-male platforms and start including women, young/old people and other diversities (Kennet et al. 2012: 33).
Stop putting pesticides and weed killer in your garden and/or chemicals on your lawns.
Start supporting politicians/policies that sustain people from 'cradle to grave'.
Start enabling a future economy and imagining a bright future for humans.
Start questioning all the supply chains of everything you use.

Conclusion

The simple conclusion is that heterodoxy is advised to replicate the holistic attributes of green economics, going beyond its past achievements to become fully pluralist, diverse, creative and inclusive – to establish some heterogeneity in its heterodoxy! The mainstream economists, of course, are welcome to 'join the party'. A reconstructed and holistic economic science can then provide a sustainable basis for a Green Economy (Kennet 2012) or 'a real green new deal' as advocated by *The Guardian* Editorial (*The Guardian* 2019) and in the US Congress House Resolution (No. 109) by Alexandria Ocasia-Cortez (in 2019), by fully considering the outcomes from economic policy and evaluating the past. A fundamental barrier to achieving this has been our attachment to the 'silos' of different epistemologies, disciplines, ontologies, theories and methods (Kennet 2009). It is now time to break down the silos and consign them to the dustbin of history before it is too late and before our global economy sinks 'below the waves' forever (Tidman 2019). People now have a brand new enhanced awareness of the present emergency and crises, and a recent understanding of the need to avoid their impossibly colossal costs, that will lead us to find the inclination and courage to work together and cooperate holistically as we, and our species, are designed to do. This will be driven, at least in part, by a new comprehension of the role of, and need for, diversity and togetherness of all peoples everywhere and an economy which nurtures us and our habitat, the earth and its systems and is no longer predicated on its incremental destruction by economic decisions and policy-making. Diversity, cooperation and holistic thinking will be the keys to survival as the silos are blown down.

References

Congress House, 2019. *Resolution 109*. Recognizing the duty of the House to create a Green New Deal, Rep. Ocasio-Cortez, Alexandria. Available at: www.congress.gov/bill/116th-congress/house-resolution/109/text, accessed 19 November 2019.

Espinosa, P., 2019. *Our House is on Fire*. Speech to United Nations Research Organisations at the COP24 Katowice, Poland, Climate Conference, December 2018.

Fielgar, H. and Kennet M., 2016. *Introducing Migration, Voices for Social and Environmental Justice*. Reading: The Green Economics Institute.

Friedman, D., 2018. *Oxford Union Debate*, Oxford. Available at: www.youtube.com/watch?v=Bpn645huKUg, accessed 17 November 2019.

GEITV, 2019. United Nations Climate Change Conference, SB50, Bonn. Interview with Young Climate Protesters. GEIClimateTV. Available at: https://vimeo.com/345685818, accessed 19 November 2019.

Guterres, A., 2018. Climate Change and the Need for Green Economics. Speech to the United Nations Climate Change Conference, SB50, June, Bonn, Germany. GEIClimateTV. Available at: https://vimeo.com/308572170, accessed 19 November 2019.

Hall, S., 2015. Exon Knew About Climate Change Almost 40 Years Ago. *Scientific American*, 26 October. Available at: www.scientificamerican.com/article/exxon-knew-about-climate-change-almost-40-years-ago, accessed 19 November 2019.

Hermann, A., 2018. *United Nations Agenda 2030*. Reading: The Green Economics Institute.

Hoeshele, W., 2010. *The Economics of Abundance: A Political Economy of Freedom, Equity, and Sustainability*. Abingdon: Routledge.

IPBES (Intergovernmental Science–Policy Platform for Biodiversity and Ecosystem Services of the United Nations) 2019. *Global Assessment on Biodiversity and Ecosystem Service. Science and Policy for People and Nature*. Available at: https://ipbes.net/global-assessment-report-biodiversity-ecosystem-services, accessed 19 November 2019.

Kamaruddin, N. and Kennet M., 2013. *The Greening of Asia and China*. Reading: The Green Economics Institute.

Kennet, M., 2007. Editorial. Background and Rationale for this Next Step in Green Economics. *International Journal of Green Economics*, Vol. 1 (3/4).

Kennet, M., 2009. Green Economics: Emerging Pedagogy in an Emerging Discipline. In J. Reardon, ed., *The Handbook of Pluralist Economics Education*. London and New York: Routledge.

Kennet, M. (ed.) 2012. *The Green Economics Reader*. Reading: The Green Economics Institute.

Kennet. M., 2014. Socio-ecological Transformation and Green Economics: New Perspectives for Solutions to the Most Pressing Problems of Today. In C. Brook and M. Kennet, *Rebalancing the Economy*. Reading: The Green Economics Institute.

Kennet, M., 2019. Introduction to Green Economics. What We Do and Why We Do It. Available at: www.greeneconomicsinstitute.org.uk. accessed 19 November 2019.

Kennet, M., Felton J., Gale D'Oliveira, M. and Winchester, A., eds., 2012. Actions for Our Readers in Green Economics. In *Women's Unequal Pay and Poverty*. Reading: Green Economics Institute.

Kennet, M. and Heinemann, V., 2006. Foreword. *International Journal of Green Economics*, Vol. 1 (1/2).

Lord, C., 2012. *Green Economics and a Citizen's Income*, edited by J. Felton. Reading: The Green Economics Institute.

Marks, K., 2019. The World is Running Out of Fresh Water. *Owlcation*, 6 October. Available at: https://owlcation.com/stem/10-Worst-Drying-Lakes-in-the-World, accessed 19 November 2019.

Moon, B.K., 2008. *Green Economics speech to the United Nations*. Available at: www.un.org/sg/en/content/sg/articles/2008-10-22/age-green-economics, accessed 19 November 2019.

NASA, 2019. *Global Climate Change, the Vital Signs of the Planet*. Available at: https://climate.nasa.gov/evidence accessed, 19 November 2019.

Nelsen, A., 2013. Jeremy Rifkin Warns Europe: Don't Repeat Obama's Mistakes. *Euractiv*, 21 March. Available at: www.euractiv.com/section/energy/news/jeremy-rifkin-warns-europe-don-t-repeat-obama-s-mistakes, accessed 19 November 2019.

Nutburn, M., 2019. 5 Benefits of a Sustainable Supply Chain. In *Supply Management*. Available at: www.cips.org/en/supply-management/opinion/2019/july/five-benefits-of-a-sustainable-supply-chain, accessed 19 November 2019.

Oversight Committee of Congress, 2019. 'So, They Knew': Ocasio-Cortez Questions Exxon Scientist on Climate Crisis Denial. *The Guardian*, 23 October. Available at: www.theguardian.com/business/video/2019/oct/23/exxon-alexandria-ocasio-cortez-congress-testimony-climate.

Pierce, A., 2009. The Queen Asks Why No-one Saw the Credit Crunch Coming. *The Telegraph*, 5 November 2008. Available at: www.telegraph.co.uk/news/uknews/theroyalfamily/3386353/The-Queen-asks-why-no-one-saw-the-credit-crunch-coming.html, accessed 19 November 2019.

Prothero, D., 2018. *When Humans Nearly Vanished, The Catastrophic Eruption of Mount Tolba*. New York: Smithsonian Books.

Reddy, S., 2019. Arctic Soil Becomes a Carbon Source Due to Winter Emissions. NASA climate website. Available at: https://climate.nasa.gov, accessed 19 November 2019.

Rostow, W., 1953. *The Stages of Economic Growth*. Oxford: Wiley, on behalf of the Economic History Society.

Russell, B., 1946. *History of Western Philosophy: And its Connections with Political and Social Circumstances from the Earliest Times to the Present Day*. London: George Allen and Unwin Ltd.

Schumacher, E.F., 1974. Small is Beautiful. In W. Bloom, ed., *Holistic Revolution*, 1st edition. London: Penguin Press.

Shiva, V., 1993. *Monocultures of the Mind, Perspectives on Biodiversity and Biotechnology*. Malaysia: Zed Books.

Snowdon, B. and Vane, H., 2005. *Modern Macroeconomics*. Cheltenham: Edward Elgar.

Stern, N., 2007. *The Economics of Climate Change: The Stern Review*. Cambridge: Cambridge University Press.

Tezza, E. and Tezza L., 2019. *Evaluating Corruption: Something Rotten Round the World*. Reading: The Green Economics Institute.

The Guardian, 2019. Editorial. *The Guardian* View of a Green New Deal: We Need It Now. *The Guardian*, May. Available at: www.theguardian.com/commentisfree/2019/may/12/the-guardian-view-on-a-green-new-deal-we-need-it-now, accessed 19 November 2019.

Tidman, Z., 2019. Flood stricken Venice hit by high tide leaving most of the City under water. *The Independent*, 17 November. Available at: www.independent.co.uk/news/world/europe/venice-flooding-70-per-cent-under-water-luigi-brugnaro-a9206361.html, accessed 19 November 2019.

Tondo, L. and Kelly, A., 2017. Raped, Beaten, Exploited: 21st Century Slavery Propping up the Sicilian Economy. *The Guardian*, 12 March. Available at: www.theguardian.com/global-development/2017/mar/12/slavery-sicily-farming-raped-beaten-exploited-romanian-women, accessed 19 November 2019.

United Nations News, 2019. The Green Economy is the Future. *UN News*, April. Available at: https://news.un.org/en/story/2019/04/1037461, accessed 19 November 2019.

Wainer, A., Kennet, M. and Grabauskaite, O., 2015. *Biodiversity Loss, The Variety of Life Under Threat*. Reading: The Green Economics Institute.

Watts, J., 2019. Arctic Warming: Scientists Alarmed by Crazy Temperatures. *The Guardian*, 27 February. Available at: www.theguardian.com/environment/2018/feb/27/arctic-warming-scientists-alarmed-by-crazy-temperature-rises, accessed 19 November 2019.

Watts, N., et al., 2019. The Lancet Countdown on Health and Climate Change: Ensuring that the Health of a Child Born Today is not Defined by a Changing Climate, *The Lancet Countdown*. Vol. 394 (16 November, 10211), pp. 1836–1878.

6 Value within the resource-based view of the firm

An approach drawing on the temporal single system interpretation of Marx

Thoralf Dassler

Introduction

Resource-based Theory (RBT) (e.g., Barney, 1991, 1993; Prahalad and Hamel, 1990; Teece et al., 1997; Wernerfelt, 1984) is mainstream management's approach to explaining production in general, and the origin of economic value within the firm in particular (e.g., Barney, 2001, 2002; Dierickx and Cool, 1989; Hoopes et al., 2003; Kraaijenbrink et al., 2010). RBT commonly asserts that value is produced when firms hold superior resources and use these in ways that are superior compared with what competitors do.

The assertion naturally triggers the question of how much value firms produce. Quantification and measurement of value are, however, left to markets, through the formula 'value equals willingness to pay' (Barney, 1986; Hoopes et al., 2003; Schmidt and Keil, 2013). This formula clearly recognises that market factors exert an influence on the amount of value firms receive during sale, but does not consider firm-specific factors of production.

Because sale prices recover the costs of production and, normally, leave a profit, a rather specific question arises. That is, how much of the firm's profit is determined by firm-specific factors, and how much is determined by factors of the market?

Addressing this question in this chapter requires quantification of the value firms produce, yet the resource-based literature has not provided an explanation. Instead, RBT "simplifies strategic analysis with an implicit assumption of homogeneous and im-mobile product markets" (Priem and Butler, 2001, p. 30; see also, Adner, 2002; Powell, 1992; Priem, 2007). The need for this assumption arises because of the theoretical disconnects identified by Molloy et al. (2011, p. 1496). They have shown that "… measures of intangible [resources] are often assigned with little theoretical conceptualization of the intangible construct or connection with RBT" (Molloy et al., 2011, p. 1496). Intangible resources are the useful characteristics that people, that is, variable capital inputs, deliver while performing job roles.

However, the focus on intangible resources alone in the current resource-based literature (e.g., Chadwick, 2017) obscures the extent of the issue. This is because intangible resources, that is, variable capital inputs, are omitted. The reason for this omission is the view that the useful characteristics of variable inputs are all that matter. This view draws on the Austrian School of Economics.

The discussion in this chapter takes the Marxian stance that commodities not only carry utility, but are also crystals of abstract labour (Marx, 1867 [1990]). Abstract labour, in other words, constitutes the common element across variable and constant capital inputs. This means that the subsequent discussion quantifies the production value relation between constant and variable capital—as opposed to seeking the source of value differentials in variable capital alone.

Addressing the question of how much of the profits individual firms receive is determined by firm-specific factors, and how much is determined by market factors, draws on the Temporal Single System Interpretation (TSSI) of Marx (e.g., Freeman, 2010; Kliman, 2007, 2010; Kliman and McGlone, 1999). This is because it is compatible with the assertion of RBT that value is created within the firm.

This application of the TSSI to address an unresolved management question would be of interest to the field of Marxian economics for the following reasons. First, the application follows Toms' (2010, p. 647) call that "RB[T] can become a coherent theory of firm behaviour, if it adopts and can integrate the labour theory of value". Second, it addresses the objection raised by non-Marxian economists that the labour theory does not account for demand conditions and their effect on prices. This is because addressing the RBT's unresolved question requires individual sales prices, instead of only the average prices that economists usually consider.

Finally, the discussion in this chapter has implications beyond the immediate context of the question. That is, the application of the TSSI of Marx does not shield RBT from the ugly realities of recurrent crises within capitalism. Unlike simultaneous approaches to valuing capital inputs, the TSSI allows for crises to be caused by capitalist production itself (Freeman, 2018). This aspect of the subsequent discussion is of particular relevance for RBT because it is placing value production within the firm.

The chapter's structure is straightforward. The discussion starts with a brief review of the various interpretations of Marx's value theory to justify why the TSSI is preferred. Because of the need to explain and quantify value production within the firm, the discussion proceeds to a review of Marx's transformation of values into the prices of production. On this basis the discussion then addresses the question of how much of the profits a firm receives is determined by factors within the firm, and how much by factors of the market. The final section before the chapter concludes reflects on the wider implications.

Contending interpretations of Marx

This section briefly reviews three interpretations of Marx's *Capital* in the particular context of addressing the unresolved issue within RBT. A critique of the interpretations is available in Kliman (2007). The first three contend that input and outputs should be valued simultaneously, whereas the final interpretation, the TSSI, values inputs and outputs sequentially.

Simultaneous readings

These come in three variations, dual system, single system and value-form. All share the view that inputs from the start of production should be revalued to match the input prices at the end of production. In other words, the prices of new inputs, purchased when products are sold, are used to revalue the input prices from the start of production. This is achieved using current replacement costing.

The *Simultaneous Dual System Interpretation*, or SDSI, traces its origin to Tugan-Baranowsky (1905) who proposed a stationary equilibrium approach for calculating value and production prices (Freeman, 2018). The work of Bortkiewicz (1952 [1907]) then separated values and prices into two systems (Kliman, 2007, p. 32). The SDSI renders Marx logically inconsistent (Kliman, 2001, 2007), which means that only one of the three aggregate equalities in Marx's (1893 [1991], ch.9) transformation procedure holds. These are the economy's total value equals total price, total surplus value equals total profit, and total value rate equals total price rate of profit. As will be seen, the equalities are required to hold when addressing the unresolved question within RBT.

The *Simultaneous Single System Interpretation*, or SSSI, considers that prices and values are, quantitatively speaking, part of a single system. Kliman (2007) has shown that this interpretation preserves the three aggregate equalities of Marx's transformation procedure, yet only in a formal-mathematical, non-substantial, sense. In addition, value becomes redundant at best (Steedman, 1977) because only physical units are required for 'valuing' outputs. This physical quantities approach leads to the mathematical result that "[v]alues can be negative, and surplus-value can be negative although profit is positive" (Kliman, 2007, p. 77f). This reasoning draws on Sraffa (1960).

The *Value-Form Interpretation*, also known as New Interpretation or New Reading of Marx, shares the view that inputs and outputs should be valued simultaneously. The Value-Form Interpretation has been critiqued previously, for example, in Freeman and Kliman (2008) and Kliman (2011). The critique should be developed further outside of the context of this chapter, in light of the recent work of Nagatani (2019) and of Pitts (2018).

Here it may be added that Value-Form proponents have introduced a tautology to Marx's (1867) value theory. This is because they acknowledge that abstract labour originates in production, but argue that sales markets are also required for labour to become fully abstract. Pitts (2018, p. 13), for example, expresses this as "[a]bstract labour both produces value and is produced by it". Heinrich (2013) also identified the tautology, yet does not acknowledge that it was introduced by his reading of Marx.

In summary, Kliman (2007) shows that simultaneous interpretations either spirit away parts of the value firms produce, or adds extra production value from nowhere. This means that simultaneous valuation, by definition, cannot explain economic crises from within capitalism's mode of production (Freeman, 2018). Thus, this approach to valuation is not only unsuitable when explaining capitalism's reality. Simultaneous valuation is also incompatible with RBT, which proposes that firm-specific resources and their deployment produce value. The subsequent discussion therefore does not draw on simultaneous readings.

The TSSI of Marx

Husson, writing as Perez (1980),[1] was the first to argue that Marx's value theory should be read temporally, as a sequence in time. Later, Kliman proposed the term 'temporal single system interpretation', or TSSI. Prominent writers (e.g., Freeman, 2010; Kliman, 2007, 2010; Kliman and McGlone, 1999) agree that values and prices constitute a single system throughout Marx's *Capital*. But in contrast to all simultaneous interpretations, the TSSI holds that, at the point of sale, input values should be left as they were at the start of production.

A temporal reading makes the transformation procedure in chapter 9 of *Capital III* logically consistent, which means that the procedure's three aggregate equalities hold in a substantive way (instead of only a formal-mathematical sense). The TSSI therefore allows for value to be created during the process of capitalist production, and for value to exist prior to exchange. This means that the TSSI does not require markets to explain the source of value. As will be seen, markets are only required to explain the difference between the amount of value that firms produce and the amount that firms receive during sale.

Relevant criticisms of the TSSI have been addressed before 2017, for example, in Potts (2014) and Potts and Kliman (2015). Yet Mohun and Veneziani (2017, p. 1415) conclude, again, that "[a]t a purely logical level, there is nothing to discuss about" Marx's transformation procedure "and there is no hope of 'solving' it". This is because, allegedly, the procedure "is irredeemably inconsistent". Mohun and Veneziani (2017) base this conclusion on a resuscitation of their earlier under-determination and inconsistency critique of the TSSI, in Mohun and Veneziani (2009). It is, however, curious that (i) their 2009 article is relegated to an endnote in Mohun and Veneziani (2017); and (ii) their 2017 article does not mention Freeman and Kliman's (2009) rebuttal of the under-determination and inconsistency critique.

In addition, and this constitutes a misrepresentation of the TSSI, Mohun and Veneziani (2017, p. 1415) argue that "[t]he TSSI insists on … historical cost pricing (Kliman and McGlone 1999, p. 34)". Besides *not* having said this on page 34, Kliman and McGlone (1999, p. 41) actually wrote:

> [i]f an item produced yesterday is warehoused until used as an input today ... the cost of reproducing the item when it enters into production is neither yesterday's price nor tomorrow's price, but today's price. The present interpretation is thus consistent with Marx's rejection of historical valuation.

Kliman (2007) reiterates this point. The TSSI thus uses pre-production reproduction costs—that is, neither historic nor current replacement costing.

In summary, the TSSI makes Marx's original texts, and in particular his transformation procedure in chapter 9 of *Capital III*, logically consistent. This also makes the TSSI compatible with RBT because both approaches hold that value is created within firms. The discussion in the remainder of this chapter therefore draws on temporal reasoning to address the RBT's unresolved question of how much of the profit an individual firm receives is determined by firm-specific factors, and how much by market factors during sale. To prepare the answer, the discussion now revisits Marx's transformation of production values into production prices.

The transformation of production values into production prices under the TSSI

Marx's transformation procedure is often viewed as somewhat mysterious and more difficult than it actually is. This is not necessarily the case under the TSSI, which this section attempts to show.

Individual and social amounts of labour

In *Capital III*, Marx (1893 [1991], ch.9, p. 257) explicitly states that the

> prerequisite [for the prices of production] is the existence of a general rate of profit, and this presupposes in turn that the profit rates in each particular sphere of production, taken by itself, are already reduced to their average rates.

This poses the question of how the reduction works. Marx (1861–1863 [1988], emphasis in original) argues that "competition within the *same* sphere of production brings about ... the determination of the *value of the commodity in a given sphere* by the average labour-time required".[2] Table 6.1 illustrates how averages materialise within a particular sphere of production.

Marx (1893 [1991], ch.10, p. 184) argues that an equal rate of surplus value, $\frac{s}{v}$, is required for capitalism to function (100 per cent is assumed for convenience).

Table 6.1 Individual values and a sphere's average value; $\frac{s}{v} = 100\%$

	Capitals $c + v$	*Used up c* u_c	*Cost-Prices* $k = u_c + v$	*Surplus Values* s	*Production Values* $k + s$
	$17_c + 3_v$	11	14	3	17
	$14_c + 5_v$	9	14	5	19
	$8_c + 9_v$	9	18	9	27
	$19_c + 2_v$	14	16	2	18
	$22_c + 1_v$	7	8	1	9
Σ	$80_c + 20_v$		70	20	90
Ø	$22_c + 4_v$		14	4	18

Note: ø: average; *c*: constant capital; *v*: variable capital.

Source: Author's design.

The sphere's total profit rate obtains as $\frac{s}{c+v} = \frac{20}{80_c + 20_v} = 0.20$ or 20%, which equals the sphere's average rate, $\frac{4}{16_c + 4_v} = 0.2$ or 20%. It is evident that the sphere's profit rate differs quantitatively from the actual, that is, the firm-specific, rates.

Marx explicitly assumes throughout *Capital I* that commodities sell at their values, produced by the capital of socially necessary (i.e., average), composition. However, this does not also mean that individual and socially necessary compositions of capital, as well as individual and socially necessary labour-time, are the same. Instead, individual amounts only *count* as the same, only count as socially necessary, as $16_c + 4_v$ for the sphere in Table 6.1. This differs from assuming they 'are' the same. It is therefore doubtful that Marx implicitly assumed they are, as Burns (2017, p. 495) concludes, because this assumption is not required. Nevertheless, the difference between individual and average value is relevant for addressing the unresolved question within RBT in subsequent sections.

Marx's transformation of production values into production prices

Table 6.2 uses the same figures as Marx's transformation procedure in chapter 9 of *Capital III*, drawing on socially necessary labour for spheres I to V.

Two aspects require clarification, as follows. First, the Table shows that the socially necessary values, which the spheres *produce*, are transformed into the production prices of the spheres. These prices represent the value the spheres *receive* if commodities sell at the sphere prices in Table 6.2 (Kliman, 2007).

Table 6.2 Transformation of production values into production prices

	Capitals $c+v$	Used up c u_c	Cost-Prices $k=u_c+v$	Surplus Values s	Production Values $k+s$	Production Prices $k+22$	+/−
I	80_c+20_v	50	70	20	90	92	+2
II	70_c+30_v	52	81	30	111	103	−8
III	60_c+40_v	51	91	40	131	113	−18
IV	85_c+15	40	55	15	70	77	+7
V	95_c+5	10	15	5	20	37	+17
Σ	390_c+110_v		312	110	422	422	0
Ø	78_c+22_v			$s_\varnothing+\pi_\varnothing$			

Note: *Soc.Nes.*: socially necessar $s_\varnothing$: economy-wide average surplus value; $\pi_\varnothing$: economy-wide average profit.

Source: Adapted from Marx (1893 [1991], ch.9, p. 256).

This distinction is crucial for subsequently addressing the unresolved question within RBT.

Second, Table 6.2 also shows that Marx (1893 [1991], p. 256) allocates the economy's aggregate surplus or profit, of Σ110$, equally among spheres I to V. Expressed differently, the economy's average profit, $\pi_\varnothing=22$, is added to the socially necessary cost-price of each sphere.

Marx (1861–1863 [1988], emphasis in original) explicitly argues that the surplus should be distributed equally because "competition between the *different* spheres of production brings about … the *creation of the same general rate of profit* in the *different* spheres through the levelling out of the different market-values". Using the figures in Table 6.2, this means that the economy's aggregate profit rate materialises as $\frac{\sum s}{\sum(c+v)}=\frac{\sum \pi}{\sum(c+v)}=\frac{110}{500}=0.22$, or 22%. If sold at the prices in Table 6.2, then each sphere will receive, on average, profits as follows (Marx, 1893 [1991], pp. 182ff, provides an extended explanation):

- Each of the spheres in Table 6.2 advances $c+v=100$ relative to the aggregate of 500. Each sphere thus receives a profit that corresponds with $\frac{100}{500}*110=\frac{1}{5}*110=22$, and a sphere's production price materialises as $p_p=k+22$, or $k+k*0.22$. This case is discussed in detail in Dassler (2016, p. 255).
- If spheres differ in size and thus advance a sum of $c+v$ that differs from 100, then the economy's aggregate, $\sum s+\sum \pi$, differs from the 110 in Table 6.2. $\frac{\sum s}{\sum(c+v)}=\frac{\sum \pi}{\sum c+v}$ and $\sum Values=\sum Prices$ also differ from 0.22 and 422, respectively. This means that the equation that measures

profits takes the form $\frac{c+v}{\sum(c+v)}\sum\pi$. A sphere's production price thus materialises as $p_p = k + k\frac{\sum s}{\sum(c+v)}$, assuming that all c and turns over in the same period as all v.

This means that firms draw profits according to the capital they advance. Importantly, however, the transformation procedure does not require actual sales. This is the case under the TSSI because, first, input prices are measured using pre-production reproduction costs. These are not revalued at the point of sale. Second, Marx argues throughout *Capital* that sale and financial speculation do not add new labour, which means that surplus value is the only source of profit (see also, Freeman, 2010; Kliman, 2001). The aggregate equality $\sum s = \sum \pi$ is therefore determined, in a substantive sense, before sale and remains unaltered during sale.

Addressing the unresolved question within RBT

The first part of this section discusses the implications of the transformation procedure for an individual sphere, and specifies what market factors and firm factors are. The second part discusses the relationship between production and sales prices. The third part proposes a method for measuring the effects of firm-specific production and market factors on the profits that individual firms receive.

Implications of the transformation procedure for a single sphere

Table 6.3 shows the implications for sphere I, to which the discussion in the remainder of the section refers.

It is important bear in mind that, first, product sale does not produce new abstract labour, it merely redistributes the amount of this labour. This means that the total amount of value firms A to E receive is limited to the $p_p = 92$ in Table 6.3. Second, the discussion in the remainder of this section measures the resources individual firms have in place as $c_i + v_i$, and the deployment of these resources (i.e., their usage) as $k_i + s_i$ (with $i = A \ldots E$). Similarly, $k_i + \pi_i$ measures market factors that comprise the following scenarios:

1. Supply equals demand. If one sets aside the factors that trigger individual firms to sell at individual prices, then these firms each sell at the $p_\oslash = 18.40$ in Table 6.3. This is because of price competition among firms *AE* ahead of sale. This scenario means that $p_\oslash$ does not only constitute a theoretical property of Marx's value theory, but $p_\oslash$ actually materialises in reality.
2. Supply and demand may differ, and the factors that trigger individual sales prices are still set aside. This means that the firms in Table 6.3 sell

Table 6.3 Values, prices and profits in sphere I; $\pi_\varnothing = 22\%$

	Capitals $c+v$	*Cost-Prices* $k_i\ (a)$	*Values Produced* u_c	*Individ. Prod. Prices* $k_i + (c_i + v_i)0.22$	*Sphere* ∅ *ProdPrice* $(70+22)/5$	*Profits* $18.4 - k_i$
A	$17_c + 3_v$	14	17	18.40	18.4	4.40
B	$14_c + 5_v$	14	19	18.18	18.4	4.40
C	$8_c + 9_v$	18	27	21.74	18.4	4.40
D	$19_c + 2_v$	16	18	20.62	18.4	4.40
E	$22_c + 1_v$	8	9	13.06	18.4	4.40
Σ	$80_c + 20_v$	70	90	92	92	22
∅				18.40	18.40	

Note: The total production price is $p_p = 22$; the average production price is $p_\varnothing = 18.40$.
Source: Author's design; (a): figures come from Table 6.1.

at one price that differs from $p_\varnothing = 18.40$. This scenario indicates that the production price constitutes a theoretical property because competition among producers enforces a price that differs from $p_\varnothing$. Nevertheless, $p_\varnothing$ carries practical relevance, representing the average value the sphere in Table 6.3 receives.

3. In addition to scenarios (1) and (2), individual sales prices may be allowed. This scenario accommodates the mainstream's views on the role of price bargaining.

The relationship between production and sales prices

This section draws on Marx (1893 [1991], ch.10) to discuss the three scenarios in some detail. This preparatory effort is required because of the complexities involved when addressing the unresolved question within RBT. The following cases may materialise in practice (for a similar discussion, see Behrens, 1976).

Case 1: All firms sell at $p_\varnothing$

Though firms A to E receive the same value, of $p = 18.40$ in Table 6.3, each firm receives the individual profits $\pi_i = 18.40 - k_i$. Firm E, in other words, receives the highest individual profit, of $\pi_D = 18.40 - 8 = 10.40$, while firm C receives the lowest profit, of only $\pi_A = 18.40 - 18 = 0.40$. It is a coincidence in Table 6.3 that $p_A = p_\varnothing$.

Case 2: All firms sell at one price that differs from $p_\varnothing$

Marx (1893 [1991]), in Chapter 10, introduces the 'market-production-price'. This generalised production price, which may be represented as p_G, accommodates the dynamic interplay of supply and demand. It is important to note that p_G represents a quantity of abstract labour from the seller's perspective. The same quantity constitutes *value* from the buyer's perspective Marx, 1893 [1991], pp. 264f). However, the following sub-cases require attention in the context of Table 6.3.

- $p_G = p_\oslash = 18.40$. The labour-time produced equals the labour-time demanded so that the commodity's average production price, the $p_\oslash = 18.40$ in Table 6.3, determines the commodity's average market or *sales* value (not the production value before the transformation procedure). Because the sphere in Table 6.3 consists of five firms, the commodity's total sales value is determined as $5 * p_\oslash = p_p = 92$. This means that all firms *receive* the same amount of value.
- $p_G < p_\oslash = 18.40$. The labour-time demanded is smaller than the labour-time supplied, and the commodity's average sales value (not production value before the transformation) therefore falls below $p_\oslash = 18.40$. Depending on how far demand falls, the individual production price of either $p_B = 18.18$ or $p_E = 14.06$ determines p_G. The sphere's total sales value is thus determined as either $5 * p_B = 90.90$ or $5 * p_E = 65.30$, so that all firms again receive the same amount of value.
- $p_G > p_\oslash = 18.40$. The labour-time demanded is greater than the labour-time supplied. Either $p_D = 20.62$ or $p_C = 21.74$ determines p_G in this scenario, depending on how far demand rises. Total sales value (not production value) is determined as either $5 * p_D = 103.10$ or $5 * p_c = 108.70$. Once again, all firms receive the same amount.

Case 3: Firms sell at individual prices—$\pi_i \neq p_G$

As shown, Marx straightforwardly facilitates the pure case of all firms receiving the same amount of value when the commodity sells at π_G. In practice, however, firms sell at individual prices, π_i, which mainstream economists explain as the result of price bargaining between individual producers and their buyers. In other words, mainstream thinking considers that price bargaining establishes the sales prices of firms A to E in Table 6.3. In contrast, the understanding discussed thus far suggests that price bargaining explains why, and by how much, π_i *deviate from* p_G. In short, π_i 'oscillate' around p_G; the latter is not static or fixed.

A method for measuring the effect of firm-specific and market factors

The discussion has now progressed to the point at which the question may be addressed as to why, and by how much, the amount of value that firms produce differs from the amount they receive. In other words, the discussion now addresses the question of whether firm-specific $c + v$ (i.e., firm-specific factors in resource-based terminology) or market factors exert a greater influence.

This requires the TSSI of Marx because of its compatibility with the RBT's proposition that value is produced within the firm. Simultaneous approaches, in contrast, are incompatible with this proposition. This is because, as discussed, they either spirit away parts of the value a firm produces, or bring in extra production value from nowhere.

Production factors were previously expressed as $k_i + s_i$, and market factors as $k_i + \pi_i$. The latter captures three factors, that is, price competition among producers, the dynamic interplay of supply and demand, and price bargaining. Because k_i appears in a firm's production value as well as in the firm's sales price, the question of the effects of firm-specific $c + v$ and market factors reduces to π_i in relation to s_i.

The following cases materialise in practice, depending on the strength of the factors in relation to one another. 'Same direction' within these cases means +, so a firm, during sale, receives more than the surplus value it has produced; 'opposite directions' means −, so a firm receives less than the surplus value it has produced.

Firm-specific $c + v$ exert a greater influence than market factors. If both factors exert influence in the same direction, then $s_i < \pi_i < 2s_i$. Conversely, if both factors exert influence in opposite directions, then $s_i > \pi_i > 0$. *Firm-specific $c + v$* determine more than 50 per cent of profit in both cases.

Firm-specific $c + v$ and market factors exert equal influence. Both factors may exert influence in the same direction, which means that the firm receives $\pi_i = 2s_i$. In other words, exactly 50 per cent of π_i are determined by firm-specific $c + v$, and the remaining 50 per cent by market factors. Conversely, both factors may exert influence in opposite directions. This means that the firm sells at $\pi_i = 0$.

Market factors exert a greater influence than firm-specific $c + v$. If both factors exert influence in the same direction, then $\pi_i > 2s_i$. This means that *market* factors determine more than 50 per cent of the profit the firm receives. It is possible that a firm receives the entire surplus value produced by the sphere, yet this would be rather unusual in practice. Conversely, both factors may exert influence in opposite directions, so that $\pi_i < 0$. This means that the firm operates at a loss, which is not unusual.

Two special cases. One such case exists as $\pi_i = s_i$. This means that market factors cancel each other out to exert zero influence. Firm-specific production factors thus determine exactly 100 per cent of the profit a firm receives. Another special case exists as $\pi_i \neq s_i$, which indicates that a firm does not itself produce surplus value. All profit this firm receives represents surplus value produced by other firms because this firm's $c + v$ exerts zero influence.

Cases for which direction is relevant represent absolute as well as relative profits. Quantitatively speaking, this means that these profits either represent a blend of the surplus value an individual firm produces, plus surplus value that other firms produce, or these profits represent only parts of the surplus value an individual firm produces because other firms receive portions of it.

Table 6.4 The effects of $c + v$ and market factors

Direction into which factors exert influence	*$c + v$ exerts greater influence*	*Bothe factors exert equal influence*	*Market factors exert greater influence*
same direction	$s_i < \pi_i < 2s_i$	$\pi_i = 2s_i$	$\pi_i > 2s_i$
opposite direction	$s_i > \pi_i > 0$	$\pi_i = 0$	$\pi_i < 0$
direction not relevant	$\pi_i = s_i$ (a)	—	$\pi_i \neq s_i$ (b)

Note: (a): market factors exert zero influence. (b): firms does not produce s_i, firm-specific $c + v$ thus exerts zero influence.

Cases in Table 6.4 for which direction is not relevant either only represent absolute surplus value—$\pi_i = s_i$, or only relative surplus value—$\pi_i \neq s_i$.

Further discussion

The discussion thus far may be generalised as: the smaller the value a firm produces individually, the greater the value this firm receives during sale. Vice versa, the greater the value a firm produces individually, the smaller the value this firm receives. In short, *less value produced means more value received; more value produced means less value received.* This applies under normal conditions. Rare cases of extreme price bargaining, though not altering the amount of value produced, may substantially alter the amount that firms would normally receive. This is because the individual price at which firms sell may substantially differ from the price at which firms sell without bargaining.

In contrast, the RBT's current approach is, as discussed previously, to measure utility using the formula 'utility equals willingness to pay' (e.g., Barney, 1986; Hoopes et al., 2003; Schmidt and Keil, 2013). This is the case even though Bentham's (1843) notion of a cardinal utility—that is, an additive utility—has been rejected repeatedly (e.g., Behrens, 1979; Heinrich, 2011; Marx, 1863 [1988]; Pareto, 1916).

This situation reveals the Austrian School of Economics, established by Menger (1871) and Böhm-Bawerk (1896). One of its main propositions is that value, as utility, is created when a buyer is willing to pay for what is on offer. This also means that utility is measured as the price a buyer is willing to pay. It is important to note that RBT has adopted this quantification mechanism, but argues instead that utility is created within the firm.

Expressed differently, RBT continues to tie itself to the Austrian School's peculiar quantification of 'willingness to pay'. The formula intends to establish the magnitude of value, yet, logically speaking, the magnitude must be presented *before* the potential buyer is able to reach a decision of whether to pay. Reality also does not support the view that 'willingness to pay' establishes the magnitude of value because prices are displayed before a decision is reached.

The formula seems to have emerged out of a desire to cover the real source of surplus value in production, and to cover the source of social conflict that comes with capitalism's method of producing the surplus. This desire led to Böhm-Bawerk's (1896) assertion that the amount of value firms receive in sale, as sales price and profit, is all that matters. This view is an obstacle that RBT struggles to overcome. To succeed, RBT would benefit from adopting the TSSI of Marx as discussed in this chapter.

Nevertheless, it might seem surprising that 'willingness to pay' remains relevant for RBT. This is because this willingness explains why, and by how much, p_i deviate from the sphere's p_G. Of course, $p_G$is, in temporal fashion, presented prior to the buyer's decision. This is the case even though $p_G$remains hidden from view and only the individual prices, p_i, are apparent in practice.

Conclusions

Using the TSSI of Marx, the discussion has addressed an unresolved question within RBT. That is, how much of the profits individual firms receive is determined by firm-specific $c + v$, and how much by factors in the firm's product market. The answer is summarised in Table 6.4.

Further conceptual work is required, however. In particular, the theoretical disconnects identified by Molloy et al. (2011) should specifically be addressed using abstract labour. Another unaddressed question is the explanation of the origin of surplus value within the remit of RBT. This is a rather pressing matter because contemporary resource-based research acknowledges that a skilled workforce has a positive impact on the profits individual firms receive. But this utility-based research is currently unable to explain exactly how and why skills account for superior individual profits.

The main reason for the lack of progress within the relevant texts is the prevailing reluctance to abandon the formula 'value equals willingness to pay', which, as discussed, is incompatible with RBT. This reluctance seems to stem from a determined attempt to keep the source profit hidden. This is motivated, on the one hand, by the need to keep hidden the main cause of ongoing social conflict and economic crises. On the other hand, there is an attempt to deprive those interested from access to Marx's political economy. This is because Marx has, unlike any other thinker in history, uncovered the dirty realities of the capitalist mode of production. So those who benefit from appropriating surplus value as profit, without paying an equivalent, have a strong incentive to keep Marx's views suppressed at all costs.

Notes

1 Now available in English, as Husson (2018).
2 In English, this passage appears in the 1861–1863 Economic Manuscript. Parts of the manuscript were published as Theories of Surplus Value in German.

References

Adner, R. (2002). When are technologies disruptive? A demand-based view of the emergence of competition. *Strategic Management Journal*, 23(8):667–688.

Barney, J. B. (1986). Strategic factor markets: Expectations, luck, and business strategy. *Management Science*, 32(10):1231–1241.

Barney, J. B. (1991). Firm resources and sustained competitive advantage. *Journal of Management*, 17(1):99–120.

Barney, J. B. (1993). Looking inside for competitive advantage. *The Academy of Management Executive*, 9(4):49–61.

Barney, J. B. (2001). Is the resource-based 'view' a useful perspective for strategic management research? Yes. *The Academy of Management Review*, 26(1):41–56.

Barney, J. B. (2002). *Gaining and sustaining competitive advantage.* Upper Saddle River, NJ: Prentice Hall.

Behrens, F. (1976). *Grundriss der Geschichte der Politischen Ökonomie, volume II: Die Marx'sche Politische Ökonomie.* Berlin: Akademie-Verlag.

Behrens, F. (1979). *Grundriss der Geschichte der Politischen Ökonomie, volume III: Die Bürgerliche Politische Ökonomie bis zur Allgemeinen Krise des Kapitalismus.* Berlin: Akademie-Verlag.

Bentham, J. (1843). *Works of Jeremy Bentham.* Oxford: Oxford University Press.

Böhm-Bawerk, E. (1896). Zum abschluß des Marx'schen systems. In H. Meixner and M. Turban (eds), *Etappen Bürgerlicher Marx-Kritik, Bd. 1*, pages 47–132. Giessen: Andreas Achenbach.

Bortkiewicz, L. (1952 [1907]). Value and price in the Marxian system. *International Economic Papers*, 2:5–60.

Burns, T. (2017). Marx, the labour theory of value and the transformation problem. *Capital & Class*, 41(3):493–510.

Chadwick, C. (2017). Towards a more comprehensive model of firms' human capital rents. *Academy of Management Review*, 42(3):499–519.

Dassler, T. (2016). The significance of Marx's Value for Strategy theory: Competitive advantage and the issue of tautology within the resource-based view of the firm. *Capital and Class*, online first, 40(2):245–262.

Dierickx, I. and Cool, K. (1989). Asset stock accumulation and sustainability of competitive advantage. *Management Science*, 35(12):1504–1511.

Freeman, A. (2010). Trends in value theory since 1881. *MPRA—Munich, Personal RePEc Archive*, 48646:1–37.

Freeman, A. (2018). Introduction to value and price: A critique of neo-ricardian claims. *Capital & Class*, 42(3):509–516.

Freeman, A. and Kliman, A. (2008). Simultaneous valuation vs. the exploitation theory of profit: A summing up. *Capital & Class*, 32(1):107–117.

Freeman, A. and Kliman, A. (2009). No longer a question of truth? The knell of scientific bourgeois Marxian economics and a positive alternative. *Marxism 21*, 6(3):302–317.

Heinrich, M. (2011). *Die Wissenschaft vom Wert: Die Marx'sche Kritik derpolitischen Ökonomie zwischen wissenschaftlicher Revolution und klassischer Tradition.* Münster: Westfälisches Dampfboot, 5th edition.

Heinrich, M. (2013). Crisis theory, the law of the tendency of the profit rate to fall, and Marx's studies in the 1870s. *Monthly Review*, 1 April.

Hoopes, D. G., Madsen, T. L., and Walker, G. (2003). Guest editor's introduction to the special issue: Why is there a resource-based view? Toward a theory of competitive heterogeneity. *Strategic Management Journal*, 24(10):889–902.

Husson, M. (2018). Value and price: A critique of neo-Ricardian claims. *Capital & Class*, 42(3):517–535.

Kliman, A. (2001). Simultaneous valuation vs. the exploitation theory of profit. *Capital & Class*, 25(1):97–112.

Kliman, A. (2007). *Reclaiming Marx's 'Capital': A refutation of the myth of inconsistency.* Lanham, MD: Lexington Books.

Kliman, A. (2010). The disintegration of the Marxian school. *Capital & Class*, 34(1):61–68.

Kliman, A. (2011). On capitalism's historical specificity and price determination: Comments on the value-form paradigm. *Critique of Political Economy*, 1(1):177–196.

Kliman, A. and McGlone, T. (1999). A temporal single system interpretation of Marx's value theory. *Review of Political Economy*, 11(1):33–59.

Kraaijenbrink, J., Spender, J. C., and Groen, A. (2010). The resource-based view: A review and assessment of its critiques. *Journal of Management*, 36(1):349–372.

Marx, K. (1861–1863 [1988]). *Economic manuscripts 1861–1863. Vol. 30 of Collected Works.* New York: International Publishers.

Marx, K. (1863 [1988]). *Theories of Surplus Value. Vol. 26 of Collected Works.* Berlin: Karl Ditz; Published Rosa Luxemburg Foundation.

Marx, K. (1867 [1990]). *Capital, Vol. I: The process of production.* London: Penguin Books.

Marx, K. (1893 [1991]). *Capital, Vol. III: The process of capitalist production as a whole.* London: Penguin Books.

Menger, C. (1871). *Grundsätze der Volkswirthschaftslehre.* Wien: Braumüller.

Mohun, S. and Veneziani, R. (2009). The Temporal Single-System Interpretation: Un derdetermination and inconsistency. *Marxism 21*, 6(3):277–301.

Mohun, S. and Veneziani, R. (2017). Value, price and exploitation: The logic of the transformation problem. *Journal of Economic Surveys*, 31(5):1387–1420.

Molloy, J. C., Chadwick, C., Ployhart, R. E., and Golden, S. J. (2011). Making intangibles 'tangible' in tests of resource-based theory: A multidisciplinary construct validation approach. *Journal of Management*, 37(5):1496–1518.

Nagatani, K. (2019). Value-form and the mystery of money. *Capital & Class*, Online First, 1–20.

Pareto, V. (1916 [1935]). *The mind and society.* London: Jonathan Cape.

Perez, M. (1980). Tvaleur et prix: Un essai de critique des propositions néoricardiennes. *Critiques de l'économie politique nouvelle,* série 10(Janvier–Mars):122–149.

Pitts, F. H. (2018). A crisis of measurability? Critiquing post-operaismo on labour, value and the basic income. *Capital & Class*, 42(1):3–21.

Potts, N. (2014). An unacceptable misrepresentation: Dismissing Marx's value theory by deliberately distorting the temporal single system interpretation of Marx. *World Review of Political Economy*, 5(1):66–116.

Potts, N. and Kliman, A. (eds) (2015). *Is Marx's theory of profit right? The simultaneist–temporalist debate.* Lanham, MD: Lexington Books.

Powell, T. C. (1992). Strategic planning as competitive advantage. *Strategic Management Journal*, 13(7):551–558.

Prahalad, C. K. and Hamel, G. (1990). The core competence of the corporation. *Harvard Business Review*, 68(3):79–91.

Priem, R. L. (2007). A consumer perspective on value creation. *Academy of Management Review*, 32(1):219–235.

Priem, R. L. and Butler, J. E. (2001). Is the resource-based 'view' a useful perspective for strategic management research? *Academy of Management Review*, 26(1):22–40.

Schmidt, J. and Keil, T. (2013). What makes a resource valuable? Identifying the divers of firm-idiosyncratic resource value. *The Academy of Management Review*, 38(2):206–228.

Sraffa, P. (1960). *Production of commodities by means of commodities: Prelude to a critique of economic theory.* Cambridge and New York: Cambridge University Press.

Steedman, I. (1977). *Marx after Sraffa.* London: New Left Books.

Teece, D. J., Pisano, G., and Shuen, A. (1997). Dynamic capabilities and strategic management. *Strategic Management Journal*, 18(7):509–533.

Toms, S. (2010). Sustained competitive advantage and the modern labour theory of value. *Accounting, Auditing & Accountability Journal*, 23(5):647–670.

Tugan-Baranowsky, M. (1905). *Theoretische Grundlagen des Marxismus.* Leipzig: Duncker & Humblot.

Wernerfelt, B. (1984). A resource-based view of the firm. *Strategic Management Journal*, 5(2):171–180.

7 The economic imbalances of our days and the heterodox economics alternative

Arturo Hermann

Macroeconomic imbalances and the structural transformations of the system

As noted by several authors and witnessed by historical events, modern economic systems[1] are increasingly moving away from a purely capitalistic system – composed of private agents acting within a self-sustaining mechanism, the market, with the state playing only the role of a passive superstructure.

There are many reasons for this phenomenon, a noteworthy group of them referring to the role of the public sector in managing the complexity and contradictions of the "mixed economies" of our days. Among its many functions, the public sector plays a central role – directly through public spending and more indirectly through credit creation – in the formation of effective[2] demand (and hence of profits for firms).

On that account, it is interesting to note that, in the absence of such factors, no significant aggregate profit[3] would be possible for firms. As a matter of fact, labour cost[4] constitutes an aggregate cost for the system of firms. This cost can be brought to zero if workers spend all their earnings, but can never become a source of profit. But, interestingly, not even the entrepreneurs' investment expenses can create an aggregate profit for the firms as a whole. In such a case, in fact, the revenues of the entrepreneurs of the investment sector must correspond to the expenses[5] of the entrepreneurs of the consumption sector, so that the net result[6] for the firms would be zero.

As a consequence, aggregate profit must derive from sources "external" to the system of firms: these sources – not considering, for the sake of simplicity, international trade,[7] whose balance is zero at world-level, and entrepreneurs consumption, which, as noted in note 3, is relatively unimportant – take two interrelated[8] forms: public spending and net credit creation.

As regards public spending, the relevance of this phenomenon has been first underscored by Adolph Wagner, who remarked that economic and social development carries with it an enlargement and diversification of the functions of the public sector.

An implication of this analysis is that a "perfect" private economy is unlikely to be attained in the modern world. Such an economy, in allowing little growth, little innovation and little change, can have as its correlate only very simple economic systems, based on vicinity and direct personal relations. But, as soon as these systems start growing, the role of public sector becomes paramount, paradoxically enough, also for the growth of profit associated with modern capitalistic institutions (in reality, mixed economies). For these reasons, it appears clearly that the neoclassical idea of a *crowding out* effect of public spending on the private sector can display, if anything, only a limited effect on our economies.

With regard to the much related issue of credit creation, many contributions[9] of the theories of "chartalism", "endogenous money" and Modern Monetary Theory (MMT) underscore the monetary nature of our economies, the non-neutrality of money, the role of the public sector (meant in a broad sense, and then also including Central Banks) in guaranteeing the value of money and in orienting the banks in their policies of credit creation. In this sense, as highlighted by many authors, money is a highly institutional phenomenon. We will now briefly consider some macroeconomic implications of these aspects.

Here we note the impressive increase in public spending, not only in absolute, but also in relative terms, as shown by the ratio of public spending on GDP. The available data clearly make evident this trend. The values of the ratio have shifted, for the most important OECD countries, from around 10 per cent in the early twentieth century, to 20 to 30 per cent in the 1970s, and then to 40 to 50 per cent in recent years. In the last 15 years, also as a result of the "austerity policies", the ratio of public spending to GDP diminished in some countries, and remained stable or slightly increased in others. However, and very interestingly for the theme of this chapter, there has occurred in the same period a parallel and notable increase[10] of the ratios of public debt/GDP and private debt/GDP for virtually all countries, with values particularly impressive for the latter. This can be a good indication that the reduction in public spending, in order not to negatively influence effective demand, needs to be accompanied by a parallel process of credit creation.

The role of structural factors

As we have seen, a central trait of the modern "mixed economies" lies in a chronic tendency of effective demand to lag behind the supply of full employment (however defined). We will now turn our attention to a set of structural factors that tend to reinforce this phenomenon: in particular, both the growing productivity of labour and the satiation for certain categories of goods combine to render the objective of full employment more difficult to achieve.

These aspects constitute a significant explanation of the tendency of socio-economic systems to move from work activities resting on "the economic motive" to activities – social, cultural, scientific, artistic – based more on the expression of the real needs and inclinations of persons.

In this regard, what are the effects of technological progress on job creation? The increase in productivity requires a growing amount of goods for guaranteeing the same level of employment. Of course, firms can introduce new products on the market, but this would not solve that structural issue. In fact, even if new jobs are created in these fields, the increase in productivity extends also, and perhaps even more, to the new products. This could contribute towards explaining that every innovative wave tends to create fewer and fewer jobs. For instance, it is easily observed that, whereas the durable goods typical of the 1960s and 1970s involved one hundred thousand workers, the innovative cycles of today's high-tech products would employ no more than some one thousand workers.

All this suggests that a kind of "forced" overconsumption is the only, and very imperfect way, in our present economies, to attain some kind of full employment level.

How many high-tech items, cars, clothes, etc. should we buy to sustain effective demand? For a host of economic, social and environmental reasons, this system is untenable in the long run. In this respect, the problem becomes identifying the set of institutional and policy arrangements for moving along a new avenue of economic and social progress.

Towards an economy of a "steady state"

A central aspect of a novel economic system relates to building a society less based on the "economic motive" and more on the unfolding of the true inclinations of persons.

This comports that this system will be fully compatible with limited growth, a steady state, or de-growth. The objective of our work is not that of indicating what option is preferable but how to facilitate the move towards this path of progress.

A relevant contribution to these issues has been provided by J.M. Keynes, in particular in the final part of the *Essays in Persuasion.* This can appear a bit surprising because Keynes, owing to his proposals for recovering from economic depression, is often depicted as the theorist of the short period. This opinion tends to be reinforced by his famous expression "in the long run we will be all dead".

However, from the reading of the *Essays* we discover that the long-term perspectives of economy and society play a central role in his analysis. For Keynes, focusing attention on short-term problems constitutes only a part of a more profound awareness of the structural transformations of society. The pith of these changes will centre on a substantial shortening of working time, made possible by the increase in productivity. The main obstacle to the attainment of this potential rests, not in a technical but in a psychological difficulty, which can be related to an unconscious feeling of guilt related to the presence of the *superego*. He pinpoints, with great psychological intuition, the difficulty of people to employ leisure time for a better realization of their personalities. In his words,

> We are being afflicted with a new disease of which some readers may not yet have heard the name, but of which they will hear a great deal in the years to come – namely, *technological unemployment*. This means unemployment due to our discovery of means of economising the use of labour outrunning the pace at which we can find new uses for labour … But this is only a temporary stage of maladjustment. All this means in the long run [is] *that mankind is solving its economic problem* … Yet [despite this opportunity] there is no country and no people, I think, who can look forward to the age of leisure and of abundance without a dread. For we have been trained too long to strive and not to enjoy … [hence, in this perspective, economics] … should be a matter for specialists – like dentistry. If economists could manage to get themselves thought of as humble, competent people, on a level with dentists, that would be splendid!
>
> (Keynes, 1963 [1931], 364, 368, 373; original emphasis)

Stagflation and other highly debated aspects of our economies

Introduction

In this paragraph we wish to put forward a "heterodox" interpretation of a number of central and interrelated phenomena of our economies. Considering the complexity of these highly researched and debated issues, we do not advance, of course, any claim of completeness. In this sense, the main aim of this section is to steer a debate on these aspects.

The tenuous relation between the Phillips Curve and Keynes' Theory

As is known, the idea that a moderate rate of inflation can help stimulate the economy and reduce unemployment is generally attributed to Keynes. This idea seemed to have received a strong confirmation by the "Phillips curve".

It refers to a seminal contribution by Alban William Phillips who – in his 1958 article in *Economica*, "The Relationship between Unemployment and the Rate of Change of Money Wages in the UK 1861–1957" – identified a negative relationship between the rate of unemployment and the rate of variation of money wages. As the variation of money wages often went in the same direction as the variation of prices, the Phillips curve is generally appraised as evidence of the inverse relation between inflation and unemployment. If things run in such a way, the only problem for policy action is to calculate the curve for its specific context and then choose which combination of inflation and unemployment is preferable.

When in the 1970s stagflation appeared, this was promptly taken as evidence of the failure of Keynesian economics. And, on that basis, a massive neo-liberal "counter revolution" was triggered by monetarists, "new classical" and other theories chiefly resting on the basic assumptions of neoclassical economics.

It often took the form of sophisticated mathematical models which, however, were based on metaphysical and wildly unrealistic postulates: namely, that an economic system can reach optimal allocation of resources and full employment only if not interfered with on the part of the public sector. Every intervention in this respect can display only a transitory positive effect on employment, while in the long run the result will be more inflation and more unemployment.

However, in our view, to appraise the Phillips curve as a test for the validity of Keynes' theory is ungrounded. This, at least, for the following reasons:

(A) The Phillips' article, as also clearly indicated in the title, only highlights the circumstance that, over a defined historical period, the rate of increase of money wages was related to a diminution of the rate of unemployment. With regard to our theme, it is significant that, while identifying such a correlation, he never dreamed of equating *tout court* increase of money wages with inflation (expressed as the rate of change of retail prices). Hence, the widespread idea, that the Phillips curve constitutes evidence of the negative relation between inflation and rate of unemployment, is rather ungrounded.

As a matter of fact, he underscored that, although the rate of increase of money wages and inflation are in most cases correlated, such a relation is by no means perfect. This is because other factors as well can heavily impinge on the rate of inflation. He mentioned in particular the reduction of costs due to technical progress, imported inflation and the dynamics of effective demand, and was well aware of the complexity of causality relations between these phenomena. He was, in any case, more prone to thinking that the money wages move upward was a reaction to prices increase, rather than the other way around.

(B) If, as already noted, in Phillips' analysis inflation and employment are very imperfectly correlated, we can note that a strong correlation of these phenomena finds little ground also in Keynes' theory.

True, he underscored – with various qualifications and by partly adopting a Marshallian approach – in the *General Theory of Employment, Interest and Money* (Keynes, 1936, in particular, Chapters 2, 3, 19) that a moderate rate of inflation, by entailing a diminution of real wages (and of real interest rates) and a parallel increase of the "marginal efficiency of capital", is likely to increase the propensity[11] to invest. More generally, he remarked that, in a period of slump, an expansionary monetary policy leading to a moderate rate of inflation would be preferable to a restrictive policy causing a deflation and a reduction of effective demand.

However, he regarded both inflation and deflation as unfair and destabilizing phenomena that should not be left to the caprices of *laissez faire* but would require instead an active control by public policies. These aspects appear clearly in the following passages:

> Of the two (inflation and deflation) perhaps Deflation is, if we rule out exaggerated inflations such as that of Germany, the worse; because it is worse, in an impoverished world, to provoke unemployment than to disappoint the *rentier*. But it is not necessary that we should weigh one evil against the other. It is easier to agree that both are evils to be shunned. The Individualistic capitalism of to-day, precisely because it entrusts saving to the individual investor and production to the individual employer, *presumes* a stable measuring-rod of value, and cannot be efficient – perhaps cannot survive – without one.
>
> For these grave causes we must free ourselves from the deep distrust which exists against allowing the regulation of the standard of value to be the subject of *deliberate decision*.
>
> (J.M. Keynes, 1963 [1931]: 103–104; original emphasis)

This and other passages constitute striking evidence that Keynes:

(I) preferred price stability and considered both inflation and deflation unjust and destabilizing phenomena. Hence, he considered a moderate rate of inflation (mainly induced by an expansive monetary policy) useful at times only as a palliative and temporary remedy to counteract economic depression.

(II) He never posited a kind of universal "mechanical relation" between rate of inflation, growth of GDP and employment. Hence, in order to orient these complex relations, much more than a palliative cure is needed.

(III) He regarded the increase of real wages advisable only if linked to the "progress of technique and equipment"; namely, to a parallel increase of the labour productivity. Hence, as in this way income distribution between wages and profits would remain unaffected, there is in his theory, for good or bad, little room for an income distribution more favourable to wages.

(IV) What Keynes advocates, at the end of *General Theory*, is a "certain socialisation of investment" as a central instrument for better attaining the objectives of macroeconomic stability, individual freedom, scientific progress and full employment. This sounds appropriate, but leaves the issue of how to realize in practice these objectives, somewhat unaddressed.

For all these reasons, we are inclined to think that the weak aspects of Keynes' theory do not lie in being too "Keynesian" but, at least for some aspects, in being "too neoclassical": in particular, as also analysed in other works,[12] (i) for retaining some aspects of neoclassical theory of market labour; and

(ii) for not clarifying the central (and most often irreplaceable) role of public spending[13] (and credit creation) in the composition of effective demand.

On that account, the phenomenon of stagflation has little to do with the "failures" of Keynesian policies but, rather, witnesses the typical features of the system: in particular, the tendency to push up prices (and hence, mark-ups) and wages when demand is brisk. In this sense, one relevant aspect of modern economies is that demand-led and cost-led inflation reinforce each other in a complex way.

Perhaps, what is needed to make headway in this field is a better collaboration between Keynes' approach, institutionalism and theories of social justice, psychology and psychoanalysis. We will address in the following paragraphs a number of these aspects.

Can price and wage flexibility ensure full employment?

Let us start from the typical assumptions of neoclassical theories, partly shared also by new-Keynesian economics,[14] which can be so summarized: (i) if prices and wages were perfectly flexible, no involuntary unemployment would exist; (ii) public spending can increase GDP in the short run, but in the long run will crowd out private investments, reduce GDP and increase prices. In this regard, we can make the following remarks.

For (i), the reason why prices are rather sticky lies in the circumstance that, normally, it is more profitable for firms to follow this pattern. This is related to the phenomenon of satiation (as highlighted, for instance, by Skidelsky and Skidelsky, 2012) for a large category of products which, by lowering the price elasticity of demand, makes it unprofitable for firms to cut down prices.

The same reasoning can be applied to wages. Fully flexible wages (especially downward), by further weakening the contractual power of the workers, would not spur firms to hire more workers. Rather, such a course would induce firms to further reduce wages and prolong working hours. More generally, if prices and wages were wildly flexible, no reliable social life would be possible.

Also the hypothesis (ii) is very unrealistic. In particular, the orthodox tenet of the "crowding out effect" does not hold true in real economies. In fact, a reduction of public spending (even if deemed useful) is rarely replaced by a corresponding increase in private spending. This is one of the reasons why, as also noted before, the ratio of public spending[15] on GDP has increased among OECD countries in the long period: from around 10 per cent of the 1910s–1920s, to 20 to 30 per cent of the 1970s to 40 to 50 per cent of the latest decades.

The same applies to credit creation as a central means to finance consumption and investment and then to create effective demand. This takes place especially when – as is very often the case – the process of debt repayment is slow and imperfect. Also in this case, the ratio of private debt on GDP has sharply increased in the long run, ranging now in the various OECD countries from 150 per cent to 400 per cent of GDP (with the highest values often occurring in the most developed countries).

Other aspects on which heterodox economics can cast a better light can be found in the policies of inflation-targeting of the early 1980s, which led to a sharp increase in real interest rates. Now, while it is highly doubtful that these policies were effective and relevant for curbing inflation, what more realistically took place was that the sharp increase of real interest rates fuelled the widespread financialization[16] of the system.

On that account, high real interest rates have a negative effect on GDP, because the cost of borrowing for firms increases, and the Keynesian marginal efficiency of capital shrinks (the difference between expected rate of profit and real interest rate). This comes about also because high real interest rates are often accompanied by "credit rationing".

A phenomenon that, by favouring the stronger companies and putting at a disadvantage small and medium-sized firms, has pushed the concentration of economic activities into few dominant groups. And, last but not least, high real interest rates have contributed to disseminating the "psychology of financial rent" to all social classes.

Another related and negative effect of high real interest rates has been the massive increase in public (and private) debt, whose ratios on GDP have approximately doubled from the early 1980s – with the advent of neo-liberal oriented policies on both sides of the Atlantic. In fact, such policies were often accompanied in most OECD countries – perhaps to give them a *semblance* of a Keynesian perspective – by large public budget deficits.

For these reasons, then, lowering real interest rates would be beneficial for promoting investment. To this can be added the idea – put forward by Keynes in the final chapter of *General Theory* – that the diminution of the real interest rate (that he associated with the "euthanasia of the rentier") would also lessen the rate of profit. Hence, a parallel reduction of inequalities would ensue. This kind of approach will shift attention, in the analysis of investments' incentives, from the all-important role attributed to profits, to the ways of enlivening "animal spirits": namely, a tendency to start initiatives not strictly related to the "economic motive".

Conclusion

As emerges from the previous account, the explanations of the phenomenon of stagflation and other economic imbalances as a failure of "Keynesian policies" is wholly inadequate for identifying the real reasons for such imbalances. Such reasons can be located in the structural tendency of effective demand to lag behind the supply of full employment. This phenomenon was reinforced in a vicious circle by the growing financialization of the economic system. A phenomenon which, in turn, was fuelled by the inflation-targeting policies leading to high real interest rates. This picture was complemented by high rates of profit for the stronger groups, most often accompanied by increasing economic inequalities and a lower "capacity to consume" of the working classes. However, these profits were much more employed in financial speculation than in productive investments. All these imbalances were reinforced by the tendency to adopt national policies of "beggar-thy-neighbour".

Institutional economics, social valuing and democratic planning

The institutional economics perspective

Institutional economics originated in the United States in the first decades of the twentieth century. Its cultural roots can be identified in the philosophy and psychology of Pragmatism – in particular in the theories of Charles Sanders Peirce, John Dewey and William James – and in the German historical school, whose principles were developed by a scholar, Richard T. Ely, who had considerable influence on the formation of the first generation of institutionalists.

The principal founders of institutional economics were Thorstein Veblen, John Rogers Commons, Walton Hale Hamilton, Wesley Mitchell and Clarence Ayres. Relevant contributions were also provided by L. Ardzooni, A.A. Berle, J.C. Bonbright, J.M. Clark, M.A. Copeland, J. Fagg Foster, I. Lubin, Gardiner C. Means, Walter Stewart and many others.

Significant contributions with important connections to institutional economics were provided by, amongst others, John Kenneth Galbraith, Fred Hirsch, Albert Hirschman, Gunnar Myrdal, Karl Polanyi and Michael Polanyi.

Within institutional economics, two main fields can be identified: (i) the *old (or original) institutional economics*, constituted by the first institutionalists and by subsequent scholars who shared their main concepts; and (ii) the *new institutional economics* (NIE), composed of later scholars adopting principles having important references in the Neoclassical and Austrian schools.

We will focus chiefly on the *old institutional economics* (from now we will indicate it as OIE or institutionalism). In this regard, it is interesting to observe the significant links between the OIE and, amongst others, the following theories: (i) various strands of sociology and social psychology, including the "Sociological or Ecological School of Chicago", the social psychology of William James, George Herbert Mead and William Ogburn; (ii) a number of theories of technological innovation, often referred to as neo-Schumpeterian, which share important concepts with the OIE: for instance, the importance of path-dependency processes in explaining the characteristics of science, technology and innovation in any given context.

As noted by numerous authors, the OIE does not present a completely unitary framework. Within this ambit, three main strands can be identified:

(I) An approach first expounded by Thorstein Veblen, stressing the dichotomy between ceremonial and instrumental institutions; the role of habits of thought and action; the cumulative character of technology in its relations with the workmanship and parental bent propensities;

the role of business enterprise in modern economy and its effects on business cycles.

(II) An approach initiated by John Rogers Commons, which focuses attention on the evolutionary relations between economy, law and institutions; the nature of transactions, institutions and collective action, also in their relations to business cycles; the role of conflicts of interest and the social valuing associated with them; the nature and evolution of ownership, from a material notion of possession to one of relations, duties and opportunities; and the role of negotiational psychology for understanding economic and social phenomena.

(III) An approach developed by Walton Hale Hamilton, Wesley Clair Mitchell and other scholars, dealing with "market imperfections" at the micro and macro level and their effects on economic systems. The aspects more widely investigated are market power, the duplication of firms and the inefficiency of many industrial sectors, the insufficient capacity of middle-low income classes to consume, and the dynamics of business cycles.

Notwithstanding several differences between these approaches, the elements of convergence are remarkable. For instance, between (a) the concepts of ceremonial and instrumental institution, (b) the various propensities of the persons in their social evolution, (c) the process of social valuing, and (d) the institutional analysis of markets and transactions.

In this sense, the observed differences tend more to concern the issues addressed rather than the basic aspects of the OIE. The general sentiment pervading these initiatives was one of optimism about the possibilities of social progress and was by no means confined only to institutional economists, as it involved the philosophy and psychology of pragmatism, and various strands of psychology, sociology and political science.

The psychological contributions of institutional economics

Within institutional economics, Veblen and Commons in particular have elaborated important psychological-oriented concepts, which can be employed in the definition and investigation of the processes of social and cultural change. As we will try to show, these concepts are not only important for heuristic reasons, but also because they, by allowing a better process of social valuation, can improve the effectiveness of policy action. Now we summarize these concepts.

(I) Veblen's Theory of Instincts

In the case of Veblen, his book, *The Instinct of Workmanship and the State of the Industrial Arts* (1990 [1914]), examines the role of two fundamental instincts (or propensities), "workmanship" and "parental bent", in economic and social development and, consequently, in the characteristics of production and consumption. Both propensities are intended in a broad sense: "workmanship" meaning not only technical abilities but the whole of manual and intellectual activities applied toward achieving a certain end, and "parental bent" meaning an inclination to look after the common good that extends beyond the sphere of the family alone.

In Veblen's analysis, these propensities tend, under ideal circumstances, to strengthen one another; this constitutes an important insight confirmed by studies in psychology and psychoanalysis, which stress the need for the person to enhance his or her intellectual, social and emotional potential through the construction of adequate interpersonal relations.

Related to these aspects, Veblen's analysis presents other pivotal observations regarding the relationship of "personification" established by the worker with his or her tools when he or she ascribes to them anthropomorphic qualities. Indeed, one reason why the worker tends to consider his or her tools as symbolic "co-workers", might derive from the fact that the worker's relation with technology also embodies an emotional/relational involvement – in other words, a social relationship – which deeply influences his or her role and motivations in the workplace and in the social context.

(II) Commons' Theory of Reasonable Value and of Negotiational Psychology

Commons has also provided significant contributions to the analysis of interrelations between economic and psychological factors in collective life. In his *Institutional Economics, Its Place in Political Economy* (1934), he elaborated upon the concept of negotiational psychology, aimed at interpreting the conflicts and dynamics of collective action as expressed through the complex web of transactions and institutions. Indeed, negotiational psychology involves the idea of conflict between different feelings and values, which find their manifold expressions in the dynamics of individual and collective action. Within this process, the importance attributed to social psychology appears in the following passages,

> If it be considered that, after all, it is the individual who is important, then the individual with whom we are dealing is the Institutionalized Mind. Individuals begin as babies … They meet each other, not as physiological bodies moved by glands, nor as "globules of desire" moved by pain and pleasure, similar to the forces of biological and animal nature, but as prepared more or less by habit, induced by the pressure of custom, to engage in those highly artificial transactions created by the collective human will.
> (Commons, 1990 [1934]: 73–74, 88, 91, 106)

Hence, the individual and collective element constitute two necessary aspects of collective action; this entails a shift of the analysis from a "person-to-nature" to a "person-to-person" relation with the related importance of an interdisciplinary approach for its understanding.

In this perspective, psychological sciences can contribute to a better understanding of the ontological foundations of reasonable value in any given context, in particular as regards its most problematic aspects, which tend to be grounded, in a partly implicitly and unconscious way, in deep-seated patterns of thought and action.

A psychoanalytic perspective

The foregoing contributions can be usefully complemented by considering a number of psychoanalytic concepts. These works highlight, especially in the more recent theories of "object and interpersonal relations",[17] that persons have an intrinsic need to establish sound interpersonal relations in order to express the various aspects of their personality.

In this sense, group life acquires significance for persons in that it allows, in a dynamic interaction, (i) to give and receive affection, (ii) to shape individual and social identity and (iii) to unfold intellectual faculties.

But, very importantly for social analysis, a group can also become a way for expressing predatory instances largely resting on neurotic conflicts. This happens not only in overtly aggressive and intolerant groups but also in more "ordinary" groups. In the latter instances, it is likely that positive and negative aspects are merged in a very tangled way. But, why are neurotic aspects likely to be present, in various degrees, even in the more altruistic groups? The basic reason is that human development is a highly complex process which is likely to also involve, again in various degrees, trouble and difficulty.

To begin with, birth itself, as stressed in particular by Otto Rank, constitutes a trauma for the child. Then, the child feels "fused and identified" with the mother, and, hence, the subsequent process of differentiation and discovery of another person, the father, is likely to engender complex relations of identification, but also of fear, rivalry and conflict.

The child understands that it is no longer "at one" with the mother, and that, therefore, the parents may even "leave it aside" in their common life. Of course, the child loves its parents and needs their affection and protection but, at the same time, can desire to be "at one" with the mother or the father and so, on these grounds, may develop a feeling of rivalry toward the parent of the opposite sex and also – in connection with its feeling of being "left aside" – of hostility and mistrust for both.

The consideration of these factors is not tantamount to downplaying the variety of cultural expressions. On the contrary, a better understanding of the needs and difficulties of human development can contribute to bringing attention to the numberless ways through which cultural evolution takes place.

As noted by Freud (in particular, 1912–1913, 1921 and 1930) and by subsequent psychoanalysts, group cohesion tends to be based[18] on the following processes: (i) libidinal and emotional links amongst the members of the group; (ii) projection of individual aggressiveness into people and/or institutions lying outside the group; (iii) identification with the group leader – who symbolizes the parental instance (typically, the father) – in order to repress the conflicts related to the *Oedipus* complex.

These processes – which operate in part at an unconscious level and may be partly driven by neurotic conflicts – can help to explain the scission that often occurs within groups between "the good and right", lying inside the group, and "the bad and mistaken", lying outside its boundaries.

All these contributions stress the role of groups and organizations for expressing the needs and conflicts of the person. For instance, to the person, the group may represent an idealized *ego*; and, in this connection, its "morals" and "code of conduct" symbolize parental figures that, through a process of "internalization", play the role of *superego*.

In this regard, it is important to note that the instance of the *superego* certainly stems also from a normal human tendency to establish sound interpersonal relations, and, accordingly, to behave with affection and solicitude towards each other and continually improve the "bright aspects" of personality. However, whereas in non-neurotic situations the "code of conduct" emerging from such tendencies asserts itself as a genuine behaviour, in neurotic situations leading to the formation of the *superego* things run in a completely different way: here, the tendency of improving personality tends to be, under an appearance of goodness and morality, subordinated to the expression of neurotic content at cross-purposes with such a tendency.

Implications for economic and social issues

The above discussion implies that, for a deeper understanding of these phenomena, in the study of these conflicts, both individual and collective dimensions should be considered, whatever the particular focus of the analysis.

In this perspective, a psychoanalytic perspective can also be employed for the study of these issues. On that account, it can be very interesting to analyse how people perceive and interpret their economic and social realities and the reasons that can hinder the attainment of a more equitable and sustainable society.

In this respect, the psychoanalytic perspective can help acquire a better understanding of the neurotic reasons underlying an irresponsible attitude towards the environment. A good explanation for such behaviour can be traced back to a predatory attitude, which can have its roots in the unsatisfactory early (and later) relationships of persons with their families and social groups. On that account, a better clarification of these conflicts constitutes a key factor for their solution.

Another, and related, aspect pertains to how people tend to perceive and interpret the increase in public spending of the past decades. In this situation, a vicious circle tends to arise: in consequence of the structural tendency towards an increase in public spending, the opinion that the only remedy to the present crisis consists in a progressive reduction of public spending has gained ground, even across various sectors of the progressive domain.

In these situations, in which the only faith in economic progress rests on a kind of wild and unregulated competition, the market tends to be psychologically perceived as an inflexible and punitive *superego* (we have to work hard in order to obtain an adequate income to live on). In that vision, the only possible thing we should do is to comply with the "needs of the market", without any further enquiry on the adequacy of the system to respond to the profound needs of economy and society. Similar remarks can be made for the psychologies of debt and credit creation.

In this regard, the *superego* can constitute an important explanation of the difficulty to move towards a society of "free time" and, more generally, towards an equitable and sustainable society.

The *superego* represents the psychological instance through which cultural values (with their inner conflicts) are internalized by the child. For this reason, it constitutes a fundamental tie between individual and collective psychology. The *superego* can be considered the heir of the *Oedipus* complex, since it arises from the internalization of the prohibitions and of the moral and cultural values – as perceived by the child – of the child's parents and also of later institutional figures such as teachers and other opinion leaders.

Implications for economic planning

The stress put by many institutional economists on political economy brings to the fore the issue of economic planning. Should it exist at all, and, in the affirmative case, what kind of economic planning is preferable?

As we have tried to show, the idea of a perfect and optimising market, conceived of as an exogenous and self-equilibrating mechanism, is a kind of wishful thinking.

For these reasons, a kind of economic planning is always necessary for attaining the objectives of policy action. We shift then to the second question, namely, what kind of economic planning is preferable?

On that account, OIE provides interesting contributions,[19] which present far-reaching implications for many issues of political economy. OIE identifies three kinds of economic planning:

(I) The first is corporate planning, which is the reality of modern capitalism. In this system, the operation of "free market forces" is heavily conditioned by the interests of big corporations. They possess a wide array of instruments to influence the structure of all the relevant markets in which they are engaged. In Dugger's words,

> "The corporation is privately efficient [in the pursuit of its goals], but it is not socially efficient because its low-cost, high-productivity performance benefits those who control it, generally at the expense of those who depend upon it but frequently also at the expense of the society at large"
>
> (Dugger, 1988: 239).

Corporate planning is highly hierarchical, since the key decisions are made by the top managers, with little involvement of workers and citizens at large.

(II) Then comes totalitarian planning, which is a system characterised by a public purpose which is pursued through a highly hierarchical structure. Such organizations are flawed by a fundamental lack of accountability and democratic representation, even though they have sometimes achieved important results in building infrastructures and poverty alleviation.

(III) We switch then to the third alternative, democratic planning. This system, although it does not always work miracles, is definitely more promising. By allowing a more complete expression of the experiences, motivations and conflicts of the involved subjects, such a system improves the process of social valuation, and then the capacity of policy action to respond to the profound needs of society.

One central difference of democratic planning in respect to corporate and totalitarian systems resides in the capacity to self-correct – by a process of trial and error – its own shortcomings.

In this respect, the relevant aspect of democratic planning is its flexibility, which calls for its application to a wide array of contemporary issues, often reaching out to a supranational dimension. These include building peaceful relations, reducing gross inequalities between persons and economic areas, and, as a pivotal theme traversing the previous issues, solving environmental problems.

Some relevant issues of democratic planning

The previous discussion raises two relevant issues for democratic planning:

(I) How can the objectives of economic planning be defined in real situations? For instance, does the egalitarian criterion imply an absolute equality of conditions, or does it allow for some income inequalities intended as a reward for quality and merit?

(II) Even more fundamentally, how can we "scientifically demonstrate" – even if we agree with it – that the "instrumental value criterion" – for instance, in Marc R. Tool's definition, "the continuity of human life and the non-invidious re-creation of community through the instrumental use of knowledge" – should be a criterion inherently better than others?

(I) Social value and reasonable value

Point (I) is related to the notion of social valuing, which can be so defined,

> To conceive of a problem requires the perception of a difference between 'what is going on' and 'what ought to go on'. Social value theory is

> logically and inescapably required to distinguish what ought to be from what is ... The role of social value theory is to provide analyses of criteria in terms of which such choices are made.
>
> (M. Tool, in Hodgson, Samuels and Tool, 1994: 406, 407)

A significant contribution has been provided by Commons through the introduction of the concept of reasonable value, which pinpoints the conflicting and context-specific nature of the process of social valuing. These concepts are set forth in the following passages,

> The problem arises out of the three principles underlying all transactions: conflict, dependence and order. Hence, reasonable values are reasonable transactions, reasonable practices, and social utility, equivalent to public purpose ... Reasonable Value is the evolutionary collective determination of what is reasonable in view of all changing political, moral, and economic circumstances and the personalities that arise therefrom to the Supreme bench.
>
> (Commons, 1990 [1934]: 681, 683–684)

In this sense, the social value process goes to the very heart of the nature of the political economy, which is considered not an activity stemming from the application of abstract laws but as a collective and evolutionary decision-making process involving many institutions. In this sense, political economy has a close relation with law and ethics,

> If the subject-matter of political economy is not individuals and nature's forces, but is human beings getting their living out of each other by mutual transfers of property rights, then it is to law and ethics that we look for the critical turning points of this human activity.
>
> (Commons, 1990 [1934]: 57)

(II) Instrumental value and cultural relativism

The above point (II) "how can we 'scientifically demonstrate' that 'the continuity of human life and the non-invidious re-creation of community through the instrumental use of knowledge should be a criterion inherently better than others'?", is related to the "instrumental value" criterion (refer, in particular, to Veblen, 2012 [1904], 1990 [1914], 1990 [1919]; Ayres, 1961; and Tool, 1986, 1988).

It refers, as noted before, to the fundamental distinction between (i) an economy oriented to serviceability, based on the instinct of workmanship, which is held to be reinforced by the "rationalising role" of technological progress; and (ii) an acquisitive economy, often ingrained in "ceremonial and past binding institutions", oriented to maintain and increase invidious distinctions of wealth and status.

But how can we establish, in real circumstances, which is the more "instrumental" or "better" policy option? To provide a simple example, building a bridge for connecting the two sides of a river will normally be appraised in our societies as a very instrumental or reasonable choice. But what could be our reaction if the local populations declare that they do not need any bridge because they do not welcome "any new foreign contact"?

Probably, instinctively we will tend to consider such a choice as unreasonable and driven by ceremonialism and backwardness. At the same time, however, many of us would also resort to the notion of cultural relativism[20] set forth by institutional economics.

In this way, however, it can become difficult for the observer to form a sufficiently articulated idea of the adequacy of such societies to attain, for its members, economic and social development of good standing. Moreover, given that the orientations and values of social scientists can vary widely, it is evident that in the social sciences there seems to exist an "intrinsic impossibility" to identify some "objective" criteria for the analysis of social structures.

How can these limiting perspectives of social sciences – cultural monism (which is a kind of reductionism), on the one hand, excess of "cultural relativism" on the other – be overcome?

In this respect, the central question becomes how to identify criteria for assessing the "intrinsic validity" – and hence the ethical foundations – of instrumental value criterion (and of the corresponding policy action). On this matter, such validity can be found not so much in some abstract universal principles of social usefulness fostered by technological progress but, rather, in linking these principles to the actual needs of the person.

For instance, in the previous example it is certainly inappropriate to say that building a bridge is an intrinsically superior choice for these populations. However, it is also limiting to say that every choice is appropriate at the hands of cultural relativism. There are undoubtedly no simple, all-encompassing solutions. Needless to say, we can study well the psychology of local people in order to try to understand whether these persons are realised in society. However, any decision concerning their societies should remain with them.

As a more general reflection, if we assume, following many insights from institutional economics, psychology and psychoanalysis, that the propensities of workmanship and parental bent lie at the heart of the true expression of the needs of the person, the ethical principles of solidarity and participation become endowed with a more precise scientific content since they are based on a systematic analysis of the ontological foundations of human needs in their social and cultural expressions.

In this respect, the distinction between the instrumental value principle led by technological progress and ceremonialism resting on irrational beliefs are interesting but, in the absence of more qualification, tends to be biased by a sort of technological determinism. In this situation, the only hope for social progress rests upon the rationalising role of technology. But technological progress, notwithstanding its enormous relevance in many fields, is not sufficient, *per se*, to warrant such a course for all fields of social life.

In fact, the circumstances whereby our societies seem (and perhaps for some aspects are) more rational than older ones – in the sense that we are less ready than our ancestors to impute animistic traits to objects – does not warrant that the ceremonial,[21] predatory and neurotic aspects play a minor role in economic and social relations.

A relatively simple solution for these issues would require a broader conception of technological progress (and of workmanship instinct) – a conception including not only the technological side, but all scientific advances taking place in natural, social and psychological sciences. As a matter of fact, these advances, by improving the process of social valuing, would also promote a more effective policy action.

This perspective also calls for a broader conception of scientific enquiry according to which also qualitative[22] phenomena are amenable to scientific analysis (for instance, in assessing the proficiency of a musician).

Conclusions

In conclusion, how can the theories addressed in this chapter help to frame a more effective policy action for the major economic imbalances of our time?

In this instance, the neoclassical conception of markets as self-sustaining mechanisms easily leading to "perfection", if not interfered with by public action, appears clearly unrealistic.

Conversely, a more factual account would consider that markets are not abstract mechanisms but institutions created and maintained by public action.

The same line of reasoning can be applied to macroeconomic imbalances. In this respect, a more realistic theoretical background would help achieve a better coordination of many relevant dimensions of policy action. We can mention, among others:

(I) Macroeconomic policies targeted at driving, in a sustainable way, effective demand to the level of supply of full employment; this requires, within a principle of subsidiarity, an adequate and efficient level of public spending; progressive taxation; a permanent low level of interest rate; and a reform of the banking system aimed at discouraging speculative ventures and promoting productive activities.
(II) Policies for promoting human capital in the workplace, through an ongoing upgrading of the workers' competencies, coupled with the improvement of their motivation and participation. These should be coupled with policies aimed at fostering scientific, cultural and technological development; and other structural policies directed at building a more equitable and sustainable society.

In this regard, the addressed theories, although different in many respects, present notable complementarities, in the sense that the aspects overlooked by some are more completely considered by others. Hence, the theories addressed in this chapter (and others as well) can make headway towards a more effective policy coordination. This would involve a horizontal level, between policies: in particular macroeconomic (fiscal and monetary) and structural (in particular, environmental, industrial, research and innovation, and social); and a vertical level, between institutions (supranational, national, sub-national, and local).

Such coordination would be greatly fostered by a process of social valuation involving all the considered dimensions of policy action.

Acknowledgements

The themes developed in the first and third sections of this chapter are also addressed in particular in the following publications: A. Hermann, *The UN 2030 Agenda for Sustainable Development*, Green Economics Institute, June 2018; A. Hermann, "The Tendency of Effective Demand to Lag Behind the Supply of Full Employment", in G.P. Lima and M. Madi (eds.), *Capital and Justice*, WEA Books; A. Hermann, *The Systemic Nature of the Economic Crisis: The Perspectives of Heterodox Economics and Psychoanalysis*, London and New York, Routledge, April 2015.

Notes

1 However, as this system seemed to approach that ideal in various respects, the theoretical foundations of these theories were little questioned. Needless to say, even in that period public intervention had played a relevant role in promoting and maintaining the institutions of capitalism.

2 We have addressed these aspects also in Hermann (2015, 2017, 2018).

3 By the expression "aggregate profit" we mean an amount of profit which exceeds the "normal" incomes of all the workers engaged in the private sector, including the so-called executive salaries.

4 By labour cost we mean the wages and salaries that firms need to pay in order to extract surplus value in the workplace. It is also interesting to note that, as we will see, since the net balance of investment expenses is zero (as the revenue of the entrepreneur is a cost for another), wage and salary bills constitute the only cost for the system of firms. This aspect helps to explain the distributional conflicts of capitalistic systems and the related tendency of firms to reduce labour costs.

5 This also implies that investment expenses cannot freely increase to compensate a reduction in consumption. As a matter of fact, investment expenses are instrumental – and hence closely related – to the production of consumption goods. For this reason, if there are not adequate sales for such goods, the firms which have made investment expenses for producing consumption goods would go bankrupt.

6 In this respect, our approach differs in some aspects from the analysis of Michal Kalecki (1954), which considers profits stemming from the following elements: investment expenses, consumption of capitalists, consumption of workers, public budget deficit, surplus of trade balance. More generally, the relevance of Kalecki's analysis lies in the circumstance that brings together various aspects of Keynesian and Marxist theories, in particular by considering the issues of accumulation and by expressly linking the rate of profit to the degree of monopoly power.

7 Needless to say, this is a gross simplification. As underlined by many authors in the Marxist tradition (a pioneering contribution, important also for the debate that steered a path on these issues, was provided by Rosa Luxemburg, 2003 [1912]), foreign markets, especially in developing countries, have played (and still play) a paramount role in absorbing the potential surplus value (or the structural excess of supply) originating in the stronger countries. The main ways to achieve this were, and still are, to create new markets for consumption and infrastructures (like railroads) heavily financed by long-term loans.

8 A little more formally (see also Hermann 2015 and 2017), we can express these relations in the following way:

1. $P + L \equiv C + S \equiv Y \equiv C + I + G \equiv a_1m_1G + (1-a_1)m_2G + a_2m_3C_2D + (1-a_2)m_4CD + ... + a_3m_5ID + (1-a_3)m_6ID + m_7C_p + m_8I_p$

where P denotes the aggregate profit of private firms, L the sum of labour incomes, including "executive salaries", C and S aggregate consumption and aggregate saving, including "executive salaries", I the total investment, G public spending, CD the amount of aggregate consumption generated by credit creation, ID the amount of investment generated by credit creation, m the values of multipliers for the different categories of income, $a_{1,}$ $a_{2,}$ $a_{3,}$ and $(1-a_1)$, $(1-a_2)$ and $(1-a_3)$ the ratios of the effective demand accruing to private profits and to labour incomes, $C_p + I_p$ the sum of autonomous consumption and investment originated in the private sector. CD and ID indicate that, in a monetary economy, purchasing power is mostly created through a process of credit creation (both short- and long-term based) made available to borrowers. In this context, P constitutes a fraction of the aggregate income and is equal to:

2. $P \equiv a_1m_1G + a_2m_3C_2D + a_3m_5ID$

9 Among the many references on these issues, see in particular Knapp (1924), Fontana and Realfonzo (2005), Hein (2013), Rochon and Rossi (2017) and Wray (2015, 2019). For more recent contributions refer to the interesting articles contained in Real-World Economics Review (RWER), issue 89. Available at: www.paecon.net/PAEReview/.

10 For more details on the data for public spending, and public and private debt, refer to the following links: https://data.oecd.org/gga/general-government-spending.htm; https://data.oecd.org/gga/general-government-debt.htm; http://stats.oecd.org/Index.aspx?DataSetCode=FIN_IND_FBS, in OECD.StatExtracts http://stats.oecd.org/.

11 However, as noted below, the "animal spirits" are also likely to play a relevant role in investment decision.

12 More details of these aspects can be found in the recent WEA online Conference. Available at: https://the2008crisistenyearson.weaconferences.net/papers/the-economic-imbalances-of-our-time-and-the-perspective-of-circular-economy/. Also noted is that the neo-liberalist stance, despite its extreme failure in solving economic problems, still holds credit these days. This can be due to the role of the psychoanalytic superego, which renders the implementation of an alternative and progressive paradigm more difficult.

13 In fact, as incredible it may seem, Keynes hardly ever mentioned public spending in his *General Theory*. Also the role of credit creation in providing new effective demand is not clearly addressed. Needless to say, he elaborated upon relevant

concepts linked to monetary issues, such as the preference for liquidity and the marginal efficiency of capital.

14 As we know, in the development of J.M. Keynes' theory, two main courses can be identified: **(i)** the post-Keynesian, tending to unfold the innovative aspects of his theory; and **(ii)** The new-Keynesian which, while criticizing various aspects of neoclassical theories, tends to share with neoclassical economists the idea that, at least in theory and in the long run, perfect flexible markets would lead to full employment (however defined).

15 We have addressed these aspects in Hermann (2015, 2017).

16 For interesting contributions on these issues refer, without any claim of completeness, to Hilferding (1910), Minsky (2008), Arestis (2018), Fontana and Realfonzo (2005), Hein (2013), Rochon and Rossi (2017) and Vercelli (2017).

17 We have addressed these issues, in particular, in Hermann (2015).

18 This does not imply that Freud disregarded the positive aspects of group cohesion but only that he gave prominent attention to the problematic aspects of group dynamics.

19 For significant contributions on these issues, refer to Commons (1990 [1934], 1995 [1924]), Clark (1939), Dugger (1988), Hamilton (1919), Hodgson, Samuels and Tool (1994), Mitchell (1924), Tool (1986, 1988), Slichter (1924), Trebing (1988) and Tugwell (1924).

20 By cultural relativism (especially in its extreme forms) we mean a type of analysis which, in the valuable attempt to be "neutral" and to avoid the dangers of "simplification" and "reductionism", tends to consider the distinctive features of a given context as the typical expressions of cultural pluralism and, as such, is not accessible to further scientific investigation.

21 A couple of other points worth mentioning are the following:

(i) if it is true that in most cases ceremonialism is based on a past-binding expression of power and status, it is also true that not any social celebration should share the same destiny. In this respect, much would depend, of course, on the profound meaning we attach to such celebrations.

(ii) In Veblen–Ayres' tradition of the OIE, institutions are mainly appraised as a negative factor – as a locus of power and ceremonialism – which stands in the way of the affirmation of the instrumental values driven by technological progress. This view disregards the circumstance that, as already noted, technological progress is not driven by its "immanent rationality" but is heavily conditioned by the economic and social objectives attached to technology.

22 We have addressed these aspects also in Hermann (2018).

References

Arestis, P. (ed.) (2018) *Alternative Approaches in Macroeconomics: Essays in Honour of John McCombie*. London: Palgrave Macmillan.

Ayres, C.E. (1961) *Toward a Reasonable Society*. Austin, TX: University of Texas Press.

Clark, J.M. (1939) *Social Control of Business*. New York: McGraw-Hill.

Commons, J.R. (1990 [1934]) *Institutional Economics: Its Place in Political Economy*. New Brunswick, NJ: Transaction Publishers. Originally published by the Macmillan.

Commons, J.R. (1995 [1924]) *Legal Foundations of Capitalism*. New Brunswick, NJ: Transaction Publishers. Originally published by the Macmillan.

Dugger, W.M. (1988) "An Institutionalist Theory of Economic Planning", in M.R. Tool (ed.), *Evolutionary Economics*, vol. II. New York: Sharpe.

Fontana, G. and Realfonzo, R. (eds.) (2005) *The Monetary Theory of Production: Tradition and Perspectives*. London: Palgrave Macmillan.

Freud, S. (1912–1913) *Totem und Tabu*. Lipsia, Vienna and Zurich. Internationaler Psychoanalytischer Verlag. Translated in English as (1990) *Totem and Taboo*, Standard Edition. New York: Norton.

Freud, S. (1921) *Massenpsychologie undIich-Analyse*. Lipsia, Vienna and Zurich. Internationaler Psychoanalytischer Verlag. Translated in English as (1990) *Group Psychology and the Analysis of the Ego*. Standard Edition. New York: Norton.

Freud, S. (1930) *Das Unbehagen in der Kultur*. Lipsia, Vienna and Zurich. Internationaler Psychoanalytischer Verlag. Translated in English as (1990) *Civilization and Its Discontents*. Standard Edition. New York: Norton.

Hamilton, W.H. (1919) "The Institutional Approach to Economic Theory", *The American Economic Review*, 9 (1): 309–318. Supplement, Papers and Proceedings of the Thirty-First Annual Meeting of the American Economic Association (March).

Hein, E. (2013) *The Macroeconomics of Finance-Dominated Capitalism – and Its Crisis*. Cheltenham: Edward Elgar.

Hermann, A. (2015) *The Systemic Nature of the Economic Crisis: The Perspectives of Heterodox Economics and Psychoanalysis*. London and New York: Routledge.

Hermann, A. (2017) "The Tendency of Effective Demand to Lag behind the Supply of Full Employment", in G.P. Lima and M. Madi (eds.), *Capital and Justice*. London: WEA and College Publications.

Hermann, A. (2018) "The Decline of the 'Original Institutional Economics' in the Post-World War II Period and the Perspectives of Today", *Economic Thought*, 7 (1): 63–86.

Hilferding, R. (1910) *Das Finanzkapital. Eine Studie über die jüngste Entwicklung des Kapitalismus*. Vienna: Wiener Volksbuchhandlung (*Marx-Studien*, vol. III). Translated in English as *Finance Capital. A Study of the Latest Phase of Capitalist Development*, (edited by T. Bottomore). London: Routledge & Kegan Paul, 1981.

Hodgson, G.M., Samuels, W.J. and Tool, M.R. (eds.) (1994) *The Elgar Companion To Institutional and Evolutionary Economics*. Cheltenham: Edward Elgar.

Kalecki, M. (1954) *Theory of Economic Dynamics*. London: George Allen and Unwin.

Keynes, J.M. (1936) *The General Theory of Employment, Interest and Money*. London: Macmillan. Quotations taken from Edison Martin Imprint 2013.

Keynes, J.M. (1963 [1931]) *Essays in Persuasion*. New York: W.W. Norton.

Knapp, G.F. (1924) *The State Theory of Money*. London: Macmillan.

Luxemburg, R. (2003 [1912]) *The Accumulation of Capital*. London and New York: Routledge.

Minsky, H. (2008) *Stabilizing an Unstable Economy*. New York: McGraw Hill.

Phillips, A.W. (1958) "The Relation between Unemployment and the Rate of Change of Money Wage Rates in the United Kingdom, 1861–1957", *Economica*, 25 (100): 283–299.

Rochon, L.P. and Rossi, S. (eds.) (2017) *Advances in Endogenous Money Analysis*. Cheltenham: Edward Elgar.

Skidelsky, R. and Skidelsky, E. (2012) *How Much Is Enough? Money and the Good Life*. New York: The Other Press.

Slichter, S.H. (1924) "The Organization and Control of Economic Activity", in R.G.Tugwell (ed.), *The Trend of Economics*. New York: A. Knopf.

Tool, M.R. (1986) *Essays in Social Value Theory: A Neoinstitutionalist Contribution*. New York: Sharpe.

Tool, M.R. (ed.) (1988) *Evolutionary Economics*, 2 volumes. New York: Sharpe.

Trebing, H.M. (1988) "The Regulation of Industry: An Institutionalist Approach", in M.R. Tool (ed.), *Evolutionary Economics*, 2 volumes. New York: Sharpe.

Veblen, T. (1990 [1914]) *The Instinct of Workmanship and the State of the Industrial Arts*. New Brunswick, NJ: Transaction Publishers.

Veblen, T. (1990 [1919]) *The Place of Science in Modern Civilization and Other Essays*, New Brunswick, NJ: Transaction Publishers. Originally published by the Viking Press.

Veblen, T. (2012 [2004]) *The Theory of Business Enterprise*, London: Forgotten Books. Originally published by Charles Scribner's Sons.

Vercelli, A. (2017) *Crisis and Sustainability: The Delusion of Free Markets*. London: Palgrave Macmillan.

Wray, L.R. (2015) *Modern Money Theory*. New York: Palgrave Macmillan. Second edition.

Wray, L.R. (2019) "Alternative Paths to Modern Money Theory", *Real-World Economics Review*, 89, 1 October, pp. 5–22. Available at: www.paecon.net/PAEReview/issue89/Wray89.pdf.

Part III

Money and monetary regimes

8 Central banking and income inequality

The impact of monetary policy on income distribution

Jalal Qanas

Introduction

Since the 2007–2008 Global Financial Crisis, income inequality and income distribution matters have gained increasing attention not only in academia but also from professionals in advanced economies. Mainstream economists also joined this concert, with Piketty's famous work, *Capital in the 21st Century* (2014). This income inequality has been rising since the early 1980s. Since 2010, median family incomes have fallen, while the mean has risen. Inequality keeps rising. A Morgan Stanley study, carried out in 2014, has also identified the rise in inequality, due to the growing proportion of poorly paid and insecure low-skilled jobs; the rising wage premium for educated people; and the fact that government (tax and spending) policies are less redistributive than they used to be a few decades ago. In that same year, a report was written by the chief US economist of Standard & Poor's, and another from Morgan Stanley, agreeing that inequality is not only rising but having damaging effects on the US economy. Janet Yellen, the chairman of the FED, recognised in her 2014 speech the growing gap between the rich and the poor, and she highlighted the risk of increasing income inequality to the American economy. However, concerns of inequality as a socioeconomic matter remain very limited among mainstream central banks. This is because Mainstream Economics views inequality as an outcome of a capitalist economy. In contrast, post-Keynesian economics see it as an inherent component of capitalist economy.

This chapter discusses inequality from a central banking perspective, debating inequality and causes and consequences from mainstream versus post-Keynesian perspectives. The main focus will be on the view of the interest rate as a distributive variable, highlighting what is called the fair rate of interest, 'Pasinetti's rate', as an alternative policy rate to tackle income inequality. However, a fair rate of interest by itself does not solve the inherent inequality, it should be combined with different measures, notably with fiscal policy through a long-term public investment that ensures that the unproductive rentier class disappear as Keynes wished. Thus, central banks as a public entity should essentially take responsibility to promote social justice and fairness, not only for the current generation but for the next one as well. The key argument presented is that central banks, because of their pivotal position between the government, the banking sector, and society, should take responsibility for the fight against increasing inequality instead of only focusing on the nominal anchor of inflation targeting. The importance of the fair interest rate, compared to other alternative interest rates, is that the one that maintains purchasing power in relation to labour hours and money borrowed or lent, maintains the distribution of income between borrowers and lenders over time. From the fair rate perspective, central bank inflation targeting, as currently practiced, is not distributionally neutral in that it enables the capitalist class to take favourable financial positions.

The chapter illustrates that if the central bank incorporated a 'fair rate of interest rule' it would reduce inequality by distributing income from the rentiers class to other productive classes. That is consistent with Keynes' policy recommendation against the unproductive rentier class.

This chapter discusses inequality from a central banking perspective. First, inequality will be defined, as inequality could take different forms. The section that follows will discuss how central bankers view inequality, causes, and consequences. That is mainly drawn from a mainstream perspective. The third section will follow a post-Keynesian approach to inequality causes and consequences in a modern financialised economy. Then the fair rate on interest will be discussed as a solution. Finally, a conclusion will be drawn.

Definition of inequality

Rising inequality has recently become a major concern in advanced economies, as not only does it affect economic activity but it also affects social justice and fairness. Inequality could take different forms in a modern capitalist economy: inequality of wealth, income, financial exclusion, race, gender, globalisation, technological progress, education, and more importantly institutional set-up of our society. Inequality matters as it not only impacts upon our society today, but it also has a long-run impact on the next generation.

Usually, mainstream studies focus on quantifying and simplifying inequality to limited and straightforward scope, such as wealth inequality, income inequality, opportunity inequality. However, social justice, holistic well-being, and morally problematic issues are ignored. For instance, should we care about inequality in well-being, in social primary goods (Rawls, 1999), capabilities (Sen, 1992), opportunities, or some other relevant domain? For instance, Piketty (2014) has justified that the current levels of inequalities are unjust in themselves.

According to Fontan et al. (2016), some recent theorists of justice suggest that what is relevant for justice is some measure of the means, resources, or capacities of the individual to pursue her life plans rather than the actual welfare level she attains (see, for example, Dworkin, 1981). For example, inequalities in income or wealth are more straightforward to ascertain than inequalities in opportunities or capabilities. Further, egalitarian theories of justice, in particular, have become more sophisticated than a simple call for equality in outcome. As a result, general claims about justice tend to focus on the inadmissibility of certain kinds of inequalities rather than call for outright equality (Fontan et al., 2016). For instance, the notion of equality of opportunity implies that people of equal talent should have equal opportunities or, put differently, that one's social background should not have any differential impact on one's life prospects. Second, we might employ Rawls's difference principle, which, as standardly understood, requires that institutions ensure inequalities in income and wealth maximise the expectations of the least advantaged (Rawls, 1999). Third, prioritarian views argue that we should be sensitive to both the 'size of the cake' and the interests of those who receive the smallest slice, but without imposing a strict constraint as a maximum threshold (Parfit, 1997). Given its structure, prioritarianism promises to be particularly useful when it comes to trade-offs between containing inequalities and promoting economic growth. Other theories such as sufficientarian approaches view that what counts is not what people have relative to others, but that they have enough. The advocates of the sufficientarian approach aim to establish a minimum threshold of the currency of justice in question that everyone should attain (for example, Frankfurt, 1987; Casal, 2007).

Trends and facts of inequality

In almost all OECD countries income inequality has increased, but the timing and the trends differ considerably (OECD, 2011; WIR, 2018). Anglo-Saxon countries already began to experience rising trends in inequality in the late 1970s and early 1980s. By the end of the 1980s, the phenomenon of rising inequality became more widespread, and by the 2000s, countries that were previously considered (more) egalitarian also became affected. High-income concentration is also indicated by the development of top income shares (Piketty and Saez, 2003, 2014). Starting in 1980, top income shares increased tremendously in Anglo-Saxon countries, and much of this increase was driven by a rapid rise in wage income and entrepreneurial income, whereas top shares in Continental European countries developed rather more moderately (Atkinson et al., 2011).

In recent decades, income inequality has increased in nearly all countries, but at different speeds, suggesting that institutions and policies matter in shaping inequality. Since 1980, income inequality has risen rapidly in North America, China, India, and Russia. Inequality has grown moderately in Europe (see Figure 8.1). From a broad historical perspective, this increase in inequality marks the end of a post-war egalitarian regime that took different forms in these regions.

The divergence in inequality levels has been particularly extreme between Western Europe and the United States, which had similar levels of inequality in 1980 but today are in radically different situations. While the top 1 per cent

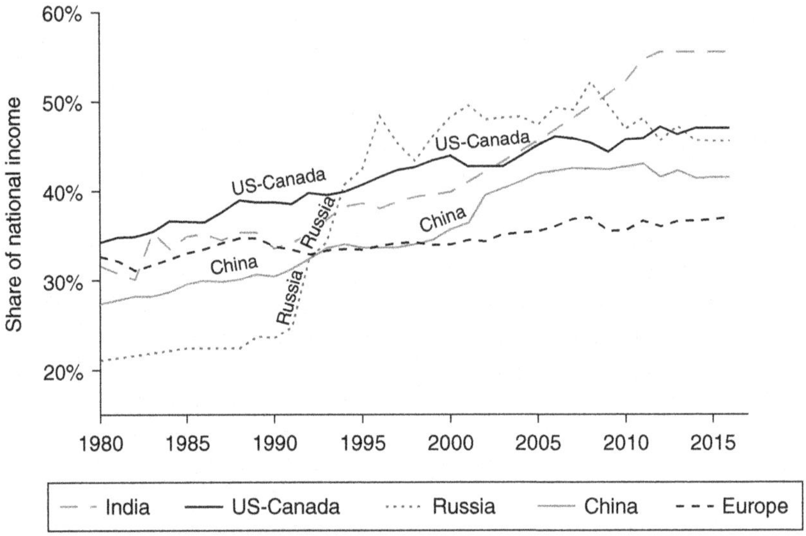

Figure 8.1 Top 10% income shares across the world, 1980–2016.
Source: WID.world (2017). See wir2018.wid.world for data series notes.

income share was close to 10 per cent in both regions in 1980, it rose only slightly to 12 per cent in 2016 in Western Europe while it shot up to 20 per cent in the United States. Meanwhile, in the United States, the bottom 50 per cent income share decreased from more than 20 per cent in 1980 to 13 per cent in 2016 (Figures 8.2 and 8.3 below).

The global top 1 per cent earners have captured twice as much of that growth as the 50 per cent poorest individuals. The bottom 50 per cent has nevertheless enjoyed important growth rates. The global middle class (which contains all of the poorest 90 per cent income groups in the EU and the United States) has been squeezed (see Figure 8.4 below).

In terms of inequality measurement, the most commonly discussed measure of income and wealth inequality is the Gini coefficient. It compares the income or (wealth) distribution of a population to a perfectly equal distribution – in which every citizen of a city or country has equal income or wealth. The Gini coefficient is a summary statistic that measures the dispersion of incomes on a scale of zero (everyone has exactly the same income) to one (one person has all the income).

Figure 8.5 shows the increase of Gini coefficient in USA, UK, and Germany, particularly starting from the 1980s. And it shows inequality in the UK increasing from the 1980s to 1990s and then 'flat' since around 1990, with the decline since the Global Financial Crisis. That is a reflection of the above graphs, where the Anglo-Saxon countries have experienced an increase in

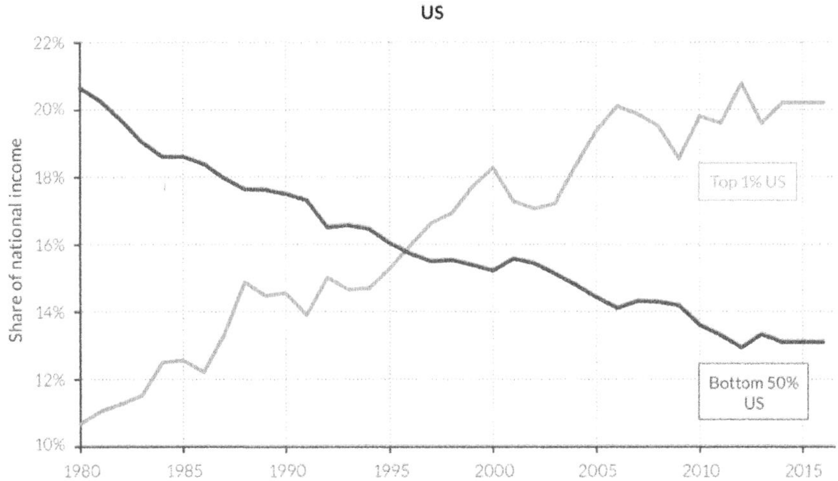

Figure 8.2 Top 1% vs. bottom 50% national income shares in the US and Western Europe, 1980–2016: Diverging income inequality trajectories.

Source: WID.world (2017). See wir2018.wid.world for data series and notes.

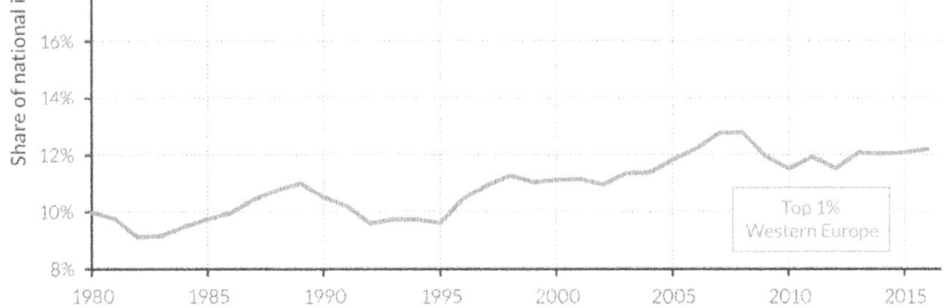

Figure 8.3 Top 1% vs. bottom 50% national income shares in the US and Western Europe, 1980–2016: Diverging income inequality trajectories.

Source: WID.world (2017). See wir2018.wid.world for data series and notes.

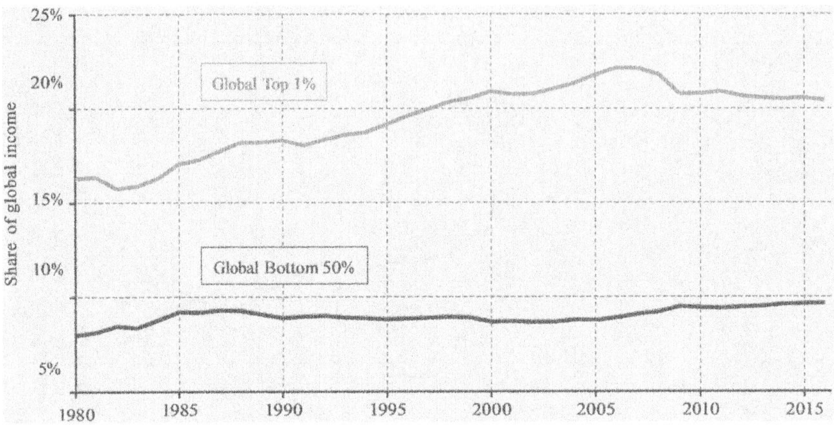

Figure 8.4 The rise of the global top 1% versus the stagnation of the global bottom 50%, 1980–2016.

Source: WID.world (2017). See wir2018.wid.world for data series and notes.

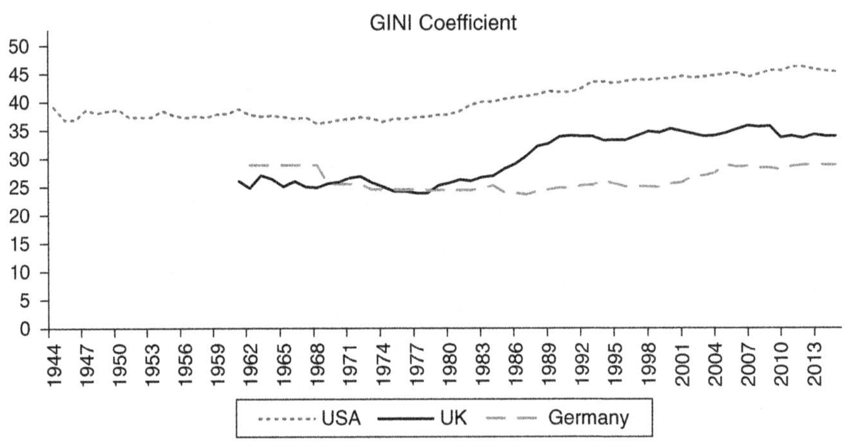

Figure 8.5 Gini coefficient USA, UK, Germany 1944–2015.

Source: OECD Database.

income inequality, starting in the 1980s (that is, after the rise of neoliberalism based on globalisation and financialisation) while Germany experienced a flat from 1960s to around 2000, with an increase from the introduction of the euro 2000 to 2006, and then flat afterward.

However, the Gini coefficient has been criticised on the grounds that it is simple and unintuitive and relatively insensitive to the tails of the distribution, which are the most dynamic parts of the distribution (Palma, 2011). Palma noticed that in most countries, the middle class – defined as those in the fifth to ninth income deciles, or the 40 to 90 per cent – take in around half of the total income. 'The (relative) stability of the income share of the middle is a strikingly consistent finding, for different data sets, countries and time periods' (Cobham and Sumner, 2014). Given that insight, there seems to be less reason in using the Gini ratio, which is sensitive to changes in the middle of the income spectrum but relatively blind to shifts at the extremes. The Palma ratio divides the income share of the top 10 per cent by that of the bottom 40 per cent, for instance, top 1 per cent, 10 per cent, ratio of top 10 per cent to bottom 10 per cent. The result is a metric that is, in Cobham and Sumner's (2014) words, ' "over"-sensitive to changes in the distribution at the extremes, rather than in the relatively inert middle'. The Palma ratio has another advantage: its real-world meaning is easy to grasp. It is not the product of statistical wizardry, but simple division: the highest-earning 10 per cent of the population make X times more than the lowest-earning 40 per cent. The Gini ratio, Cobham and Sumner (2014) write, 'yields no intuitive statement for a non-technical audience'. The best we can do is something like: on a scale of 0 to 1, this country is 0 or unequal, and another one is 1 or equal. This debate needs much further research, which is beyond the scope of this chapter.

To sum up, understanding the economics of inequality from different perspectives is an important matter in order to find the right policy levers that promote social justice and fairness, not only for the current generation but for the next one as well. In contrast, income inequality does not play a prominent role in mainstream discussions of crises.

Mainstream, central banker's and inequality

Central bankers, following neoclassical economics, view inequality as an outcome of the capitalist economy rather than an inherent component of it. That is because neoclassical economics, in its canonical form, views income in terms of the returns to factors of production. Abstracting from questions of power, inequality thus arises from differing marginal productivities of labor and capital. Different endowments of skills, talents, and scarce factors of production inequality, therefore, reflect one's ability to earn in the marketplace. In contrast, as is discussed in the following section, heterodox approaches view differences in power as an essential component of one's ability to earn income. Thus, it is not shocking that there is a late and weak recognition of mainstream economics to this crucial phenomenon. That is so because of their beliefs in free and self-adjusting market mechanisms, labor market flexibility, the major assumption of general equilibrium and their ignorance of the nature and crucial role of money in a monetary production economy, and its impact on the real economy in the short and long run. Academic contributions such as Stiglitz (2012) and Piketty (2014) have fuelled debate on issues of inequality.

Furthermore, the role of macroeconomic policies in inequality, such as central banking policy, has been understated or even ignored by mainstream economists. The conventional monetary policy focus on inflation targeting ignores any link whatsoever with inequality. The increasing power of central banks and the use of unconventional monetary policy in the post-crisis period have invigorated mainstream economists to question the impact of such policy on causing or worsening inequality. As a result of these unconventional policies, such as quantitative easing, the distributive consequences have become more prominent (Ertürk, 2014). Arguably, the increasing concern of inequality as a socioeconomic matter has remained very limited in the mainstream central banks' intellectual apparatus. Usually, mainstream economics studies inequality at best within the scope of causes and impact on economic activities, for example its role in declining economic growth, or negatively impacting consumption and spending, or the impact on price (Goda, 2013). The fact that inequality is not prominent in mainstream research can also be seen from the fact that the vast majority of Dynamic Stochastic General Equilibrium (DSGE) models were based on one rational representative agent (with some exception, such as the work from Kumhof and Ranciere (2010), and Kumhof et al. (2012)). That means that 'there are no distributive issues [and] no scope for exploitation [because] what the worker loses through lower wages, he/she gets back in his/her role as "owner" through higher profits' (Stiglitz, 2011, p.598). Furthermore, DSGE models normally disregarded the possibility of excess indebtedness, as no financial market was included in most models. In other words, according to the vast majority of mainstream theories and models, inequality will have neither a negative impact on aggregate demand nor will it lead to over-indebtedness. Even if capital markets are taken into account mainstream theories of consumption '... see no link between the inequality of (permanent) income and aggregate personal consumption, and hence no need for government action ...' (van Treeck and Sturn, 2012, p.1). The reason for this view is that households are expected to be able to smooth fluctuations in income with the help of financial markets. And that inequality is seen to be rather influenced by transitory changes (e.g., depending on the age of the individual) and not by permanent changes in lifetime income (Krueger and Perri, 2006).

More importantly, some mainstream economists have recently gone a step further by realising the impact of monetary policy on income distribution (Nakajima, 2015). These studies focused on the impact of interest rate policy and quantitative easing policy on the income distribution gap between the rich and the poor. However, their main argument was raised due to the low interest rate after the crisis that could deteriorate safe assets investments. For instance, these economists criticised quantitative easing policies (liquidity facilities) that went mainly to banks in replacement of their risky assets in order to restore their balance sheets and liquidity and restore their willingness to lend. But, instead, they refused to do so because of the uncertainty and low confidence in the state of the economy, which deteriorated the economy further, increasing the income distribution gap. According to Nakajima (2015), monetary policy affects income distribution through two channels: first, the inflation channel, where labor and low-income households hold mainly cash assets compared to high-income households (which hold financial assets); second, the income channel, through the impact of the policy rate on employment (labor income) and the income of financial assets. However, he argued that these redistributive effects would average out (no impact) in the long run. For instance, the Survey of Consumer Finances (Yellen, 2014) identified that wealthier households receive a significant amount of financial and business income, whereas other households rely primarily on labor income or transfers. This survey indicated that

> among working-age households in the US the bottom 60 per cent of the wealth distribution, 'Main Street', receive virtually none of their income from financial assets, whereas 'Wall-Street', the 5 per cent wealthiest households, receive 41 per cent of their income from financial assets.

Controversially, most central banks' mission statements promote 'social justice' and the 'good of the people' objectives. But mainstream economists view of the 'good of the people' is to be focusing on one 'nominal objective' a low and stable rate of inflation to generate financial and economic stability. Furthermore, these neoclassical economists have not even allowed 'social justice' and distributive concerns to play a minimal role in their mandates. For instance, the Bank of England's mission is to promote 'the good of the people of the United Kingdom by maintaining monetary and financial stability' (BoE, 2014). For the European Central Bank (ECB), Article 3 of the Treaty on the Functioning of the European Union (the Lisbon Treaty) mentions that the ESCB (European System of Central Banks) shall support the general economic policies in the Union, as long as it does not jeopardise the price stability objective, and the Treaty also explicitly mentions social justice as one such objective.

In addition to insufficient attention, the assumption of the long-term neutrality of money underpins mainstream and central bank approaches to the distributive impact of monetary policy. That is to say, even though central bankers generally accept that monetary policy could have some temporary redistributive effects in the short run, this does not hold in the long run. Moreover, the short-run distributive consequences are unintended, which little can be done about. For example, Bank of England (BoE) officials such as David Miles (2012), argued that any monetary policy action will have some distributional impacts. In the same vein, Ben Bernanke emphasises that the effects are temporary:

> It is true that in the short run, some of the tools that we have involve changing asset prices, so higher stock prices and things of that sort, but

> we can't affect those things in the long run. It is only a short-run transmission mechanism that is involved there.
>
> (Bernanke, quoted in Fontan et al., 2016)

As already discussed there are reasons to be doubtful of this assertion. To repeat, the asymmetric nature of business cycles mitigates against any long-run corrections of short-run distributive consequences of monetary easing as, according to Nakajima (2015) there is a good chance that the redistributive effects do not average out because business cycles are known to be asymmetric. Thus more research is needed to identify these effects.

The Global Financial Crisis has, however, shifted the debate. Most strikingly, post-2007–2008 crisis, central bankers almost uniformly recognise that the distributive effects of the unconventional monetary policy are not minor. The main mechanism identified is that the high level of asset purchases pushes up the price of assets, which are disproportionally held by the wealthiest households (BoE, 2012). Mark Carney (2014), former governor of the BoE said: 'the distributional consequences of the response to the financial crisis have been significant'. However, Central bankers continued to argue that these effects are 'unintended and temporary'. For instance, ECB officials emphasised that the distributive effects of the unconventional monetary policy are 'unintended consequences', and Haldane (2014) from the BoE stressed that this policy 'was taken with the best of intentions'. 'Collateral effects', or 'side effects', thus all illustrate that these central banks share the idea that the effects are temporary and unintended.

Furthermore, they have also justified their actions in saving the global economy from collapse: 'Extraordinary times heralded truly extraordinary measures' (Haldane, 2014). Further: '[A] central bank with a clear mandate to safeguard price stability needs to act forcefully when push comes to shove. These distributional side effects then need to be tolerated' (Fontan et al., 2016). In addition, central bankers stress that the post-2007 policies will not stay with us for long, and they will revert to the pre-2007 policies soon. Carney from the BoE talked about 'extreme circumstances, such as in the wake of a financial crisis' (Carney, 2014), and his colleague Haldane maintains that 'extraordinary monetary measures will of course not last forever' (Haldane, 2014). Arguably, major central banks argued that they cannot do much to address inequality. For instance, while emphasising that the FED cannot do much, Bernanke also gestured toward a sort of trickle-down effect: 'We can only hope to address the overall state of the labor market and hope that a rising tide will lift all ships, so to speak' (Bernanke, quoted in Fontan et al., 2016).

In sum despite central bankers' recognition of the monetary policy consequences on inequality, they believe that fighting inequalities is not the mandate of any modern central bank and it does not fall within central banking scope. In contrast to mainstream, post-Keynesians have been concerned with the increased risk of income distribution to our economy long before the recent crisis.

Post-Keynesians and inequality

In his 'General Theory of Employment, Interest, and Money', Keynes (1936, p.372) states that one of 'the outstanding faults of the economic society [is] its arbitrary and inequitable distribution of wealth and incomes'.

Post-Keynesian economics, in contrast to mainstream economics, views inequality as an inherent component of an unstable capitalist economy. The theories of John M. Keynes mainly inspire post-Keynesian economics but 'post-Keynesians [also] derive inspiration from a variety of [other] sources ... such as Marx, ... Kalecki, Kaldor, Leontief, Sraffa, Veblen, Galbraith, Andrews, Georgescu-Roegen, Hicks or Tobin, or from other disciplines (sociology, history, political science, psychology, and anthropology)' (Lavoie, 2006, p.18). Further, 'Issues of class, power, and distribution of income and wealth are at the heart of [post-Keynesian] analysis' (Arestis, 1996, p.114).

In terms of income inequality, post-Keynesians distinguish between functional and personal income distribution. The functional income distribution is a matter of class: it measures how much of the national income goes to workers (wage-share) and how much of the national income goes to capitalists and rentiers (profit-share); whereas the personal income distribution measures how far the national income is equally distributed among individuals/households. Post-Keynesians argue that an increase in the functional income distribution tends to have negative impacts on the economy if the economy is wage-led (Onaran and Galanis, 2014). Similarly, an increase in the inequality of the personal income distribution can have negative consequences for the stability of the economy because poorer segments of the population have a higher marginal propensity to consume than richer segments of the population. That is, an increase in income inequality is expected to lead to a decrease in aggregate consumption demand (Palley, 2002; Dutt, 2011; Stockhammer, 2012). Indeed, Keynes and Kalecki believed that an increase in inequality would lead to a weakened propensity to consume that, in turn, weakens demand for investment and consumption.

Furthermore, post-Keynesians argued that in a financialised economy, inequality becomes more complex. Particularly, in theory, workers receive their income only out of wages, while capitalists receive their income out of profits, and rentiers receive their income through dividends, interest payments, rents, and capital gains. However, in reality, many households occupy various contradicting class positions; for example, capitalists and workers receive also rentier income, and managers occupy the class position of capitalists (as they execute power in firms), and workers (as they are employed and receive wage income), and can be rentiers (through their stock options) at the same time (Stockhammer, 2004). Post-Keynesians also found that the negative consequences of an increase in income inequality might not be immediately visible in a finance-dominated economy. In particular, the negative consequences of rising inequality may not be immediately apparent if the poorer segments of the population are able to accumulate debt to finance their consumption, due to greater availability of finance (such as mortgages) and because of rising asset prices (such as houses prices).

However, the debt-led consumption model is unsustainable. That means that, in the long-run, income is redistributed from poorer households to richer households and the consumption of poor households consequently will be constrained. Eventually, this will most likely lead to a debt-burdened recession (Palley, 1994; Bhaduri et al., 2006; Dutt, 2006, 2011), or, instead, translate into a financial crisis if rising asset prices and financial innovation enable poor households to engage in Ponzi finance to keep their living standards constant (Hein and van Treeck, 2008; Bhaduri, 2011). Furthermore, Stockhammer (2010) found that the crisis could be understood as a combined effect of deregulation and rising inequality.

Post-Keynesians, among other heterodox economists, draw on a wide range of income distribution theories. For instance, the Kaleckian approach of income distribution between labor and firms is based on the mark-up price power of firms as they protect their profit share (Goda, 2013). Furthermore, according to Barba and Pivetti (2009) in the 'Production of Commodities by Means of Commodities', Sraffa (1960) analyses the extent to which monetary authorities can control the interest rate, recognising the powerful position central banks have in improving banks' liquidity. Furthermore, they argued that Sraffa explained that the conflict of interest among firms, policymakers, and the political class could put at risk the economy's stability, giving rise to further conflict among social classes. In addition, Sraffa identified that financial innovations accelerate when financial firms have liquidity problems and their growth is affected, and such acceleration makes monetary policy less effective and monetary authorities less influential. Sraffa's approach to money and banking serves as the basis for the analysis of distributive variables during a particular economic period and is of particular use when looking to the effects of financialisation on income distribution.

To sum up, in contrast to mainstream dogma, post-Keynesians view inequality as a core element of the unstable capitalist economy, and they offer different approaches to understand this important matter. They view conflict among competing classes as a central component of distributive outcomes. Before these insights are integrated into our model, we first consider post-Keynesian approaches to interest rates and monetary policy.

Post-Keynesians interest rates and monetary policy

In contrast to neoclassical economics, post-Keynesians focus more on the relationship between the interest rate and monetary policy, rather than on the relation between monetary policy and inflation. As discussed by Rochon and Setterfield (2007, 2011), the interaction between the interest rate and monetary policy is approached in two different ways in the endogenous money approach. The activist approach considers the interest rate to move counter-cyclically, in order to ensure strong growth and full employment. The 'parking-it' approach, on the other hand, proposes to set nominal, or real interest rates, and change them carefully and in moderation. This approach recognises that changes in interest rate do not always have the desired effects on unemployment, growth, and capacity utilisation. What is more, the utilisation of an interest rate for macro stabilisation is rather seen as uncertain, and fiscal policy is preferred for such purpose.

Nevertheless, given the importance the interest rate has on affecting real variables, there are three views on how to use such a powerful tool. The 'Smithin rule' proposes that central banks should keep interest rates as low, and as close to zero, as possible. Similarly, the 'Kansas City rule' recommends a nominal interest rate equal to zero. In contrast, the Pasinetti or Fair interest rule proposes to set the interest rate to a fair level, in relation to the impact on labor (Rochon and Setterfield, 2007).

In the Pasinetti rule the interest rate should be equal to the rate of growth of labor productivity, so when wage earners incur credit, they can always have a constant purchasing power, and rentiers are seen as a 'necessary evil' (Lavoie, 1996). Furthermore, in an economy where the profit rate is constant, the growth rate and therefore, the fair rate will be equal to the growth rate of wages. When the economy is subjected to price inflation, then the fair rate will be equal to the average rate of wage inflation (Lavoie, 1999). In other words, the fair interest rate is the one that maintains purchasing power in relation to labor hours and money borrowed or lent and maintains the distribution of income between borrowers and lenders over time. From the fair rate perspective, central bank inflation targeting as currently practiced is not distributionally neutral in that it enable the capitalist class to take favorable financial positions.

Brancaccio and Fontana (2012) proposed an interest rate rule that takes into consideration the solvency conditions of macro agents involved in the production process and interrelates the Keynesian analysis of income and employment with the Sraffian analysis of income distribution, while explicitly showing the relationship between real and monetary variables and the role of credit in the economy. They have used the rule to show how households' unsustainable debt-financed consumption, along with increasing inequality on income distribution, led to the 2007 financial crisis in the US. Central banks did not identify, nor address households' growing indebtedness. The latter is the result of the FED's policy which merely focuses on the financial sector's liquidity, and as Taylor (2009) pointed out, its refusal to treat this crisis as a solvency crisis rather than a liquidity one.

In addition, Moore (1989) analysed the effects of the interest rate as a distributive tool between industrial capital, financial capital, and labor, and he argued that if the increase in interest rate was temporary, it will not affect the mark-up price, as firms will have absorbed the change. However, a permanent increase in the interest rate may affect the production costs, which leads to an increase in the mark-up price, affecting distribution between wage and non-wage income. That will result in a transfer of income from industrial to financial capital, as well as a decrease in the wage-share in the national income. Further, Epstein (1992) analysed the impact that social groups have on central bank policymaking. He identified three social groups affected by central bank policy: labor representing wage earners, industry representing firms, and finance representing the financial sector. Using a Kaleckian and Marxian analysis he studied the weight each sector has on central bank policymaking, and in order to do so, he analysed the relation between capital and labor, finance and industry, central bank and the state, and nation with the world, to then interrelate the results. His study illustrated that the Kaleckian approach is more comprehensive and able to relate to the real world, than the Marxian model. In addition, he found that by using the interest rate tool, the central bank set its policy in favor of the financial sector, instead of firms and wage earners, serving in this way only to benefit certain social groups rather than the society as a whole.

All the interest rate rules that are discussed above view the interest rate as a distributive variable and consider that monetary policy acts through changes in income distribution among wage earners and rentiers. As Lavoie (1996) expressed: '[the] interest rate is an important determinant of the distribution of income between social classes and presumably between individuals'. In such a sense, monetary policy could contradict itself over time, depending on whether the distributional purpose of the policy is to maintain the rentier class or not.

In terms of Keynes' own views, according to Lavoie and Seccareccia (2017), Keynes had originally planned a whole chapter, not on the wage/profit relation but, instead, on the critical 'Influence of Changes in the Distribution of Income between the Rentiers and Earners' (Keynes 1979, p.63). Further, Keynes (1923, quoted in Lavoie and Seccareccia, 2017) identified that an economy consists of the 'Rentiers' or the 'Investing Class', the 'Business Class', and the 'Earning Class'. Keynes refers to the 'rentiers' as the 'functionless investor' – a separate income class whose interests were fundamentally opposed to those whom he considered the productive classes of capitalist entrepreneurs and workers. For Keynes, in contrast to the mainstream view of the interest rate as a simple cost of borrowing, interest rates played a much more crucial role via the income channel or what we could describe as the income distribution transmission mechanism (Lavoie and Seccarecia, 2017). He further wrote that, through central bank intervention: 'The monetary authority often tends in practice to concentrate upon short-term debts and to leave the price of long-term debts to be influenced by belated and imperfect reactions from the price of short-term debts ...' (Keynes 1936, p. 206; also see Seccareccia and Lavoie 2004, pp. 165–166). In that sense, monetary policy determined short-term rates and, in turn, representative opinion or rentier expectations of the future behavior of the central bank would impact, albeit imperfectly, on the long-term rate of interest. Thereby making interest rates a 'highly conventional' phenomenon instead of a 'real' phenomenon determined by productivity and thrift, as in the loanable funds theory. Consequently,

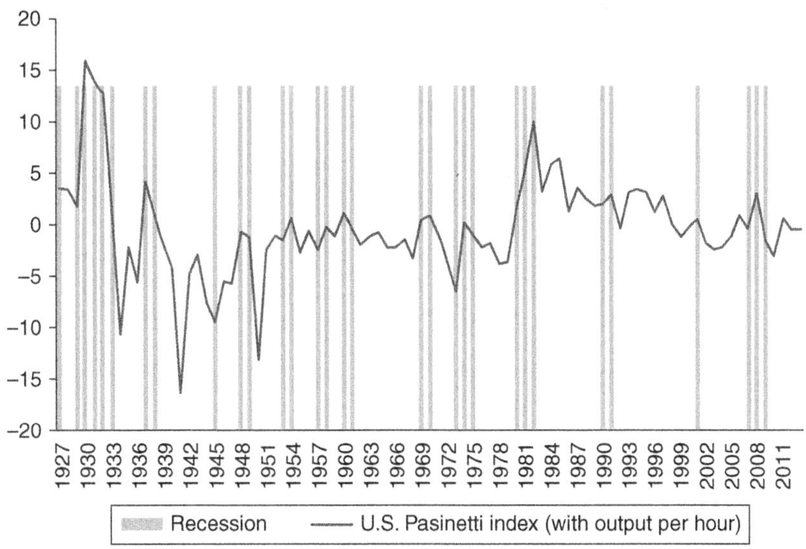

Figure 8.6 The Pasinetti Index for the United States, 1926–2013.
Source: Lavoie and Seccareccia (2017).

monetary policy decisions and conventions were at the very heart of interest rate determination.

Turning to empirical evidence, Lavoie and Seccareccia (2017) measured the intensity of the transfer between the rentier and non-rentier sectors historically, using the Pasinetti Index for the United States and Canada 1926–2013 (the Pasinetti Index, as measured in percentage terms, is the gap between real long-term interest rates and labor productivity growth per person employed). As shown in Figures 8.6 and 8.7 there was, for instance, a massive transfer in favor of rentiers during the Great Depression, which eventually turned in the opposite direction, in favor of the non-rentier sector by the early post-war years which, with only minor fluctuations, lasted until the late 1970s. As is evident from the two figures in both the US and Canada, the 1980s witnessed 'the revenge of the rentiers' (Smithin, 1996) as the transfer persisted in favor of rentier income until the mid-1990s. There was a subsequent decline during the late 1990s, but with some important fluctuations around a positive value until the financial crisis. Broadly speaking, it appears that whenever the transfer in favor of rentiers was becoming positive, it would be associated with a recessionary environment.

To summarise, there has been a marked increase in inequality in recent years. Distributional factors have been of secondary importance within neoclassical economics, which also views monetary policy as having no effect on inequality in the long run. For post-Keynesians, in contrast, distributional conflicts play

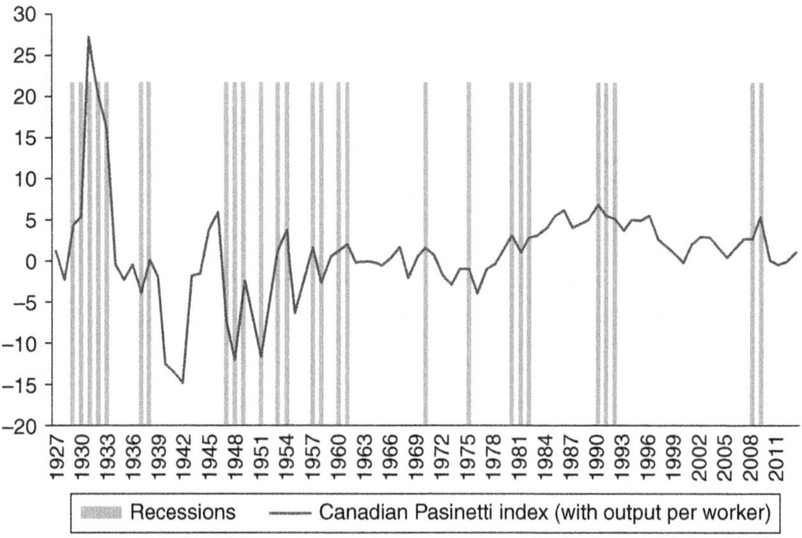

Figure 8.7 The Pasinetti Index for Canada, 1926–2013.
Source: Lavoie and Seccareccia (2017).

a central role in capitalist development. As outlined here, the interest rate and monetary policy play an important role in the competition for resources.

Conclusion

The impact of central banking on income distribution has increasingly gained attention, not only by mainstream economists but also by professionals. Within this framework, the interest rate is viewed as either being irrelevant or having only short-run effects on income inequality. In contrast, post-Keynesians have long emphasised that the interest rate is a distributive variable. In contrast to inflation-targeting policy, using the 'fair rate' of interest, as proposed by post-Keynesians, is related to the role of central banks as a social regulator stabiliser by affecting income distribution between workers and rentiers, without harming economic activity, but instead stabilising economic activity. So, a central banking policy that incorporates income inequality matter in its mandate, such as a fair rate of interest, will mitigate the negative impact that the unproductive rentier class has on the economy.

Here, this chapter is not proposing a rule that fits all. Instead, it is argued that these points raised in the chapter contribute to the ongoing debate on income inequality. The main argument is that central banks should view income inequality as an urgent matter, and they must be actively doing something to solve it rather than fuelling it with their inadequate policy. However, monetary policy cannot effectively address the increasing inequality without the help of government. Thus, a fair rate of interest, with income policies and long-term public investment, is vital in the fight against income inequality.

References

Arestis, P., 1996. Post-Keynesian Economics: Towards Coherence. *Cambridge Journal of Economics*, 20(1): 111–135.

Atkinson, A. B., T. Piketty and E. Saez, 2011. Top Incomes in the Long Run of History. *Journal of Economic Literature*, 49(1): 3–71.

Bank of England (BoE), 2012. *The Distributional Effects of Asset Purchases*. London: Bank of England. Available at: www.bankofengland.co.uk/publications/Documents/news/ 2012/nr073.pdf, (accessed 23 May 2016.

Bank of England (BoE), 2014. One Mission, One Bank: Promoting the Good of the People. Available at: www.bankofengland.co.uk/-/media/boe/files/speech/2014/one-mission-one-bank-promoting-the-good-of-the-people-of-the-uk.

Barba, A., and M. Pivetti, 2009. Rising Household Debt: Its Causes and Macroeconomic Implications: A Long-Period Analysis. *Cambridge Journal of Economics*, 33(1): 113–137.

Bhaduri, A., 2011. A Contribution to the Theory of Financial Fragility and Crisis. *Cambridge Journal of Economics*, 35(6): 995–1014.

Bhaduri, A., K. Laski, and M. Riese, 2006. A Model of Interaction between the Virtual and the Real Economy. *Metroeconomica*, 57(3): 412–427.

Brancaccio, E. and G. Fontana, 2012. 'Solvency Rule' versus 'Taylor Rule': An Alternative Interpretation of the Relation between Monetary Policy and the Economic Crisis. *Cambridge Journal of Economics*, 37: 17–33.

Carney, M., 2014. *Inclusive Capitalism: Creating a Sense of the Systemic*. Presentation at Conference on Inclusive Capitalism, London, 27 May.

Casal, P., 2007. Why Sufficiency Is Not Enough. *Ethics*, 117(2): 296–326.

Cobham, A., and A. Sumner, 2014. Is Inequality all about the Tails? The Palma Measure of Income Inequality. *Significance*, 11: 10–13.

Dutt, A. K., 2006. Maturity, Stagnation and Consumer Debt: A Steindlian Approach. *Metroeconomica*, 57(3): 339–364.

Dutt, A. K., 2011. Power, Uncertainty, and Income Distribution: Towards a Theory of Crisis and Recovery. Paper presented at FMM Conference, Berlin, 28–29 October.

Dworkin, R., 1981. What is Equality? Part 1: Equality of Welfare. *Philosophy & Public Affairs*, 10(3): 185–246.

Epstein, G., 1992. Political Economy and Comparative Central Banking. *Review of Radical Political Economics*, 24: 1.

Ertürk, I., 2014. Reconceptualizing Central Bank Unconventional Policies: Long Positions on No Growth Capitalism, in C. Goodhart, D. Gabor, J. Vestergaard, and I. Ertürk (eds.), *Central Banking at a Crossroads: Europe and Beyond*, London: Anthem Press, pp. 217–228.

Fontan, C., F. Claveau, and P. Dietsch, 2016. Central Banking and Inequalities: Taking off the Blinders. *Politics, Philosophy & Economics*, 15(2016): 319–357.

Frankfurt, H., 1987. Equality as a Moral Ideal. *Ethics*, 98(1): 21–43.

Goda, T., 2013. The Role of Income Inequality in Crisis Theories and in the Subprime Crisis. Post Keynesian Economics Study Group Working Paper 1305.

Haldane, A. G., 2014. *Unfair Shares*. Speech at Bristol Festival of Ideas, 21 May.

Hein, E. and T. van Treeck, 2008. 'Financialisation' in Post-Keynesian Models of Distribution and Growth: A Systematic Review. IMF Working Paper No. 10/2008.

Keynes, J. M., 1936. *The General Theory of Employment, Interest and Money*. New York: Harcourt Brace.

Keynes, J. M., 1979. *The General Theory and After: A Supplement*, in D. Moggridge (ed.), Vol. 29 of *The Collected Writings of John Maynard Keynes*. New York: Cambridge University Press.

Krueger, D. and F. Perri, 2006. Does Income Inequality Lead to Consumption Inequality? Evidence and Theory. *Review of Economic Studies*, 73(1): 163–193.

Kumhof, M. and R. Ranciere, 2010. Inequality, Leverage and Crises. IMF Working Paper No. 268.

Kumhof, M., C. Lebarz, R. Ranciere, A. W. Richter, and N. A. Throckmorton, 2012. Income Inequality and Current Account Imbalances. IMF Working Paper 12/08.

Lavoie, M., 1996. Monetary Policy in an Economy with Endogenous Credit Money, in E. Nell and G. Deleplace (eds.), *Money in Motion*. London: Macmillan, pp. 532–545.

Lavoie, M., 1999. Fair Rates of Interest and Post-Keynesian Economics: The Canadian Case. Paper presented at the University of Bourgogne.

Lavoie, M., 2006. *Introduction to Post-Keynesian Economics*. Houndmills: Palgrave Macmillan.

Lavoie, M. and M. Seccareccia, 2017. Understanding the Great Recession: Some Fundamental Keynesian and Post-Keynesian Insights, with an Analysis of Possible Mechanisms to Achieve a Sustained Recovery. Institute of New Economic Thinking Working Paper No. 37.

Miles, D., 2012. *Asset Prices, Saving and the Wider Effects of Monetary Policy*. Speech at Manchester Business Conference, 1 March.

Moore, B. J., 1989. The Endogeneity of Credit Money. *Review of Political Economy* 1(1): 65–93.

Nakajima, M., 2015. *The Redistributive Consequences of Monetary Policy*. Federal Reserve Bank of Philadelphia Research Department, Second Quarter.

Onaran, O. and G. Galanis, 2014. Income Distribution and Growth: A Global Model. *Environment and Planning A*, 46(10): 2489–2513.

Organization for Economic Cooperation and Development (OECD), 2011. *Divided We Stand: Why Inequality Keeps Rising*. Paris: OECD Publishing.

Palley, T. I., 1994. Debt, Aggregate Demand, and the Business Cycle: An Analysis in the Spirit of Kaldor and Minsky. *Journal of Post Keynesian Economics*, 16(3): 371–390.

Palley, T. I., 2002. Economic Contradictions coming Home to Roost? Does the U.S. Economy face long-term Aggregate Demand Generation problem? *Journal of Post Keynesian Economics*, 25(1): 9–32.

Palma, J. G., 2011. Homogeneous Middles vs. Heterogeneous Tails, and the End of the 'Inverted-U': It's All About the Share of the Rich. *Development and Change*, 42: 87–153.

Parfit, D., 1997. Equality or Priority? *Ratio (New Series)*, X3: 202–221.

Piketty, T., 2014. *Capital in the Twenty-First Century*. Cambridge, MA: Harvard University Press.

Piketty, T. and E. Saez, 2003. Income Inequality in the United States, 1913–1998. *Quarterly Journal of Economics*, 118(1): 1–39.

Piketty, T. and E. Saez, 2014. Inequality in the Long-Run. *Science*, 344: 838–843.

Rawls, J., 1999. *A Theory of Justice*. Revised ed. Cambridge, MA: Belknap Press of Harvard University Press.

Rochon, L-P. and M. Setterfield, 2007. Interest Rates, Income Distribution and Monetary Dominance: Post-Keynesians and the 'Fair Rate' of Interest. *Journal of Post Keynesian Economics*, 30(1): 13–42.

Rochon, L-P. and M. Setterfield, 2011. Post Keynesian Interest Rate Rules and Macroeconomic Performance: A Comparative Evaluation, in C. Gnos and L-P. Rochon (eds.), *Credit, Money and Macroeconomic Policy*, Cheltenham: Edward Elgar, Chapter 7.

Seccareccia, M. and M. Lavoie, 2004. Long-Term Interest Rates, Liquidity Preference and the Limits of Central Banking, in M. Lavoie and M. Seccareccia (eds.), *Central Banking in the Modern World: Alternative Perspectives*. Cheltenham: Edward Elgar, pp. 164–182.

Sen, A., 1992. *Inequality Re-examined*. New York: Russell Sage Foundation.

Smithin, J. N., 1996. *Macroeconomic Policy and the Future of Capitalism: The Revenge of the Rentiers and the Threat to Prosperity*. Cheltenham: Edward Elgar.

Sraffa, P., 1960. *Production of Commodities by Means of Commodities*. Cambridge: Cambridge University Press.

Stiglitz, J., 2011. Rethinking Macroeconomics: What Failed, and How to Repair it. *Journal of the European Economic Association*, 9(4): 591–645.

Stiglitz, J., 2012. *The Price of Inequality*. London: Penguin Books.

Stockhammer, E., 2004. Financialisation and the Slowdown of Accumulation. *Cambridge Journal of Economics*, 28(5): 719–741.

Stockhammer, E., 2010. Neoliberalism, Income Distribution and the Causes of the Crisis. Research on Money and Finance Discussion Papers No. 19.

Stockhammer, E., 2012. Financialization, Income Distribution and the Crisis. *Investigación Económica*, LXXI(279), 39–70. Available at: www.redalyc.org/articulo.oa?id=60123307003, (accessed 20 June 2020).

Taylor, J. B., 2009. *Getting Off Track: How Government Actions and Interventions Caused, Prolonged, and Worsened the Financial Crisis*. Stanford, CA: Hoover Institution Press.

van Treeck, T. and S. Sturn, 2012. Income Inequality as a Cause of the Great Recession? A Survey of Current Debates. ILO Conditions of Work and Employment Series No. 39.

World Inequality Report (WIR), 2018. *World Income Database*. Available at: http://wir2018.wid.world/files/download/wir2018-full-report-english.pdf, (accessed 1 March 2018).

Yellen, J., 2014. *Perspectives on Inequality and Opportunity from the Survey of Consumer Finances*. Speech at Conference on Economic Opportunity and Inequality, Federal Reserve Bank of Boston, Boston, MA, 17 October.

9 Getting the Financial Crisis wrong

The dead end that is Neoclassical macro modeling

John T. Harvey

Introduction

Nobel Laureate Paul Krugman famously explained in a 2009 *New York Times* column why he thought economists "got it so wrong" when it came to the 2008 Financial Crisis (Krugman 2009). There, he writes:

> During the golden years, financial economists came to believe that markets were inherently stable—indeed, that stocks and other assets were always priced just right. There was nothing in the prevailing models suggesting the possibility of the kind of collapse that happened last year.
>
> (Krugman 2009)

This was, according to Krugman, "the result of mistaking beauty for truth." One of our most recent Nobels goes much further, arguing that, "In the last three decades, the methods and conclusions of macroeconomics have deteriorated to the point that much of the work in this area no longer qualifies as scientific research" (Romer 2016: 1). The state of Neoclassical macroeconomics is so abysmal that even their own PhD students avoid it:

> In the interviews, macro received highly negative marks across schools. A typical comment was the following: "The general perspective of the micro students is that the macro courses are pretty worthless, and we don't see why we have to do it, because we don't see what is taught as a plausible description of the economy. It's not that macroeconomic questions are inherently uninteresting; it is just that the models presented in the courses are not up to the job of explaining what is happening. There's just a lot of math, and we can't see the purpose of it."
>
> (Colander 2005: 180)

The consequence of this is not simply that fewer Neoclassical economists are specializing in macroeconomics—that is probably a good thing. Much worse, theory determines policy and the policy informed by these fatally flawed macro models has brought us concepts like austerity, deregulation, and right-to-work laws. It has contributed materially to both the destruction of our environment and the worldwide return to nationalism, tribalism, and fascism. It is creating poverty and tragedy at a time when the basic economic problem has been solved for decades.

The only thing wrong with the reservations expressed by Krugman, Romer, and the economics PhD students is that they do not go far enough. In their estimation, reform is sufficient. They believe that we can keep the Neoclassical core and simply tweak things here and there. However, as I am sure the readers of this volume would agree, the truth is that the problems are so deeply seated that we have no choice but to look beyond the mainstream.

This chapter will argue just that. The things that make Neoclassicism "Neoclassical"—including but not limited to general equilibrium modeling, risk and rationality assumptions, and Friedman's positivism—all condemn their analyses to irrelevance even before pen is put to paper. These mean that not only is it impossible for them to include a remotely realistic financial sector, but when even they can see that they have fallen short they lack a methodology that provides a roadmap to redemption. Tragically, while well-founded and realistic models that eschew those foundational elements already exist—as we see annually at Association for Heterodox Economics (AHE) conferences—these are ignored.

The chapter will proceed as follows. In the next section, the manner in which its foundational elements make it impossible for Neoclassicism to explain macroeconomic fluctuations is explained. There is also mention of viable alternatives. The role of the AHE in developing a parallel literature is then briefly reviewed. Concluding comments follow.

What's wrong with Neoclassical macro?

In answer to the title of this section, many things. But for purposes of this discussion I will limit them to three: general equilibrium modeling, risk and rationality, and Friedman's positivism. The first two render it impossible to include a realistic financial market and the third means that Neoclassical economists lack a useful guide to how to proceed when models fail.

Beginning with the first, even first-year economics students understand the concept of equilibrium, if only in its graphical form. It involves specifying the relevant relationships in equation form and then solving for the unknowns. Hence, we model the behavior of households and firms to discover the equilibrium price and quantity; or the behavior of businesses and labor-market participants to discover the equilibrium wage and level of employment; or the behavior of landlords and families to discover the equilibrium rent and quantity of apartments; and so on. Naturally these become more sophisticated as we move from undergraduate to graduate to professional economist, but the basic concepts are still the same: a set of simultaneous equations is solved to determine its properties in equilibrium. Even dynamic stochastic general equilibrium models, despite their fancy name, are essentially the same.

Unfortunately, regardless of how complex you make the system or how well specified the individual equations are, you necessarily capture only snapshots in time. Or, rather, not "in time" at all, for that is what is missing from general equilibrium. There is a reason why it is called solving a set of "simultaneous" equations. Consider the point of equilibrium on a simple market diagram. We know that, at present, price is P_0 and quantity is Q_0, but how did earlier events lead us to this point? Furthermore, how will these circumstances affect future developments? The answer is not at all, for there is no past or present in this model. One could decide to specify a new demand curve, drawing it to the right of the original, which raises both price and quantity; but even with this there is no logical order. An observer looking at both equilibria could not determine which represented the first and which the second. General equilibrium is a timeless world. We make up stories for our classes about the transitions from one point to the next, but regardless of how compelling we make them they remain ad hoc fabrications that are completely independent of the model itself.

Unfortunately, macroeconomics is inherently a story about transitions from one period to the next. The real world is path-dependent. The fact that firms are reaching target levels of capacity today means that they will reduce investment tomorrow. This lowers aggregate profits and leads to recession. The fact that agents are successfully meeting their debt-repayment schedule today induces both them and lenders to increase debt-to-income ratios tomorrow. These events are not random, but causal and connected in time. It is impossible to model this using a method that considers each outcome to be completely independent of every other one.

Nowhere is this more obvious than in the financial sector. Its raison d'être is to connect past to present to future. I wish to purchase something today but pay for it tomorrow; the bank incurs costs today in anticipation of future income; debt incurred in January carries through—net of further borrowing and repayments—to February. However, general equilibrium models cannot track debt levels from one period to the next; they cannot show bankruptcies occurring as incomes fall short of projections; and they cannot take into account the manner in which past events affect (in a very predictable manner) agent confidence.

All this is precisely why they do not bother to try. Since the embarrassment of the Financial Crisis, a great deal has been made over the fact that mainstream models omit banking, finance, and debt. Take for example Joseph Stiglitz's criticisms. Though he is a mainstream economist himself, he is spot on. Their models, he writes, contain:

> no financial markets (who is lending to whom?); no scope accordingly for excess indebtedness (who owes money to whom?) or for deleveraging (who is reducing their indebtedness to whom?); no problem of debt restructuring; no meaningful capital structures (since the single individual is bearing all the risk, it is obvious that nothing can depend on whether

> finance is provided in the form of debt or equity); no role for bankruptcy; no agency problems; no externalities.
>
> (Stiglitz 2011: 598)

University of Pennsylvania Wharton school professor Franklin Allen argues similarly:

> … many economists used mathematical models that failed to account for the critical roles that banks, and other financial institutions play in the economy. "Even a lot of the central banks in the world use these models," Allen said. "That's a large part of the issue. They simply didn't believe the banks were important."
>
> (Wharton School 2009)

Krugman and his co-author, too, make such an admission: "… one might have expected debt to be at the heart of most mainstream macroeconomic models … however, it is quite common to abstract altogether from this feature of the economy" (Eggertsson and Krugman 2012: 1470–1). By "abstract altogether from" they mean "omit."

To their credit, Eggertsson and Krugman try to remedy this situation. However, as argued above, this is futile so long as one continues to operate under the same assumptions and practices. Indeed, because they are so handicapped, their "improvement" involves resorting to a variation of the loanable funds theory:

> Imagine a pure endowment economy in which no aggregate saving or investment is possible, but individuals can lend to or borrow from each other. Suppose, also, that although individuals all receive the same endowments, they differ in their rates of time preference. In that case, "impatient" individuals will borrow from "patient" individuals.
>
> (Eggertsson and Krugman 2012: 1473–4)

In stark contrast to how a modern (or even historical) credit-money financial system actually operates, net savers provide the loanable funds borrowed by net spenders. In the real world, it is not necessary for "impatient" individuals to wait for "patient" individuals. Debt is created at a keystroke and without need for prior savings or deposits—one reason why financial institutions can so quickly raise capital-to-asset ratios to dangerous levels. None of this is possible in Eggertsson and Krugman's new-and-improved approach. Not surprisingly, it is a general equilibrium model (Eggertsson and Krugman 2012: 1473). They were beat before they started.

Let us imagine for a moment that this were not a problem, that Neoclassicism embraced dynamic modeling at least in addition to, if not instead of, general equilibrium. There exists another immovable roadblock: the assumption that agents operate in an environment of risk and that their behavior is marked by (a very narrow definition of) rationality. As is well known, risk implies that all possible futures and their likelihoods are known. Armed with this information, market participants can generate objective mathematical forecasts of the future and take actions based on these. A key takeaway from this is that even in the face of disappointment, agents do not panic. Incorrect forecasts are a result of bad luck, not bad decisions.

For example, say that it was necessary to predict whether an outcome would be 1, 2, or 3. Say further that we know that there is a 45 percent possibility of a "1," a 40 percent possibility of a "2," and a 15 percent possibility of a "3." The rational agent would forecast "1." This is so because despite the fact that there is a better-than-even chance that the outcome will not be "1," it is nevertheless the most likely of the three and therefore the logical choice. When the realized result is "2," agents do not say to themselves, "What the heck was I thinking! Next time I'm picking '2!'" Instead, and assuming no change in the underlying probability distributions, they will once again predict "1"—and they will continue to do so indefinitely. No sudden re-evaluations, panics, or crashes are possible.

Keynes, of course, took issue with such characterizations of the decision-making process. While assuming complete information about future eventualities and their likelihoods makes the math easy and offers a determinate solution to the question "How will agents choose?" it does so by oversimplifying to the point of irrelevance. The real world is uncertain. We only ever know a fraction of the information necessary to make our decisions. In reality,

> human decisions affecting the future, whether personal or political or economic, cannot depend on strict mathematical expectation, since *the basis for making such calculations does not exist* … it is our innate urge to activity which makes the wheels go round, our rational selves choosing between the alternatives as best we are able, calculating where we can, but often falling back for our motive on whim or sentiment or chance.
>
> (Keynes 1936: 163; emphasis added)

People rely on "whim or sentiment or chance" not so much because they are irrational—that would imply that they had sufficient information to make an objective forecast but simply ignored it—but because in an uncertain world it is the only means of reaching the point where we are willing to commit to a course of action.

Now we have a logical and predictable role for waves of optimism and pessimism and for crisis and collapse. In this uncertain world, when things appear to be going well, agents are encouraged and become even more willing to act. Bubbles, which Neoclassicism has struggled to explain, become a logical outcome. Crashes do as well. When a decision turns out poorly, panic can result and lead agents to make the sort of drastic revisions to forecasts that were impossible in the above risk model. Lacking the objective anchor of a complete mathematical expectation, market sentiment can vary over a wide range very quickly and very violently. Throughout all this, agents are affected by others' behavior and may herd. In short, we get the stuff of the real-world financial markets.

Unfortunately, this is not how Neoclassicism models finance (when they bother to do so at all). Nor is this limited to the classroom. Take, for example, the US Federal Reserve's FRB/US model. There, "Equity prices equal the present discounted value of corporate earnings, where the discount rate equals the expected real yield on 30-year Treasury bonds plus an endogenous equity premium" (Brayton, Laubach, and Reifschneider 2014). In other words, since we are assuming that future outcomes and probability distributions are known and that agents act rationally on this information, we might reasonably build our model assuming that forecasts are always correct. Equities are priced just right in the sense that they accurately reflect future issuer earnings (recall Krugman's comments on this above). Little wonder that no central bank had any inkling that a financial crisis was on the horizon. Perhaps even more concerning is the fact that more than enough time had passed for the above-cited model (from 2014) to have been revised. It was not, and today even the popular press concedes that "Central bankers face a crisis of confidence as models fail" (Giles 2017).[1]

How can general equilibrium models assuming risk and rationality explain real-world upturns, downturns, and crises? They are forced to invoke what Paul Romer identifies as "imaginary shocks" to explain fluctuations. It boils down to a sophisticated way of saying "stuff happens." And,

> Once macroeconomists concluded that a macroeconomic aggregate could fluctuate in the absence of any decision by any person, macroeconomists piled on extra imaginary driving forces. The resulting menagerie, together with my suggested names now includes:
>
> * A general type of phlogiston that increases the quantity of consumption goods produced by given inputs
> * An "investment-specific" type of phlogiston that increases the quantity of capital goods produced by given inputs
> * A troll who makes random changes to the wages paid to all workers
> * A gremlin who makes random changes to the price of output
> * Aether, which increases the risk preference of investors
> * Caloric, which makes people want less leisure.
>
> (Romer 2016: 5)

While readers of this volume might take issue with Romer's broader point (i.e., that monetary policy has a significant impact on economic behavior), there is little with which to quibble above.

The begging question becomes, however, if even a Neoclassical Nobel Laureate can see that obvious and glaring problems exist, why is nothing done? This brings us to the third methodological roadblock put up by

Neoclassicism. Here, too, Romer is on target: the issue is the widespread acceptance of Milton Friedman's positivism. In a more reasonable world, Neoclassical macroeconomists would be worried about their obvious failures. They would have retreated after the widespread recognition of the fact that they missed the target and revised their approach. But the standard defense invokes Milton Friedman's (1953) methodological assertion from unnamed authority that "the more significant the theory, the more unrealistic the assumptions" (Romer 2016: 5).

> More recently, "all models are false" seems to have become the universal hand-wave for dismissing any fact that does not conform to a favorite model. The noncommittal relationship with the truth revealed by these methodological evasions and the "less than totally convinced ..." dismissal of fact goes so far beyond post-modern irony that it deserves its own label. I suggest "post-real."
>
> (Romer 2016: 5)

Hence, there is no incentive to do what might actually be fruitful when a model fails, which is to look to real-world phenomena like banking, finance, and the psychology of human decision-making. Instead, they seek another clever, unique, and unrealistic way to erect a model that justifies their preconceptions. The trick is to make it so complex that even journal referees do not bother to check (Romer 2016: 15). It is worth repeating Romer's condemnation from above: "In the last three decades, the methods and conclusions of macroeconomics have deteriorated to the point that much of the work in this area no longer qualifies as scientific research" (Romer 2016: 1).[2]

Macroeconomics and the AHE

Of course, it is not true that, as claimed by Krugman, all economists missed the mark. Far from it, many were raising red flags leading up to the Financial Crisis hit—including those involved with the AHE. Steve Keen, for example, the winner of the Revere Award[3] for having been the economist to have most accurately predicted the Financial Crisis, has been a participant. Nor was his participation unique. Reviewing the programs from every conference from the inaugural meeting (1999) through to just as the crisis was emerging (2008), yields no less than thirty-three presentations dealing directly or indirectly with macroeconomic instability.[4] Given a total of 680 paper presentations over that period, this yields nearly 5 percent. Compare that to the number of papers on the same topic appearing in the *Economic Journal* of the *Royal Economic Society*, the organization that inadvertently created the AHE. There, I could find roughly ten of the 894 articles published, or just over 1 percent. Furthermore, all but one of those assumed that any instabilities were exogenous in origin (reducing the coverage to just over 0.1 percent). There were zero mentions of Minksy, Kalecki, or Marx and only four of Keynes.

In short, the AHE conference has, since 1999, provided an otherwise absent opportunity for the exposition and cross-fertilization of ideas from those economists who are far more concerned with explaining and solving real-world problems than in publishing in the "right" journals. Let us hope that our universe is more rational than appears at present. If so, the AHE will prove to have been on the right side of history.

Conclusion

I give talks to civic groups on occasion and usually focus on issues related to economic theory or the economics discipline. My assumption is that the lay-person can read up on the details of the trade war with China or review Wall Street's analysis of the Fed's latest move, but it takes an economist to explain an economist. Since the passing of the tenth anniversary of the Financial Crisis, my favorite topic has been Neoclassical macro modeling and why it was so unsuccessful in predicting the collapse, where I give some version of what I explained above. I always cringe when I reach the point where I explain that mainstream models rarely include a financial sector. Surely the audience must think that I am lying or just plain ignorant. How on earth can this possibly be true? How could highly educated, well-funded, hard-working, and presumably well-meaning social scientists do such a thing? Fortunately, I speak for free and have not had to face angry crowds demanding refunds.

But, as the readers of this volume know, it is absolutely true. Nor is this, given the deep-seated nature of the reasons why, about to change. If the Financial Crisis was not sufficient, nothing will be. Unfortunately for us, this is totally lost on the lay public who continue to quite naturally assume that the macro models developed by central banks, governments, and scholars at elite universities are based on rational, common-sense principles. Joan Robinson's words ring true here: "The purpose of studying economics is not to acquire a set of ready-made answers to economic questions, but to learn how to avoid being deceived by economists" (Robinson 1978: 75). As we cannot expect every citizen to earn a PhD in economics, it remains one of the key charges of associations like the AHE to be that (mostly) loyal opposition. It is up to us to avoid being deceived by economists.

Notes

1 Although they, like the Neoclassical critics, are missing the mark regarding the source of the problems.

2 Incidentally, I happened to serve with Paul Romer on a panel just before his Nobel and as I was aware of the article cited here, I asked him about it. He said he was roundly criticized for the paper, but not for its substance. Rather, his Neoclassical colleagues were outraged that he would impugn the scholarly contributions of their revered ancestors: Friedman, Lucas, Sargent, etc.

3 See https://rwer.wordpress.com/2010/05/13/keen-roubini-and-baker-win-revere-award-for-economics-2/.

4 I tried to make these determinations conservatively. There was no doubt more. The conference programs can be found here: https://hetecon.net/?page=ahe_conferences.

References

Brayton F., Laubach T., and Reifschneider, D.L. (2014) The FRB/US Model: A tool for macroeconomic policy analysis. *Board of Governors of the Federal Reserve System* (US), April 3.

Colander, D. (2005) The making of an Economist Redux. *Journal of Economic Perspectives* 19(March, 1): 175–98.

Eggertsson, G., and P. Krugman. (2012) Debt, deleveraging, and the liquidity trap: Fisher-Minsky-Koo approach. *The Quarterly Journal of Economics* 127(3): 1469–513.

Giles, C. (2017) Central bankers face a crisis of confidence as models fail. *The Financial Times*, October 11. www.ft.com/content/333b3406-acd5-11e7-beba-5521c713abf4.

Keynes, J.M. (1936) *The General Theory of Employment, Interest and Money*, London: Macmillan.

Krugman, P. (2009) How did economists get it so wrong? *The New York Times*, September 2. www.nytimes.com/2009/09/06/magazine/06Economic-t.html.

Robinson, J. (1978) *Contributions to Modern Economics*, New York: Academic Press.

Romer, P. (2016) The trouble with macroeconomics. *The American Economist* 20(10): 1–20.

Stiglitz, J. (2011) Rethinking macroeconomics: What failed, and how to repair it. *Journal of the European Economic Association* 9(4): 591–645.

Wharton School (2009) Why economists failed to predict the Financial Crisis, *Knowledge@Wharton*, May 13, available at: https://knowledge.wharton.upenn.edu/article/why-economists-failed-to-predict-the-financial-crisis/, accessed October 31, 2019.

Part IV

Development issues and the role of public action

10 Center and periphery in global value chains

An interpretation based on the pioneers of development

Cristina Fróes de Borja Reis and Fernanda Graziella Cardoso

Introduction

In the post-Second World War context, some pioneering authors of Development Economics (Rosenstein-Rodan, Nurkse, Hirschman, Kalecki and Prebisch, among others) placed industrialization as the pathway towards overcoming sub-development, retaking the argument of "nascent industry" from List (1856). Roughly, wealthy countries – the center – were manufactures exporters, while poor countries – the periphery – were staple exporters and manufactures importers. After more than a half century, the world vastly changed, so that production progressively became more internationalized in global value chains (GVC), impacting export specialization both in the center and at the periphery. But would the classical center-periphery configuration continue to be valid? Would the industrialization still be the most promising path to promote economic development? If so, what type of industrialization? If it would not, which is the most promising path? These questions are the object of reflection of this chapter.

The expression "center-periphery" has its origins in the idea of the international division of labor, rescued from the theorists of imperialism by Prebisch (2000 [1949]), mediated by the thesis of the long-run tendency towards the deterioration in terms of exchange between primary and manufactured goods. The author concluded that at the periphery the achievement of industrialization was needed in order to avoid the income gap in relation to the center. In the absence of market conditions enabling industrialization, Prebisch and other pioneers believed that a broad and profound State action, as both planner and investor, was necessary. Only in this way would the *Big Push* investment strategy, recommended by Rosenstein-Rodan (1969 [1943]) and maximizing the potential of backward and forward linkages emphasized by Hirschman (1958), be capable of overcoming the vicious cycle of poverty clarified by Nurkse (1957 [1953]), especially the structural heterogeneity between the wages and productivity of the tradable and non-tradable sectors, such as remarked by Furtado (2008 [1975]) and others – key concepts that will be debated throughout this chapter.

Indeed, with the advance of industrialization from the 1950s until the 1970s, the structural heterogeneity was furthered to the degree that industry could not entice a dynamic strong enough to absorb the most abundant factor of some "underdeveloped"[1] regions: labor. As a result, the elevated inequality among regions or among social classes was not confronted, which was the other defining and imprisoning condition of the underdevelopment. In addition, as Furtado (2008 [1975], p. 86) observed in Brazil during that period called developmentalist: "the society modernized before the economy had developed." In fact, despite the advance of the industrial matrix and the supposed modernization, especially the small economic elite's emulation of consumption standards from developed countries, the inequalities have grown.

Later, the uneven societies from the periphery would have to deal with a new blow: the debt crisis of the 1980s. On the other hand, at that time the international flow of capital, goods and services brought deep transformations in the international division of labor. Led by multinational companies, production has become geographically fragmented around the world not just through exports, licensing or direct investments (Dunning, 2001), but also through more flexible forms of contracts that ruled movements of outsourcing, modularization, relocation and different types of services from third parties. This productive and trade network of players and countries were named, in the present century, global value chains,[2] which currently account for more than 70 percent of global exports (OECD, 2018).

Taking this context, the chapter seeks to identify how current some of the lessons are about economic development possibilities associated with industrialization suggested by Development Economics pioneers. Such intent helps to interpret the insertion of periphery countries into the GVC's consequences, culminating, potentially, in a renewed conception of what is center and periphery in the twenty-first century.

The chapter is divided in two sections, in addition to the introduction and the conclusions. The first section discusses the history of Development Economics ideas, recognizing some of the main contributions from a couple of selected pioneering authors. The second section returns to the center-periphery concept, reconciling it with the new context of GVC, from the structuralist approach, based on some variables shown by modern map visualization resources from macroeconomic databases. The conclusions summarize the main findings of the chapter.

Classical development: Industry as protagonist

In this section, we bring back some central concepts for classical development theory, which in our view was based on three pillars: center-periphery relations, industrialist strategy, and direct intervention of the State as planner and investor.

Established in order to address the socioeconomic-specific problems faced by underdeveloped nations, Development Economics gained form and expression after the Second World War, in the Cold War context. To a certain extent, this literature had more of a reformation character – especially due to the influence of Keynes' thoughts – rather than a revolutionary one. In general, in addition to showing the particularities of the underdeveloped nations, this theory's pioneers proposed some development strategies. Here we discuss some main definitions and conclusions on development from Rosenstein-Rodan, Nurkse, Hirschman, Kalecki and Prebisch, whose work contemplates the elements that characterize the basis of developmentalist thinking.[3] Among so many other questions, these pioneers helped to understand why obedience to the Ricardian comparative advantages theory would not be an adequate choice for underdeveloped countries; why industrialization would not occur spontaneously; and why underdevelopment and its underlying poverty have a retroactive tendency. Or, in other words, why underdevelopment was a historical trap (Furtado, 1992) that, therefore, demanded a specific overcoming strategy.

Rosenstein-Rodan (1969 [1943]) emphasized the need to promote industrialization for overcoming underdevelopment. Industrialization, as related to greater levels of productivity, would be essential for the dissolution of a generalized characteristic of underdeveloped nations: the existence of low-paid disguised unemployment. In order to industrialize, it became necessary to confront the great initial difficulty related to the circular causation between income and industrialization. This means that industrialization tends to develop more where there is greater availability of income, generating industrial concentration and reinforcing the initial condition of structural heterogeneity inside a nation.

In order to reverse this tendency, Rosenstein-Rodan (1969 [1943]) recommended the planning for large-scale industrialization with investments necessarily coordinated by the State. The State planning of large-scale industrialization would guarantee a political, economic and social balance among diverse sectors during the process of change, leading to block transformation. The crucial areas for planning would relate to labor training and investment promotion, seeking to take the best advantages from positive technological externalities.[4] Thus, the effects of positive productive chain linkages could be intensified, allowing the formation of a big push, necessary to trigger the development process. When the industrialization process matures, the nations that were previously underdeveloped will participate in the international division of labor more virtuously.

From a similar thinking stream, Nurkse (1957 [1953]) suggests that balanced growth strategies should be conceived in world terms. In the author's opinion, the underdeveloped nations should diversify their exports in the direction of manufactures in parallel to developing their internal market. The industrialization strategy would be fundamental to overcome what Nurkse defined as the vicious cycle of poverty, whose circular relationship complicates capital formation. In underdeveloped countries, there is little capital available because the income level is very low, due to low salaries and productivity.

Under this circumstance, continues Nurkse, the process of productive transformation should be planned. The State, in addition to directly capturing and allocating resources, should provide institutional guarantees and incentive policies for the society to work to overcome the vicious cycle of poverty. Moreover, the State should be aware of the adverse effects from the increasing demand for luxury goods that comes with the modernization process due to the demonstration effect – that is, the emulation of consumer patterns of higher-income countries. Its consequence could be the growing pressure for importing these goods and/or the concentration of investments in those goods' productive industries. In the first case, the multiplier effects from industrialization would be transferred abroad; in the second case, unbalanced industrial growth would reduce the potential for structural change (Nurkse, 1957 [1953].

Hirschman (1958) emphasizes some specific effects – the backward and forward linkages – allowed by productive investments in industrial sectors, inspired by the Canadian staple theory (Innis, 1933). The author affirms that the change – and imbalances – triggered by the industrialization process may generate positive development effects. In Hirschman's approach, investment constitutes the key variable needed to overcome the difficulties confronted by underdeveloped nations, following a dynamic which, in every new investment wave in certain manufacturing or other sectors, would enjoy the advantages of linkages generated by the previous wave, in its turn creating new external economies to be profited by more sectors. According to the author, the lack of interdependence and linkages between the sectors of the national economic system is precisely a typical characteristic of underdeveloped nations. In general, their economies were based mainly on agriculture, especially sustenance agriculture, characterized by rare (or weak) linkage effects. He thinks that promoting the industrialist strategy in that context would improve the productive structure complexity, potentially generating backward and forward linkages (Hirschman, 1958). As a result, the economy's multiplier effect increases, fostering the effective demand principle developed by Keynes (1985 [1936]) and Kalecki (1985 [1939]) some years before.

However, Kalecki (1980 [1968]) clarified that the abnormality of unemployment and underemployment in underdeveloped countries was more related to the productive capacity's limitation than to effective demand insufficiency. In particular, the author points out the basic necessities (food) supply bottlenecks, whereby any increase in available jobs would imply inflation in food prices. Therefore, to avoid inflationary pressures, expansion in agricultural productivity was also required for a successful industrialist strategy. Otherwise, the initial condition of structural heterogeneity would remain. Thus, for Kalecki, the crucial problem of underdeveloped nations is productive capacity, so investment is important not only to increase effective demand, but more importantly to improve supply conditions.

In sum, according to Kalecki, there would be, in the meantime, at least three obstacles to the increasing of investments: the low volume of private investment, which might be not enough to achieve a desirable economic development rate; the lack of available resources to produce capital goods; and even if the first two issues were resolved, the just-mentioned inflationary pressures, related to an inadequate supply of primary goods for the additional demand generated by employment growth. Thus, and likewise the Latin-American structuralists, Kalecki highlights the need for promoting agricultural reform in order to rationalize agricultural production. Moreover, for confronting the numerous obstacles to the industrialization process, planning the volume and the investment structure are desirable, seeking a relative balance among the productive sectors. Then, the author recommends governmental intervention either through direct investment or through planning.

Prebisch (2000 [1949]) focuses his critiques towards the comparative advantage's theory, according to which the fruits of technical progress would tend to be equally distributed among the nations participating in international trade. For this rationale, it is more efficient for some nations relatively abundant in land/natural resources to specialize in the production of primary goods, not needing to or should not industrialize. However, Prebisch believed that center-periphery relationships prevailed, so that in the center the economic cycles are triggered by technological progress, while the periphery has to absorb the effects of technological progress and economic growth from the center.

The development strategy recommended by Prebisch – and by other structuralists from the Economic Commission for Latin America and the Caribbean (ECLAC, established by the United Nations after the Second World War) – was to transform the productive structure, modernizing it through industrialization, escaping from the deterioration in terms of trade that would adversely impact the primary exports from the periphery. Given the continuous technical progress in the center, the deterioration in terms of trade would be an inevitable and irreversible trend. The deterioration comes from the difference between primary and manufactured goods income elasticities: the first low, and the second high. Thus, maintaining the traditional international division of labor between primary export periphery nations and manufactures export central nations would strengthen the income gap between nations.

According to Prebisch (2000 [1963], p. 455), "the proof of the dynamic robustness of a system lies in its ability to bring velocity to the development rate and to progressively improve the income distribution." For this goal, structural changes would be essential, fighting some privileges, like the luxury goods consumption by the highest income earners, and the land tenure regime concentration.

For Prebisch (2000 [1963]), like Kalecki affirmed, the production and productivity gains in the primary sector should be better retained in the internal market, rebalancing the income distribution between the urban and the rural sides of a nation. Both in terms of investment planning and income/wealth redistribution, the State plays the crucial role of developer and executor.

However, in order to achieve satisfactory improvements in the living standard of the people, in addition to the productive structure transformation, a profound social (and State) transformation is required. Otherwise, the benefits of structural change would be the usufruct of the elites, perpetuating and even accentuating existing inequalities and disparities.

In his vast contribution to the Development Economics' literature, Celso Furtado discusses how, in each technological–industrial paradigm from the center, the external insertion of periphery States led them to a development-averse historical path. In this sense, Furtado (1974) highlights some key development barriers: (i) wealth and income concentration – so that the interests of the elites from the center economies prevail in all political spheres, including the international trade; (ii) labor exploitation in the peripheral countries – so that any or a small part of the additional surplus from trade is appropriated by local elites; (iii) the orientation of the industrialization process to attend the elites – so that real wage levels are kept low; (iv) the rising cost of the technology required to upgrade local production in order to imitate consumption standards from center countries, which facilitates the penetration of transnational corporations (TNCs) into the domestic markets; (v) the need to cope with the rising costs of domestic production in foreign currency, paving the way for a less complex export profile (essentially primary, in the author's context); and (vi) macroeconomic imbalances related to the exchange rate volatility and the external constraints of the balance of payments.

Thus, to promote structural change in the production matrix from the insertion into the world system, some institutional mechanisms should be implemented to avoid those barriers suggested by Furtado and to promote equality. He also underlines the need for formidable agricultural modernization, which includes deep and extensive land reform and de-concentration. Agriculture modernization for Furtado means a complex process that transforms social structures in the countryside in geographical, demographic, and cultural terms. This would allow for productivity and profitability increase in subsistence agriculture, improving the domestic food supply and the participation of small and medium-sized farms in exports.

Similarly, there should be conditions in place so that the political and institutional arrangement can become more democratic and prevent rent-seeking behavior: first, to increase the workers' bargaining power and enlarge the wage share in the surplus; and, second, to make sure that profits (in the exporting sectors, in particular, but also in the rest of the economy) are going to be reinvested in the diversification and sophistication of economic activities, promoting competition and de-concentrating markets – improving the pattern of "*desarollo hacia dentro*."

Having made a brief synthesis of some thoughts from the structuralist approach, we highlight the following conclusions: despite the differences and even possible incompatibilities, the elements discussed by the pioneers point to the need for structural change and reforms – related to various areas, especially those with distributive impacts – and for State planning. Finally, for the pioneers, without the promotion of industrialization and its expected outcome (although not guaranteed) of a more complex productive structure, implying a better multiplier effect on income and employment, the periphery would be doomed to the historical underdevelopment historical trap, with unequal income/wealth distribution. Despite its theoretical and ideological problems, as commented on in the pages ahead, import substitution industrialization in the second half of the twentieth century became an economic policy guideline for the development strategy, especially carried out by Brazil and other Latin-American countries as an alternative to maintaining their old roles in the classic international division of labor.

The new center and periphery division in the context of global value chains

What is center and what is periphery in the twenty-first century? Judging by per capita income criteria, the current interstate distribution is not very different from the time of the pioneers or from the end of the 1970s, when the financial and productive globalization led by large TNCs from developed countries began, consolidating the international financial system based on the flexible dollar (Serrano, 2002).

Taking the Gross Domestic Product (GDP) per capita in purchasing power parity (PPP), according to the International Monetary Fund (IMF), a clear division between "North/South" is still evident. As seen in Figure 10.1, despite the general increase in GDP from 1980 to 2016, the wealthiest economies remain practically the same (GDP above US$25,000 PPP in 2016, or above US$5,000 PPP in 1980): Western and Northern Europe, USA, Canada, Australia, New Zealand, Japan and Saudi Arabia. The periphery of the systems comprises the other countries, the vast majority of the world – from which only the Asian Tigers (Taiwan, Hong Kong, Singapore and South Korea) have leveraged income standards, while only Libya fell from the wealthiest group.

Nevertheless, economic development is a complex process whose success cannot be summed up just by per capita GDP. The debate stimulated by the pioneers about that concept was extended in the following decades, acknowledging – already from the mid-sixties, according to Arndt (1987) – that development goals need to incorporate distributive objectives, in the economic, political and social dimensions. To a certain extent, the structuralist thinkers – Prebisch, Furtado and Kalecki, for example – had realized the non-sufficiency of the industrialist strategy to solve the deep-rooted underdevelopment problems – problems that would cause the early exhaustion of the industrialist strategy itself. As previously explained, without the combination of the base reforms – agricultural, taxation and political – industrialization at the periphery could accentuate two of its main problems: structural heterogeneity and wealth concentration.

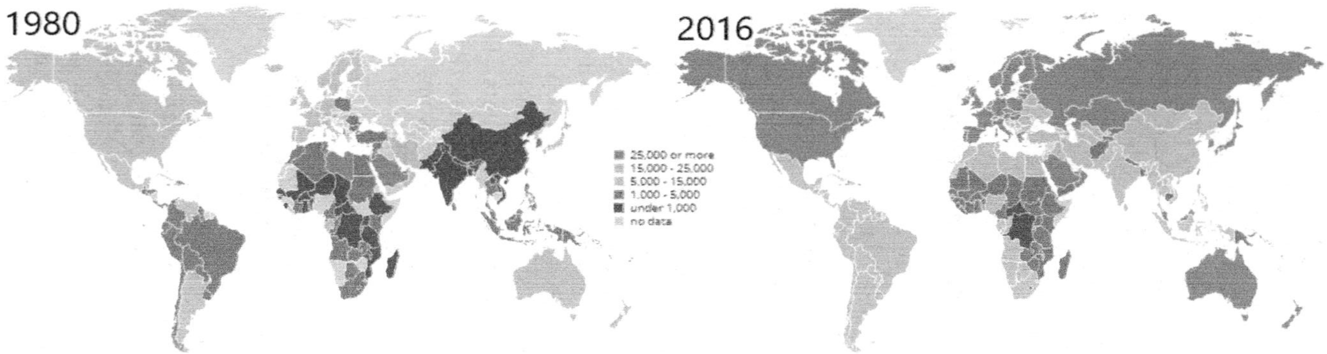

Figure 10.1 Maps of per capita Gross Domestic Product, in purchasing power parity, averages in 1980 and 2016.

Source: IMF, World Economic Outlook, Datamapper: www.imf.org/external/datamapper/PPPPC@WEO/OEMDC/ADVEC/WEOWORLD/CHN?year=1980 www.imf.org/external/datamapper/PPPPC@WEO/OEMDC/ADVEC/WEOWORLD/CHN?year=2016

In Latin America, the intuition of the pioneers revealed itself to be correct: due to the absence of reforms and a deep process of structural change during the industrialization process, a remarkable imbalance in domestic income distribution remained beside the permanence of a big income gap in relation to the center. Thus, in 2016, according to World Bank Data, almost the totality of the world's extreme poverty (measured by daily income less than $1.90 a day) was located in the countries that do not belong to the highest per capita GDP country group. Especially in some countries of sub-Saharan Africa, the extremely poor were around 50 percent of the population.

In spite of the permanence of brutal income inequality among countries, since the 1980s, the market, production and finance patterns have experienced a profound transformation triggered, on the one hand, by new forms of company internationalization, and on the other by the restructuring of geopolitical relations after the end of the Cold War, with the rise of Asian economies, especially Japan, China and Korea. In this context, the progressive fragmentation of the productive chain led by TNCs of advanced countries involved the transfer of a series of chain activities and tasks, not only productive stages, to underdeveloped countries.

The different engagements into GVC since the 1980s, framed by the new information and telecommunication technological paradigms (Perez, 2002), were associated to the industrial and financial globalization processes that reformulated the productive specialization in both the periphery and the center. Less than half of the countries with the highest share of manufactures of the total merchandises exported in 2016,[5] seen in Figure 10.2, were on the map in 1980 – when the traditional center/periphery division was starting to change. However, in the group of 2016 there are many countries with low- or medium-income levels. Even if the share of high-technology manufactures of total manufactures exports are considered, expressive contrasts in the income level between the countries from center and periphery still persist, according to World Bank Data.

Comparing GDP per capita and the share of manufactures in exports, we identify countries playing both in the manufacturing and primary goods markets. There are periphery countries that export manufactured goods, but they are still far from achieving the income level that exists in the center. Similarly, many center States export primary goods, like the USA or Norway. In addition, the services exports should also be taken into account. They have become more important in terms of size and relevance (around one-quarter of total exports of goods and services, according to WTO data), accounting for some of the highest added value in the other sectors' productive chains.

In this sense, Rodrik (2006) highlights the importance of what is exported so as to understand the economic development of a country. For analyzing the relationship between the trade profile and the development path, Hidalgo and Hausmann (2009) suggest the index of economic complexity. The index combines the diversification criteria (quantity of products exported by a country) and the ubiquity criteria (quantity of countries that export every

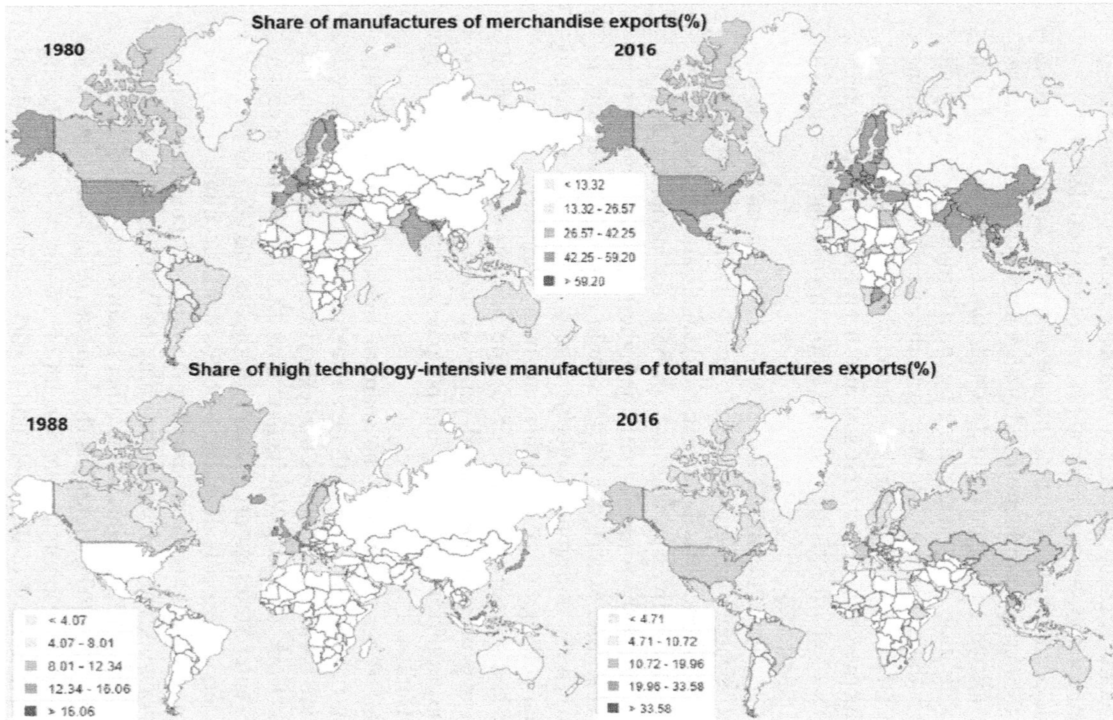

Figure 10.2 Share of manufactures exports of total merchandise exports (above) and share of high-technology manufactures of manufactures exports, in percentage, 1980 and 2016.

Source: World Bank, charts grouped together by the authors. See https://data.worldbank.org/indicator/TX.VAL.MANF.ZS.UN?end=2018&start=1962&view=chart; https://data.worldbank.org/indicator/TX.VAL.MANF.ZS.UN?end=2016&start=1962&view=map; https://data.worldbank.org/indicator/TX.VAL.TECH.MF.ZS?end=2016&start=2007&view=map; https://data.worldbank.org/indicator/TX.VAL.TECH.MF.ZS?end=2016&start=2007&view=map.

product). The economic complexity is higher the less ubiquitous and more diversified the exported products are. Examining the complexity, Hartmann et al. (2017, p. 11) find a "strong and robust correlation" between the countries' productive structures and income inequality: the more complex the first, the lower the inequality. In general, among the more complex products (a list with more than 1000 items) there are high-technology-intensity manufactured goods. The 30 most complex countries have mostly, but not exclusively, high income (the best exception is China, whose exports rapidly acquired more complexity in the last three decades, but the income levels are still low). Also, there are wealthy countries that are not at the top of the list – mainly because of the ubiquity factor: Norway, United Arab Emirates and Australia. Nonetheless, the 70 least complex countries of the ranking have low income, which reinforces the argument on the importance of industrialization for economic development.

The point is that to overcome structural heterogeneity between high-productivity tradable and low productivity non-tradable sectors, public policies and or institutional reforms are needed – with regard to property rights, the macroeconomic regime, the industrial policies etc. – as Kalecki and the Latin-American structuralists have asserted.

As Figure 10.3 illustrates, in 2016, except for Argentina, most countries with high average value-added per worker in agriculture (a proxy for labor productivity) also have high income per capita. So, we claim that this variable continues to symbolize the center/periphery division. More than simply increasing productivity, what distinguishes developing from developed countries is the modernization in agriculture (Senghaas, 1985), understood as a complex process that changes the social structures related to geographic, institutional and demographic-specific contexts – integrating the economy and reducing the inter-sectorial inequalities.

Retaking the structuralist argument, the agricultural productivity increment of overall economy – not only in the staple production – is a necessary condition for economic development. But it is not sufficient because it should be accompanied by structural change towards more complex activities of the internal economy. Likewise, trade complexity, in the direction of manufacturing products of higher technology-intensity, seems to be a necessary condition for development, but not sufficient. As Gala, Rocha and Magacho (2018) interpreted, the more sophisticated the productive industrial tissue, the greater the workers' knowledge and qualifications, probably lifting the wage levels and working conditions. However, this hypothesis may not hold in the realm of imperfect goods and labor markets, with uneven distribution of power in favor of big companies, which gives them means to keep high profit margins and low wage shares in the surplus.

Moreover, the economic complexity indexes are not precise enough to evaluate the consequences of trade specialization for development. First because the index deals with gross data, nothing is said about the foreign origin added value in exports. Second, the index is all about merchandise, not

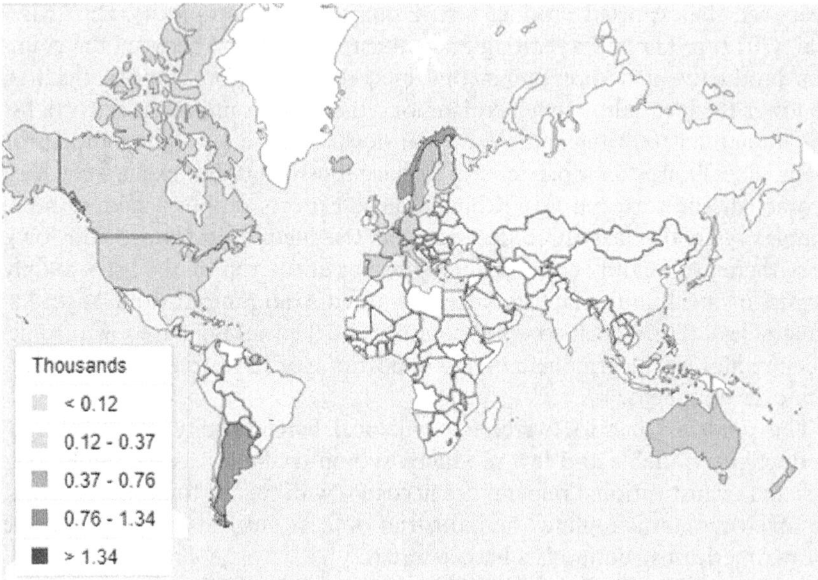

Figure 10.3 Value-added per worker in agriculture, 2016 (US$ 2010).
Source: World Bank. See https://data.worldbank.org/indicator/NV.AGR.EMPL.KD?end=2016&start=1991&view=map.

available for tradable services. And third, the index is only for the trade profile, not for the production profile, preventing the analysis of its correlation, as well as of the mechanisms by which the foreign insertion affects, and is affected by, the productive structural changes.

Table 10.1 shows the share of foreign value-added in gross exports (backward GVC index) of some selected countries in 1995 and 2016, the last year available at TiVA (OECD/WTO, 2013). As a general trend, the index has grown in the last two decades, although it reached its peak in the first years of the 2010s. However, there is no one rule regarding the relationship between the indexes and economic development. The different sizes of the economies, their different trade specializations and schemes of regional interaction confer on each case an authentic character of GVC integration. There are big economies with low backward indexes, although they are actually integrated to the GVCs, such as the USA. In opposition, countries like Russia and Brazil are also big economies presenting low backward indexes, but are indeed less integrated to GVC. There are others with high indexes related to poor GVC insertion through low value-added activities, such as Philippines. And there are still others with high indexes that are performing high value-added activities in the chain, like Luxembourg or Germany.

Table 10.1 Share of foreign value-added in total gross exports, in %, 1995 and 2016

OECD Members			*OECD Non-members*		
Country	*1995*	*2016*	*Country*	*1995*	*2016*
Australia	12.07	10.05	Argentina	5.74	6.87
Austria	21.44	26.58	Brazil	7.83	10.22
Belgium	31.02	33.85	Brunei	7.28	7.71
Canada	24.38	20.64	Bulgaria	30.04	32.19
Chile	13.88	12.38	Cambodia	12.82	28.56
Czech Republic	30.57	37.67	China	33.88	16.65
Denmark	23.17	28.1	Columbia	8.46	10.07
Estonia	35.97	34.47	Costa Rica	22.07	16
Finland	24.16	25.91	Croatia	20.79	19.17
France	17.31	22.06	Cyprus	20.9	23.61
Germany	14.88	20.26	Hong Kong, China	21.69	24.81
Greece	16.35	21.5	India	9.36	16.13
Hungary	29.87	44.14	Indonesia	12.57	11.32
Iceland	17.38	20.32	Latvia	22.69	7.69
Ireland	38.49	41.67	Lithuania	24.57	36.08
Israel	21.9	17.19	Malaysia	30.5	59.27
Italy	17.24	21.97	Malta	49.99	25.27
Japan	5.61	11.38	Philippines	30.06	23.39
South Korea	22.33	30.37	Romania	21.17	21.63
Luxembourg	41.02	67.4	Russia	13.26	10.23
Mexico	27.34	36.41	Saudi Arabia	4.19	4.91
Netherlands	23.23	27.03	Singapore	42.38	39.45
New Zealand	16.85	12.8	South Africa	13.17	22.54
Norway	19.9	13.7	Taipei	30.72	29.79
Poland	16.11	26.9	Thailand	24.29	32.51
Portugal	27.37	28.03	Tunisia	24.69	29.91
Slovakia	31.93	44.51	Vietnam	21.31	43.6
Slovenia	32.29	31.55	Rest of the world	13.49	10.8
Spain	19.16	21.62			
Sweden	26.29	19.71			
Switzerland	17.62	25.76			
Turkey	8.94	16.53			
United Kingdom	18.25	15.36			
United States	11.46	9.04			

Source: OECD/TiVA.

So, none of those indexes are definitive enough to demonstrate the center/periphery division. But their assessment enables a suggestion for building a structuralist interpretation on the international division of labor between the center and periphery: if before it opposed specialization in, respectively, manufactured goods to primary products, today it separates high added value, let's say sophisticated, from not sophisticated GVC activities specialization. In actual fact, instead of sophistication, the GVC literature works with the notion of upgrading, understood as the economic and social improvement of activities and tasks performed by workers from companies and countries, moving from low added value to relatively high added-value activities that leverage both material working conditions (Barrientos, Gereffi and Rossi, 2011; Barrientos et al., 2011, Reis and Barroso de Souza, 2018).

However, as Milberg and Winkler (2011) affirm, the association between economic and social upgrading in GVCs must be cautious, because it is does not simply happen by the functioning of the market, as is supposed by mainstream theories. For example, spillover and multiplier effects are not automatic, especially considering that the productivity gains in a chain might be captured by the leading companies – as the pioneers had also asserted, especially so of Furtado (1974). As discussed in the first section, the bridge between commercial and productive structures relies on institutional and structural pillars. Roughly, the development literature's main structural determinants are initial endowments, linkages, sunk costs and technology. The main institutions' determinants are the class struggles, property rights, education, culture, the State and its policies – especially, the macroeconomic regime, industrial, commercial and technological policies.

The Development Economics pioneers affirmed that in order to develop, poor countries needed to build productive capacity and to expand the aggregate demand, for example, public spending or indebtedness, funding for private investment and consumption, or a new push coming from the external demand (both due to increasing liquidity in world markets or to a new export market for underdeveloped economies). In particular, some of the ideas of those authors can be adapted to identify a couple of aspects that influence how the GVC insertion impacts the periphery's development: (a) income and wealth inequalities, particularly in rural areas; (b) the characteristics of the commodities markets; (c) the intensity of the linkage effects on the main tradable sectors; (d) the reinvestment of primary exports revenues; (e) the macroeconomic regime and external constraints; and, more broadly, (f) the international and national competition for power and wealth, between capitalists (companies) and classes.

The first above-mentioned aspect (a) pertains to the means of production and land appropriation by a privileged minority – oligopolists – in the primary, industrial or service sectors. Their great market power gives them extra political strength, so that their interests are prioritized by public policies. Moreover, in the case of rural inequality, there is also structural heterogeneity, so that modern agro-export production coexists with problems in the supply of goods for basic necessities (food), generating all those negative effects previously discussed.

The aspect (b) occurs when export specialization compromises medium and long-term development due to its decreasing terms of trade in relation to imports. The deterioration in terms of trade, however, is a controversial concept, mainly due to its empirical inconsistency, which may arise when its analyses choose different commodities baskets and/or time periods.

But, considering the entire twentieth century, the deterioration in terms of trade between primary products and manufactured goods is clearly observed, though there have been short cycles of valuation – such as in the 1990s and 2000s (ECLAC, 2007).

Both the unlimited offer of labor and the assumption that the developing countries' production does not affect the commodities prices in world markets, result in low pay, exogenously determined, subsistence wage levels. The periphery economies' income flow depends on the modern tradable sector's investment tax and demand for labor. The multiplier effect of those last variables will determine the gross product, to be distributed among the classes in the form of wages, rents and profits. Notably, the investment tax of the export sector depends on the profit rate of its capitalists and on the increased global demand (Findlay and Lundahl, 2002).

The fundamental mechanism to elevate the wage level is productivity growth, which depends on the market dynamism of the staple exported. Productivity would tend to be greater if modern tradable sector production were more sophisticated, leading to a positive wage valuation tendency.

Regarding the intensity of the linkage effects (c), Hirschman's theoretical contribution was well incorporated in the recent material-space works from Sociology and Geography. The space and material characteristics are key parameters for technological progress, and for markets evolution, shaping the (geo)political forces, too (Bunker and Cicantell, 2005). The transformation from a less complex specialized economy to a diversified, not ubiquitous, and sophisticated economy is related to innovations' creation and diffusion in those industries that implement new productive processes capable of increasing productivity, linkage effects and learnerships that dynamize the rest of the productive structure. Nonetheless, for the diversification to generate upgrading, there might be significant linkage effects between suppliers (upstream) and buyers (downstream) across value chains (Doner, 2009). But if the industries, both from upstream or downstream, are oligopolies or protected by market barriers, their asymmetric power may prevent the full spread of linkage effects.

With regard to (d) the exports' revenues constitute a crucial resource for the reduction of external constraints in developing countries' balance of payments, according to Prebisch (2000 [1949]), Furtado (1974) and Tavares (1972). The productive and trade specializations bring foreign currencies that, when the macroeconomic regime is appropriate, provide additional income to the government and self-finance capital to the companies in the tradable sectors (Ocampo and Parra, 2006). If the income from taxes upon these tradable sectors is reversed into efficient and qualified public consumption and investment, and/or if the profits are reinvested in higher value-added industries and services, the export sector fosters structural change in the economy, which potentially might sustain the development process in the long run. Nonetheless, this virtuous development cycle depends on the property rights system of the society, the market regulations, the institutions' ability to alleviate power inequalities between capitalists and workers and, in consequence, the degree of democracy in the society.

The macroeconomic regime and the external constraint (e) can limit development, as warned by the pioneers and their critics, such as Tavares (1972, 1985). Virtuous structural transformation depends on macroeconomic coherence: alignment between fiscal/monetary policies and development's social objectives (Biancarelli and Rossi, 2014), ensuring a competitive real exchange rate, capital control, long-term investment funding, energy and food security, technology transfer etc. As ECLAC (2014) summarizes, the macroeconomics for development must have an integrated approach that prioritizes productive change and improves social capacities and opportunities, considering the growth's cycle and the long-term trend. Therefore, the State continues to play a fundamental role, as it is responsible for leading the development plan and the structural reforms for achieving the redistribution of productivity gains.

Finally, and considering the previous aspects, (f) the periphery development possibilities from integration into GVC are scarce in international capitalist competition (Fiori, 2004). Otherwise, there would not be such a small number of developed countries, shocking world poverty and its implications such as hunger and thirst, and the repaginated center and periphery division in the twenty-first century. The material expansion from the accumulation cycles since the 1950s, which had at its core the external investments of American manufacturing TNCs, the arms' race during the Cold War, and most recently against terrorism,[6] built the new international division of labor. But it has kept its old formula: the deep concentration of property rights regarding land, energy, raw materials and capital, plus labor exploitation and inter-State competition.

Thus, as a general conclusion from this section, the current center/periphery division separates those countries that generate and benefit more or less from technological progress. The groups of center and periphery countries have hardly changed since the mid-twentieth century. There is still an expressive income difference between the wealthy countries and the others, which coincides, even if not exactly, with the differences in export complexity patterns and with the differences in agriculture productivity. However, in the current GVC context, the mere manufactured/primary product division is not valid when it comes to distinguishing between center and periphery. In addition, it must be acknowledged that this structure benefits minority groups both in the center and periphery, establishing associated dependence relationships that pressure States to defend their interests.

Conclusions

This chapter proposed the reconciliation between the current organization of international production and the lessons of the pioneers of Development Economics. This is relevant when considering that, more than 60 years after their work, the division between wealthy and poor nations still continues, although the international production configuration has significantly changed. At any rate, the international division of labor continues to be essential in understanding the development of nations.

More specifically, the pioneers' theoretical discussion about the mechanisms that make the external insertion virtuous, still possesses appropriated elements to interpret the possibilities of economic development through the insertion in the GVC. In the current center-periphery dynamics, the roles of both center and periphery countries in merchandise and service trade become more diffused, so that their distinction mirrors more the sophistication degree of its chain activities than its sectorial classification (commodities/manufactures/services). Moreover, center and periphery can also be distinguished by the deep agricultural modernization present in the former, which raises wages and mechanization in the rural areas and inflationary effects prevail during the expansive period of the economic cycle.

The elimination of structural heterogeneity at the periphery designates greater chances of success for a productive and trade specialization strategy in terms of inclusive development. However, integration to the GVC does not necessarily increase the productivity of non-tradable sectors, depending on the structural and institutional features of the society, such as the State action (especially, industrial policies and macroeconomic regimes), that shapes the productive structure and its consequences over employment and income in the other sectors of the economy – thus impacting class relations and wealth and power distribution.

Acknowledgments

This text is the English version of our paper published in Portuguese, at Revista de Economia Contemporanea (Cardoso and Reis, 2018). The research leading to these results has received funding partly from the Coordenação de Aperfeiçoamento de Pessoal de Nível Superior – Brasil (CAPES) – Finance Code 001 and partly from the People Programme (Marie Curie Actions) of the European Union's Seventh Framework Programme (FP7/2007-2013) under REA grant agreement no. 600209 (TU Berlin – IPODI).

Notes

1 Term used by the pioneers instead of "backward" economies, so that both were later replaced by "developing" economies. As criticize some authors in defense of South epistemologies, the concept of development was always Eurocentric and must be reconsidered in order to mirror the local values and needs (Santos, 2006; Reis, Barbosa and Cardoso, 2019).

2 As became famous due to the Global Value Chain Initiative (GVCI, 2018).

3 Other pioneer authors also contributed significantly to the developmentalist thought, but for the sake of scope and space, we have selected just a couple of fundamental ideas related to countries' insertion in the international division of labor. For learning more about the pioneers, see Cardoso (2018).

4 Technological externalities happen when the production function of one firm is affected by the production function of other firms, so that positive economies arise from specialized work formation and complementary investments that generates a higher rate of return than from isolated investments.

5 Countries that presented manufactures share in total exports above 70% in 2016, according to the World Bank: Austria, Belgium, Botswana, Camboja, China, Czech Republic, El Salvador, Germany, India, Ireland, Israel, Italy, Jordan, Korea, Luxembourg, Macedonia, Mexico, Morocco, Pakistan, Palau, Panama, Phillipines, Poland, Portugal, Romenia, Singapore, Slovak, Slovenia, Spain, Sri Lanka, Swede, Switzerlans. Thailand. Tunisia, Turkey, UK and Vietnam (USA 64%).

6 Foster, 2006.

References

Arndt, H.W. (1987). *Economic Development – the History of an Idea*. Chicago, IL/ London: The University of Chicago Press.

Barrientos, S., Gereffi, G. and Rossi, A. (2011). Economic and Social Upgrading in Global Production Networks: A New Paradigm for a Changing World. *International Labour Review*, 150(3–4), pp. 319–40.

Barrientos, S., Mayer, F., Pickles, J. and Posthuma, A. (2011). Decent Work in Global Production Networks: Framing the Policy Debate. *International Labour Review*, 150(4), pp. 299–317.

Biancarelli, A., and Rossi, P. (2014). A política macroeconômica em uma estratégia social-desenvolvimentista. *Revista Brasileira de Planejamento e Orçamento*, 4(1), pp. 21–38.

Bunker, S. and Cicantell, P. (2005). Matter, Space, Time, and Technology: How Local Process Drives Global Systems. In Cicantell, P., Smith, D.A. and Seidman, G. (eds.), *Nature, Raw Materials, and Political Economy*. London: Elsevier.

Cardoso, F.G. (2018). *Nove Clássicos do Desenvolvimento Econômico*. Jundiaí: Paco Editorial.

Cardoso, F.G. and Reis, C.F.B. (2018). Centro e Periferia nas Cadeias Globais de Valor: uma interpretação a partir dos pioneiros do Desenvolvimento. *Revista de Economia Contemporânea*, 22, pp. 1–31.

Doner, R. (2009). *The Politics of Uneven Development: Thailand's Economic Growth in Comparative Perspective*. Cambridge: Cambridge University Press.

Dunning, J. (2001). The Eclectic (OLI) Paradigm of International Production: Past, Present and Future. *International Journal of the Economics of Business*, 8(2), pp. 173–190.

ECLAC. (2007). *Progreso técnico y cambio structural em America Latina*. Documento de proyecto. Economic Commission for Latin America and Caribbean, United Nations.

ECLAC. (2014). *Mudança estrutural para a igualdade: uma visão integrada do desenvolvimento*. Santiago, Chile: United Nations.

Findlay, R. and Lundahl, M. (2002). Resource-Led Growth – A Long-Term Perspective: The Relevance of the 1870–1914 Experience for Today's Developing Economies. *Working Paper*, no. 162, UNU WIDER.

Fiori, J.L. (2004). Formação, expansão e limites do poder global. In Fiori, J.L. (ed.), *O Poder Americano*. Editora Vozes: Petrópolis.

Foster, J.B. (2005). Naked Imperialism. *Monthly Review*, 57(4), p. 1.

Furtado, C. (1974). *O Mito do Desenvolvimento Econômico*. Rio de Janeiro: Paz e Terra.

Furtado, C. (1992). *Brasil – a construção interrompida*. São Paulo: Paz e Terra.

Furtado, C. (2008 [1975]). *Economia do Desenvolvimento – curso ministrado na PUC-SP em 1975. Arquivos Celso Furtado 2*. Rio de Janeiro: Centro Internacional Celso Furtado de Políticas para o Desenvolvimento, Editora Contraponto.

Gala, P., Rocha, I. and Magacho, G. (2018). The Structuralist Revenge: Economic Complexity as an Important Dimension to Evaluate Growth and Development. *Brazilian Journal of Political Economy*, 38(2), pp. 219–236.

Global Value Chain Initiative (GVCI). (2018). Duke University. Available at: https://globalvaluechains.org/about-us (accessed April 2018).

Hartmann, D., Guevara, M.R., Jara-Figueroa, C., Aristarán, M. and Hidalgo, C.A. (2017). Linking Economic Complexity, Institutions, and Income Inequality. *World Development*, 93, pp. 75–93.

Hausmann, R., Hidalgo, C.A., Bustos, S., Chung, M.C.S., Jimenez, J. , Simoes, A. and Yildirim, M.A. (2015). *The Atlas of Economic Complexity – Mapping Paths to Prosperity*. Center for International Development at Harvard University, Harvard Kennedy School, Macro Connections MediaLab, MIT.

Hidalgo, C.A. and Hausmann, R. (2009). The Building Blocks of Economic Complexity. *Proceedings of the National Academy of Sciences*, 106(26), pp. 10570–10575.

Hirschman, A.O. (1958). *The Strategy of Economic Development*. New Haven, CT: Yale University Press.

Innis, H. (1933). *Problems of Staple Production in Canada*. Toronto: The Ryerson Press.

International Monetary Fund (IMF). *Data Mapper*. Available at: www.imf.org/external/datamapper/index.php (accessed February 2020).

Kalecki, M. (1980 [1968]). A diferença entre os problemas econômicos cruciais das economias capitalistas desenvolvidas e subdesenvolvidas. In Miglioli, J. and Fernandes, F. (eds.), *Kalecki. Coleção Grandes Cientistas Sociais*, Editora Ática.

Kalecki, M. (1985 [1939]). *Teoria da dinâmica econômica. Coleção os economistas*, 2nd edition. São Paulo: Editora Nova Cultural.

Keynes, J.M. (1985 [1936]). *A Teoria Geral do Emprego, do Juro e da Moeda. Coleção Os Economistas*, 2nd edition. São Paulo: Editora Nova Cultural.

List, F. (1856). *The National System of Political Economy*. Philadelphia, PA: J.B. Lippincott.

Milberg, W. and Winkler, D. (2011). Economic and Social Upgrading in Global Production Networks: Problems of Theory and Measurement. *International Labour Review*, 150(3–4), pp. 341–365.

Nurkse, R. (1957 [1953]). *Problemas da Formação de Capital em Países Subdesenvolvidos*. Rio de Janeiro: Editora Civilização Brasileira, [1953].

Ocampo, J.A. and Parra, M.A. (2006). The Dual Divergence: Growth Successes and Collapses in the Developing World since 1980. *DESA Working Paper*, no. 24, June.

OECD. (2018). Trade Policy Implications of Global Value Chains. *Trade Policy Brief*. Organization for Economic Cooperation and Development.

OECD/TiVA. *Trade in Value Added*. Available at: http://stats.OCDE.org/Index.aspx?DataSetCode=TIVA_OCDE_WTO (accessed August 2019).

OECD/WTO. (2013). *Interconnected Economies: Benefiting from Global Value Chains*. Preliminary Version. Geneva: Organization for Economic Cooperation and Development, World Trade Organization.

Perez, C. (2002). *Technological Revolutions and Financial Capital*. Cheltenham: Edward Elgar.

Prebisch, R. (2000 [1949]). O desenvolvimento econômico latino-americano e alguns de seus principais problemas. In Bielschowsky, R. (ed.), *Cinquenta anos de pensamento da CEPAL*. Rio de Janeiro: Record, vol. 1.

Prebisch, R. (2000 [1963]). Por uma dinâmica do desenvolvimento latino-americano. In Bielschowsky, R. (ed.), *Cinquenta anos de pensamento da CEPAL*. Rio de Janeiro: Record, vol. 1.

Reis, C.F.B., Barbosa, M.S. and Cardoso, F.G. (2019). The South's Thoughts on Development: Links between Latin America and Africa. *Revista de Economia Mundial*, 52, pp. 191–216.

Reis, C.F.B. and Barroso de Souza, A. (2018). Drawing Value Curves: Lessons from Financial Statements of the World's Biggest Manufacturing Corporations. *Revue d'économie industrielle*, 163, p. 229.

Rodrik, D. (2006). *Industrial Development: Stylized Facts and Policies*. John F. Kennedy School of Government, Harvard University. Available at: ksghome.harvard.edu/~drodrik/industrial%20development.pdf.

Rosenstein-Rodan, P. (1969 [1943]). Problemas de Industrialização da Europa Oriental e Sul-Oriental. In Agarwala, A.N. and Singh, S.P. (eds.), *A Economia do Subdesenvolvimento*. Rio de Janeiro: Cia Editora Forense.

Santos, M. (2006). Por uma epistemologia existencial. In Lemos, A., Silveira, M., and Arroyo, M. (eds.), *Questões territoriais na América Latina*. São Paulo: CLACSO.

Senghaas, D. (1985). *The European Experience – A Historical Critique of Development Theory*. New Hampshire: Berg Publishers.

Serrano, F. (2002). Do ouro imóvel ao dólar flexível. *Economia e Sociedade*, 20.

Tavares, M.C. (1972). *Da substituição de importações ao capitalismo financeiro*. Rio de Janeiro: Zahar.

Tavares, M.C. (1985). *Acumulação de capital e industrialização no Brasil*. Campinas: Editora da Unicamp.

World Bank. *World Development Indicators*. Available at: http://data.worldbank.org/products/data-visualization-tools (accessed February 2020).

11 Models of fair public ownership

Lessons from Singapore and Hong Kong

Andrew Purves

Introduction

So often, the debate about public ownership is based on a narrative that sets the public interest against the private interest. In this debate in Western democracies, one can characterize the period since the Second World War as having been 'a game of two halves'. In Britain during the war, a social democratic narrative emerged, where the interests of society would be put first. This social welfare model was presented in the UK with the publication of the Beveridge Report in 1944, and its main recommendations were introduced during the following three decades. Living standards rose dramatically, and public provision of housing, healthcare, and education became the normal expectation. We 'never had it so good'.[1]

However, this direction was challenged by many, including Margaret Thatcher, British Prime Minister 1979–1991, leading to a reversal of public ownership and provision during the next 40 years, and the victory of the private interest. While this was driven primarily by ideology at least in the UK (see, for example, Hayek, 1944), there was an appetite for change, the 1980s were as much about curtailing the power of the unions as the resurgence of free market principles, and the intended efficiency from competition.

We have now reached an intellectual and philosophical point at which voters are challenging the assumptions of globalization, the dominance of financial interests and multinational companies protected by undemocratic supranational organizations. This is in part a response to a sustained period of rising inequality, and a smaller share of national wealth flowing to labour, but also reflects a desire to rebuild the idea of local community and sharing of resources at a time of environmental stress.

This chapter considers how two jurisdictions took a different path over these years. Hong Kong and Singapore have developed a somewhat unique approach, based on distinctive models of public asset ownership, which has been either missed, misinterpreted or ignored by many economists and social scientists, but is now being rectified (see Phang, 2007; Cullen, 2014; and Haila, 2016). The context for this is the resurgence of interest in the importance of society working together, and the public benefit of recognizing the collective value of public assets, highlighted by Detter and Fölster (2015). Not only do Hong Kong and Singapore offer good examples of efficient use of public assets, but in doing so, these two cities have transformed themselves from colonial backwaters to thriving international centres for trade and services. Their respective GDPs per capita[2] have overtaken that of the UK, their former colonial master. Much of the progress is due to their approach to public asset ownership.

Some dismiss the lessons that can be learned from these two jurisdictions for various reasons: their small size; their reliance on an external hinterland for resources; their authoritarian 'one party' governance. But this would be a mistake. Many of the principles applied in a pragmatic way in Hong Kong and Singapore can be adapted easily for larger, more democratic countries. In the case of Singapore, the idea of giving all people a stake, in the form of property ownership, was advocated as a vital element of nation-building, although, 'ownership' was not absolute, or permanent. In the current climate of public disenchantment with politicians, this could offer a way to re-engage with civic society. There is one caveat – particularly in the case of Hong Kong, the problem of the high price of land has not been avoided, in fact, it could be said that the Hong Kong administration pursues a policy of high property prices, given that so much of their revenue is derived from land values. This problem could be overcome, however, with a proper distinction of what constitutes the public interest in land or property against the private interest.

In this chapter, I will briefly review what we mean by public assets. I will then give examples of public ownership from Hong Kong and Singapore, focusing on land use, housing, state-owned companies, and provision of public transport including airports. The chapter concludes that our discussion of public ownership in Hong Kong and Singapore provides many insights into a model of *fair public ownership*.

What are public assets? What makes public ownership of them fair?

Governments may own assets: it might be to fulfil a public purpose – a government building, for example a parliament or offices to house civil servants; a police service; land for military bases and exercises; a sewage treatment works; a road network or public transport infrastructure – these would generally be built to facilitate the creation of wealth by and for society as a whole. They are often considered to be public assets, as it would be difficult for an individual to build these for himself, and once built they tend to benefit all members of the society. These assets have value, not just for today, but for the future (Detter and Fölster, 2015). A concentration and focus on GDP growth by governments and economists has left a blind spot for policymakers that is beginning to be illuminated (Hamilton and Hepburn, 2016) – public assets are being recognized for their potential to enhance growth, rather than simply being a cost.

There are other, less tangible public assets, more akin to collective services, sometimes referred to as intangible capital (Hamilton and Liu, 2014). Important examples of these are a common language, the rule of law upheld by a network of courts or a national currency issued by a central bank. This chapter will concentrate on the more tangible assets of property and infrastructure.

Some of these assets have always been in public ownership without controversy, but others have come into existence first as private assets, sometimes created by charitable institutions. During the nineteenth or early twentieth century these assets were transferred into public ownership, and in many countries there was a deliberate effort to create facilities for education, health or pension provision for all citizens as a matter of right, under public direction and ownership.

However, in the latter half of the twentieth century, a new direction was forged – the Washington Consensus (Williamson, 1990) – and was promoted around the world. Different governments were more or less zealous about transforming the public into private, depending on the ease with which it could be done, or the political will it could muster to make the change. In some of the privatizations, there was a good deal of artifice involved to introduce the idea of competition, which lay at the heart, and was perhaps the prime motivator, of the process, and gave rise to relatively short-term gains: once a public utility has been sold, it cannot be done so again.

There can be a good deal of interpretation as to what is public or private, for example, natural resources can be considered as public assets, and licence fees collected for their exploitation; or the radio spectrum can be auctioned to the highest bidder; on the other hand, common land used by nomadic peoples for centuries might be usurped and leased to overseas companies (Pearce, 2012).

What is the right model of public ownership? What factors should determine whether an asset is in public or private ownership? Is this simply a matter of economic efficiency? Does the market dictate that all goods and services should be in private ownership? Are there some goods and services which can only be provided to the public as a whole, and therefore by publicly owned agents?

What if there was a different way to imagine public assets, not as tools of ideological correctness, of competition, but as sources of income, an alternative to taxation as a source of public revenue (Burgess, 1993)? Or: as the means by which public services, such as transport, could be delivered cost effectively? Or: as a mechanism to ensure a measure of fairness in the distribution of income and wealth? By addressing such questions, we perhaps begin to discern the outlines of a model of fair public ownership.

Public ownership of land

With these issues in mind, I now turn to the examples of Hong Kong and Singapore to illustrate what might be possible in this new era of debate about what constitutes public assets, and how best to use them. Each, in their different way, has exploited the idea of public assets to the full, and realized their value for the benefit of all. I first give a little history, and recognition, that in these two jurisdictions, perhaps the most significant public asset in this context is land.

Both Hong Kong and Singapore became British colonies during the nineteenth century, and have grown from being the island homes of small fishing villages to two of the most significant cities in Asia. Singapore is independent, while Hong Kong, since 1997, has been a Special Administrative Region (SAR) within the People's Republic of China, with its own administration governed by the Basic Law for 50 years, as agreed between the UK and China when sovereignty was returned to China.

All land in Hong Kong is owned by the government of the Hong Kong special administrative region. It is made available to individuals and companies through a lease of varying length and with certain conditions, in return for an annual rent (Government Rent). There is a long and convoluted history of how this system evolved, which I will not go into here.[3] The guiding principles can be found in articles 6 and 7 of the Basic Law referred to above. It is worth quoting these in full:

- **Article 6**

  The Hong Kong Special Administrative Region shall protect the right of private ownership of property in accordance with law.

- **Article 7**

  The land and natural resources within the Hong Kong Special Administrative Region shall be State property. The Government of the Hong Kong Special Administrative Region shall be responsible for their management, use and development and for their lease or grant to individuals, legal persons or organizations for use or development. The revenues derived therefrom shall be exclusively at the disposal of the government of the Region.[4]

What this means, in principle, is that the revenues derived from the land itself, or its location value,[5] can be used for public revenue. In practice, this is what the leaseholder is prepared to pay at public auction for the right to 'own' the lease. At the same time, the revenues generated by the leaseholder, through whatever activity or investment and development occurs on the land, belong to the leaseholder. The leaseholder's interest and security of tenure is protected in law. As Anne Haila says:

> The land question is not only an economic question concerning the efficient use and management of land as property rights scholars assume, it is also a *moral, social, political and ideological question*. Land can be used

> either for the public good or to maximise rental income, and its use, management and ownership necessitate justification.
>
> (Haila, 2016:219; original emphasis)

In the case of Hong Kong, in the financial year 2016/17, out of total public revenue of HK$498bn land premiums totalled HK$67bn (13 per cent) (Government of Hong Kong, 2016) – made up from a combination of new lease sales as well as lease modification agreements. A new lease sale is an agreement to lease for 30, 50 or perhaps 70 years a particular piece of land, with permission for a particular kind of development, for example a residential apartment block of a certain height, within a certain time period. On the other hand, lease modification premiums are charged in return for a change of use, or to allow redevelopment of a particular piece of land (e.g., from industrial to residential), or for new, higher buildings on an existing leasehold piece of land. Lease modification premiums are paid to the Urban Renewal Authority, after agreement on the new use and development parameters, and payment can be phased over a period of time, or 'in kind', for example by building a new school as part of the new development. In this latter way, the Hong Kong government benefits from the ongoing rise in land values due to population growth or economic development more generally, while the leaseholder can maximise his return on investment in buildings. This distinction, and separation of location value from use value is grounded in insights given by Adam Smith (1986 [1776]), David Ricardo (1973 [1817]) and Henry George et al. (2017 [1879]).

Returning to Hong Kong's General Revenue account, an additional HK$50bn (10 per cent) in 2016/17 came in from Stamp Duties, from the sale and purchase of property. A further HK$20.7bn (4 per cent) came from investment income, including income from the Land Fund held by the Hong Kong Monetary Authority. The Land Fund was established in 1983, when agreement was reached between the UK and China on the return of sovereignty to China. These figures exclude revenue from Government Rent, general property tax or personal taxes on rental income. Taking all these streams together, almost 30 per cent of public revenue in Hong Kong is derived from land values.

These receipts are healthy, and depend on high land values, which gives rise to high property prices – a problem for young people. One could argue that not enough land is made available for lease, which is in part responsible for the high cost of housing. One could also propose an increase in the Government Rent (currently only 3 per cent of rateable value on new leases), which would have the effect of bringing down the upfront cost of new lease premiums at public auction. David Webb, an active investor, estimates that 'land premiums in current auctions would be between 32 per cent and 40 per cent lower for GR30 leases than for the current GR3 leases' (Webb-site Reports, 2010b). A GR30 lease would carry Government Rent at 30 per cent of rateable value per annum, as opposed to 3 per cent for the GR3 lease, which would have the advantage of spreading the income from the lease over the full term, thereby further reducing the need for general taxation.

Turning to Singapore, the government by 2002 owned 90 per cent of the land, but this was not always the case. On gaining independence first from Britain, and then after expulsion from the Malaysian Federation in 1965, the new Singapore government deliberately went about buying land. It inherited all land originally owned by the colonial administration, as well as a system of ownership which comprised an ad hoc patchwork of leasehold land (of different length) and some freehold plots.[6] In 1949, 31 per cent of land was in public ownership, which had increased to 49 per cent by 1965. The Land Acquisition Act 1966 accelerated the process, allowing the compulsory purchase of land 'needed for any public purpose, by … any statutory board … for any residential, commercial or industrial purposes' (Motha and Yuen, cited in Haila, 2016:73).

The previous owners were compensated, but never at more than existing use values, and often at historic use values. One of the early dates for valuation was 30 November 1973, although this was later amended to January 1986, January 1992 and January 1995, as the country became more prosperous. Lee Kuan Yew, Prime Minister of Singapore from 1959–1990,[7] explained these fixed points for valuations:

> I saw no reason why private landowners should profit from an increase in land value brought about by economic development and the infrastructure paid for with public funds.
>
> (Lee, 2011:97)

Public land is managed through statutory boards, such as the Housing Development Board (HDB) and the Jurong Town Corporation (JTC), which have specific purposes. The JTC was set up in 1968, and charged with developing land and buildings for commerce and industry. In the year to 31 March 2015, its revenue was S$1.9bn, mainly derived from land and building rental income (Jurong Town Corporation, 2016). Its net assets were S$19.6bn with a net annual surplus of S$1.3bn. As a statutory body it transfers any annual surplus to the Government's Consolidated Fund. As of May 2013, JTC managed 43 estates that covered 7,100 hectares of land area, providing 3.2 million square metres of ready-built space for 5,100 customers (Jurong Town Corporation, 2013). Its strategy is to build 'clusters' of facilities for particular industries, which encourages innovation sectors to invest in Singapore.

It is more difficult to gauge the exact annual income from land sale premiums in Singapore as they are not recorded as part of annual government revenue. However, as well as land managed by the HDB and JTC, the Singapore Urban Redevelopment Authority (URA) handles land lease sales on behalf of the government to private developers, and earns a fee, rather like an agency, on those sales. Its own accounts declare the fee income, and they also publish a list of all land sales together with the 'successful tender price' every six months. In 2016, the sales of eight 99-year leases are listed, with a total tender price of S$5,083m (URA, 2017). It is also possible to estimate revenue from land sales in Singapore from statistics based on the International Monetary Fund's Special Data Dissemination Standards (SDDS). In 2015/16, sales of non-financial assets came to S$15.5bn (Department of Statistics Singapore, 2017), although this may include assets other than land and may not take account of any purchases in the same year. These receipts are retained in reserves rather than being recorded as annual revenue.

Either way, the public ownership of land in both Hong Kong and Singapore offers each jurisdiction a significant source of income to benefit society, without depriving private users or investors of the opportunity to generate wealth through their own investment and activities *on* and above the land. This illustrates the possibility for governments elsewhere to levy a tax on location value, without disrupting the economic activity that takes place (Stiglitz, 2015). Such a levy would bring vacant land into use, and encourage the best use of all land. Although both Hong Kong and Singapore 'own' the land, there is no need to take land into public ownership – only to make an annual levy on the location value.

Public ownership in housing

Next we turn to the question of housing, an issue often referred to as being in 'crisis' or 'broken' in many Western countries, including the UK (Department for Communities and Local Government, 2017). Both jurisdictions are relatively small and experienced rapid population growth in the second half of the twentieth century. Conditions were poor, with extensive shanty or slum dwelling in both cities evident well into the 1970s. Both governments decided to act to provide better housing.

In Hong Kong, the decision was made to provide basic public rental housing in large high-rise estates. The early estates provided little more than two or three rooms to a family, with shared cooking and washing facilities on every landing. In time, the estates became more sophisticated, with independent flats containing their own facilities. At ground level, there were shops, restaurants, schools and some leisure facilities or public space and gardens. Today, about 30 per cent of the population lives in these public housing units, and many of the early estates have been replaced (Hong Kong Housing Authority, 2018). Rents are low, (HK$1,540 per month on average, including all management fees, see Hong Kong Housing Authority, 2017) and from the 1980s schemes were established to allow residents to buy their flats, such as the Home Ownership Scheme (HOS) or Tenant Purchase Scheme (TPS). Since inception about 10 per cent of the population have taken advantage of these schemes, often with subsidized loans. Subsidies are available for any residents unable to pay their rent, due to unemployment, disability or old age.

In Singapore, a new form of ownership was devised. Singapore citizens who satisfied certain income and wealth criteria were able to buy flats under a 99-year non-renewable lease at a subsidized price. After a certain period of time, the flat could be sold, and a second, perhaps larger flat could be bought, again with the subsidy. Any further move would be to a flat in a private development, or, for the really successful, a so-called landed property, which was a rare freehold purchase. Over time, residents were able to borrow from their own Central Provident Fund[8] (CPF) account, (a compulsory individual saving scheme linked with their employment), to help purchase these apartments.

Ownership of these HDB apartments peaked at 87 per cent of the population in 1990, falling back to 82 per cent in 2009.[9] Home ownership remains high in Singapore at 95 per cent of the population, the balance being both public and private rental. The public rental sector could be described as social housing, with heavily subsidized rents, while the private rental sector largely serves itinerant foreign workers in Singapore. The HDB housing was never social housing. The motivation was to give all Singapore citizens a stake in the new nation. According to Lee Kuan Yew, if you were going to ask the people to work hard, they would need rewards: 'What we have attempted in Singapore is asset enhancement, not subsidies. We have attempted to give each person enough chips to be able to play at the table of life' (Kwang et al., 1998:159). This was a recurring theme in his speeches and writing: 'My primary preoccupation was to give every citizen a stake in the country and its future. I wanted a home owning society' (Lee, 2011:95).

To what extent are HDB flats public assets? How can the state own 90 per cent of the land, but at the same time, 95 per cent of the population own their houses? The trick is that the state remains the freeholder, while the citizens are leaseholders; on expiry, the property reverts to the state. In other countries with leasehold systems of ownership, the freeholder is usually another individual, who can command a premium for the renewal of the lease.

Singapore can offer to each successive generation the same opportunity to take a stake in their nation, at a subsidized price, using their own savings to purchase an apartment on the same non-renewable, 99-year leasehold basis. If the owners die before the expiry, the remaining years of a lease can be bought from their estate, while the newly refurbished flat can be sold again to the next generation. The difference in price between, say, a lease with ten years remaining, and the new 99-year lease is treated as public revenue, after the expense of refurbishment. Once again, in the words of Lee Kuan Yew (1965), who flirted with socialism in his early years, but later became a prominent champion of the free market: 'We believe it is immoral that the ownership of property should allow some to exploit others'.

So, the state of Singapore has secured an asset, through the public ownership of land, which can offer each generation the same opportunity to prosper and build their own assets for use, but not in perpetuity (at least for the individual). An estimate of this distribution of asset wealth amongst the population has been calculated by (Phang 2018:145): '… assuming that the bottom 50 per cent of households live in 4 room or smaller HDB flats, their share of Singapore's gross housing wealth in 2015 was estimated at 25%', with implications for equality: 'Singapore's housing policies have resulted in gross housing wealth distribution approximating capital ownership distribution in Piketty's ideal society'.[10]

Public companies

Singapore's HDB was born out of the colonial Singapore Improvement Trust (SIT) whose assets were transferred to the new state at independence. Along with holdings in land, which included military establishments and ports, were the Post Office and telecommunication infrastructure.

All of these assets were managed by the Ministry of Finance at first, and in 1974, many of these, particularly the trading companies, were brought together in an investment holding company called Temasek, which adopted commercial principles of management and investment. The value of assets transferred in 1974 was S$354m, whereas, as of 31 March 2016, the value of the same holding company was S$242bn.[11] While many of its holdings are in the original companies and assets, it now has investments in companies all over the world. For example, it owns 51 per cent of SingTel, Singapore's main telephone company.[12] In financial services, it owns 16 per cent of Standard Chartered, an international bank, and 30 per cent of DBS, a bank incorporated in Singapore. In transportation, it owns 56 per cent of Singapore Airlines, and 54 per cent of SMRT Corporation, which operates much of Singapore's public transport network. In property it owns 100 per cent of Mapletree, a Singapore developer, and 25 per cent of A. S. Watson Group, a retailer with outlets throughout South East Asia.

Temasek has delivered 15 per cent Total Shareholder Returns since inception in 1974, a compounded annualized measure which includes dividends paid to its single Shareholder, the Singapore Ministry of Finance. It is difficult to estimate how much has been paid in dividends over the years. Since 2015, a Net Investment Returns Contribution (NIRC) has been declared in the annual Government Budget process, with a revised figure of S$9.9bn for 2015. Total government operating revenue in that year was S$64.16bn, and total expenditure was S$68.41 – before the NIR contribution (Government of Singapore, 2016).

This is a most unusual form of public asset for a government to hold, particularly at a time following an extended period of the privatization of state assets in other countries. The literature on this subject often concludes that state ownership of firms is generally inefficient compared to private ownership (Megginson and Netter, 2001), although Seiferling and Tareq (2015:21), conclude that: 'Unlike past contributions, this paper finds that government acquisition of equities on their own, are not indicative of fiscal gimmickry, as average returns over time for transparent governments tend to be relatively profitable'. Others highlight Singapore's strategy as a protective measure against global shocks, such as the Asian financial crisis of 1997, and 'that it serves to sustain the legitimacy of the nation state' (Clark et al., 2013:xv). Singapore seems to have avoided the pitfalls of picking losers instead of winners. Temasek, through its ownership of 'government linked companies' (GLCs) which account for 37 per cent of Singapore's stock market value, and government linked real estate investment trusts (GLREITs) at 54 per cent of the REIT market, scores well on transparency, independent governance and accountability, as well as performance. As one recent report concludes:

> The findings bring into question the unfavourable literature on government ownership. SGX-listed GLCs and GLREITs are well managed, efficient, and profitable. They play a vital economic role in transforming Singapore from a developing third world country to its current status as a globalised city-state.
>
> (Sim et al., 2014:8)

This success is rarely recognized in any discussion or report of Singapore as a free market economy. Reference is always made to low levels of taxation, small government and the ease of doing business in Singapore. Hong Kong and Singapore are often listed as first and second in the Economic Freedom Index published by the Heritage Foundation, an influential pro-free-market think tank.[13] Very few commentators (Detter and Fölster excepted) refer to the public ownership of land or trading companies in Singapore, or the consequent enjoyment of income derived from these assets.

The logic of this form of public ownership is to provide income to the government – an alternative to general taxation. Resource-rich countries (particularly oil producing countries, such as Norway, Qatar, the UAE) have relied on the sale of these assets to finance public spending during the last 70 years, and have created Sovereign Wealth Funds to manage the investments derived from the sale of these resources. But both Hong Kong and Singapore lack these natural resources, and yet enjoy investment income for government revenue.

Public transport: Railways

In most developed economies, public transport is subsidized, and operated either directly by publicly owned companies or through private franchises. What if public transport could be self-financing or profitable?

An example is provided by the Hong Kong Mass Transit Railway (MTR). Hong Kong is one of the most densely populated cities in the world, with over 7 million people occupying 1,100 square km – an average density of 6,650 per square km, rising to 46,000 per square km in downtown Kowloon. The government realized the best way to improve mobility, and promote productivity, would be to develop an underground railway. The research work took place in the 1960s, and by 1973 tender documents were ready. A Japanese company,

Mitsubishi, won the HK$5bn contract, however, the sudden increase in energy prices forced them to withdraw. This allowed the Hong Kong government to rethink the project, and a decision was made not only to scale down the initial system, but to grant development rights to the main contractor in return for building the railway. It had been recognized that in other countries when you build a public railway, the land along the route, and particularly around the stations, tends to increase in value. A public statutory corporation was established in Hong Kong to manage the process: the Mass Transit Railway Corporation (MTRC), wholly owned by the government, with a share capital of HK$2bn. Existing leaseholders along the route were bought out by the government at pre-railway prices, and the land was then sold (leasehold) to the MTRC in return for equity. Having the land to offer as collateral, the MTRC could issue Corporate Bonds and raise conventional loans from banks to begin building infrastructure. It was then able to auction the development rights to build apartments, hotels or office blocks above the stations to property developers at post-railway prices. The difference paid for the railway.

The premiums people were willing to pay for apartments above the stations ranged from 15 to 80 per cent depending on the location and proximity to the station entrance (Cervero and Murakami, 2008). In some cases, the MTRC retained ownership of these assets, particularly shopping centres built on the station podium, to provide ongoing rental income. The licence given to the MTRC to operate the railway is coterminous with all the land leases sold to them, so that if they were to lose the licence to operate the railway, they would lose the benefit of land ownership. On average, between 2001 and 2005, the MTRC generated revenue from the following sources: Railway 28 per cent, Property Development 52 per cent, Property Investment and Management 10 per cent, Non-fare (such as advertising) 10 per cent. While most Western governments subsidize their public transport system to varying degrees, Hong Kong's MTRC is consistently profitable, with profits rising from HK$5,962m (£458m) in 2006 to HK$10,894m (£838m) in 2015.[14]

The MTRC has continued to use this method to finance new routes, and work with the Hong Kong Planning Authority to develop New Towns. At a meeting in March 2014 with Sharon Liu, Chief Town Planning Manager of the MTRC, she confirmed to me that when a new project is proposed, the first question is: 'How much land do we need to cover the cost of building the railway?' This encapsulates the logic behind the whole process.

Public transport: Airports

A similar method was employed to build a new airport in the 1990s. Hong Kong International Airport (HKIA) is operated by the Airport Authority Hong Kong, a statutory body, created in 1995 to develop the new airport, wholly owned by the Hong Kong government. The airport was built on land reclaimed from the eastern tip of Lantau Island, and has two runways. Hong Kong lies within five hours' flying time of half the world's population, and in 2015, 68.5 million passengers passed through Hong Kong airport (Hong Kong Airport, 2016). There is a plan to build a third runway. Operating revenue in the year to March 2016 was HK$18.2bn, with a profit for the year of HK$8.4bn. Total equity in the business was HK$52.5bn.[15]

Of the operating revenue, HK$7.5bn comes from retail licences and advertising, HK$4.2bn from landing charges, and HK$2.5bn from airside service franchises. Under the operating statute, the airport authority was granted a lease for the entire site from 1 December 1995 to 30 June 2047 (50 years after the 1997 handover of sovereignty). In return, the authority had to create the land (by reclamation), and build the airport. The airport has a total debt-to-capital ratio of 5 per cent, although with the commitment to build a third runway (with a budget of HK$141bn) this is due to rise in the coming years. This explains why no dividend was declared in 2016, in contrast to the dividend of HK$5.3bn paid to the Hong Kong government in 2015.

Singapore's Changi Airport is similarly owned by the Singapore Ministry of Finance, and operated by a statutory corporation, Changi Airport Group (CAG). In 2014, it handled 54.1 million passengers, the seventh busiest airport in the world for international passengers. Total revenue in the year to March 2015 was S$2.1bn, with profit after tax of S$781m; its equity was S$6.1bn.[16]

While HKIA holds equity positions in airports in China, CAG holds equity positions in airports in several countries, including India, Brazil, Saudi Arabia and Russia. Not only do the airports in Hong Kong and Singapore serve their own populations, but they also export their expertise around the world, for profit.

Public ownership of airlines and airports has a long history, due perhaps to the close relationship of the development of aircraft for military as well as passenger use, and the commandeering of airfields not in public ownership at times of war. Gradually, during the last 25 years, national governments have divested themselves of ownership of national carriers in some developed economies, whereas in emerging economies, particularly in the Middle East, governments have invested heavily in airlines as a means of promoting a positive image and national identity.

The argument about whether the airports themselves should remain in public ownership or be sold to private investors has been ideological rather than pragmatic. Perhaps the public in some countries where the decision has been made to privatize were swayed by the poor standard of service offered in the publicly owned facility. One would need to conduct a detailed analysis of the investment programme, and profitability of individual cases, to arrive at a conclusion, but one can ask fundamental questions about what is creating value for the operator, and whether this value should belong to the public revenue or private investors.

Given the large-scale nature of the infrastructure required, and the impact (of noise and pollution, for example) on those living near an airport, to what extent are private operators able to make decisions independently of government agencies? If provision of air transport is public transport, at least as far as the airport infrastructure is concerned, should private owners have the privilege of exploiting the traveller for shareholder profit? Given that the location and very existence of an airport has national implications for people and business efficiency, can the delivery of air transport infrastructure be left to the private sector? Where does the value created arise? Most travellers in the UK would have a preference for which airport to use, and this preference is reflected in the landing charges that apply at the different airports. Heathrow is clearly the most popular, followed by Gatwick, Stansted and Luton. But the traveller's preference is more about airport location, the destinations to which operators fly from that airport, and the ease with which one can get to the airport, than about the facilities offered by the airport operator. In the UK context, all the main international airports are in the South East, which has major implications for growth and regional development, as well as the road and rail network necessary to service them.

The British Airports Authority was created in 1965, to take responsibility for the state-owned airports at Heathrow, Gatwick and Stansted. It subsequently acquired the airports in Glasgow, Edinburgh, Aberdeen and Southampton. The Authority was privatized in 1986, through a stock market listing. The company is now owned by a consortium led by Spanish infrastructure investor Ferrovial, which includes, incidentally, the Singapore Government Investment Corporation, and has invested heavily in new terminals at Heathrow.

New York's main airports, JFK and La Guardia, are owned by the public through the Port Authority of New York and New Jersey, together with other transport infrastructure including roads, ports and railways. It returns an annual profit to the two States, but has been criticized in the past for poor facilities and a general lack of investment.

In seeking to address the question of who creates the value that arises at a well located airport, in 1998, UK Deputy Prime Minister John Prescott challenged the idea that landing slots belonged to the airlines: 'The slots do not belong to British Airways. They belong to the community' (*The Guardian*, 1998).[17] In practice, however, Prescott's philosophy has not applied. The loss-making airline British Midland (BMI) was sold by Lufthansa in 2012 to International Airlines Group (IAG):

> IAG, the company that owns BA and Iberia, will pay Lufthansa £172.5m ($276.2m) for BMI. But IAG isn't really buying the airline, per se. Instead, this deal appears to be a play for BMI's valuable slot pairs – rights to take-off and land – at London Heathrow, the world's busiest airport for international travel. Regulators are making IAG give up 14 of BMI's 56 daily slot pairs at Heathrow, but the deal will still increase IAG's total ownership of slots at the airport from an already dominant 43% to 51%, according to an analysis by Dow Jones.
>
> (*The Economist*, 2012)

In fact, in Europe the airlines in possession of landing slots are treated, de facto, as the owners. In the case of Hong Kong and Singapore, by contrast, the argument so far has been won for the public revenue, with landing slots being under the control of the airport authority. In trying to assess what is a fair ownership structure for airports, given the very public nature of the asset, we perhaps need an honest debate about who creates the value: the traveller or the operator? If it is the traveller, to what extent should the profit go to a private operator? Is it enough to collect some of this value through Corporation Tax (easily avoided), or should more be collected by another means, such as a location value tax?

To conclude our discussion of international airports, in 2016, Singapore's Changi Airport was voted the world's number one airport by passengers, for the fourth year running as collated by Skytrax. Hong Kong is number five, Heathrow number eight, whereas both JFK and La Guardia are outside the top 100 (World Airport Awards, 2017). We can conclude that ownership status alone does not guarantee the quality of the facility.

Conclusion

What are the main lessons from Singapore and Hong Kong as to what constitutes fair public ownership?

Perhaps, most significantly, it seems reasonable for governments to retain control and ownership of land. This is in order to guarantee residents affordable housing and to generate public revenue, and/or to offer efficient and cheap public transport facilities. The alternative seems to be ever more complex and devious methods of imposing general taxation to subsidize the otherwise high cost of transport infrastructure, and to pay ever rising levels of housing benefit to hundreds of thousands of people in full employment to compensate for the lack of affordable housing.

To be sure, all is not a Garden of Eden in Singapore or Hong Kong. There are high levels of inequality in both jurisdictions, and at least in Hong Kong housing costs (beyond publicly rented flats) are the highest in the world, leading to serious over-crowding and often squalid conditions in the private rental and private ownership sectors. House prices in Singapore are also high, if one excludes the initial subsidy available for the purchase of HDB properties. However, this largely stems from a failure to recognize the origin of much of the public wealth in each jurisdiction, and to devise a system to manage and use it for the benefit of all.

More research is necessary to answer some of the questions posed here, as well as a more honest recognition of who generates location value in a rapidly urbanizing world. But research such as this has the potential to unleash income, or public revenue, which is otherwise retained for private benefit. Where ownership has already passed into private hands, it is not necessary to nationalize or take land back into public ownership. Control can be reasserted by imposing an annual charge on the location value of all land, ensuring that private owners pay for the services that they enjoy as a result of public investment, and the demands of their community. Changes in value after public investment will be captured so long as the location value is assessed periodically, perhaps every two years, as it is in Hong Kong. If such a rental charge were set at a sufficiently high level, many other forms of general taxation could also be reduced, or, as is the case in Hong Kong and Singapore, need not exist at all.

Acknowledgements

This chapter is an edited version of a paper published in 2019: Purves, A. (2019) ‘Models of fair public ownership: Lessons from Singapore and Hong Kong’, *International Journal of Public Policy*, Vol. 15, Nos. 1/2, pp. 59–75.

Notes

1 Harold Macmillan, British Prime Minister, in a speech in 1957 to fellow conservatives in Bedford. Available at: http://news.bbc.co.uk/onthisday/hi/dates/stories/july/20/newsid_3728000/3728225.stm (Accessed 8 December 2017).

2 GDP per capita in Singapore is now 7th, Hong Kong 18th, and the UK 40th in global ranking. Available at: www.indexmundi.com/g/r.aspx?v=67 (Accessed 21 January 2018).

3 The best account of this can be found in Nissim (2007), but a summary can also be found on David Webb’s website (Webb-site Reports, 2010a, 2010b). Also of interest would be Smith’s account (1966) of Mill’s ‘Other Island’.

4 See www.basiclaw.gov.hk/en/basiclawtext/images/basiclaw_full_text_en.pdf (Accessed 6 December 2018).

5 In simple terms, the location value is the premium someone is prepared to pay to occupy a piece of land in a particular location compared to the same sized plot of land in a less advantageous location.

6 A brief history of land ownership in Singapore is taken from Haila (2016, chapter 5).

7 The period from 1959 to 1965, was before the independence of Singapore.

8 For more information on the CPF see www.cpf.gov.sg/Members/AboutUs/about-us-info/cpf-overview (Accessed 5 January 2018).

9 HDB Annual Report 2008/09.

10

> To my knowledge, no society has ever existed in which ownership of capital can reasonably be described as ‘mildly’ inegalitarian, by which I mean a distribution in which the poorest half of society would own a significant share (say one fifth to one quarter) of total wealth … Of course, how one might go about establishing such an ‘ideal society’ – assuming that such low inequality of wealth is indeed a desirable goal – remains to be seen.
>
> (Picketty, 2014: 258)

11 All figures in this section are taken from the Annual Review of Temasek Holdings, available through their website: www.temasek.com.sg (Accessed 6 December 2018), unless otherwise specified.

12 Temasek owned 100 per cent of SingTel until 1993, when part of the company was sold to investors. Some of the offering was to Singapore Citizens at half the market value, with incentives over time to retain the shares.

13 See www.heritage.org/index/ (Accessed 6 December 2018). The 2016 Global Go To Think Tank Index Report ranks Heritage 12th among the top think tanks worldwide.
14 All figures from MTRC annual report and accounts.
15 HKIA Annual Report and Accounts 2016.
16 All figures taken from CAG report and accounts 2015.
17 The context was in a potential merger of British Airways and American Airlines, that BA would be forced to give up some of their landing slots to other competitors. Could BA sell the slots or not?

References

Burgess, R. (1993) *Public Revenue without Taxation*, Shepheard-Walwyn, London.

Cervero, R. and Murakami, J. (2008) *Rail + Property Development: A model of Sustainable Transit Finance and Urbanism*, UC Berkeley Center for Future Urban Transport, Berkeley, CA.

Clark, G., Dixon, A.D. and Monk, A.H.B. (2013) *Sovereign Wealth Funds: Legitimacy, Governance and Global Power*, Princeton University Press, Princeton, NJ.

Cullen, R. (2014) 'Hong Kong's remarkable land revenue regime: Why it works so well' *The Asian Business Lawyer*, Vol. 14 (Fall), pp. 193–222.

Department for Communities and Local Government (2017) *Fixing Our Broken Housing Market*, Department for Communities and Local Government, UK Government, London.

Department of Statistics Singapore (2017) *Data Dissemination Standard* [online].

Detter, D. and Fölster, S. (2015) *The Public Wealth of Nations: How Management of Public Assets Can Boost or Bust Economic Growth*, Palgrave Macmillan, London.

George, H., Peddle, F.K. and Peirce, W.S. (2017 [1879]) *Progress and Poverty*. Annotated works of Henry George, volume 2. Fairleigh Dickinson University Press, Lanham, MD.

Government of Hong Kong (2016) *The 2016–17 Budget* [online]. www.budget.gov.hk/2016/eng/pf.html (Accessed 6 December 2018).

Government of Singapore (2016) *Budget 2016* [online]. www.singaporebudget.gov.sg/budget_2016/RevenueandExpenditure (Accessed 23 December 2018).

Haila, A. (2016) *Urban Land Rent: Singapore as a Property State*, John Wiley & Son, Chichester.

Hamilton, K. and Hepburn, C. (Eds.), (2016) *National Wealth: What is Missing? Why it Matters*, Oxford University Press, Oxford.

Hamilton, K. and Liu, G. (2014) 'Human capital, tangible wealth, and the intangible capital residual', *Oxford Review of Economic Policy*, Vol. 30, No. 1, pp. 70–91.

Hayek, F. (1944) *The Road to Serfdom*, Routledge, London.

Hong Kong Airport (2016) *About the Airport* [online]. www.hongkongairport.com/eng/business/about-the-airport/welcome.html (Accessed 6 December 2018).

Hong Kong Housing Authority (2018) *Public Housing* [online]. www.housingauthority.gov.hk/en/public-housing/ (Accessed 5 January 2018).

Hong Kong Housing Authority (2017) *Rent Enquiry Services* [online]. www.housingauthority.gov.hk/en/public-housing/rent-related-matters/rent-enquiry-services/index.html (Accessed 6 December 2018).

Jurong Town Corporation (2016) *Annual Report* [online]. www.jtc.gov.sg/news-and-publications/annual-report/Documents/JTC-AR2015/files/pdf/JTC-AR2015-Financial-Statement.pdf (Accessed 6 December 2018).

Jurong Town Corporation (2013) *JTC Today, Moving Ahead* [online]. www.jtc.gov.sg/About-JTC/Pages/JTC-Today.aspx (Accessed 12 July 2013).

Kwang, H.F., Fernandez, W. and Tan, S. (1998) *Lee Kuan Yew: The Man and His Ideas*, Singapore Press Holding, Times Editions, Singapore.

Lee, K.Y. (2011) *From Third World to First: The Singapore Story, 1965–2000*, Harper Collins Publishers, New York.

Lee, K.Y. (1965) *Speech to Asian Socialist Conference*, 6 May 1965, Quoted in full, in Kwang, H.F., Fernandez, W. and Tan, S. (1998) *Lee Kuan Yew: The Man and His Ideas*, Singapore Press Holding, Times Editions, Singapore, page 388.

Megginson, W.L. and Netter, J.M. (2001) 'From state to market: A survey of empirical studies on privatization', *Journal of Economic Literature*, Vol. 39, No. 2, pp. 321–389.

Nissim, R. (2007) *Land Administration and Practice in Hong Kong*, Second Edition, Hong Kong University Press, Hong Kong.

Pearce, F. (2012) *The Land Grabbers: The New Fight over Who Owns the Earth*, Transworld Publishers, London.

Phang, S.Y. (2018) *Policy Innovations for Affordable Housing in Singapore*, Palgrave Macmillan, Switzerland.

Phang, S.Y. (2007) 'The Singapore Model of Housing and the Welfare State', in Groves, R. et al. (Eds.), *Housing and the New Welfare State: Perspectives from East Asia and Europe*, Ashgate Publisher, Aldershot, pp. 15–44.

Piketty, T. and Goldhammer, A. (2017) *Capital in the Twenty-first* Century. Belknap Press, Cambridge, MA.

Ricardo, D. (1973 [1817]) *The Principles of Political Economy and Taxation*, London, J.M. Dent.

Seiferling, M. and Tareq, S. (2015) *Fiscal Transparency and the Performance of Government Financial Assets*, IMF Working Paper, [www.imf.org/external/pubs/ft/wp/2015/wp1509.pdf (Accessed 6 December 2018)

Sim, I., Thomson, S. and Yeong, G. (2014) *The State as Shareholder: The Case of Singapore*, Centre for Governance, Institutions & Organizations, National University of Singapore, Singapore.

Smith, A. (1986 [1776]) *The Wealth of Nations*, Penguin, Harmondsworth.

Smith, H. (1966) *John Stuart Mill's Other Island: A Study of the Economic Development of Hong Kong*, Institute of Economic Affairs, London.

Stiglitz, J. (2015) *Life Cycle Savings vs. Inherited Savings*, Working Paper, National Bureau of Economic Research, www.nber.org/papers/w21191, 2015 (Accessed 6 December 2018).

The Economist (2012) 'In which British Airways buys a money-losing airline to the detriment of its own passengers', *The Economist*, 1 April 2012.

The Guardian (1998) 'Prescott risks turf dispute', *The Guardian*, 12 August 1998.

Urban Redevelopment Authority (2017) *Past Sale Sites*. Available online: www.ura.gov.sg/Corporate/Land-Sales/Past-Sale-Sites (Accessed 23 December 2018, statistics quoted compiled by author).

Webb-site Reports (2010a) *Hong Kong Land Lease Reform, Part 1* [online]. https://webb-site.com/articles/leases1.asp (Accessed 5 March 2017).

Webb-site Reports (2010b) *Hong Kong Land Lease Reform, Part 2* [online]. https://webb-site.com/articles/leases2.asp (Accessed 5 March 2017).

Williamson, J. (1990) *What Washington Means by Policy Reform, in: Latin American Adjustment: How Much Has Happened?* Peterson Institute for International Economics, Washington, DC.

World Airport Awards (2017) *World's Top 10 Airports* [online]. www.worldairportawards.com/Awards/worlds_best_airport.html (Accessed 8 February 2017).

12 The other side of paradise

The cost of tourism in the Caribbean

Wendy Sealy and Simon Mouatt

Introduction

The development of indigenous tourism in the Caribbean is inhibited by several challenges such as the inability to achieve economies of scale and scope through structural and resource constraints. These challenges are further exacerbated by the heavy prominence of transnational conglomerates who own and operate most of the hotels, airlines, cruise ships, travel agencies and tour operators that market and control tourism on the islands. Foreign domination of the foregoing sectors has contributed to substantial leakage of foreign exchange revenues – weakening exchange rates, social polarization, social exclusion and social degradation. While most Caribbean islands achieved constitutional independence from Europe, this did not necessarily involve a restructuring of economic relationships or a shattering of colonial ideologies. Today, the legacy of slavery and the plantation society underpins much of the regional contemporary culture, values and economic relationships, despite the attainment of political independence. This chapter aims to trace the nature and antecedents of foreign domination and control of Caribbean tourism and explores possible policy solutions to combat transnational intervention and economic dependency.

Mass tourism has become a significant source of revenue for many Caribbean states. According to the World Travel and Tourism Council report, 30.1 million tourists visited the Caribbean in 2017. In Barbados, tourism makes a 25 percent contribution to the gross national income, in Antigua 27 percent and in the Bahamas and St. Lucia 28 percent (Caribbean Development Bank, 2017). Tourism supports over 800,000 jobs and generates over US$35.5 billion in revenue per year (Caribbean Tourism Organization, 2018). However, tourism has not been a panacea for the Caribbean's social or economic ills. Many locations are still struggling to become fully fledged, attractive destinations (Séraphin, 2018). Thus, the ultimate objective of Destination Marketing Organisations (DMOs) is to achieve better performance in the longer term (Gowreesunkar, Cooper & Dubarry, 2009). Yet, this is difficult to achieve due to the number of competitors, short product and service lifecycles, and changing consumer preferences (Mihalache & Mihalache,

2016). The destinations also find it difficult to gain scale economies because Caribbean islands are small, with high imports, foreign exchange leakage, small marketing budgets, little access to entrepreneur networks and a lack of opportunities for indigenously derived strategies (Gowreesunkar, Van der Sterren & Séraphin, 2015). Many scholars have noted the structural similarities between tourism and the plantation economies of the seventeenth and eighteenth centuries (Beckles, 1990; Britton, 1982; Brohman, 1996; Kondo, 2008; Lewis, 2002; Pattullo, 2006; Strachan, 2002; Weaver, 1988). Some authors refer to Caribbean tourism as the 'new plantocracy' (Beckles, 1990), 'plantation tourism' (Weaver, 1988) or 'apartheid tourism' (Elliott & Neirotti, 2008). These similarities include the dominant role of expatriate capital, management and control; profit repatriation; the seasonality of employment; the need for a large component of unskilled local labor; and the reliance on a narrow range of monolithic tourist markets. What is also evident is the industry's tendency to respond to external, rather than local, needs. Using the structural method thesis, these scholars argued that the periphery was dependent on the core in the historic development process, where growth was distorted and benefited only a small proportion of society. Globalization and the power of international investors were identified as the agents of dependency which inhibit any indigenous national development (Clancy, 1999). Thus, the core-periphery structure of the plantation system remains intact well into the twenty-first century, resulting in a tourism industry which perpetuates underdevelopment and dependency.

Historical background

Colonial rule in the Caribbean involved 500 years of domination, subjugation, conquest, genocide, miscegenation, settlement, piracy, slavery, extra-regional migration and indentured servitude. This mass exploitation has its roots in seventeenth and eighteenth-century mono-crop agricultural production, mainly sugar, for European markets. By the eighteenth century, sugar had surpassed grain as the most valuable commodity in European trade and by the eighteenth and nineteenth centuries, Caribbean plantations produced 80 to 90 percent of all sugar consumed in Western Europe (Beckles, 1990). During the sugar revolution, and after the obliteration of the indigenous Amerindians, the social stratification system of most Caribbean islands comprised a minority planter class consisting of wealthy European plantation owners and a majority black labor class comprising African slave labor and later the indentured servants from Asia and Ireland. By the time of emancipation in 1833, Caribbean societies remained socially and economically the same with sugar remaining the dominant mono-crop export. Years of colonial rule, post-colonial political conflict and natural disasters make Caribbean economies vulnerable to external exigencies.

The Caribbean islands achieved independence in the 1960s, but this did not necessarily involve a restructuring of economic relationships or a shattering of colonial ideologies. During the post-war (1950–1978) period, the islands underwent an economic transformation. By the 1960s, proponents of capitalists and neoliberalist ideologies influenced a more outward-oriented approach to economic development with less emphasis on staple crops and more emphasis on foreign direct investment (FDI). Multilateral lending agencies, such as the Inter-American Development Bank, the World Bank, the International Monetary Fund, and the United Nations Development Agency, promoted tourism as a viable economic and social development tool for third world countries. Access to IMF structural adjustment funding became conditional on the implementation of policies designed to reduce state intervention in economic affairs and the adoption of more outward market-oriented economic growth and free trade (Edmonds, 2015). These policies influenced a shift away from agriculture and indigenous industries to policies which emphasized the expansion of hitherto ignored sectors such as tourism. Such policies hindered the sustainable development of indigenous business and exacerbated economic dependency. Cuba and the Dominican Republic, for instance, notwithstanding together having the 'lion's share' of tourists in the Caribbean in 2017, with 3,903,958 and 5,969,377 arrivals respectively, remain two of the poorest countries in the region (Caribbean Tourism Organization, 2018). The Dominican Republic is regarded as 'a rich country populated by poor people' (Black, 1986, p.236). Tourism development in the Dominican Republic, as in Cuba and several other Caribbean nations, is structured along the lines of large-scale, foreign investment, which appropriates most of the profit (Meyer, 2006). Today, tourism represents to many islands what sugar was a century ago: a mono-crop controlled by foreigners and a few local elites.

Dependency theory

In his inauguration speech after World War II, President Harry Truman had introduced the concept of US-led international cooperation to facilitate development in the South, with the promise of goodwill and technical assistance from the rich countries (Truman, 1945). Yet, the subsequent application of so-called modernization theory, to provide the necessary technological knowledge to developing countries as they progressed through various stages towards the Western model, failed to materialize. It was not long before critics emerged. Raul Prebisch, for instance, a dependency theorist from Argentina, and Executive Secretary for the United Nations Economic Commission for Latin America and the Caribbean (ECLAC), pointed out in 1950 that peripheral countries that had been subjected to colonial powers remained dependent on primary products for export earnings (Prebisch, 1950). He argued that since industrialization raised the standard of living, if developing countries were to implement import-substitution policies (by supporting the infant manufacturing companies that were embracing technology) this would protect their hard-earned foreign exchange earnings by substituting Western manufacturing imports with domestic production. The subsequent strengthening of their currency would then enhance their relative spending power in the world. Prebisch had earlier surmised, in the Prebisch–Singer hypothesis, that the relative terms of trade for primary products, in relation to manufactured ones, tended to decline over time (backed by some empirical evidence). The diverging profit margins over time derived from the lack of market power of primary product producers, suggesting that if they failed to diversify their sectors there was little prospect of development for the economies of Latin America and the Caribbean (Nafziger, 1997, p.502).

In the post-colonial period, it was apparent that little had changed in structural terms for the developing countries. Thomas noted in 1987 that they had simply 'traded one form of dependence for another' (Thomas, 1987, p.9) and there were calls from Amartya Sen to create a new vision of development that addressed the necessary 'entitlements and capabilities' (Sen, 1984, p.9). Trade rules agreed during the General Agreement on Tariffs and Trade (GATT) negotiations, for instance, were biased against developing countries and thus served to galvanize their dependence on primary products (Thomas, 1987, p.65). Trade barriers in the West blocked certain kinds of manufactured exports from the South, and these were estimated by the World Bank to constitute between 2.5 and 9 percent of developing countries' GDP in 1992 (Nafziger, 1997, p.509). In addition, high-tech manufacturing firms in the West jealously guarded intellectual capital and competitive advantage, showing no signs of a willingness towards a technology transfer.

The present neoliberalism of today, beginning in the 1980s, has arguably worsened the prospect of development for the indigenous businesses of the Caribbean since the so-called Washington consensus has driven the implementation of a set of economic policies that now mitigate against it. The deregulated global financial architecture, for instance, has led to floating exchange rates, easy access to financial markets, colossal sums of mobile capital and increased speculation. These changes have served to facilitate the growth of FDI by transnationals, especially in tourism. The previously mentioned IMF structural adjustment policies, forced on peripheral debtor nations during the 1980s in the wake of the Latin American debt crisis of 1982, insisted on reduced public spending (and economic planning), the privatization of state assets, increased exports, currency devaluation and measures to attract FDI. The devaluation of local currency, in particular, has led to cheaper access to local resources/assets for the transnational tourist enterprise and more competitive holiday packages to attract and penetrate the lucrative markets of the West. In addition, by maintaining a high level of profit repatriation, the transnationals of the West are guaranteed continued business as the currency remains weak.

In terms of the standard of living for Caribbean people, the impact of structural adjustment has been largely negative, especially in the so-called 'lost decade' of the 1990s (Melville, 2002). If the situation is to be improved we argue that the original dependency theory of the 1950s needs to be reformulated for the twenty-first century, since margins for manufacturing have been surpassed by service sector markups, particularly in those companies that engage a measure of intellectual capital. The island states of the Caribbean are, therefore, advised to engage in forms of protectionism towards the nascent indigenous firms from the service sector, for example, those associated with tourism, in order to experience meaningful economic development. Indigenous tourist firms will, in this sense, practice export-substitution rather import-substitution, since their activity will replace the tourism exports of transnationals from the richer nations (this could be coupled with import-substitution in service sectors serving the domestic economy). If these policies are pursued in conjunction with policy measures to encourage economies of scale and scope there is every chance of success.

Transnational hotels – nature and impact

The Caribbean region is almost a mono-product area with sea-sand-sun tourism, and the economy has not been adequately developed in favor of the local community due to transnational hotel chains, airlines and tour operators, where many companies are vertically integrated (Sealy, 2018). Transnationalism also reinforces the asymmetrical distribution of power between the post-colonial core-periphery. The hotel chain encourages a particular kind of mass, enclaved, institutionalized, standardized, packaged tourism that leads to foreign exchange leakage, social polarization, social exclusion and the loss of cultural integrity in the region. Their superior skills of entrepreneurialism also undermine the latent development of peripheral developing tourist regions (Clancy, 1999; Neblett & Green, 2000). International hotel chains such as Marriott, Sheraton, Starwood, Sandals, Best Western, Holiday Inn, Hilton, Renaissance, Radisson, Ritz Carlton, Four Seasons and several others have invested heavily into Caribbean tourism. Many of these establishments are based in North America or Western Europe. The economic leakages incurred by these resorts are said to be anything from 37 percent in Jamaica to as much as 90 percent in the Bahamas (Pattullo, 2006). These leakages include repatriated profits, higher imports, salary repatriation and tax concessions (Cabezas, 2008; Pattullo, 2006). The payments to transnational firms by travel agents, tour operators and conference organizers are also often made to bank accounts located outside of the region (Sealy, 2014, 2018). Other leakages include opportunity costs from resource damage, ecological deterioration and tax evasion (Meyer, 2006).

Due to an under-capitalized and peasant indigenous agricultural sector, only 16 percent of fruit and 20 percent of fish consumed in Caribbean hotels are sourced locally (Caribbean Development Bank, 2017). More than 60 percent of total food consumption for almost all Caribbean states is imported, with half of them importing more than 80 percent of the food they consume (Ewing-Chou, 2019). Pattullo (2006, p.53) notes how tourists in the

Caribbean do not eat the mangoes, breadfruit and bananas produced on Caribbean farms but instead 'drink orange juice from Florida, eat a banana from Columbia and stab at pineapple chunks from Hawaii'. Even when local produce is available they are either not available in sufficient quantity or are rejected as inferior by the international hotel developers and visitors (Sealy, 2018). The antecedent of this problem lies in centuries of colonialism and slavery, which has ensured that the mono-crop plantation culture remains dependent on foreign produce.

All-inclusive hotels

On several islands, all-inclusive hotels dominate the industry. In Jamaica, all-inclusive resorts make up 53 percent of the island's hotel rooms. Additionally, all-inclusive resorts account for 79.4 percent of the larger hotels with 100 rooms or more. In St. Lucia, all-inclusive resorts make up 51 percent of all hotel rooms (McElroy & de Albuquerque, 1998) and in the Dominican Republic 95 percent of all resorts are all-inclusive (Cabezas, 2008). All-inclusive resorts are tourism enclaves characterized by a single payment that the visitor makes to its tour operator, or travel agent, in their home countries, which covers meals, beverages, sightseeing and recreational activities, so that no money changes hands at the destination (Turner & Troiano, 1987). The concept has proved to be very successful from a marketing perspective, as the customer knows exactly how much their vacation will cost. The problem is that visitors arrive at the destination but do not venture outside the resort because all the vacation needs are catered for. The concept has been criticized profusely in the Caribbean for producing 'zero-dollar tourism' economies (King, Dwyer & Prideaux, 2006). All-inclusives have also established business units within their resorts to ensure that tourists do not venture out. Resorts own and operate their own boutiques, gifts shops, watersports operations, tour buses and minimarts. Because visitors are discouraged from venturing outside to spend money in locally owned firms, opportunities for restaurants, retail and taxi drivers, are decreased (Williams, 2012).

Some 75 to 80 percent of the vacation expenses of all-inclusive package tours are allocated to tour operators, airlines, hotels and other global corporations headquartered in a foreign country (Kondo, 2008) with very little, if any, of the expenditure reaching the destination. In several countries, the per capita spending of visitors (Pattullo, 2006) has dropped considerably due to all-inclusive resorts. In the Dominican Republic, the earnings per tourist have decreased per-room spending from a high of US$318 in 1982 to the current low of US$154 (Cabezas, 2008). The all-inclusive resort is, thus, another consequence of the colonial legacy, which encourages mass tourism tied to the colonial tradition of high-volume, low value-added, mono exports (Mycoo, 2006). The result is mass visitation but a lower economic multiplier impact within the host community.

Labor and employment

Tourism is often recognized for its ability to generate high employment multipliers. Direct and indirect tourist employment accounts for 50 percent of all employment in the Virgin Islands, 37 percent in Jamaica and 35 percent in the Bahamas (Meyer, 2006). However, much of this is in low-skilled or semi-skilled work and wages are poor. Just as with sugar production, tourism employment tends to be mainly seasonal, casual and/or sporadic work. The potential to be laid off creates a high degree of anxiety and uncertainty for workers and their families in the region.

While tourism employs a high number of workers, wages are at least 20 percent less than those paid by other sectors and are considerably less than those paid in the metropole. In Cuba, Haiti, Dominican Republic, Jamaica, St. Lucia, Trinidad and Tobago and several other islands, the annual minimum wage is under US$5,000.00. The gross national income, per capita, of the USA and Canada is three times that of Barbados, and more than ten times that of Jamaica. The average tourist is therefore able to spend more on a weeks' vacation than the minimum wage earner in the Caribbean can earn in a year (Toppin-Allahar, 2015). This wide wealth disparity between the average tourists visiting most Caribbean islands and the majority of the local population creates tension, agitation and irritation between host peoples and guests (Doxey, 1976). Caribbean islands also tend to suppress the minimum wage level to please foreign investors. Yet, by maintaining low wages, the economic benefits of any enhanced tourist inflow and visitor expenditure does not reach most of the workers in the tourist trade but is retained by the international conglomerates as profits (Sealy, 2018; Williams, 2012; Wong, 2015).

In places like the Dominican Republic, tourism has done little to upskill the talents of Dominican workers. This is because senior positions are filled by foreign professionals from North America or Europe. Cabezas (2008) notes that in the Dominican Republic natives are relegated to positions of servitude in low-paid jobs. These practices have led to locally trained executives and mid-level managers migrating to find work abroad, creating a 'brain drain' (Sealy, 2018). When locals do benefit from tourism, it is usually the local elites, particularly those with lighter skin, who benefit from high-paying jobs or middle management positions (Goodwin, 2008). This is a consequence of the brainwashing brought about by colonialism, which has created a pigmentocracy in the region where the highest social status is based on lightness of skin color rather than achievement. In Barbados, where there is a high concentration of foreigners in senior positions, to address this problem, the Government of Barbados entered into an agreement with Marriott resorts in the 1990s which ensured that for every American coming to take up a position, one Barbadian worker would be sent to the USA to work and train in the Marriott corporation. Several migrated to work in the USA with some returning several years later to take up senior positions in the Marriott resort on the island or at other hotels. However, on several islands, tourism hiring practices has reinforced the colonial notion of black inferiority and white supremacy (Sealy, 2018).

Exclusion, polarization, marginalization

In the face of globalization, Caribbean governments are pressurized to abolish alien landholding legislation. This move in many islands has reduced national sovereignty over land development, thereby giving corporations power over decisions that may not be in the best interests of locals (Mycoo, 2006). In many islands, foreign owners and operators of tourism facilities have acquired exclusive rights over extensive tracts of land and shoreline. In Jamaica, all but 19 of the island's 488 miles of coastline had been privatized by 1992 (Goodwin, 2008). In Jamaica, land immediately above the high-water mark can be privately owned. Licenses can also be issued to privatize the water for 25 meters out to sea. The hotels argue that such measures are necessary to ensure that guests are not harassed by 'drug-pushers' and 'beach bums' (Eriksson, Noble, Pattullo & Barnett, 2009). In the Bahamas, hoteliers purposely restrict access to beaches by constructing fences or delineating specific areas of the beach to ensure that locals cannot utilize the facilities (Thomas, 2016). In Barbados, large tracts of land have also been acquired by foreign developers. Many of these areas were previously places of recreation for locals. As this Barbadian puts it:

> All I can see these golf courses doing is creating more and more areas in this island that are off-limits to locals. Areas where I used to play as a child have now been developed and fenced in for only those who can afford it.
>
> (Sealy, 2009)

In 2018, Barbadians staged a protest in response to a dispute between owners of the Crane Beach Resort and beach vendors over access to the beach (Brathwaite, 2018). In Cuba, attractions such as Varadaro Beach, which was once accessible to native Cubans, is now available only to foreign tourists (Elliott & Neirotti, 2008). Due to tourism, many Caribbean nationals are excluded from land that once served agricultural purposes, and from shorelines and land formerly used for fishing and recreation.

Cruise tourism

If Caribbean people derive few benefits from all-inclusive visitors, then they derive even less from cruise passengers. It is estimated that only 12 percent of the revenue generated from cruise passengers stays in the port of call (Goodwin, 2008). The daily spending per person for ship passengers is 55 percent lower than the spending per person for long-stay tourists. Furthermore, the little spending that cruise tourists do occurs in duty-free shops owned by foreign companies that sell imported goods (Sealy, 2018). Of the more than 70 cruise ships that travel through the Caribbean, 90 percent are owned and operated by multinational corporations, ensuring that the revenue generated flows out of the Caribbean. Ship construction materials and furniture are mostly imported, and the food and beverages consumed are frequently bought overseas in the country where the ship is registered.

Just like the all-inclusive resorts, cruise-ship passengers can stay on board and not go to port, which reduces the revenue for the local community. Like the all-inclusive hotels, all services and amenities are provided on board the ship ensuring that most of the profits go to the owners of the cruise lines, and only a small fraction is left in the seaports where the ships land. Opportunities for ports to make money from cruise-ship passengers are restricted to the port fees charged as a tax by governments, and if the visitor decides to leave the ship, local enterprises could make money from ship to shore excursions or from the selling of trinkets. The economic benefits accrued by these small operators are miniscule in comparison to those extracted by transnational cruise-ship owners. Consequently, the overall market for cruise tourism in the Caribbean translates into even lower earnings for the region, since its participation in the profits is restricted to port fees and a few hours of shopping in duty-free ports (Goodwin, 2008; Sealy, 2018). Regional economic development is clearly not being enhanced by the existence of the cruise ships.

Cultural assassination

The development of tourism has modified the culture to meet the expectations, fantasies and preconceived notions of the tourists as portrayed in the brochures of overseas tour operators. Fake performances and staged authenticity are a common feature of the Caribbean industry, and many of the indigenous cultural attributes are purposely objectified, commoditized and corrupted for Western consumption (Wong, 2015). Many of the tour operator brochures portray the image of the Caribbean as a utopia with poor natives. The thematic framework of paradise often mimics past colonial regimes, despite the fact that the Caribbean is socially, culturally and environmentally different from the conjured-up images of the tourism brochure. At a famous West Coast resort in Barbados, employees are not allowed to wear any ostentatious fine jewelry because they are not allowed to look better off than the foreign guests that they serve. Many hotels dress their staff in fake colonial costumes to project notions of black servitude. In some hotels, to reinforce colonial servitude, the practice of stooping and bowing in the provision of services to tourists is mandatory. Many visitors to the Caribbean are oblivious to the realities of Caribbean life as the brutal hardship and suffering endured by the slaves during the colonial era are conveniently omitted from the entertainment plots and narratives of hotel entertainment.

In Barbados, a recurring narrative concerns hotel management opposition to black female workers wearing their natural afro hair, or braided or dreadlocked hairstyles, calling it unprofessional and requesting that these women chemically relax their hair. In the absence of anti-discrimination or equality legislation these women are forced to comply or fightback. In 1986, a female employee of a south coast hotel was dismissed for wearing a braided hairstyle (Sealy, 2015). The employee later won a case against her employer.

This Barbados incident is an example of how assaults on Caribbean culture have spurred rebellion, revolution, cultural affirmation and other forms of resistance (Beckles, 1990). Every single ethno-cultural group that came to the Caribbean had been forced to acknowledge the superiority of the ruling culture while resisting, rejecting, destroying or devaluing their own creole heritage (Beckles, 1990). Unfortunately, Caribbean people have been forced to 'assimilate' the culture of the ruling-class to advance themselves. 'Assimilation' was an ideological tenet of French colonial policy in the nineteenth and twentieth centuries (Girvan, 2012). The French taught their colonial subjects that, by adopting the French language and culture, they could eventually become 'French' (McNamara, 1989). One of the perverse effects of these historic policies is that Caribbean people judge each other based on the constructs created by the colonizer. The white and Anglo-American-European identities have established themselves in Caribbean life and tourism as definitions of what is proper and acceptable. As a result, creole manifestations of Caribbean identity are rejected and replaced by a hegemony of Western culture in terms of language, fashion, music, food, dress and lifestyle.

Tour operators and wholesalers

Tour operators (UK term), and wholesalers (US term), have an important role in the marketing and promotion of Caribbean tourism and so destinations reach mass customers at relatively low marketing cost. Caribbean resorts are dependent on tour operators and wholesalers for as much as 50 percent of business. In Barbados, hotels report that as much as 90 percent is tour operator/wholesaler generated (Sealy, 2014). In the UK, tour operators are also vertically integrated into airlines, travel agencies and hotels, giving them oligopolistic powers over air capacity, price, product, promotion and customer buying behavior (Bastakis, Buhalis & Butler, 2004; Buhalis, 2000; Gartner and Bachri, 1994; Stuart, Pearce & Weaver, 2005). This oligopolistic power allows the tour operators to exert pressure on accommodation providers for rooms to be contracted at the lowest possible rates. The rates offered to tour operators by hotels are much lower than rates published by hotels to the public and can represent discounts of 20 to 60 percent off the published rack rates (Sealy, 2018).

Tour operators are notorious for the techniques they use to drive accommodation rates down for hotels. These include creating illusions of poor demand by withholding advanced bookings until the hotel lowers its rates. When the hotel offers cheaper rates, the tour operator then releases the previously held bookings to the hotel. Mystery shopping studies also reveal that tour operators would force the hotel to drive rates down, but these discounts would not be passed onto customers (Sealy, 2014, 2018). Tour operators use the practice of 'switch-selling' or 'directional-selling' to divert customers to other destinations where they have investments. They sometimes mislead customers by putting them off certain properties by citing unfounded issues or by telling them that the hotel is full or 'unavailable' so that the customer books a property owned by the tour operator (Picazo & Moreno-Gill, 2018). Tour operators can manipulate the competition among the various hotels and destinations within the same competitive set since they control the airlift capacity and price (Papatheodorou, 2006). These unscrupulous practices put hotels who depend on tour operator channels in a vulnerable position. If customers choose to book with the hotel direct, hotels also risk punitive penalties from tour operators if they take the direct bookings (Sealy, 2014).

Tour operators would often misquote travel statistics, employ intimidation tactics or play hotels against each other at the destination to compel them to give further rate reductions (Andriotis, 2003; Bastakis, Buhalis & Butler, 2004). Furthermore, tour operators may also withhold payment until the last minute, sometimes leaving hotels in serious overdrafts and scrambling for cash to pay local suppliers and staff. The visitor pays the tour operator in advance for their holidays but, the large tour operators require a 30 to 45 days credit facility, but many do not pay on time. Buhalis (2000) notes that these delayed payments allow the tour operators to earn as much as 25 percent of their revenue from interest on hotels' money as it sits in their banks in the metropole. Frequently, the failure of tour operators to pay on time has resulted in hotels applying for additional overdraft facilities to meet financial and operational obligations and paying interest on the credit facility.

The constant reduction in net rates will lead to the inability of the smaller hotels to maintain their physical facilities and service standards. The deterioration of the tourism product also leads to a poor destination and product image, and to a reluctance by customers to pay a premium price. The further deterioration of the product showers the tour operator with additional power to negotiate for even cheaper rates, which, consequently, leads to a further drop in prices. Buhalis (2000) warns that the concentration of bargaining power in European tour operators will reduce the profit margins of small and medium-sized tourism firms and their ability to reap returns on their investments.

Recommendations

The neo-colonial economy appropriates local resources in peripheral places and concentrates them in the hands of foreign organizations in metropolitan countries for profit. When a country's natural resources are packaged and sold by foreign enterprises, a substantial portion of the profits and value-added is captured by the metropole and therefore does not accrue to the destination country. These leakages result in the local population bearing the economic and social costs of tourism while retaining relatively little economic benefit. Traditionally, Caribbean governments are more concerned about short-term fancy and pleasing foreign investors when it comes to policymaking rather than the long-term sustainability of the local population (Wilson, 1996). We argue that the role of government must be in strategic policymaking. This is critical to ensure that the destination and its local businesses are competitive. Government, the private and public sectors, and academic and civic organizations could work together to create a more enabling environment for indigenous and sustainable tourism to flourish. Several steps could be taken to mitigate the current industry.

Government policy

First, Caribbean states could encourage and facilitate policies to strengthen the competitive position of the local tourism sector. There is also a need to diversify economies in order that the dependency on mass tourism is mitigated. Strengthening inter-sectoral linkages, particularly between tourism and the agro-industries, to reduce foreign exchange leakage via food imports, is a key imperative. This could include the development of market associations that make it easier for hotels and restaurants to source local produce and goods. Governments could also put limits on the import of food that can be produced locally. The Sandals Program in Jamaica, for instance, is an agro-tourism initiative, which has grown from ten farmers supplying two hotels in 1994, to 80 farmers in 2004. Due to the program, sales increased in three years from US$60,000 to US$3.3 million (Caribbean Development Bank, 2017). Jamaica, as a result of this and other agricultural initiatives, is the most food self-sustaining country in the region. There are political constraints, of course, not least of which is the pressure from international institutions, such as the IMF, transnational firms and the pervading neoliberal paradigm.

Second, promoting the removal of barriers to a single market for Caribbean goods and services could enhance the growth of indigenous tourist business, and their attainment of the necessary economies of scale and scope to effectively compete with foreign transnationals. Inter-island economic integration would also serve to strengthen the regulatory environment that foreign operators are subjected to when they invest in the Caribbean, so that their corporate operations serve the wider development needs of the islands. However, there are several barriers to Caribbean free trade, such as island differences in language, culture, governance, history and the specific nature of their development problems. These barriers, coupled with the sheer number of sovereign independent jurisdictions and other geopolitical ties, make such obstacles difficult to navigate.

Third, island states could incentivize the diversification of holiday offerings away from the sea, sun and sand concept. This could be achieved through regulatory management of accommodation to prevent over-supply. Stronger regulations to limit the existence of all-inclusive resorts, perhaps through the taxation system, could also be considered. Gambia, the African nation, made the decision to ban 'all-inclusives', as they contributed nothing to the local economy (Kondo, 2008).

Fourth, facilitating the use of the sharing-economy channels, such as Airbnb, can encourage more home stays and alternative accommodation choices for visitors. These types of tourists spend more on groceries and dining outside of their holiday residence than tourists in other accommodation (Caribbean Development Bank, 2017). This would allow a wider spread of tourism benefits into the local economy and filter down to the indigenous population. In general, the island regulators need to ensure that hotel development resonates with the ethos, values and needs of the destination.

Fifth, island states could create an enabling environment for small tourist firms to grow with access to financial incentives and training opportunities to incentivize smaller business innovators. What is also needed within many countries is an indigenous craft industry that would encourage all-inclusive and cruise-ship tourists to venture outside the resorts/ships for Caribbean-made, distinct and unique handicrafts. In many Caribbean islands, almost all souvenirs offered to tourists are generic and imported from Asia, which contributes to more foreign exchange leakages.

The private sector – strategies for small hotel entrepreneurs

Indigenous hotels can compete with transnationals by reassessing their market strategy position through identifying unique, tangible and intangible features, enabling a differentiation of their product to attract and satisfy niche markets. The focus of these small hotels should be to reduce their dependency on mass-market inclusive tour traffic while increasing bargaining power and pursuing other market segments. Several initiatives could be easily implemented. These include:

- Attract independent travelers by added value components such as early check-in, late checkout, free dinners, free parking and retail discounts replacing monetary reductions. Focus on creating an amazing experience instead of discounting (Tan & Dwyer, 2014).
- Provide bespoke all-inclusive packages and dynamic packages that are customized rather than standardized to independent travelers.
- Ensure websites and social media communicate the different ways hotel bookings can be made, linked to distribution gateways for all geographic and psychographic segments.
- Train reservation staff to upsell hotel features and services to potential direct customers.
- Cooperate with third-party websites such as Lastminute, Orbitz, Expedia, and e-Long to diversify distribution channels and to reach a broader customer base. They also expect low prices, but these websites allow the

customers greater control in the selection of their vacation choices (Dong & Ling, 2015).

- Market properties independent of tour operators via PR – such as press releases or travel writer free stays in exchange for publicity on special interest tourism.
- Develop database profiles of clients who can potentially return as repeat visitors, and recommend friends, and also gain discounts via loyalty schemes.

Destination marketing companies

Poon (1994) argues that the future of Caribbean tourism will depend on innovativeness, leading to indigenous development. Ethical tourism, for example, would focus on fair-trade products, improved working conditions and ecology protection, a branding that is becoming increasingly popular with the discerning Western tourist. Another example is the community event, such as the Barbados Oistins Fish Fry, a weekly event where fishermen, fish sellers, farmers, local chefs and craft people sell vegetables, fish and beverages, prepare meals and sell handicrafts to thousands of tourists and locals. This event evolved organically due to tourists' desire for authentic Caribbean experiences.

Diversifying tourism offerings involves much effort in delivering specialized and special interest products. Niche markets have more focused and targeted media outlets and offer opportunities for strategic alliances with a cadre of more specialized tour operators and their networks. Research has highlighted that niche or luxury operators tend to be more concerned about service quality and value for money than price. They tend to be more cooperative, appreciative and concerned about having amicable relationships with hotels than mass tour operators (Sealy, 2018).

Destination marketing companies should also pursue diasporic tourism. Previous research by Séraphin, Korstanje and Gowreesunkar (2019) shows that diasporic tourism generates significantly more benefits to underperforming destinations than mass tourism. This is not seasonal; diasporic visitors visit main tourist areas as well as secondary regional sites; they consume local products and use local services, which facilitates the filtration of tourism expenditure into the local economy. The diaspora also act as ambassadors of their culture in their adopted countries and thus contribute to the marketing of destinations.

Mass tour operators have a strong influence on the nature of the information communicated to clients before and during the holiday, which influences the consumption patterns and expectations of the visitor. Consequently, tourists often lack information and awareness about the cultural, environmental and economic impacts of their touristic activity. Caribbean destinations should change the consumption patterns of the tourists through the application of information-based communications instruments (Goodwin, 2008). This could be done through social media, press editorials or movie and film tourism with the appropriate storylines.

Academic institutions and civic society

Globalization and technological change require a much higher-skilled and confident workforce. The indigenous tourism industry needs professionals who can bring expertise that would give a competitive advantage to their hotel sector. It is imperative that Caribbean educational institutions make marketing research skills a key cornerstone of their qualifications. Workers also need to be digitally literate to reach customers independently rather than depending on tour operators. It is a students' problem-solving ability that will help them as future managers to achieve a competitive advantage for their organizations and adapt to the changing environments in which hotels operate (Tan & Dwyer, 2014). Hospitality-related curricula must move away from the practical and instead mold future graduates who are technologically literate, critical thinkers and problem solvers. It is important that hospitality students be instructed in decision-making tools that can facilitate best practice and innovation to hotel management. Internships and placements outside the Caribbean will assist in broadening the horizons of future hospitality leaders and will expose them to different practices and realms of thinking.

Much wider public consultation should ideally also be part of the tourism sector decision-making process (Wilson, 1996). The authorities could implement a local communications campaign aimed at raising the level of awareness of tourism development projects to ensure that tourists have the best experience possible.

Closing remarks

The Caribbean's dependency has its roots in colonial society. On the surface, independence in the Caribbean was nothing more than a 'constitutional independence' with all of the features of an emerging neo-colonial society (Britton, 1982; Wall & Mathieson, 2006; Weaver, 1988; William, 2012; Wong, 2015). Caribbean societies today resemble a more subtle organization of the colonial economic system through neo-colonial structures and a hegemony of European culture and Western ideologies. Today, as in the past, the political economy of the Caribbean is socially, politically and economically structured in a way that facilitates the interests of the metropolitan centers as it did during the colonial era. In order to encourage the adoption of the recommendations outlined above, it would also help to jettison any remnants of the colonial mindset, whereby Caribbean public officials, or local business decision makers, continue to consider themselves the weaker party. This 'victim mentality' is more likely to be exploited by the hardnosed buyers and marketers from the West. However, although there is recognition of the importance of shattering the psychological barriers hampering true independence, this is easier said than done.

As the notable Caribbean writer, C.L.R. James (1958) once said:

> Freedom from colonialism is not merely a legal independence, the right to run up a national flag and to compose and sing a national anthem. It is necessary also to break down the economic colonial systems under which the colonial areas have been forced to live for centuries as hinterlands, sources of raw material, backyards to the industries of the advanced countries. Independence is independence, but when you continue to live in territories which still bear the shape of the old colonial territories it is extremely difficult to free yourself from the colonial mentality.

Globalization has destroyed much of the Caribbean's traditional economic and subsistence base, concentrating the jobs and income in the hands of the transnational elite. The alternatives offered, such as tourism or financial services, serve the needs of the imperial powers first, and those of the local people a distant second. Rather than advocating the implementation of import-substitution policies, the dependency theorists of today would be wiser to advise the Caribbean governments possessing strong tourism sectors to instigate policies that incentivize export-substitution, that is, the development of indigenous tourist businesses to rival the transnational corporate ones. Stephen Hymer, in his theory of transnational corporate behavior, argued that FDI only makes sense when there is a competitive advantage over indigenous firms (Dunning & Rugman, 1985). If Caribbean business can gain the necessary economies of scope and scale, and gain (importantly) access to competitive marketing in the West, it would at least be more difficult for newer Western firms to enter the market and this may even displace some current ones who might choose to divest their assets to indigenous firms. In conjunction with other policies, this may provide the capacity to enhance the standard of living for islanders and secure their long-term future.

The contemporary Caribbean is one of the most politically fragmented regions on earth. This is a direct consequence of the region's 500-year history as an area of rivalry among European powers (Girvan, 2012). The fragmentation, with continued external control, is a major impediment to the establishment of a single Caribbean market. Blocks to the consolidation of Caribbean identity remain, and a localized independent course of economic development continues to be elusive. The political and psychological decolonization of Caribbean countries is still to be achieved.

References

Andriotis, K. (2003). Dependency on Tour Operators: Problem Faced by the Cretan Tourism Business and the Views of their Owners/Managers. *International Journal of Hospitality and Tourism Administration*, 4 (3): 23–48.

Bastakis, C., Buhalis, D., & Butler, R. (2004). The Perception of Small and Medium-sized Tourism Accommodation Providers on the Impacts of the Tour Operators' Power in Eastern Mediterranean. *Tourism Management*, 25 (2): 151–170.

Beckles, H. (1990). *A History of Barbados: From Amerindian Settlement to Nation-State.* London: Cambridge University Press.

Black, J.K. (1986). Development and Dependency in the Dominican Republic. *Third World Quarterly*, 8: 236–257.

Brathwaite, S. (2018). Crane Dispute Upsets Vendors, Nation News. Available at: www.nationnews.com/nationnews/news/144380/crane-dispute-upsets-vendors, [accessed March 22, 2018].

Britton, S. (1982). The Political Economy of Tourism in the Third World. *Annals of Tourism Research*, 9 (2): 331–358.

Brohman, J. (1996). New Directions in Tourism for Third World Development. *Annals of Tourism Research*, 23 (I): 48–70.

Buhalis, D. (2000). Relationships in the Distribution Channel of Tourism: Conflicts between Hoteliers and Tour Operators in the Mediterranean Region. *International Hospitality, Leisure and Tourism Administration Journal*, 1 (1): 113–139.

Cabezas, A. (2008). Tourism and Social Exclusion in the Dominican Republic. *Latin American Perspectives*, 35 (3): 21–36.

Caribbean Development Bank (2017). *Tourism Industry Reform: Strategies for Enhanced Economic Impact.* Available at: www.caribank.org/publications/featured-publications/tourism-industry-reform-strategies-for-enhanced-economic-impact, [accessed April 9, 2018].

Caribbean Tourism Organization (2018). *Annual Statistical Report*. Available at: www.onecaribbean.org/buy-cto-tourism-statistics/annual-statistical-report/, [accessed April 25, 2018].

Clancy, M. (1999). Tourism and Development: Evidence from Mexico. *Annals of Tourism Research*, 26 (1): 1–20.

Dong, Y. & Ling, L. (2015). Hotel Overbooking and Cooperation with Third-party Websites. *Sustainability*, 7: 11696–11712.

Doxey, G. (1976). *A Causation Theory of Visitor-Resident Irritants, Methodology, and Research Inferences*, 6th Annual Conference Proceedings of the Travel and Tourism Research Association: The Impact of Tourism, San Diego, CA, pp.195–198.

Dunning, J. & Rugman, A. (1985). The Influence of Hymer's Dissertation on the Theory of the Foreign Direct Investment. *The American Economic Review*, 75 (2): 228–232.

Edmonds, K. (2015). An Elusive Independence: Neo-colonial Intervention in the Caribbean. *International Socialism: A Quarterly Review of Socialists Theory*, 146. Available at: http://isj.org.uk/neocolonial-intervention-in-the-caribbean, [accessed January 24, 2018].

Elliott, S.M. & Neirotti, L.D. (2008). Challenges of Tourism in a Dynamic Island Destination: The Case of Cuba. *Tourism Geographies*, 10 (3): 375–402.

Eriksson, J., Noble, R., Pattullo, P., & Barnett, T. (2009). *Putting Tourism to Rights: a Challenge to Human Rights Abuses in the Tourism Industry*. London: Tourism Concern.

Ewing-Chou, D. (2019). Five Overlooked Facts about Caribbean Food Security. Available at: www.forbes.com/sites/daphneewingchow/2019/02/20/five-facts-about-caribbean-food-security/#305da22c5016, [accessed March 21, 2019].

Gartner, W. & Bachri, T. (1994). Tour Operators' Role in the Tourism Distribution System: An Indonesian Case Study. In M. Uysal (Ed.), *Global Tourism Behaviors* (pp.161–179). New York: International Business Press.

Girvan, N. (2012). *Colonialism and Neo-colonialism in the Caribbean: An Overview*. Paper delivered at the IV International Seminar Africa, The Caribbean and Latin America, St. Vincent and The Grenadines, 24th-26th November.

Goodwin, J. (2008). Sustainable Tourism Development in the Caribbean Island Nation States. *Michigan Journal of Public Affairs*, (5): 1–16.

Gowreesunkar, V., Cooper, C.P., & Durbarry, R. (2009). The Role of Internal Marketing in Sustainable Destination Management: Grand Bay, Mauritius, as a Case Study. *International Journal of Environmental, Cultural, Economic and Social Sustainability*, 5 (5): 21–24.

Gowreesunkar, V., Van der Sterren, J., & Séraphin, H. (2015). Social Entrepreneurship as a Tool for Promoting Global Citizenship in Island Tourism. *Ara Journal of Tourism Research*, 5 (1): 7.

James, C.L.R. (1958). Lecture on Federation. Available at: www.marxists.org/archive/james-clr/works/1958/06/federation.htm, [accessed March 5, 2019].

King, B., Dwyer, L., & Prideaux, B. (2006). An Evaluation of Ethical Business Practices in Australia's China Inbound Tourism Market. *International Journal of Tourism Research*, 8: 127–142.

Kondo, M. (2008). The Economic Impact of All-inclusive Resorts in Jamaica. *City Tech Writer* (8). Available at: www.citytech.cuny.edu/english/docs/ctw_v3_2008.pdf, [accessed January 31, 2018].

Lewis, A. (2002). A Case Study of Tourism Curriculum Development in the Caribbean: A Stakeholder Perspective, Unpublished PhD Doctoral dissertation Buckinghamshire Chilterns University College, Brunel University.

McElroy, J.L. & de Albuquerque, K. (1998). Tourism Penetration Index for the Small-island Caribbean. *Annals of Tourism Research*, 28: 145–168.

McNamara, F.T. (1989). *France in Black Africa*. Washington, DC: NDU Press.

Melville, J. (2002). *The Impact of Structural Adjustment on the Poor*, Eastern Caribbean Central Bank, 7th Annual Development Conference, Basseterre, St. Kitts and Nevis. Available at: www.caribank.org/uploads/publications-reports/staff-papers/StrucAdj[1].pdf, [accessed June 10, 2018].

Meyer, D. (2006). *Caribbean Tourism, Local Sourcing and Enterprise Development: Dorothea Meyer Centre for Tourism and Cultural Change*, Sheffield Hallam University. Available at: www.odi.org/sites/odi.org.uk/files/odi-assets/publications-opinion-files/4038.pdf, [accessed March 20, 2019].

Mihalache, M. & Mihalache, O.R. (2016). Organisational Ambidexterity and Sustained Performance in the Tourism Industry. *Annals of Tourism Research*, 56: 128–163.

Mycoo, M. (2006). Sustainable Tourism using Regulations, Market Mechanisms and Green Certification: A Case Study of Barbados. *Journal of Sustainable Tourism*, 14 (5): 489–511.

Nafziger, E.W. (1997). *The Economics of Developing Countries*, 3rd Edition. Upper Saddle River, NJ: Prentice-Hall.

Neblett, J. & Green, W. (2000). *Linking Development, Indigenous Entrepreneurship and Tourism, with Special Reference to Barbados*. Available at: www.siue.edu/GEOGRAPHY/ONLINE/neblett.htm, [accessed March 25, 2019].

Papatheodorou, A. (2006). *Corporate Rivalry and Market Power: Competition Issues in the Tourism Industry*. London: IB Tauris.

Pattullo, P. (2006). *Last Resort: The Cost of Tourism in the Caribbean*. London: Wellington House.

Picazo, P. & Moreno-Gill, S. (2018). Tour Operators' Marketing Strategies and their Impact on Prices of Sun and Beach Package Holidays. *Journal of Hospitality & Tourism Management*, 35: 17–28.

Poon, A. (1994). *Tourism, Technology, and Competitive Strategies*. London: CABI.

Prebisch, R. (1950). *The Economic Development of Latin America and its Principal Problems*. New York: New York Department of Economic Affairs.

Sealy, J. (2015). Right to Wear Braids. *Nation News*. Available at: www.nationnews.com/nationnews/news/62241/wear-braids, [accessed March 21, 2019].

Sealy, W. (2009). An Exploratory Study of Stakeholders' Perspectives of a Mega Event in Barbados. The Case of the Golf World Cup, 2006, Unpublished PhD Doctoral dissertation Buckinghamshire Chilterns University College, Brunel University.

Sealy, W. (2014). Tourism Intermediaries. In S. Roberts, M. Best, & A. Cameron (Eds.), *Contemporary Caribbean Tourism*. Kingston: Ian Randall Publishers.

Sealy, W. (2018). *An Exploratory Study of Caribbean Hoteliers' Bargaining Power with British Tour Operators: A Barbados Case Study*. Working Paper.

Sen, A. (1984). *Resources, Values and Development*. Oxford: Basil Blackwell.

Séraphin, H. (2018). Locals' Happiness: The Missing Measurement in Caribbean Tourism Development, Words in the Bucket. Available at: www.wordsinthebucket.com/locals-happiness-the-missing-measurement-in-caribbean-tourism-development, [accessed November 10, 2018].

Séraphin, H., Korstanje, M., & Gowreesunkar, V. (2019). Diaspora and Ambidextrous Management of Tourism in Post-Colonial, Post-Conflict and Post-Disaster Destinations. *Journal of Tourism & Cultural Change*, 3: 1–20.

Strachan, I.G. (2002). *Paradise and Plantation: Tourism and Culture in the Anglophone Caribbean*. Charlottesville, VA: University of Virginia Press.

Stuart, P., Pearce D.G., & Weaver, A. (2005). Tourism Distribution Channels in Peripheral Regions: The Case of Southland, New Zealand. *Tourism Geographies*, 7 (3): 235–256.

Tan, J. & Dwyer, L. (2014). Managing Distribution Channel Conflict in the Hotel Industry. *International Journal of Marketing and Business Communication*, 3 (1): 9–19.

Thomas, A. (2016). Small Tourism Enterprises, Mass Tourism and Land Use Change: A Case Study of The Bahamas. *Caribbean Geography*, 21: 24–44.

Thomas, C. (1987). *In Search of Security: The Third World in International Relations*. London: Harvester Wheatsheaf.

Toppin-Allahar, C. (2015). De Beach Belong to We: Socio-Economic Disparity and Islanders Rights of Access to the Coast in a Tourist Paradise. *Oñati Socio-legal Series*, p.2.

Truman, H. (1945). Presidential Inauguration Speech. Available at: https://trumanlibrary.org/whistlestop/50yr_archive/inagural20jan1949.htm, [accessed June 4, 2018].

Turner, S.M. & Troiano, C.S. (1987). Notes. *Cornell Hotel & Restaurant Administration Quarterly*, 28 (3): 25–27. Retrieved October 31, 2007, from Hospitality & Tourism Complete Database.

Wall, G. & Mathieson, A. (2006). *Tourism: Change, Impacts and Opportunities*. Harlow: Pearson Education Limited.

Weaver, D.B. (1988). The Evolution of a 'Plantation' Tourism Landscape on the Caribbean Island of Antigua. *Tijdschrift voor Economische en Sociale Geografie*, 79 (5): 319–331.

Williams, T. (2012). Tourism as a Neo-colonial Phenomenon: Examining the Works of Pattullo & Mullings. *Caribbean Quilt*, 2: 191–200.

Wilson, D. (1996). Glimpses of Caribbean Tourism and the Question of Sustainability in Barbados and St. Lucia. In L. Bruguglio, R. Butler, D. Harrison & W.I. Filho (Eds.), *Sustainable Tourism in Islands and Small States*. London: Cassell, pp.75–102.

Wong, A. (2015). Caribbean Island Tourism: Pathway to Continued Colonial Servitude. *Études Caribéennes*, August–December. Available at: https://journals.openedition.org/etudescaribeennes/7524, [accessed June 3, 2020].

Part V

Improving pluralism in economics education

13 Heterodox Economic Journal Rankings revisited

Bruce Cronin

Introduction

In an influential paper, Lee and Cronin (2010) considered the place of heterodox economic journals in the increasingly restrictive journal ranking process. We noted the pervasive use of journal rankings in academic appointments, evaluations and promotions and the pressure these then place on academic researchers to publish in highly ranked journals. In economics, because well-rated journals are virtually exclusively orthodox, this puts particular pressure on academics pursuing heterodox lines of enquiry. We argued that the pursuit of publication in highly ranked economics journals was a fruitless strategy for heterodox economists because their work actually comprised a distinct body of knowledge from mainstream economics, typically different in theoretical and methodological approach, and reference and citation patterns. We proposed that a more effective publication strategy for heterodox economists would be to target those journals that provided institutional support for this separate subdiscipline. To this end, we developed a ranking of journals in which heterodox published, in terms of an assessment of their contribution to this particular body of knowledge.

The Lee–Cronin (2010) 'heterodox journal quality score' evaluated the contribution of a journal to the field. This comprised a weighted average of bibliometric impact, a position in the network of citations among the journals and a peer evaluation. It represented an attempt to measure the multidimensional contribution to a field in place of the pervasive 'impact factor', a highly reductionist metric comprising a simple count of citations of papers published in a journal over a standardised period.

The resulting 'Heterodox Economic Journal Rankings' were used by various heterodox economists as an independent validation of publication strategies, prioritising journals outside the mainstream rankings of economic journals. It provided a justification for Departments to resource heterodox economic research and supported efforts to recruit, evaluate and promote heterodox economists in their own terms. However, construction of journal rankings is a very laborious task, particularly where peer evaluation is used, and plans to subsequently update the exercise were interrupted by the untimely death of Frederic Lee in 2014 (Jo and Todorova 2015).

Meanwhile, there had been major developments in bibliometrics and journal ranking systems amidst the rising 'metric tide' in research quality evaluation (Wilsdon et al. 2015). Efforts were made to develop standardised bibliometrics that controlled for the varying citation practices in different academic disciplines. And new metrics were developed that attempted to capture wider contributions to a discipline than simply raw citations, notably the Subject Normalized Impact per Paper (SNIP) and the SCImago Journal Ranking (SJR) (González-Pereira et al. 2010), which includes a citation network centrality indicator. These developments raise the question of whether bespoke efforts to create Heterodox Economic Journal Rankings are still needed.

In this chapter, I revisit the original Heterodox Economic Journal Rankings, comparing these with the rankings of the same journals using the SNIP and SJR metrics. The analysis addresses two questions. First, to what extent do the SNIP and SJR capture the bibliometric and citation network effects that for Lee and Cronin (2010) indicated much of a journal's contribution to the heterodox economics body of knowledge? I address this question with a comparative analysis of the bibliometrics from each approach. Second, it is clear that neither the SNIP nor SJR attempt to capture the third element in the Lee–Cronin quality score, subjective quality evaluation by members of the heterodox economic community; but a question remains as to how much such peer evaluation changes over time. This is unlikely to be highly volatile and so the original peer evaluation may prove of long-lasting value. I address this question by replicating the peer review undertaken in the original study, comparing the results of the two surveys to estimate the volatility over a ten-year period.

The Heterodox Journal Quality Score

The Heterodox Journal Quality Score (HJQS) was an attempt to evaluate the relative contribution of a range of 62 academic journals to the distinctive body of knowledge identified as heterodox economics, which we argued is a distinct subdiscipline of economics, the other being mainstream economics.

As detailed in Lee and Cronin (2010), the HJQS was constructed as the weighted average of three constituent components, a Journal Bibliometric Quality Score (JBQS), a Journal Social Network Quality Score (JNQS), combined as a Total Citation Score (TCS = JBQS + JNQS) and a Journal Peer Evaluation Quality Score (JPEQS). These components were constituted as follows:

$$\text{HJQS} = 0.5\,(\text{TCS}/14 + \text{JPEQS}/5) \tag{1}$$

The JPEQS was a novelty for bibliometric analysis. But we saw this as an essential ingredient in assessing the contribution of a journal to the development of an emerging subdiscipline.[1] The JPEQS component was derived from

405 responses to a questionnaire distributed to subscribers to the Association for Heterodox Economists' email list in 2008, rating the perceived quality of each of 62 heterodox journals on a 1–5 scale, weighted by familiarity on a 3-point scale. Because I revisit this in this chapter, it is worth restating its derivation:

$$\text{JPEQS} = (1/\text{R}) \sum_{i=1}^{n_j} \left(z_j \times v_j \right)$$

$$= TS / n_j \times n_j / R \qquad (2)$$

where:
R is the total number of respondents;
n_j is the total number of respondents who had some or considerable familiarity with the jth journal;
z_j is equal to 1 or 0.5 when the respondent has considerable or some familiarity with the jth journal; and
v_j is equal to 1 … 5 depending on the research quality score chosen by the respondent for the jth journal.
TS is the sum of v_j

The HJQS provided a valuable reference point for heterodox economists attempting to expand space for heterodox views in a field dominated by mainstream economics. However, there were several practical and theoretical limitations to the HJQS. Construction of the HJQS was labour-intensive. Citation data were drawn manually for each journal from the Web of Science. Citations from and to heterodox journals were manually coded. The administration of the JPEQS questionnaire was also labour-intensive and the response rate relied greatly on Fred Lee's high personal standing within the heterodox economics community. Theoretical limitations include the somewhat idiosyncratic development of journal quality and network metrics and their combination with the qualitative evaluation, all of which are based on arbitrary assumptions of equal weightings to various components. While a pioneering and valuable tool for many in 2010, each subsequent year delivers a diminishing return from the original investment. Meanwhile, firmer theoretically grounded developments in bibliometrics offer potential alternatives.

Recent developments in bibliometric journal ranking

Since the construction of the Lee–Cronin (2010) index there have been some major developments in journal bibliometrics. In the last two decades, Dutch academic publisher Elsevier has been a major investor in the field with the establishment of the Scopus bibliometric database in 2002 disrupting the traditional domination of bibliometrics by Clarivate's Web of Science product, a spin-off from Thomson Reuters.[2] Elsevier won an agreement over Clarivate to use Scopus as the bibliometric evidence base for the 2014 UK Research Evaluation Framework exercise (REF), though Clarivate regained the contract for the 2021 REF.[3] There is some suggestion that REF 2014 evaluators were influenced by the Scopus metrics, either explicitly where citation metrics were formally employed, as with the Economics and Econometrics Panel, or implicitly where citation metrics were formally excluded from evaluation, as in the case of the Business and Management Panel. A comparison of journal impact factors and the REF 2014 assessment of published outputs found a strong association between journals ranked in the first quartile of the Scopus SJR or SNIP metrics and REF evaluations of outputs as 3* or 4* (Wilsdon et al. 2015).

As well as providing greater journal coverage than the Web of Science, a more accessible user interface and a free online basic version, Scopus introduced some more sophisticated metrics than the simple citation count-based two-year Journal Impact Factor (JIF), which had been the workhorse of bibliographic research since 1964 (Garfield 2006). Scopus provides free online access to three principal journal ranking metrics, CiteScore, SNIP and SJR. CiteScore is the three-year mean annual citations of a journal. SNIP weights citations by the mean citations of journals in the field, normalising citation rates by disciplinary practices. SJR, the SCImago Journal Rank, is weighted by both subject-specific citation rates and citing journal prestige. As SNIP and SJR are subject-normalised, they can be used to compare journals in different fields; the mean SNIP and mean SJR values for all journals is 1.0 (Research Intelligence 2018).[4]

While Lee and Cronin (2010) had recognised the *social* role of journals of citation networks in building a disciplinary field and had incorporated network metrics in our journal quality metric, bibliographic researchers had been exploring the *mathematical* value of including network measures in bibliographic metrics to enhance their accuracy. An early attempt to weight journal citations by the number of times the citing journals were cited themselves (Pinski and Narin 1976) was found to be inconsistently affected by the size and typology of the particular network of citations. But later applications of the PageRank algorithm developed by Google (Page et al. 1998) iteratively weight citations by the probability of a journal being cited, a function of its current citation rate and citation typology (Palacios-Huerta and Volij 2004; Bollen et al. 2006; Ma et al. 2008; Bergstrom 2007). The SJR is a subject and size normalised version of this approach, so that a citation from a highly cited journal within a subject area has more impact than a citation from a less-cited journal within the subject or one outside the subject (González-Pereira et al. 2010).

So the subject normalisation of the SNIP and SJR and the prestige factor in the SJR metric play a similar role to the incorporation of subject and network metrics into the Lee–Cronin (2010) journal quality score; journals are given additional weighting where they contribute to the transfer of knowledge within a particular discipline.

Comparing HJQS and new bibliometrics

To what extent do the new subject-normalised journal quality metrics reflect the qualities sought in the HJQS? If the new metrics provide largely similar results to the HJQS then the laborious task of compiling a separate heterodox journal quality ranking is rendered redundant. However, if the different metrics prove to be measuring substantially different things, then the case for compiling a specialised ranking remains.

The comparison of the SNIP and SJR with the HJQS proceeded in three steps. First, the SNIP and SJR metrics for 2008 were downloaded for those HJQS journals listed in Scopus and the characteristics of the series were compared; data were available for 54 of the 62 journals in the HJQS list.[5] Second, a regression analysis was undertaken of the relationship between the HJQS and the two new bibliographic series. Third, a questionnaire was administered among the heterodox economics community, to determine the extent to which the qualitative evaluation of the journals had changed.

This analysis was then used to develop a proxy for the HJQS in 2008 from the bibliometrics for 2008 and the qualitative evaluation of 2008. The proxy HJQS* was validated by a comparison with the original HJQS. Then the HJQS* for 2017 was estimated from the 2017 bibliometrics for an expanded range of 147 heterodox journals derived from the Heterodox Economics Directory (Kapeller and Springholz 2016).

While the HJQS is actually a ranking, derived from ordinal data, all values are unique, so it is reasonable to treat the HJQS and its component scores as continuous variables and analyse via linear regression. This is more parsimonious and more useful in developing proxy metrics than attempting to derive rankings from the probabilities of an ordinal regression.

A set of simple linear regressions was undertaken between the HJQS and its components and the SNIP and SJR respectively:

$$\mathrm{H} = \alpha + \beta_1 \mathrm{B} + e \tag{3}$$

Where:

H is the HJQS and each of its components (JRQS, JNQS, TCS, JPEQS); and
B is each of the new bibliometrics SNIP and SJR.

As the HJQS is comprised of a citation-derived element (TCS) and a qualitative evaluation (JPEQS), the new bibliometrics are likely to provide more of a proxy for the former than the latter. So, an alternative model was also tested:

$$\mathrm{H} = \alpha + \beta_1 \mathrm{B} + \beta_2 \mathrm{JPEQS} + e \tag{4}$$

A proxy for the HJQS_{2008} for the 54 journals for which new bibliometrics were available was developed substituting estimations for TCS, derived from equation (3), into the original HJQS equation (1). Since JPEQS is given from the data it does not need to be estimated.

$$TCS^*_{j,\,2008} = \alpha + \beta_1 B_{j,\,2008} \tag{5}$$

$$HJQS^*_{j,\,2008} = 0.5\,(TCS^*_{j,\,2008}/14 + JPEQS_{j,\,2008}/5) \tag{6}$$

Where $j = 1 \ldots 54$ journals in common to HJQS and Scopus in 2008.

Then estimates for $HJQS_{2017}$ were derived from the bibliometric data for 2017 for an expanded set of 147 journals.

$$TCS^*_{j,\,2017} = \alpha + \beta_1 B_{j,\,2017} \tag{7}$$

$$HJQS^*_{j,\,2017} = 0.5\,(TCS^*_{j,\,2017}/14 + JPEQS_{j,\,2017}/5) \tag{8}$$

where $j = 1 \ldots 147$ journals from the Heterodox Economics Directory listed in Scopus in 2017.

The 2017 JPEQS for the expanded set of journals is derived from the 54 responses to a questionnaire distributed to subscribers to the Heterodox Economics email list hetecon.jisc.ac.uk. The questionnaire responses also provided an indication of the volatility of the JPEQS. Qualitative evaluation is likely to be more stable and persistent than citation-based bibliometrics as users' evaluations of academic journals take time to develop and are likely to remain settled for some time. Thus, the JPEQS metric is likely to need only periodic updating.

Results

The HJQS, SNIP and SJR have widely differing ranges around different means, as reported in Table 13.1 for all journals and Table 13.2 for the subset of 62 journals covered by the HJQS. While the HQJS and SJR data are rankings rather than continuous variables, since all values are unique, means and symmetry measures are reported in Table 13.2 to indicate the approximate distributions.

To the extent that the data approximate continuous ranges, as reported in the last column of Table 13.3, the SJR, HJQS and JPEQS variables are significantly non-normally distributed, the HJQS variables are non-normally

Table 13.1 Descriptive statistics – all journals 2008

Statistic	*SNIP*	*SJR*	*HQJS*
N	16468	17156	62
Max	9.905	107.104	0.542
Min	0.000	0.100	0.087
Mean	1.000	1.000	0.233

Table 13.2 Descriptive statistics – HJQS journals 2008

Statistic	*SNIP*	*SJR*	*HJQS*	*JRQS*	*JNQS*	*TCS*	*JPEQS*
N	54	54	62	62	62	62	62
max	2.153	2.223	0.5419	5.2277	4.3320	8.0970	2.9173
min	0.0000	0.1000	0.0873	1.0708	0.2167	2.2646	0.0247
median	0.7615	0.3525	0.2214	2.6425	1.8461	4.5375	0.4802
mean	0.8376	0.4777	0.2327	2.7458	1.9958	4.7378	0.6300
sd	0.5782	0.4226	0.0890	0.9311	0.9060	1.3985	0.5436
variance	0.3343	0.1786	0.0079	0.8671	0.8209	1.9560	0.2955
skewness	0.5706	2.04328	0.8114	0.2540	0.4275	0.4066	1.7524
kurtosis	2.6842	7.5283	4.0288	2.5808	2.6237	2.5732	7.14396

Table 13.3 Skewness/kurtosis tests for normality

Variable	*Obs*	*Pr(Skewness)*	*Pr(Kurtosis)*	*– joint –*	
				Adj chi2(2)	*Prob>chi2*
SNIP	54	0.0712	0.8411	3.48	0.1759
SJR	54	**0.0000**	**0.0004**	26.13	**0.0000**
HJQS	62	**0.0094**	0.0820	8.49	**0.0143**
JRQS	62	0.3759	0.6069	1.08	0.5815
JNQS	62	0.1439	0.6849	2.40	0.3009
TCS	62	0.1634	0.5930	2.33	0.3125
JPEQS	62	**0.0000**	**0.0004**	24.89	**0.0000**

skewed and the SJR and JPEQS variables display both non-normal skewness and kurtosis. So, to meet the normality distribution assumptions of linear regression, log transformations of the response variables, HJQS and JPEQS, were used.

Unsurprisingly, as reported in Table 13.4, the SNIP and SJR rankings are strongly correlated. There is a moderate correlation between the HJQS and SNIP, but not between HJQS and SJR, indicating some potential to use the SNIP as a proxy for the HJQS. There are also correlations between SNIP and the individual components of the HJQS (JRQS, JNQS, TCS and JPEQS), the strongest being with the TCS and which is the only component correlated with the SJR; the TCS is the component that draws on citation counts as do the SNIP and SJR. Surprisingly, despite making use of network metrics, the SJR is not correlated with the JNQS, which was designed to capture network effects.[6]

Table 13.5 presents the results of the linear regressions. The models demonstrate that the HJQS and each of its component metrics are significantly associated with SNIP, particularly TCS, which is the only metric associated

Table 13.4 Pearson pairwise correlations

	SNIP	*SJR*	*Log HJQS*	*JRQS*	*JNQS*	*TCS*
SJR	0.8187 ***					
Log HJQS	0.4454 ***	0.2524				
JRQS	0.3786 **	0.2431	0.5875 ***			
JNQS	0.3330 *	0.2410	0.7310 ***	0.1586		
TCS	0.4714 ***	0.3217 *	0.8637 ***	0.7691 ***	0.7526 ***	
Log JPEQS	0.3505 **	0.1627	0.8610 ***	0.2606 *	0.5582 ***	0.5331 ***

Observations: 54; * $p < 0.05$, ** $p < 0.01$, *** $p < 0.000$.

with SJR. However, the variation in the HJQS and its components explained by the association is modest, with Adj. R2 values of < 21%, indicating likely individual differences in rank between respective measures.[7]

To develop a proxy of HJQS from SNIP, an estimated TCS* is derived from the regression model (7) as per equation (4): Since JPEQS is given from the data it does not need to be estimated. An estimated HJQS* can then be derived from SNIP as per equation (5).

For example, taking a median-ranked journal from the HJQS, *Historical Materialism*, with a SNIP_{2008} of 0.762 and a JPEQS of 0.45851:

$$\text{TCS*}_{j,\,2008} = \alpha + \beta_1 \text{SNIP}_{j,\,2008} = 3.826883 + 1.146537 * 0.762 = 4.701$$

$$\text{HJQS*}_{j,\,2008} = 0.5\,(4.701\,/14 + 0.45851\,/5) = 0.2164$$

These SNIP-derived estimates compare with actual values of 0.2052 for HJQS and 4.3873 for TCS. But while absolute values of the proxy estimates will vary from actual values, more important is the relative ranking of journals. Of the HJQS top 20, three are unranked for want of SNIP metrics and five are ranked outside the HJQS* top 20. Ten journals have lower HJQS* rankings than HJQS and seven have the same or higher rankings. One journal, *International Labour Review*, has an HJQS* ranking more than one standard deviation from its HJQS ranking.

Among all HJQS journals, six were ranked in HJQS* more than one standard deviation from their HJQS rank, all but one higher. Sixteen journals were ranked lower in HJQS* than in HJQS and 37 the same or higher. As reported in Table 13.6, the distribution of HJQS* was narrower than the HJQS, reflecting the properties of the SNIP metric for these journals.

In summary, then, the JPEQS-adjusted SNIP bibliometric provides a reasonable proxy for the HJQS. It is thus feasible to construct annual HJQS* estimates, following the annual update of SNIP, combined with periodic updating of the JPEQS via surveys of the qualitative evaluation of the journals by their principal users – heterodox economists.

Table 13.5 Linear regression models

	(1)	(2)	(3)	(4)	(5)	(6)
Dependent	Log HJQS	Log HJQS	JRQS	JRQS	JNQS	JNQS
Intercept	−.7763502	−.7139502	2.287533	2.543876	1.543706	1.738125
exp(Incpt.)	.4600821	.4897059				
SNIP	.1335376 ***		.6132241 **		.5333539 *	
SJR		.1035318		.5386655		.5282433
exp(Coef.)	1.142864	1.109081				
F	12.87	3.54	8.70	3.27	6.48	3.21
Prob > F	0.0007 ***	0.0655	0.0048 **	0.0765	0.0139 *	0.0791
R^2	0.1984	0.0637	0.1434	0.0591	0.1109	0.0581
Adj R^2	0.1830	0.0457	0.1269	0.0410	0.0938	0.0400
Root MSE	0.15668	0.16933	0.87506	.91709	.88173	.90751

	(7)	(8)	(9)	(10)
Dependent	TCS	TCS	Log JPEQS	Log JPEQS
Intercept	3.826883	4.275968	−.6090008	−.467856
exp(Incpt.)			.543894	.6263437
SNIP	1.146537 ***		.2641555 **	
SJR		1.07035 *		.1677285
exp(Coef.)			1.302331	1.182615
F	14.86	6.00	7.28	1.41
Prob > F	0.0003 ***	0.0177 *	0.0094 **	0.2399
R^2	0.2223	0.1035	0.1229	0.0265
Adj R^2	0.2073	0.0863	0.1060	0.0077
Root MSE	1.252	1.3442	.41202	.4307

Observations: 54; * $p < 0.05$, ** $p < 0.01$, *** $p < 0.000$.

Table 13.6 2008 HJQS* and HJQS descriptive statistics

	HJQS 2008*	*HJQS*
Mean	0.234	0.233
Median	0.235	0.221
Max	0.484	0.542
Min	0.148	0.087
SD	0.068	0.089
N	54	62

Table 13.7 2008 JPEQS and 2017 JPEQS – descriptive statistics

	N	*Max*	*Min*	*Mean*	*Median*	*SD*
2008 – HJQS Journals						
Average Score (TS/n_j)	62	3.25	1.32	2.04	2.03	0.40
Familiarity Weighting (n_j/R)	62	0.90	0.02	0.28	0.23	0.19
JPEQS	62	2.92	0.02	0.63	0.48	0.54
2017 – HJQS Journals						
Average Score	62	4.27	2.00	3.41	3.50	0.53
Familiarity Weighting	62	0.89	0.06	0.38	0.40	0.20
JPEQS	62	3.80	0.15	1.36	1.32	0.82
2017 – Extended journals						
Average Score	147	5.00	2.00	3.75	3.73	0.73
Familiarity Weighting	147	3.80	0.02	0.21	0.15	0.20
JPEQS	147	3.80	0.09	0.77	0.46	0.76

To derive HJQS* estimates for 2017 then, it was necessary to construct a 2017 JPEQS. This was derived from an extended version of the original 2008 questionnaire, using equation (2). For the original 62 HJQS journals, the 2017 JPEQS values were highly correlated with those of 2008 (R = 0.9134 ***). Fifty-seven journals were ranked the same or higher in 2017 than in 2008 and 25 journals ranked lower. Only one journal ranking was outside the standard deviation in ranking, the *Journal of Development Studies*, 18 ranks higher.

However, as presented in Table 13.7, the 2017 values were considerably higher than in 2008, most likely reflecting the smaller sample from which the questionnaire responses were drawn. The 54 respondents in 2017 were likely motivated by valuing more highly the contribution of heterodox journals than the much larger sample in 2008. The 2017 sample generally reported greater familiarity with the journals than the 2008 sample and rated the journal quality considerably higher on average. A linear regression of individual journal JPEQS for 2008 and 2017 indicated $JPEQS^*_{2008} = -.1922658 + .6067013\, JPEQS_{2017}$ ($p = 0.000$, Adj. $R^2 = 0.8322$). So, to use the 2017 JPEQS as an equivalent proxy for the 2008 JPEQs requires an adjustment in values by these coefficients (eq. 9) and a corresponding adjustment to eq. 8, when calculating $HJQS^*_{2017}$.

$$JPEQS^*_{j,2017} = -.1922658 + .6067013\ JPEQS_{2017} \tag{9}$$

$$HJQS^*_{j,2017} = 0.5\ (TCS^*_{j,2017}/14 + JPEQS^*_{j,2017}/5) \tag{10}$$

where $j = 1 \ldots 147$ journals from the Heterodox Economics Directory listed in Scopus in 2017.

Table 13A.3 in the Appendix presents the derivation of the $JPEQS^*_{2017}$ estimates for each of the 147 journals. Table 13A.4 presents the $HJQS^*_{2017}$ estimates for the 99 journals where 2017 SNIP metrics were available, in rank order. Finally, Table 13A.5 compares the 2008 HJQS journal rankings with the 2017 proxy rankings of the original cohort. Twenty-nine of the original journals were ranked the same or higher in 2017 and 29 were ranked lower. Sixteen journals changed ranking by more than one standard deviation, all but four lower. This indicates large movements in ranking in a quarter of journals, the qualitative evaluations amplifying citations recorded in the SNIP. The main beneficiaries are cross-disciplinary and specialist journals *Ecological Economics*, *Feminist Economics*, *History of Political Economy* and the *International Review of Applied Economics*.

Where the correlation between SNIP and Log JPEQS for the original cohort of journals in 2008 was 0.3505**, in 2017 it was 0.3175*, indicating some increased disparity in qualitative evaluation from citation data in the later period. As discussed earlier, since the 2017 respondents are likely to have a greater appreciation of a wider range of journals, the small increase in disparity may simply represent a more expert evaluation. But the divergence from the SNIP over time is small, pointing to the influence of citation activity on qualitative evaluation. This supports the proposition that qualitative evaluation is not highly volatile and so a sampling at one point of time remains reliable for a lengthy period after.

Conclusion

The results demonstrate that the method presented provides a viable means of generating ongoing annual proxies for the original Lee–Cronin (2010) Heterodox Journal Quality Score. Making use of advances in mainstream bibliometric analysis, such as the SNIP, removes the laborious quantitative effort involved in the construction of the original index. And the low volatility in qualitative evaluation, relative to the bibliometrics, suggests that only infrequent sampling of the views of heterodox journal users is needed to maintain this input in the index or to extend the index to additional journals.

The HJQS journal ranking presented in Appendix Table 13A.4 represents a contemporary extension of the original vision of the index that can provide heterodox economists with a systematic tool to justify the quality of their work in terms of its contribution to a distinctive subdiscipline of economics. This is a more appropriate standard by which to evaluate the efforts of heterodox economists than to judge them in terms of contributions to orthodox economics, a subdiscipline of little relevance to the work of this important group of economists.

Notes

1 Hudson (2013) has since attempted to model the qualitative evaluation effect for orthodox economics subdiscipline by examining the variation in banding of journals among different ranking lists. He found the Association of Business School's Journal Quality List as an outlier, rating highly journals of little interest to orthodox economists.
2 See www.elsevier.com/about/press-releases/science-and-technology/scopus-comes-of-age. Scopus underpins Elsevier's expansion into research impact benchmarking (SciVal, Pure) and research networking (Mendeley, SSRN).
3 See www.ref.ac.uk/news/clarivate-analytics-will-provide-citation-data-during-ref-2021/.
4 Elsevier's competitors have not ignored these developments and both Clarivate and Wiley have introduced journal prestige metrics, though these remain less accessible, propriety rather than open sources.
5 Scopus bibliometrics were only available from 2009 for *Econ Journal Watch*, the *Journal of Australian Political Economy* and the *Quarterly Review of Austrian Economics*. In these three cases, the 2009 values were used on the assumption that these were unlikely to be greatly different from 2008.
6 An examination of the more precise Spearman rank coefficients finds the same pattern in terms of SNIP but does find modest correlations of the SJR with HJQS (0.3113*) and JRQS (0.3551*).
7 An ordered logistic regression found the SNIP associated with the HJQS and its components in a similar manner, though a less significant association with TCS and JPEQS and lower model fit, Pseudo R2s of < 4%. SJR was also similarly weakly associated with TCS but no other variables.

References

Bergstrom, C. (2007). Eigenfactor: Measuring the value and prestige of scholarly journals. *College & Research Libraries News*, 68(5), 314–316.

Bollen, J., Rodriguez, M.A. and van de Sompel, H. (2006). Journal status. *Scientometrics*, 69(3), 669–687.

Garfield, E. (2006). The history and meaning of the journal impact factor. *JAMA-Journal of the American Medical Association*, 295(1), 90–93.

González-Pereira, B., Guerrero-Bote, V.P., and Moya-Anegón, F. (2010). A new approach to the metric of journals scientific prestige: The SJR indicator. *Journal of Informetrics*, 4(3), 379–391. Available at: http://dx.doi.org/10.1016/j.joi.2010.03.002

Hudson, J. (2013). Ranking journals. *The Economic Journal*, 123, F202–F222. Available at: http://dx.doi.org/10.1111/ecoj.1206.

Jo, T.-H. and Todorova, Z. (2015). Introduction: Frederic S. Lee's contributions to heterodox economics. In Tae-Hee Jo and Zdravka Todorova (Eds.), *Advancing the frontiers of heterodox economics: Essays in honor of Frederic S. Lee* (pp. 1–18). London and New York: Routledge. Available at: https://mpra.ub.uni-muenchen.de/62568/1/MPRA_paper_62568.pdf.

Kapeller, J. and Springholz, F. (2016). *Heterodox Economics Directory: Your guide to heterodox economics*, 6th edn. Available at: http://heterodoxnews.com/directory/.

Lee, F.S. and Cronin, B., with McConnell, S. and Dean, E. (2010). Research quality rankings of heterodox economic journals in a contested discipline. *American Journal of Economics and Sociology*, 69(5), 1409–1452. DOI: 10.1111/j.1536-7150.2010.00751.x

Ma, N., Guan, J. and Zhao, Y. (2008). Bringing PageRank to the citation analysis. *Information Processing and Management*, 44(2), 800–810.

Page, L., Brin, S., Motwani, R. and Winograd, T. (1998). *The PageRank citation ranking: Bringing order to the Web*. Technical report. Stanford, CA: Stanford University.

Palacios-Huerta, I and Volij, O. (2004). The measurement of intellectual influence. *Econometrica*, 72(3), 963–977.

Pinski, G. and Narin, F. (1976). Citation influence for journal aggregates of scientific publications: Theory, with application to the literature of physics. *Information Processing and Management*, 12, 297–312.

Research Intelligence (2018). *Research metrics guidebook*. Elsevier. Available at: www.elsevier.com/research-intelligence/resource-library/research-metrics-guidebook.

Wilsdon, J. et al. (2015). *The metric tide: Report of the independent review of the role of metrics in research assessment and management*. Bristol: Higher Education Funding Council of England. DOI: 10.13140/RG.2.1.4929.1363.

APPENDIX

Table 13A.1 Spearman rank correlations

	SNIP	*SJR*	*HJQS*	*JRQS*	*JNQS*	*TCS*
SJR	0.8866 ***					
HJQS	0.4846**	0.3397 *				
JRQS	0.4162 **	0.3414 *	0.6004 ***			
JNQS	0.2589 *	0.1433	0.7173 ***	0.0992		
TCS	0.4552 ***	0.3355 *	0.8879 ***	0.7680 ***	0.6993 ***	
JPEQS	0.4188 **	0.2952	0.8617 ***	0.2774 *	0.5690 **	0.5656 ***

Observations: 54; * $p < 0.05$, ** $p < 0.01$, *** $p < 0.000$.

Table 13A.2 Comparison of linear and ordered logit regression models

	Linear		*Ordered logit*	
	SNIP sig.	*Adj. R2*	*SNIP sig.*	*Pseudo R2*
HJQS	***	0.1830	***	0.0278
JRQS	**	0.1269	**	0.0186
JNQS	*	0.0938	*	0.0109
TCS	***	0.2073	**	0.0301
JPEQS	**	0.1060	*	0.0165

Table 13A.3 JPEQS 2017

Journal	*Cohort*	*Total Score (TS)*	*(nj)*	*Average Score (TS/ nj)*	*Familiarity Weighting (nj/R)*	*JPEQS*	*JPEQS**
Advances in Austrian Economics	Original	28	11	2.545	0.204	0.519	0.122
American Journal of Economics and Sociology	Original	105	32	3.281	0.593	1.944	0.987
Antipode	Original	53	16	3.313	0.296	0.981	0.403
Cambridge Journal of Economics	Original	205	48	4.271	0.889	3.796	2.111
Capital & Class	Original	120	37	3.243	0.685	2.222	1.156
Capitalism, Nature, Socialism	Original	52	14	3.714	0.259	0.963	0.392
Cepal Review	Original	38	12	3.167	0.222	0.704	0.235
Constitutional Political Economy	Original	25	9	2.778	0.167	0.463	0.089
Contributions to Political Economy	Original	109	31	3.516	0.574	2.019	1.032
Critical Perspectives on International Business	Original	8	4	2.000	0.074	0.148	−0.102
Critical Sociology	Original	33	12	2.750	0.222	0.611	0.178
Debatte	Original	8	3	2.667	0.056	0.148	−0.102
Development and Change	Original	67	19	3.526	0.352	1.241	0.560
Ecological Economics	Original	95	26	3.654	0.481	1.759	0.875
Econ Journal Watch	Original	48	17	2.824	0.315	0.889	0.347

Table 13A.3 Cont.

Journal	*Cohort*	*Total Score (TS)*	*(nj)*	*Average Score (TS/ nj)*	*Familiarity Weighting (nj/R)*	*JPEQS*	*JPEQS**
Economic Systems Research	Original	39	12	3.250	0.222	0.722	0.246
Economics and Philosophy	Original	97	26	3.731	0.481	1.796	0.898
Economy and Society	Original	127	34	3.735	0.630	2.352	1.235
European Journal of Economics and Economic Policies: Intervention	Original	90	24	3.750	0.444	1.667	0.819
European Journal of the History of Economic Thought	Original	139	35	3.971	0.648	2.574	1.369
Feminist Economics	Original	85	22	3.864	0.407	1.574	0.763
Forum for Social Economics	Original	75	25	3.000	0.463	1.389	0.650
Historical Materialism	Original	71	25	2.840	0.463	1.315	0.605
History of Economics Review	Original	70	20	3.500	0.370	1.296	0.594
History of Political Economy	Original	120	31	3.871	0.574	2.222	1.156
International Journal of Green Economics	Original	13	6	2.167	0.111	0.241	−0.046
International Journal of Political Economy	Original	92	27	3.407	0.500	1.704	0.841
International Journal of Social Economics	Original	30	9	3.333	0.167	0.556	0.145
International Labor Review	Original	46	14	3.286	0.259	0.852	0.325
International Review of Applied Economics	Original	97	26	3.731	0.481	1.796	0.898
Journal of Australian Political Economy	Original	40	13	3.077	0.241	0.741	0.257

(continued)

Table 13A.3 Cont.

Journal	*Cohort*	*Total Score (TS)*	*(nj)*	*Average Score (TS/nj)*	*Familiarity Weighting (nj/R)*	*JPEQS*	*JPEQS**
Journal of Development Studies	Original	50	16	3.125	0.296	0.926	0.369
Journal of Economic Behavior and Organization	Original	127	30	4.233	0.556	2.352	1.235
Journal of Economic Issues	Original	154	39	3.949	0.722	2.852	1.538
Journal of Economic Methodology	Original	94	24	3.917	0.444	1.741	0.864
Journal of Evolutionary Economics	Original	89	24	3.708	0.444	1.648	0.808
Journal of Income Distribution	Original	28	10	2.800	0.185	0.519	0.122
Journal of Institutional Economics	Original	89	25	3.560	0.463	1.648	0.808
Journal of Interdisciplinary Economics	Original	18	7	2.571	0.130	0.333	0.010
Journal of Post Keynesian Economics	Original	160	41	3.902	0.759	2.963	1.605
Journal of Socio-Economics	Original	72	22	3.273	0.407	1.333	0.617
Journal of the History of Economic Thought	Original	110	27	4.074	0.500	2.037	1.044
Metroeconomica	Original	122	30	4.067	0.556	2.259	1.178
New Left Review	Original	108	29	3.724	0.537	2.000	1.021
New Political Economy	Original	71	18	3.944	0.333	1.315	0.605
Organization & Environment	Original	9	4	2.250	0.074	0.167	−0.091
Oxford Development Studies	Original	31	9	3.444	0.167	0.574	0.156
Quarterly Journal of Austrian Economics	Original	24	9	2.667	0.167	0.444	0.077

Table 13A.3 Cont.

Journal	*Cohort*	*Total Score (TS)*	*(nj)*	*Average Score (TS/nj)*	*Familiarity Weighting (nj/R)*	*JPEQS*	*JPEQS**
Research in the History of Economic Thought and Methodology	Original	50	14	3.571	0.259	0.926	0.369
Rethinking Marxism	Original	79	24	3.292	0.444	1.463	0.695
Review of African Political Economy	Original	19	6	3.167	0.111	0.352	0.021
Review of Austrian Economics	Original	29	10	2.900	0.185	0.537	0.134
Review of Black Political Economy	Original	22	7	3.143	0.130	0.407	0.055
Review of International Political Economy	Original	87	21	4.143	0.389	1.611	0.785
Review of Political Economy	Original	128	32	4.000	0.593	2.370	1.246
Review of Radical Political Economics	Original	142	37	3.838	0.685	2.630	1.403
Review of Social Economy	Original	105	29	3.621	0.537	1.944	0.987
Revista de Economía Politica/ Brazilian Journal of Political Economy	Original	33	10	3.300	0.185	0.611	0.178
Science & Society	Original	98	27	3.630	0.500	1.815	0.909
Structural Change and Economic Dynamics	Original	95	24	3.958	0.444	1.759	0.875
Studies in Political Economy	Original	21	6	3.500	0.111	0.389	0.044
Work, Employment and Society	Original	49	12	4.083	0.222	0.907	0.358
Accounting, Organizations and Society	Extended	5	1	5.000	0.019	0.093	−0.136
Alternative Routes	Extended	5	1	5.000	0.019	0.093	−0.136

(*continued*)

Table 13A.3 Cont.

Journal	*Cohort*	*Total Score (TS)*	*(nj)*	*Average Score (TS/nj)*	*Familiarity Weighting (nj/R)*	*JPEQS*	*JPEQS**
Basic Income Studies:	Extended	10	3	3.333	0.056	0.185	−0.080
Bulletin of Political Economy	Extended	28	9	3.111	0.167	0.519	0.122
Cambridge Journal of Regions, Economy and Society	Extended	43	10	4.300	0.185	0.796	0.291
Comercio Exterior	Extended	5	1	5.000	0.019	0.093	−0.136
Competition and Change	Extended	32	8	4.000	0.148	0.593	0.167
Critical Perspectives on Accounting	Extended	5	1	5.000	0.019	0.093	−0.136
Critique	Extended	32	9	3.556	0.167	0.593	0.167
Cuadernos de Economía	Extended	5	1	5.000	0.019	0.093	−0.136
Economía e Sociedade	Extended	14	3	4.667	0.056	0.259	−0.035
Economic and Political Weekly	Extended	25	7	3.571	0.130	0.463	0.089
Economic Geography	Extended	36	8	4.500	0.148	0.667	0.212
Economic Issues	Extended	30	9	3.333	0.167	0.556	0.145
Economics and Labour Relations Review	Extended	37	10	3.700	0.185	0.685	0.223
Economics and Policy of Energy and the Environment	Extended	5	1	5.000	0.019	0.093	−0.136
Economie Appliquée	Extended	30	11	2.727	0.204	0.556	0.145
Environmental Values	Extended	10	2	5.000	0.037	0.185	−0.080
Erasmus Journal for Philosophy and Economics	Extended	47	15	3.133	0.278	0.870	0.336
Evolutionary and Institutional Economic Review	Extended	11	3	3.667	0.056	0.204	−0.069
Gender, Work, and Organization	Extended	25	6	4.167	0.111	0.463	0.089
History of Economic Ideas	Extended	59	16	3.688	0.296	1.093	0.471

Table 13A.3 Cont.

Journal	*Cohort*	*Total Score (TS)*	*(nj)*	*Average Score (TS/ nj)*	*Familiarity Weighting (nj/R)*	*JPEQS*	*JPEQS**
Industrial and Corporate Change	Extended	50	12	4.167	0.222	0.926	0.369
Innovations (Revue d'économie et de management de l'innovation)	Extended	5	1	5.000	0.019	0.093	−0.136
Interdisciplinary Journal of Economics and Business Law	Extended	7	2	3.500	0.037	0.130	−0.114
Interface: A Journal for and about Social Movements	Extended	5	1	5.000	0.019	0.093	−0.136
International Critical Thought	Extended	12	3	4.000	0.056	0.222	−0.057
International Journal of Development Issues	Extended	5	2	2.500	0.037	0.093	−0.136
International Journal of Green Economics	Extended	8	2	4.000	0.037	0.148	−0.102
International Journal of Pluralism and Economics Education	Extended	61	21	2.905	0.389	1.130	0.493
International Journal of Public Policy	Extended	12	3	4.000	0.056	0.222	−0.057
International Review of Applied Economics	Extended	65	16	4.063	0.296	1.204	0.538
International Socialism: A Quarterly Journal of Socialist Theory	Extended	12	3	4.000	0.056	0.222	−0.057
Interventions Économiques	Extended	7	2	3.500	0.037	0.130	−0.114
Investigación Económica	Extended	13	3	4.333	0.056	0.241	−0.046

(*continued*)

Table 13A.3 Cont.

Journal	*Cohort*	*Total Score (TS)*	*(nj)*	*Average Score (TS/nj)*	*Familiarity Weighting (nj/R)*	*JPEQS*	*JPEQS**
Journal des Économistes et des Études Humaines	Extended	5	1	5.000	0.019	0.093	−0.136
Journal of Agrarian Change	Extended	16	4	4.000	0.074	0.296	−0.013
Journal of Economic and Social Policy	Extended	5	1	5.000	0.019	0.093	−0.136
Journal of Economic Geography	Extended	17	4	4.250	0.074	0.315	−0.001
Journal of Heterodox Economics	Extended	14	5	2.800	0.093	0.259	−0.035
Journal of Human Development and Capabilities	Extended	13	3	4.333	0.056	0.241	−0.046
Journal of Innovation Economics & Management	Extended	5	1	5.000	0.019	0.093	−0.136
Journal of Philosophical Economics	Extended	17	5	3.400	0.093	0.315	−0.001
Journal of World-Systems Research	Extended	20	6	3.333	0.111	0.370	0.032
Labor Studies Journal	Extended	8	2	4.000	0.037	0.148	−0.102
Local Economy	Extended	18	5	3.600	0.093	0.333	0.010
Momentum Quarterly	Extended	8	2	4.000	0.037	0.148	−0.102
New Labor Forum	Extended	8	2	4.000	0.037	0.148	−0.102
New Proposals: Journal of Marxism and Interdisciplinary Inquiry	Extended	5	1	5.000	0.019	0.093	−0.136
New School Economic Review	Extended	23	10	2.300	0.185	0.426	0.066
Nova Economía	Extended	12	4	3.000	0.074	0.222	−0.057
OEconomia	Extended	27	8	3.375	0.148	0.500	0.111

Table 13A.3 Cont.

Journal	*Cohort*	*Total Score (TS)*	*(nj)*	*Average Score (TS/ nj)*	*Familiarity Weighting (nj/R)*	*JPEQS*	*JPEQS**
OIKOS – Revista de Economía Heterodoxa	Extended	9	3	3.000	0.056	0.167	−0.091
Ola Financiera	Extended	10	3	3.333	0.056	0.185	−0.080
On the Horizon	Extended	17	4	4.250	0.074	0.315	−0.001
Panoeconomicus	Extended	19	5	3.800	0.093	0.352	0.021
Papers in Political Economy	Extended	16	4	4.000	0.074	0.296	−0.013
Problemas del Desarrollo	Extended	13	3	4.333	0.056	0.241	−0.046
PROKLA	Extended	10	2	5.000	0.037	0.185	−0.080
PSL Quarterly Review	Extended	44	12	3.667	0.222	0.815	0.302
Public Policy Research	Extended	5	1	5.000	0.019	0.093	−0.136
Quarterly Journal of Austrian Economics	Extended	11	4	2.750	0.074	0.204	−0.069
Realidad Económica	Extended	15	3	5.000	0.056	0.278	−0.024
Régulation Review. Capitalism, Institutions, Powers	Extended	30	8	3.750	0.148	0.556	0.145
Research in Political Economy	Extended	25	8	3.125	0.148	0.463	0.089
Research in the History of Economic Thought and Methodology	Extended	30	8	3.750	0.148	0.556	0.145
Review of Capital as Power	Extended	9	3	3.000	0.056	0.167	−0.091
Review of Keynesian Economics	Extended	90	25	3.600	0.463	1.667	0.819
Review of Social Economy	Extended	68	17	4.000	0.315	1.259	0.572
Revista Circus	Extended	9	2	4.500	0.037	0.167	−0.091
Revista de Economía Institucional	Extended	5	1	5.000	0.019	0.093	−0.136

(continued)

Table 13A.3 Cont.

Journal	*Cohort*	*Total Score (TS)*	*(nj)*	*Average Score (TS/ nj)*	*Familiarity Weighting (nj/R)*	*JPEQS*	*JPEQS**
Revista de Economía Mundial/Journal of World Economy	Extended	28	8	3.800	7.368	0.148	−0.102
Revista Outubro	Extended	8	2	4.000	0.037	0.148	−0.102
Revue Française de Socio-Economie	Extended	5	1	5.000	0.019	0.093	−0.136
Social and Economic Studies	Extended	5	1	5.000	0.019	0.093	−0.136
Socio-Economic Review	Extended	39	9	4.333	0.167	0.722	0.246
Structural Change and Economic Dynamics	Extended	55	13	4.231	0.241	1.019	0.426
Studies in Political Economy	Extended	11	3	3.667	0.056	0.204	−0.069
Thesis Eleven	Extended	15	4	3.750	0.074	0.278	−0.024
Transformation: Critical Perspectives on Southern Africa	Extended	5	1	5.000	0.019	0.093	−0.136
tripleC: Communication, Capitalism & Critique	Extended	7	2	3.500	0.037	0.130	−0.114
Urbani Izziv (Urban Change)	Extended	5	1	5.000	0.019	0.093	−0.136
Work Organisation, Labour and Globalisation	Extended	5	1	5.000	0.019	0.093	−0.136
World Economic Review	Extended	46	15	3.067	0.278	0.852	0.325
World Review of Political Economy	Extended	16	6	2.667	0.111	0.296	−0.013

Table 13A.4 Heterodox Journal Quality Score Ranking 2017

Journal	*Cohort*	*SNIP 2017*	*TCS* 2017*	*JPEQS* 2017*	*HJQS* 2017*	*HJQS* Rank*
Cambridge Journal of Economics	Original	2.299	2.299	6.463	2.111	1
Journal of Post Keynesian Economics	Original	0.996	0.996	4.969	1.605	2
Journal of Economic Issues	Original	0.766	0.766	4.705	1.538	3
Review of Radical Political Economics	Original	0.906	0.906	4.866	1.403	4
European Journal of the History of Economic Thought	Original	1.047	1.047	5.027	1.369	5
Review of Political Economy	Original	0.91	0.91	4.87	1.246	6
Economy and Society	Original	1.852	1.852	5.95	1.235	7
Journal of Economic Behavior and Organization	Original	1.351	1.351	5.376	1.235	8
Metroeconomica	Original	1.143	1.143	5.137	1.178	9
History of Political Economy	Original	1.159	1.159	5.156	1.156	10
Capital and Class	Original	0.861	0.861	4.814	1.156	11
Journal of the History of Economic Thought	Original	0.652	0.652	4.574	1.044	12
Contributions to Political Economy	Original	2.996	2.996	7.262	1.032	13
New Left Review	Original	3.927	3.927	8.329	1.021	14
American Journal of Economics and Sociology	Original	0.584	0.584	4.496	0.987	15
Review of Social Economy	Original	0.392	0.392	4.276	0.987	16
Science and Society	Original	0.581	0.581	4.493	0.909	17
Economics and Philosophy	Original	1.156	1.156	5.152	0.898	18
International Review of Applied Economics	Original	0.613	0.613	4.53	0.898	19
Ecological Economics	Original	1.702	1.702	5.778	0.875	20
Structural Change and Economic Dynamics	Original	1.68	1.68	5.753	0.875	21
Journal of Economic Methodology	Original	0.922	0.922	4.884	0.864	22
Review of Keynesian Economics	Extended	1.059	1.059	5.041	0.819	23
Journal of Institutional Economics	Original	1.258	1.258	5.269	0.808	24
Journal of Evolutionary Economics	Original	0.773	0.773	4.713	0.808	25
Review of International Political Economy	Original	2.072	2.072	6.203	0.785	26

(*continued*)

Table 13A.4 Cont.

Journal	*Cohort*	*SNIP 2017*	*TCS* 2017*	*JPEQS* 2017*	*HJQS* 2017*	*HJQS* Rank*
Feminist Economics	Original	1.193	1.193	5.195	0.763	27
Rethinking Marxism	Original	0.68	0.68	4.607	0.695	28
Journal of Socio-Economics (renamed Journal of Behavioral and Experimental Economics)	Original	0.86	0.86	4.813	0.617	29
New Political Economy	Original	1.728	1.728	5.808	0.605	30
Historical Materialism	Original	0.681	0.681	4.608	0.605	31
Review of Social Economy	Extended	0.392	0.392	4.276	0.572	32
Development and Change	Original	1.461	1.461	5.502	0.56	33
International Review of Applied Economics	Extended	0.613	0.613	4.53	0.538	34
History of Economic Ideas	Extended	0.342	0.342	4.219	0.471	35
Structural Change and Economic Dynamics	Extended	1.68	1.68	5.753	0.426	36
Antipode	Original	2.412	2.412	6.592	0.403	37
Capitalism, Nature, Socialism	Original	0.274	0.274	4.141	0.392	38
Industrial and Corporate Change	Extended	1.544	1.544	5.597	0.369	39
Journal of Development Studies	Original	1.25	1.25	5.26	0.369	40
Research in the History of Economic Thought and Methodology	Original	0.657	0.657	4.58	0.369	41
Work, Employment and Society	Original	1.775	1.775	5.862	0.358	42
Econ Journal Watch	Original	0.408	0.408	4.295	0.347	43
Erasmus Journal for Philosophy and Economics	Extended	0.013	0.013	3.842	0.336	44
International Labour Review	Original	0.925	0.925	4.887	0.325	45
Cambridge Journal of Regions, Economy and Society	Extended	2.069	2.069	6.199	0.291	46
Journal of Australian Political Economy	Original	0.239	0.239	4.101	0.257	47
Socio-Economic Review	Extended	2.179	2.179	6.325	0.246	48
Economic Systems Research	Original	1.344	1.344	5.368	0.246	49
Cepal Review	Original	0.3	0.3	4.171	0.235	50
Economic and Labour Relations Review	Extended	0.631	0.631	4.55	0.223	51

Table 13A.4 Cont.

Journal	*Cohort*	*SNIP 2017*	*TCS* 2017*	*JPEQS* 2017*	*HJQS* 2017*	*HJQS* Rank*
Economic Geography	Extended	2.363	2.363	6.536	0.212	52
Revista de Economia Politica/ Brazilian Journal of Political Economy	Original	1.262	1.262	5.274	0.178	53
Critical Sociology	Original	1.22	1.22	5.226	0.178	54
Competition and Change	Extended	1.296	1.296	5.313	0.167	55
Critique	Extended	0.635	0.635	4.555	0.167	56
Oxford Development Studies	Original	0.83	0.83	4.779	0.156	57
Research in the History of Economic Thought and Methodology	Extended	0.657	0.657	4.58	0.145	58
International Journal of Social Economics	Original	0.544	0.544	4.451	0.145	59
Review of Austrian Economics	Original	0.611	0.611	4.527	0.134	60
Advances in Austrian Economics	Original	0.514	0.514	4.416	0.122	61
Gender, Work and Organization	Extended	1.505	1.505	5.552	0.089	62
Economic and Political Weekly	Extended	0.765	0.765	4.704	0.089	63
Constitutional Political Economy	Original	0.678	0.678	4.604	0.089	64
Research in Political Economy	Extended	0.387	0.387	4.271	0.089	65
Quarterly Journal of Austrian Economics	Original	0.234	0.234	4.095	0.077	66
Review of Black Political Economy	Original	0.413	0.413	4.3	0.055	67
Studies in Political Economy	Original	0.361	0.361	4.241	0.044	68
Review of African Political Economy	Original	1.256	1.256	5.267	0.021	69
Panoeconomicus	Extended	0.847	0.847	4.798	0.021	70
Journal of Interdisciplinary Economics	Original	0.823	0.823	4.77	0.01	71
Local Economy	Extended	0.658	0.658	4.581	0.01	72
Journal of Economic Geography	Extended	2.634	2.634	6.847	–0.001	73
On the Horizon	Extended	0.396	0.396	4.281	–0.001	74
Journal of Agrarian Change	Extended	1.776	1.776	5.863	–0.013	75

(*continued*)

Table 13A.4 Cont.

Journal	*Cohort*	*SNIP 2017*	*TCS* 2017*	*JPEQS* 2017*	*HJQS* 2017*	*HJQS* Rank*
Thesis Eleven	Extended	0.411	0.411	4.298	–0.024	76
Journal of Human Development and Capabilities	Extended	0.985	0.985	4.956	–0.046	77
Problemas del Desarrollo	Extended	0.62	0.62	4.538	–0.046	78
International Journal of Green Economics	Original	0.253	0.253	4.117	–0.046	79
International Journal of Public Policy	Extended	0.258	0.258	4.123	–0.057	80
Studies in Political Economy	Extended	0.361	0.361	4.241	–0.069	81
Quarterly Journal of Austrian Economics	Extended	0.234	0.234	4.095	–0.069	82
Environmental Values	Extended	0.84	0.84	4.79	–0.08	83
Basic Income Studies	Extended	0.448	0.448	4.341	–0.08	84
Organization and Environment	Original	2.28	2.28	6.441	–0.091	85
OIKOS	Extended	1.322	1.322	5.343	–0.091	86
Critical Perspectives on International Business	Original	0.741	0.741	4.676	–0.102	87
Labor Studies Journal	Extended	0.322	0.322	4.196	–0.102	88
International Journal of Green Economics	Extended	0.253	0.253	4.117	–0.102	89
Debatte	Original	0.096	0.096	3.937	–0.102	90
tripleC	Extended	0.768	0.768	4.707	–0.114	91
Critical Perspectives on Accounting	Extended	1.953	1.953	6.066	–0.136	92
Accounting, Organizations and Society	Extended	1.816	1.816	5.909	–0.136	93
Transformation	Extended	0.331	0.331	4.206	–0.136	94
Urbani Izziv	Extended	0.296	0.296	4.166	–0.136	95
Innovations	Extended	0.288	0.288	4.157	–0.136	96
Social and Economic Studies	Extended	0.219	0.219	4.078	–0.136	97
International Journal of Development Issues	Extended	0.116	0.116	3.96	–0.136	98
Economics and Policy of Energy and the Environment	Extended	0.111	0.111	3.954	–0.136	99

Table 13A.5 Original cohort – comparison of rankings

Journal	*Rank 2008*	*Rank 2017*	*Change*
Advances in Austrian Economics	56	61	–5
American Journal of Economics and Sociology	11	15	–4
Antipode	36	37	–1
Cambridge Journal of Economics	1	1	0
Capital and Class	12	11	1
Capitalism, Nature, Socialism	28	38	–10
Cepal Review	43	50	–7
Constitutional Political Economy	35	64	**–29**
Contributions to Political Economy	31	13	18
Critical Perspectives on International Business	61	87	**–26**
Critical Sociology	52	54	–2
Debatte	62	90	**–28**
Development and Change	6	33	**–27**
Ecological Economics	42	20	**22**
Econ Journal Watch	48	43	5
Economic Systems Research	49	49	0
Economics and Philosophy	26	18	8
Economy and Society	5	7	–2
European Journal of Economics and Economic Policies: Intervention	14	NA	
European Journal of the History of Economic Thought	18	5	13
Feminist Economics	47	27	**20**
Forum for Social Economics	38	NA	
Historical Materialism	39	31	8
History of Economics Review	23	NA	
History of Political Economy	58	10	**48**
International Journal of Green Economics	29	79	**–50**
International Journal of Political Economy	27	NA	
International Journal of Social Economics	10	59	**–49**
International Labour Review	25	45	**–20**
International Review of Applied Economics	59	19	**40**
Journal of Australian Political Economy	50	47	3
Journal of Development Studies	21	40	**–19**
Journal of Economic Behavior and Organization	9	8	1
Journal of Economic Issues	2	3	–1
Journal of Economic Methodology	22	22	0
Journal of Evolutionary Economics	19	25	–6
Journal of Income Distribution (ceased 2000)	40	NA	
Journal of Institutional Economics	34	24	10
Journal of Interdisciplinary Economics	57	71	–14
Journal of Post Keynesian Economics	3	2	1
Journal of Socio-Economics (renamed Journal of Behavioral and Experimental Economics)	33	29	4
Journal of the History of Economic Thought	16	12	4
Metroeconomica	13	9	4
New Left Review	30	14	16
New Political Economy	32	30	2

(*continued*)

Table 13A.5 Cont.

Journal	*Rank 2008*	*Rank 2017*	*Change*
Organization and Environment	54	85	**–31**
Oxford Development Studies	41	57	–16
Quarterly Journal of Austrian Economics	51	66	–15
Research in the History of Economic Thought and Methodology	53	41	12
Rethinking Marxism	20	28	–8
Review of African Political Economy	45	69	**–24**
Review of Austrian Economics	37	60	**–23**
Review of Black Political Economy	60	67	–7
Review of International Political Economy	8	26	–18
Review of Political Economy	7	6	1
Review of Radical Political Economics	4	4	0
Review of Social Economy	15	16	–1
Revista de Economia Politica/Brazilian Journal of Political Economy	46	53	–7
Science and Society	17	17	0
Structural Change and Economic Dynamics	24	21	3
Studies in Political Economy	44	68	**–24**
Work, Employment and Society	55	42	13

14 Institutional practice and the inadequacy of orthodox macroeconomics

A challenge for pluralism?

James Juniper, Andrew Nadolny, George Pantelopoulos, and Martin Watts

Introduction

Macroeconomics has long been a contested area of economics, with a number of distinct schools of thought including monetarism, new Keynesianism, post Keynesianism and Marxism. However, with the dominance of orthodox macroeconomic thinking and increasing career pressures associated with the need to publish in leading orthodox journals,[1] many university teachers have become reliant on a number of orthodox macroeconomics textbooks that have extensive resources for both instructors and students, which enable assessment to be conducted efficiently, if not effectively. Yet, despite the conceptual, theoretical and policy questions which arose from the global financial crisis (GFC), some of the leading introductory textbooks have continued to cling to orthodox principles and policies at the cost of clarity and coherence (see Juniper et al., 2018).

Moreover, it is difficult to incorporate additional modelling and policy material from other sources, when teaching large first-year classes. Consequently, many instructors have eschewed pluralism as a key principle underpinning their macroeconomics courses.[2] At best, competing perspectives would be introduced in a non-compulsory later-year class, by which time particular modes of thinking have been ingrained in students. In this chapter, we argue that a meaningful and relevant learning experience in macroeconomics requires that students be exposed to competing perspectives in their first year of study.

While some macroeconomics textbooks may still contrast and assess the policy frameworks of monetarists and Keynesians, they typically do not question the legitimacy of competing perspectives by examining how the real world of Institutional Practice is depicted, that is, how the major macroeconomic institutions, such as Central Banks, treasuries and commercial banks operate. For example, how do Central Banks manage their intraday payment and settlement systems, and how do commercial banks create credit?

Modern monetary theory (MMT) is one lens through which to investigate the workings of a modern monetary system. It espouses the principles of chartalism and functional finance and is grounded in Institutional Practice. In short, the fundamental workings of a modern monetary system are not founded on the construction of theory, but rather how the key institutions say they operate in terms of their designated roles within the macroeconomy, that is, Institutional Practice.[3,4]

We would argue that the failure of other schools of thought to incorporate these Institutional Practices, which cannot be contested, leads to serious questions about their coherence and relevance to understanding the macroeconomy. These observations, in turn, raise the question as to how pluralist pedagogy is defined with respect to macroeconomics, and specifically whether it represents an appropriate set of principles by which to guide both the content and the style of teaching. In particular, given the failure of some leading textbooks to respond to the anomalies raised by the GFC, is the study of orthodox macroeconomics fit for purpose within a first-year course? We conclude that, as the dominant school of thought in macroeconomics, orthodox theory cannot be *ignored* in first-year teaching, but that the principles of MMT should be central to first-year teaching with contentious orthodox claims being subject to critical assessment.

The rest of this chapter is structured as follows. First, we provide an overview of the literature that provides a philosophical and pedagogical justification for pluralism in economics and then ask whether macroeconomics is a special case. We then summarise some important theoretical propositions arising from orthodox macroeconomics.

Through the presentation of three claims, the next section bolsters our argument that the examination of Institutional Practice highlights the fundamental differences in the respective depictions of the operation of a modern monetary system associated with the orthodox analysis, along with most economic commentary in the media, as compared to the insights of Central Bank practitioners and financial regulators.[5] We particularly emphasise the distinction between constraints on the major macroeconomic institutions that are *voluntary* and those that are *involuntary*. The final section concludes.

Pluralism and pedagogy

Martyn (n.d.) notes that the concept of pluralism 'appeals to our values of democracy, open-mindedness and critical-thinking … It frees us from both scepticism (nothing goes) and relativism (anything goes)'. However, the concept of pluralism is inherently vague (see also Dow, 2007).

Martyn quotes the International Student Initiative for Pluralist Economics (ISIPE) open letter, which outlines three features of pluralism: pluralism of theory, pluralism of method and interdisciplinary pluralism. At a superficial level, economics clearly satisfies these criteria with many theoretical approaches, without a strict demarcation between them; the existence of multiple methodologies including theoretical modelling, econometrics and behavioural experiments; and engagement with other disciplines including geography, psychology and neuroscience[6], although economics is a relatively insular discipline in terms of limited referencing of other disciplines (Aistleitner et al., 2018).

The philosophical justification for pluralism is often based on ontological claims that the nature of the world is such that it is beyond the explanation of a single theory (Dow, 2008; Holcombe, 2008), and epistemological claims that no single standard exists for declaring the one 'best' theory because all theories are fallible (Budzinski, 2008; Mearman, 2008, 2012; see also Mariyani-Squire and Moussa, 2015).[7,8]

Earl (2009) argues that considering multiple perspectives concurrently has the benefit of allowing the student to 'make tentative commitments to theoretical positions, whilst acknowledging that others exist' (Mearman et al., 2011, p. 54). The evidence supports arguments that a pluralist economics curriculum develops cognitive capacities of criticism, comparison and analysis which, in turn, cultivate judgement, an improved capacity to learn and integrate new material, and acquisition of better writing skills (Barone, 1991; Denis, 2009; Fullbrook, 2009; Reardon 2009; Mearman, 2012; Cooper and Ramey, 2014; Cantrell and Mitchell, 2017; Provencher and Ramnarain, 2018). Pluralistic thinking takes time to develop, with most students starting as dualistic thinkers and lacking the confidence to critique a theory or model (Mearman, 2012). Addressing these issues is labour-intensive for both students and instructors, with the latter, for example, providing detailed feedback on written work.[9]

The adoption of pluralist teaching practices is also a challenge to both heterodox and orthodox advocates. 'Indeed, those paradigmatically attached to the current orthodox have a strong incentive to support pluralist pedagogy since ... it promotes deeper learning of orthodox theories, by contrasting them at every point with their rivals' (Denis, 2009, p. 12).

The challenges of embedding a pluralist approach have been discussed in detail (for example, Mearman, 2008, 2012; Courvisanos et al., 2016; Peterson, 2016). Clearly, some shared perspectives on the subject matter of economics and underlying concepts at the beginning of the course are essential for students. This requires meaningful communication between the adherents of different approaches and methodologies.

However, '[t]he vision of pluralism is of an economics that accepts these approaches that seem incompatible with its way of thinking' (Martyn, n.d.). Martyn notes that Thomas Kuhn was pessimistic, arguing that science progressed by the replacement of one dominant monist paradigm, by another that resolved some of the anomalies associated with the first.[10] Likewise, Lakatos (1970) argued that a progressive research programme could be judged on both theoretical and empirical grounds. Newer theories should enable us to make better predictions, which can be checked against the available evidence. When researchers support a degenerating programme, they attempt to preserve what Lakatos calls a 'heuristic' (or a constellation of beliefs), that are allied to a 'hard core' that will not change from one theory to the next, a notion which Lakatos complemented by suggesting how beliefs, in what he called the 'protective belt', could be revised in a minimal way so as to protect the hard core against refutation. However, Kuhn (1970) made the point that scientific revolutions are needed because paradigms are also constraining, in that they limit the conception of what is possible, so that puzzle-solving capacities are weakened.

However, the advocacy of pluralism does not require justification solely on the grounds of epistemological scepticism or a presumably inescapable relativism, even while acknowledging that there is always some degree of uncertainty about the nature of things. Instead, justification can be sought from an acknowledgement that both the coherence and breadth of argument and clarity of purpose are forged in the flames of often-heated debate!

For example, when Sraffa completed *Production of Commodities by Means of Commodities*, in 1960, he benefited significantly from his earlier critical engagement with Marshallian partial equilibrium analysis (Sraffa, 1960 in Signorino, 2000). Similarly, while editing Ricardo's collected works, Sraffa, together with the Marxist historian Maurice Dobb, called for a return to the surplus approach of classical political economy. They advocated that an instantaneous 'snapshot' analysis of reproduction prices (in logical time) be combined with a long-period investigation of the determinants of social norms such as the subsistence wage bundle or dividend-retention ratios (in historical time) (Signorino, 2000). A similar approach to modelling based on convergence to long-period, stock-flow norms has been proposed by those Post Keynesians developing long-run, stock-flow-consistent macroeconomic models (see Godley and Lavoie, 2007, especially Chapter 11).

Sraffa's views were nurtured within an environment in which diversity of economic opinion was encouraged, but academics engaged in vigorous debate and polemic. These features appear to be absent today, which detracts both from progress in economics and from improved pedagogy.

For example, dedicated non-orthodox journals have emerged, such as the *Review of Radical Political Economics* (1968); *International Journal of Political Economy* (1970); *Capital and Class* (1977); *Cambridge Journal* (1977); *Journal of Post Keynesian Economics* (1978); *International Review of Applied Economics* (1987) and *Review of Political Economy* (1989), given the high probability of non-orthodox papers being rejected by orthodox journals.[11] Non-orthodox economists conduct their own conferences too, including the Union of Radical Political Economists (1968–); Association of Heterodox Economists Conference (1999–)[12]; Society of Heterodox Economists (2002–2017).

The theoretical and empirical challenges to orthodoxy raised by the GFC may have been expected to lead to greater engagement between orthodox economists and Post Keynesians but there is scant evidence that this is true. Adverse real macroeconomic outcomes have persisted over the last decade with loose conventional (and unconventional) monetary policy and fiscal austerity failing to promote sufficient economic growth, particularly in the Eurozone countries (see, for example, Sharpe and Watts, 2012; Constancio, 2015) but also in numerous developed economies, each with its own currency (Blanchard and Summers, 2017; Lavoie, 2018).

Juniper et al. (2018) examined four leading textbooks and assessed their methodologies and theoretical frameworks against some key propositions advanced by major international organisations about the monetary system in advanced developed economies, notably the role of banks, the intraday payment and settlement system and how monetary and fiscal policy is conducted. While the four texts to varying degrees have attempted to incorporate contemporary Institutional Practice into their narratives, the major contradictions that emerged when attempting to maintain an essentially monetarist perspective have been finessed. This has led to a degree of incoherence in all four textbooks. Certainly, they do not adopt a pluralist framework, so that reliance on one of these, albeit well-resourced, textbooks, would not provide students with a clear understanding of competing analytical frameworks.

The GFC has reinforced the existing arguments for pluralism in economics education according to Cantrell and Mitchell (2017), Dimmelmeier et al. (2017), Courvisanos et al. (2016), Cooper and Ramey (2014), Mearman (2012) and Denis (2009). Also, in the last 15 years or so many students in developed economies, including the UK, Europe and the USA, have expressed major misgivings about the manner in which macroeconomics (and economics in general) is taught and the inflexibility of the curriculum, as noted in Section 1.

It would be doing a grave disservice to first-year students for lecturers to present orthodox macroeconomics as a coherent, uncontested set of concepts and theories that clearly and unambiguously explain the workings of a monetary economy, which would then enable policy options to be interrogated. This conveys the wrong impression about the nature of macroeconomics. Students may find that having their monist thinking challenged in later years to be quite confronting after it had been presented as the received wisdom. They may well be reluctant to try to understand competing perspectives.

Even first-year students who are terminating their study of macroeconomics need to be provided with the analytical tools[13] to enable them to make informed judgements about current policy debates, at least at the level found in the serious media.

On the other hand, pluralism for the sake of presenting different 'schools of thought' is a pointless exercise if these different perspectives are not subject to critical scrutiny as to their institutional, theoretical and empirical legitimacy. Otherwise claims that are often ideologically based are given the same weighting as legitimate arguments grounded in institutional reality.

However, in the next two sections of this chapter, we argue that the orthodox analytical frameworks typically found in first year macroeconomics texts are such that, if subject to a rigorous assessment within a pluralist framework, would be considered deficient, due to their incoherent depiction of

Institutional Practice. Thus, based on our 'pluralist methodology', orthodox macroeconomics would not be taught at the first-year level. On the other hand, it remains dominant across colleges and universities in the Western world, so it cannot be and should not be ignored.[14] Hence, an understanding of orthodox macroeconomic principles is essential but does not need to be central to the content of a first-year course.[15]

We argue that, for a meaningful and relevant learning experience, students should be exposed to a macroeconomic perspective based on MMT which is grounded in Institutional Practice from the outset and has overall coherence, which still means that the economic consequences of different policies can be contested (see, for example, Mitchell et al., 2019). In contrast, orthodox macroeconomic thinking has been protected by the failure of its advocates to engage in serious academic debate, as argued above.[16]

Orthodox macroeconomic principles for a first-year course

Below we outline what we consider to be the key principles underpinning an orthodox first-year macroeconomics course:

- *Money creation* occurs when banks (financial intermediaries) receive new deposits from customers, hold a small fraction of these as reserves, and then lend out the remainder. If each bank follows this process, aggregate lending expands through the *money multiplier*.
- The *Central Bank* controls the monetary base[17] (stock of *high-powered money*) and hence, via the money multiplier, the money supply.
- The *money supply* is inelastic with respect to interest rates.
- Under the *quantity theory of money*, the size of the money stock determines the rate of inflation, ceteris paribus.
- Under *loanable funds theory* the interest rate adjusts to equate the demand for funds to finance investment, fiscal deficits and current account deficits with the supply of funds (savings) in an open economy.
- *Monetary policy* is considered to be the *primary arm of macroeconomic policy*, even though it has been relatively ineffective, and now a number of countries have limited capacity for further monetary stimulus in the event of another financial crisis due to the policy rate being close to the zero lower bound (ZLB).[18] The Central Bank is claimed to be independent of the political process and hence makes better decisions than an elected government.
- Reference is sometimes made to the Central Bank setting an *overnight interest rate* as its policy variable, rather than a measure of the stock of money, and the role of the Central Bank in the payments system. However, these ideas are not typically reconciled with the monetarist policy framework.
- *The government budget constraint* is considered to be analogous to that of a household in that it has to decide on the source of finance before

new expenditure can be made. The national government can finance its spending through taxes, issuing debt (i.e. selling government bonds) and increasing the monetary base. Higher taxes reduce the capacity of income earners to make spending decisions. Debt sales and money creation will have undesirable macroeconomic consequences, namely raising interest rates due to the increased demand for funds, and causing inflation, via the quantity theory of money.

- *Fiscal balance should be achieved over the course of the business cycle* (e.g. deficits in downturns, surpluses in inflationary upturns of the cycle).
- No distinction is usually made between *sovereign and non-sovereign currencies*, so ongoing fiscal deficits are considered to be unsustainable.
- The modelling of the determination of equilibrium output is typically based on aggregate demand and supply functions, both expressed as a function of the price level. Flexible wages and prices lead to the achievement of market-clearing equilibrium.
- There is a *short-run inflation rate/unemployment rate trade-off*. In the long-run, fiscal policies that attempt to lower unemployment below its (alleged) natural rate (NRU) will be inflationary and will not lower the NRU.

A first-year course that outlined the principles of MMT and engaged with these orthodox principles would expose students to many of the contemporary debates about macroeconomic theory and policy.[19]

Three claims based on Institutional Practice

A number of advanced countries, including the USA, UK, Canada and Australia, enjoy currency sovereignty, which is characterised by (i) the issue of their own currency; (ii) a floating exchange rate; and (iii) limited exposure to foreign currency-denominated debt.

In exploring Institutional Practice, we explain that despite advanced economies exhibiting currency sovereignty, their policymaking is still subject to *voluntary* constraints; Central Banks achieve their policy objectives through liquidity management operations to maintain an overnight policy rate, rather than controlling the money supply; and policymakers can be considered subject to *involuntary* constraints, because public debt is issued as a means of upholding the integrity of the intraday payment and settlement system, in addition to providing a risk-free financial asset for the non-government sector.

We now present our three claims, which are based on Institutional Practice. The first claim is that the sale of Treasury debt is a liquidity management operation in support of the target interest rate set via monetary policy and is not a fiscal financing operation.

It is accepted from a wide variety of perspectives that Central Banks are able to inject currency *ex nihilo* and are able to operate with negative equity. Governments that exhibit currency sovereignty cannot default on any obligation denominated in their own currency (Greenspan, 1997; Draghi, 2014; Eichengreen and Panizza, 2016).[20,21]

Nonetheless, policymaking is subject to a series of *voluntary* constraints, as exemplified by current institutional arrangements in the United States. Generally, the implementation of fiscal policy is subject to a 'full funding rule', which requires public debt to be sold to the non-government sector prior to any deficit spending taking place, as opposed to the Central Bank purchasing securities on the primary market. Tymoigne (2016, p. 1326) notes that the 1913 Federal Reserve Act allowed for unlimited financing of Treasury debt by the Federal Reserve. Limits were then imposed and in 1979 the option for the Federal Reserve to purchase debt on the primary market was scrapped.[22]

Moreover, Treasury must now have a positive balance to draw on its account at the Federal Reserve. Taxes and other receipts are held within special commercial bank accounts, which are then transferred into the 'Treasury General Account', held at the Federal Reserve. This account must have a positive balance (generated via tax and other receipts) before any Government spending occurs (Tymoigne, 2016, pp. 1325–1326).[23]

Nevertheless, it would appear that *voluntary* constraints, such as the 'full funding rule', can be finessed when the occasion demands. HM Treasury in Britain is subject to arrangements similar to those of the USA with respect to deficit spending.[24] Yet in the midst of the GFC, HM Treasury received a £19.5 billion 'Ways and Means' advance from the Bank of England (Saravelos et al., 2016).

Similarly, the Federal Government of Australia maintains its daily cash account with the Reserve Bank of Australia (RBA), known as the 'Official Public Account' (OPA). All government departments hold all cash reserves within a 'Consolidated Revenue Fund'. All monies collected are then transferred into the OPA (Department of Finance, 2014). As, at times, there are significant mismatches between taxation receipts and expenditures, the RBA provides an overdraft facility to the government (see, for example, AOFM, 2017, pp. 31–32). In this way, even though the Australian Government, via the Australian Office of Financial Management (AOFM), issues and sells securities to the non-government sector, it still has the backing of a sovereign power and therefore can create currency *ex nihilo*.

The AOFM (2010, p. xiv) is clear about the key role of Australian public debt within the financial system: 'Government bonds are one of the foundations of the Australian financial system, as they are *risk-free* assets that provide both liquidity and reference points for pricing. A well-functioning government bond market strengthens the resilience of the system to shocks …' (emphasis added; see also RBA, 2001, p. 6; and Garbade and Kambhu, 2006, p. 1, who discuss role of US bonds).

The sale of public debt can be viewed as an involuntary constraint, which is a consequence of the need to maintain the domestic intraday payment and settlement system in addition to the Central Bank retaining control of the interbank rate. Commercial banks require public debt for collateral when engaging with the Central Bank in the process of acquiring additional reserves. Therefore, the elimination of public debt would possibly culminate in significant volatility in the interbank market rate, as commercial banks would compete for scarce liquidity, unless private forms of collateral were accepted.[25]. Also, households desire safe liquid assets, given their greater exposure to financial volatility, particularly in countries where the provision of retirement income is becoming increasingly privatised with the reduced reliance on public pensions.[26] This need could be met by a 'National Savings Fund, fully guaranteed by the currency-issuing capacity of the government' (Mitchell, 2020).

Our second claim is that the Central Bank is unable to control the money supply. Several Central Bank practitioners, including Constancio (2011, 2015) and McLeay et al. (2014), have rebutted the claim that Central Banks target the money supply by altering the size of the monetary base. The Central Bank steers the market determined interbank rate, the interest rate at which commercial banks borrow reserves from one another, to an announced policy rate through liquidity management operations (Bank of Canada, 2019). Also, the money multiplier works in reverse: '… A further misconception surrounding reserves is that commercial banks require reserves to lend … Any observation of a stable money multiplier relationship between narrow and broad money actually reflects the reverse causality' (Rule, 2015, p. 7).

Our third claim is that in a currency sovereign economy, interest rates on Treasury debt are not determined by foreign investors. In economies including Australia and Canada, the Central Bank implements a 'corridor' reserve remuneration scheme, with the policy rate situated in the middle of the 'channel', while the lending and deposit rates constitute the ceiling and floor respectively. If there is an excess of commercial bank reserve balances, the Central Bank must drain this surplus liquidity from commercial banks through open market operations, which are typically conducted through a repurchase agreement.[27] Intervention is also required when there is an aggregate reserve shortage, otherwise commercial banks will bid up the interbank rate. Alternatively, a 'floor' system may be adopted, under which the Central Bank pays interest corresponding to the policy rate on any excess reserves.[28] Consequently, intervention is only needed when there is an aggregate liquidity shortage.

This control by the Central Bank of the interbank (overnight) rate extends to any longer-term interest rate on Government debt, which the Central Bank chooses. For example, in March 2020, RBA Governor Lowe remarked that '[t]he Bank will do what is necessary to achieve the 3-year yield target, with the target expected to remain in place until progress is being made towards the goals for full employment and inflation' (RBA, 2020, see also Bank of Japan, 2019, p. 19).

Conclusion

Heterodox economists continue to espouse the importance of pluralist principles being employed in the teaching of economics at the tertiary level.

In this chapter we warn against tokenistic attempts at the pluralist teaching of macroeconomics, by arguing that, even in a first-year macroeconomics course, there needs to be a rigorous assessment of the competing perspectives that are being outlined. These warnings arise from the failure of orthodox macroeconomists to respond to the fundamental flaws in their understanding of a (modern) monetary economy, which have been exposed by the GFC and its aftermath.

The three claims that we have substantiated highlight the deficiencies in the orthodox accounts of how key institutions, such as the central bank, treasury and the banks, operate in a modern monetary economy, in particular with respect to the functioning of the intraday payment and settlement system, and both the operation and the effectiveness of monetary and fiscal policy (see also Juniper et al., 2018).[29]

In our view, this failure to provide a coherent account of Institutional Practice, which can be incorporated into a first-year textbook, disqualifies orthodox macroeconomics from taking centre stage within a first-year course in which competing perspectives are explored. On the other hand, we argue that MMT does recognise the importance of Institutional Practice, which exhibits some common features but also differences across advanced economies. Institutional practice is integral to a number of key propositions that are derived within the MMT framework. Consequently, the principles of MMT should take centre stage within a first-year course. Whether such a course should be considered pluralist is a question of semantics.

Notes

1 Lavoie (2015) notes that Lee and Harley (1998) quickly became aware of the dangers of the adoption of the British research assessment exercise (RAE) for both pluralism in teaching and the hiring of academics with alternative views. The RAE has become the benchmark for similar processes in Australia and New Zealand.

2 The teaching of economics from a monist perspective has led to student demands for curriculum reform. These include the Post-Autistic Economics Movement in Paris, when economics students circulated a petition in June 2000, and the emergence of organisations including the Post-Crash Society at Manchester University, the Cambridge Society for Economic Pluralism and organisations at UCL, LSE and Sheffield University. In November 2011, Harvard student protesters walked out of Economics 10, arguing that there was bias inherent in the introductory economics course taught by Professor Mankiw, which then attracted the highest course enrolment in the University.

3 Here we are not considering, for example, the principles that guide the conduct of monetary policy by the Central Bank, but rather its day-to-day accommodative practices (see Section 4).

4 By contrast, orthodox theory is underpinned by abstract notions of rational choice and methodological individualism.

5 That is not to say that MMT advocates would necessarily endorse the policy advice of central bankers!

6 This concept of pluralism is silent about how economics should be taught, however.
7 For example, Critical Realists such as Roy Bhasker argue that the logic of scientific discovery requires researchers to penetrate beneath what is experienced and observed, to what is actualised by the underlying mechanisms. Although the latter cannot be directly observed, laboratory techniques can isolate key mechanisms, thus allowing identification of their causal attributes and influences. However, although natural systems are 'closed', social systems are 'open' and reflexive insofar as changing insights into, and ideas about, the social system is also an important aspect of the social system. In other words, as our ideas about society change, this changes the very way that society itself develops and functions. Somewhat earlier, 'Marx sought to pierce the "ideological veil" of capitalism, to get at its real systemic operations, which are found in the material, economic realm' (Prychitko, 2004).
8 Further support for pursuing a pluralistic approach is that economic policy impacts unevenly on members of the population, which typically leads to the emergence of interest groups propagating competing perspectives (Denis, 2009).
9 However, assessment processes are often streamlined with the absence of continuous assessment and an undesirable reliance on multiple-choice tests. Further, the attributes that universities, such as Manchester University, were trying to engender in their graduates appeared to be inconsistent with the orthodox perspective of their courses at the time (Post-Crash Economics Society Report, 2014).
10 However, Kuhn (1970) warned that science did not steadily progress in a linear fashion from myth to truth. A good example is the policy response to the GFC, namely fiscal austerity and loose monetary policy which, in part, echoed the failed policy response to the Great Depression.
11 While these journals have gained prestige amongst heterodox economists, journal ranking lists are used to assess the research of academics seeking employment or promotion in a number of countries, including Australia, the United Kingdom and New Zealand. These ranking lists tend to be dominated by orthodox journals that attract a greater readership as well as the endorsement of orthodox economists who predominate on ranking committees.
12 The first AHE Conference was a one-day fringe conference at the Royal Economics Society Conference. This accord only lasted one year!
13 The Faculty of Business and Law, University of Newcastle, Australia website refers to global citizenship: 'Our curriculum is international in focus and challenges our students to understand and question the global economy and society of which they are part' (University of Newcastle, 2018).
14 While higher education should not be considered merely as the nexus between high school and the prospect of a well-paid job, economics and business graduates who have had no exposure to orthodox macroeconomics would be disadvantaged in the job market.
15 So, we disagree with Joan Robinson who, at a seminar at Monash University, Melbourne, Australia in 1975, famously suggested that the teaching of orthodox economics should be confined to history of economic thought courses.
16 Orthodox responses to MMT, since it was given public prominence by Alexandria Ocasio-Cortez, the New York Democrat, have typically been glib and frequently in the form of tweet-length comments, as illustrated by the economic content of the US Senate motion (2019).
17 The monetary base is composed of currency in circulation plus commercial bank reserves.

18 This has not deterred the IMF from actively considering strategies to enable 'deep negative interest rates' to be imposed (see Agarwal and Kimball, 2015, 2019; see also Lilley and Rogoff, 2019)

19 We would advise against juxtaposing heterodox macroeconomic principles against those of orthodox macroeconomics, because economists appear to be facing another existential crisis over the meaning and worth of heterodox economics (Lavoie, 2019).

20 Becklumb and Frigon (2015, p. 3) note that 'The Bank of Canada's money creation for the Government of Canada is an internal government process. This means that external factors, such as financial markets dysfunction, cannot cause the federal government to run out of money'. In contrast, public debt issued by Eurozone members is denominated in a foreign currency, which cannot be created *ex nihilo* by Eurozone governments, because their own Central Banks cannot create liquidity.

21 A country that issues foreign currency-denominated public debt may suffer from macroeconomic instability in the face of a currency depreciation or market dysfunction. However, several advanced economies now only issue public debt in their respective domestic currencies. For example, during the early 2000s, the Australian Office of Financial Management retired all remaining foreign currency denominated public debt from its portfolio (AOFM, 2004, p. 39).

22 On the other hand, in Canada, the central bank is permitted to purchase up to 20 per cent of any newly issued debt on the primary market (De Guzman, 2016).

23 Treasury tax and loan accounts are the source of commercial bank reserves for borrowing and lending within the interbank market. If there were to be an inadequate supply of reserves, significant volatility in the interbank market rate would transpire, as commercial banks would compete for scarce liquidity.

24 'An overarching requirement of debt management policy is that the Government fully finances its projected financing requirement each year through the sale of debt'. In this way, the full funding rule is argued to fulfil '… the principles of transparency and predictability … to avoid the perception that financial transactions of the public sector could affect monetary conditions, consistent with the institutional separation between monetary policy and debt management policy' (HM Treasury, 2017, pp. 6–7).

25 For example, the RBA conducts outright purchases of government securities so as to inject liquidity into the banking system (Robertson, 2017). When the Australian government ran persistent fiscal surpluses in the early to mid-2000s, the RBA was forced to supplement declining stocks of Government securities with foreign exchange swaps and also began accepting a wider pool of assets as collateral when undertaking repurchase agreements in its implementation of monetary policy (see RBA, 2001, pp. 5–10).

26 On the other hand, the financial sector, which claims to be able to assess risk, receives a subsidy in the presence of riskless government bonds.

27 In a repurchase agreement, short-term government securities (t-bills) are sold to commercial banks in exchange for reserves and then later the transaction is reversed.

28 Due to the introduction of quantitative easing, Central Banks in the United States, Japan, Britain and the Eurozone all began to pay interest on excess reserves, and hence adopted a floor scheme.

29 We acknowledge that many of these aspects of Institutional Practice are also articulated by Post Keynesian macroeconomists in their work.

References

Agarwal, R. and Kimball, M.S. 2015, 'Breaking Through the Zero Lower Bound', *International Monetary Fund*, Working Paper No. 15/224.

Agarwal, R. and Kimball , M.S. 2019, 'Enabling Deep Negative Rates: A Guide', *International Monetary Fund*, Working Paper No. 19/84.

Aistleitner, M., Kapeller, M. and Steinerberger, S. 2018, 'Citation Patterns in Economics and Beyond', *Institute for New Economic Thinking*, Working Paper No. 85.

Australian Office of Financial Management (AOFM). 2004, *Annual Report, 2003–2004*, Commonwealth of Australia, Canberra.

Australian Office of Financial Management (AOFM). 2010, *Annual Report, 2009–2010*, Commonwealth of Australia, Canberra.

Australian Office of Financial Management (AOFM). 2017, *Annual Report, 2017–2018*, Commonwealth of Australia, Canberra.

Bank of Canada. 2019, 'Framework for Market Operations and Liquidity Provision'. Available from: www.bankofcanada.ca/markets/market-operations-liquidity-provision/framework-market-operations-liquidity-provision/. [Accessed 25 August 2019].

Bank of Japan (BoJ). 2019, *Minutes of the Monetary Policy Meeting on July 29 & 30*. Available from www.boj.or.jp/en/mopo/mpmsche_minu/minu_2019/g190730.pdf [Accessed 22 November 2019].

Barone, C. 1991, 'Contending Perspectives: Curricular Reform in Economics', *Journal of Economic Education*, vol. 22, no. 1, pp. 15–26.

Becklumb, P. and Frigon, M. 2015, 'How the Bank of Canada Creates Money for the Federal Government: Operational and Legal Aspects', *Library of Parliament*, Publication No. 2015-51-E.

Blanchard, O.J. and Summers, L. 2017, 'Rethinking Stabilization Policy: Back to the Future', prepared for the *Rethinking Macroeconomic Policy Conference at the Peterson Institute for International Economics*, 8 October.

Budzinski, O. 2008, 'Monoculture versus Diversity in Competition Economics', *Cambridge Journal of Economics*, vol. 32, no. 2, pp. 295–324.

Cantrell, P. and Mitchell, D. 2017, 'Enhancing Pluralism in the Undergraduate Economics Curriculum by Incorporating a Political Economy Approach', *International Journal of Pluralism and Economics Education*, vol. 8, no. 3, pp. 273–285.

Constancio, V. 2011, 'Challenges to Monetary Policy in 2012', speech at the 26th International Conference on Interest Rates, Frankfurt, 8 December.

Constancio, V. 2015, 'Monetary Policy and the Euro Area Problem', speech at the 18th Euro Finance Week, Frankfurt, 16 November.

Cooper, B. and Ramey, E. 2014, 'Pluralism at Work: Alumni Assess an Economics Education', *International Review of Economics Education*, vol. 16, no. B, pp. 63–72.

Courvisanos, J., Doughney, J. and Millmow, A. (eds.) 2016, *Reclaiming Pluralism in Economics*, Routledge, Melbourne, Victoria, Australia.

De Guzman, M. 2016, 'Market Operations and Liquidity Provision at the Bank of Canada', *Bank of Canada Review* (Autumn), pp. 12–24.

Denis, A. 2009, 'Editorial: Pluralism in Economics Education', *International Review of Economics Education*, vol. 8, vol. 2, pp. 6–22.

Department of Finance. 2014, 'Resource Management Guide No. 413. The Banking of Cash by Commonwealth Entities', *Commonwealth of Australia*, Canberra.

Dimmelmeier, A., Heussner, F., Pürckhauer, A. and Urban, J. 2017, 'Making the Incommensurable Comparable: A Comparative Approach to Pluralist Economics Education', *European Journal of Economics and Economic Policies: Intervention*, vol. 14, vol. 2, pp. 250–266.

Dow, S. 2007, 'Pluralism in Economics', in J. Groenewegen (ed.), *Teaching Pluralism in Economics*, pp. 22–39. Edward Elgar, Cheltenham.

Dow, S. 2008, 'Plurality in Orthodox and Heterodox Economics', *Journal of Philosophical Economics*, vol. 1, no. 2, pp. 73–96.

Draghi, M. 2014, Unemployment in the Euro Area, Speech by Mario Draghi, at the Annual Central Bank Symposium in Jackson Hole, 22 August.

Earl, P. 2009, 'In the Economics Classroom', in E. Fullbrook (ed.), *Pluralist Economics*, Zed Books, London.

Eichengreen, B. and Panizza, U. 2016, 'A Surplus of Ambition: Can Europe Rely on Large Primary Surpluses to Solve its Debt Problem?', *Economic Policy*, vol. 31, no. 85, pp. 5–49.

Fullbrook, E. 2009, 'Relevance of Pluralist Economics for the 21st Century', in J. Reardon (ed.), *The Handbook of Pluralist Economics Education*, Routledge, London.

Garbade, K. and Kambhu, J. 2006, 'Why is the US Treasury Contemplating Becoming a Lender of Last Resort for Treasury Securities?', *Federal Reserve Bank of New York*, Staff Report no. 223.

Godley, W. and Lavoie, M. 2007, *Monetary Economics: An Integrated Approach to Credit, Money, Income, Production and Wealth*, Palgrave Macmillan, London.

Greenspan, A. 1997, 'Maintaining Financial Stability in a Global Economy', remarks from a speech at the Annual Economic Symposium sponsored by the Federal Reserve Bank of Kansas City in Jackson Hole, Wyoming, 29 August.

HM Treasury. 2017, *Debt Management Report 2017–18*. Available from: https://assets.publishing.service.gov.uk/government/uploads/system/uploads/attachment_data/file/597297/debt_management_report_2017-18_web.pdf. [Accessed 25 August 2019].

Holcombe, R. 2008, 'Pluralism versus Heterodoxy in Economics and the Social Sciences', *Journal of Philosophical Economics*, vol. 1, no. 2, pp. 51–72.

Juniper, J., Nadolny, A., Pantelopoulos, G. and Watts, M.J. 2018, 'Same Old Wine in New Bottles: The Inadequacy of Orthodox Macroeconomics Textbooks in a Post-GFC World', paper presented to the Association of Heterodox Economists Conference at De Montfort University, Leicester, 5–7 July.

Kuhn, T.S. 1970, *The Structure of Scientific Revolutions*, 2nd edn., University of Chicago Press, Chicago, IL.

Lakatos, I. 1970, 'Falsification and the Methodology of Scientific Research Programmes', in I. Lakatos and A. Musgrave (eds.), *Criticism and the Growth of Knowledge*, pp. 91–195. Cambridge University Press, Cambridge.

Lavoie, M. 2015, 'Teaching Monetary Theory and Monetary Policy Implementation after the Crisis', *European Journal of Economics and Economic Policies: Intervention*, vol. 12, no. 2, pp. 220–228.

Lavoie, M. 2018, 'Rethinking Macroeconomic Theory before the Next Crisis', *Review of Keynesian Economics*, vol. 6, no. 1, pp. 1–21.

Lavoie, M. 2019, 'From Political Economy to Heterodox Economics and Back: Lessons from the MMT Success Story', paper presented at the Association of Heterodox Economists Conference, Lille, France, 3–5 July.

Lee, F. and Harley, S. 1998, 'Peer Review, the Research Assessment Exercise and the Demise of Non-mainstream Economics', *Capital & Class*, vol. 66, pp. 23–51.

Lilley, A. and Rogoff, K. 2019, The Case for Implementing Effective Negative Interest Rate Policy, Conference draft for presentation at *Strategies for Monetary Policy: A Policy Conference*, The Hoover Institution, Stanford University, 4 May.

Mariyani-Squire, E. and Moussa, M. 2015, 'Fallibilism, Liberalism and Stillwell's Advocacy for Pluralism in Economics', *Journal of Australian Political Economy*, vol. 75, pp. 194–210.

Martyn, R. n.d., *What Even is Economic Pluralism? Rethinking Economics*. Available from: www.rethinkeconomics.org/journal/what-even-is-economic-pluralism/. [Accessed 25 August 2019].

McLeay, M., Radia, A. and Thomas, R. 2014, 'Money Creation in the Modern Economy', *Bank of England Quarterly Bulletin*, vol. 54, no. 1, pp. 14–27.

Mearman, A. 2008, 'Pluralism and Heterodoxy: Introduction to the Special Issue', *Journal of Philosophical Economics*, vol. 1, no. 2, pp. 5–25.

Mearman, A. 2012, '"Heterodox" Economics and the Problems of Classification', *Journal of Economic Methodology*, vol. 19, no. 4, pp. 407–424.

Mearman, A., Shoib, G., Wakeley T. and Webber, D. 2011, 'Does Pluralism in Economics Education make Better Educated, Happier Students? A Qualitative Analysis', *International Review of Economics Education*, vol. 10, no. 2, pp. 50–62.

Mitchell, W.F. 2020, 'Why do Currency-issuing Governments Issue Debt? – Part 2', *Billy Blog*, 2 June. Available from: http://bilbo.economicoutlook.net/blog/?p=45108/. [Accessed 8 June 2020].

Mitchell, W.F., Wray, L.R. and Watts, M.J. 2019, *Modern Monetary Theory and Practice: An Introductory Text*, Palgrave Macmillan, London.

Peterson, J. 2016, 'The Political Economy of Employment: A Framework for a More Pluralistic, Real World Labour Economics Course', *International Journal of Pluralism and Economics Education*, vol. 7, no. 4, pp. 413–425.

Post-Crash Economics Society Report. 2014, *Economics, Education and Unlearning: Economics Education at the University of Manchester*, published by the Post-Crash Economics Society at the University of Manchester (UK), April 2014. Available from: www.post-crasheconomics.com/economics-education-and-unlearning/. [Accessed 25 August 2019].

Provencher, A. and Ramnarain, S. 2018, 'Class Debates in Intermediate Microeconomics: Social Economics and Pluralist Perspectives'. Available from: https://doi.org/10.1080/07360932.2018.1447494. [Accessed 25 August 2019].

Prychitko, D.L. 2004, *The Nature and Significance of Marx's Capital: A Critique of Political Economy*. Available from: www.econlib.org/library/Columns/y2004/PrychitkoMarx.html. [Accessed 25 August 2019].

Reardon, J. (ed.). 2009, *The Handbook of Pluralist Economics Education*, Routledge, London.

Reserve Bank of Australia (RBA). 2001, *Reserve Bank of Australia Annual Report 2001*. Commonwealth of Australia, Canberra.

Reserve Bank of Australia (RBA). 2020, Statement by Philip Lowe, Governor: Monetary Policy Decision, *Media Release*, 7 April. Available from: www.rba.gov.au/media-releases/2020/mr-20-11.html [Accessed 7 April 2020].

Robertson, B. 2017, 'Structural Liquidity and Domestic Market Operations', *RBA Bulletin*, September Quarter, pp. 35–44.

Rule, G. 2015, 'Understanding the Central Bank Balance Sheet', *Bank of England Handbooks*.

Saravelos, G., Brehon, D. and Winkler, R. 2016, 'Helicopters 101: Your Guide to Monetary Financing', *Deutsche Bank Research Special Report*, April.

Sharpe, T. and Watts, M.J. 2012, 'Policy Advice in Crisis: How Inter-governmental Organisations have Responded to the GFC', *Journal of Australian Political Economy*, vol. 69, pp. 103–133.

Signorino, R. 2000, 'Method and Analysis in Piero Sraffa's 1925 Critique of Marshallian Economics', *European Journal of the History of Economic Thought*, vol. 7, no. 4, pp. 569–594.

Sraffa, P. 1960, *Production of Commodities by Means of Commodities: A Prelude to the Critique of Neoclassical Economics*, Cambridge University Press, Cambridge.

Tymoigne, E. 2016, 'Government Monetary and Fiscal Operations: Generalising the Endogenous Money Approach', *Cambridge Journal of Economics*, vol. 40, no. 5, pp. 1317–1332.

University of Newcastle. 2018, 'Global Citizenship, Faculty of Business and Law'. Available from: www.newcastle.edu.au/about-uon/governance-and-leadership/faculties-and-schools/faculty-of-business-and-law/about-us/learning-and-teaching. [Accessed 25 August 2019]

US Senate. 2019, *Senate Resolution PAT19390*, 116th Congress, 1st Session, Government Printing Office, Washington, DC. Available from: www.perdue.senate.gov/imo/media/doc/MMT%20Resolution.pdf [Accessed 25 August 2019].

15 Pluralism and heterodox economics

Sheila Dow

Introduction

Calls for pluralism have arisen for some time now from a range of international organisations, such as the Association for Heterodox Economics, the World Economics Association and Rethinking Economics, all seeking to promote and support a broad development of economics beyond the current orthodoxy. Indeed, pluralism has been seen as a key characteristic of heterodox economics, contrasted with orthodox economics (see most recently Mearman, Berger and Guizzo 2019). But not all commentators agree (see Kvangraven and Alves 2019). Some (such as Garnett 2006) have argued that many heterodox economists are in fact monist (or 'paradigmist'), presenting their work as the preferable alternative to orthodox economics. Of these heterodox economists, some argue for the superiority of heterodoxy as a whole over orthodoxy, while others argue for the superiority of their own approach over other approaches within heterodoxy. Yet others (such as Davis 2006) have argued that in the meantime orthodox economics has itself become more pluralist.

The purpose here is to revisit the meaning and role of pluralism in heterodox economics and to make the case for pluralism's continuing centrality in heterodox economics. In the process we pursue the question of how to characterise economics in terms of pluralism and thus to consider the best path for heterodoxy to follow. In addition we attempt to address continuing concerns that pluralism may hold back the building up of knowledge, or at least be a poor strategic choice, by encouraging an 'anything goes' interpretation.[1]

Underlying differences of opinion on pluralism, some confusion has arisen from different understandings of what pluralism actually entails.[2] Is orthodox economics pluralist in the same sense as heterodox economics? We will address this question in terms of the level at which pluralism applies. Further, are some heterodox economists monist (advocating only one approach) in the same sense as the orthodoxy? We will consider whether heterodoxy (defined in terms of an alternative) can be monist at all. Can it even be dualistic (allowing for only two all-encompassing approaches)? Or are all heterodox economists in fact pluralist? These questions will be pursued in the third section.

The first need is therefore to be clear about the meaning of pluralism to be employed here, in the next section. This need epitomises issues over pluralism, since the plurality of understandings of pluralism itself creates confusion within the debates over characterisation and about the future path for heterodoxy. No one understanding can claim to be the sole correct understanding. But to move the discussion forward anyone must be clear as to how they understand and use the term, as well as be sensitive to how it is used by others. This is the essence of pluralism.

A definition of pluralism

The understanding of pluralism which will frame the discussion to follow is, first, that it means *advocacy* of plurality, and second, that it applies at different levels, including the levels of theory, method and epistemology (Dow 1997). At the level of theory, pluralism involves support for a proliferation of theories: *theoretical pluralism*. This fragmentation may result from diversity of narrowly defined subject areas, data sets, etc., or from piecemeal theoretical developments that can be expected to consolidate into an agreed theoretical core. It is this form of pluralism, within one approach, which has been most commonly identified in mainstream economics – although there is now debate as to whether this continues to be the case (see e.g. Cedrini and Fontana 2017[BIB-003]). It has always been clear that theoretical pluralism is present in heterodox economics. This plurality has generally also arisen, not only within schools of thought but also between schools of thought. At issue is whether these schools of thought each employ a different approach or whether heterodox economics too has a unified approach.[3]

Pluralism may also apply at the level of method: a *pluralist methodology*. Again, there is an asymmetry between orthodoxy and heterodoxy. McCloskey (1983) has shown that economists of all stripes employ a range of methods in their unofficial discourse. But orthodox economists privilege only mathematical formalism in their official discourse – a monist methodology (see e.g. Lawson 2017).[4] Since it is through the official discourse of publications that economists are judged, this distinction holds particular force in the sociology of the discipline. Heterodox economists on the other hand employ a wide range of methods in their official (as well as unofficial) discourse – a pluralist methodology.

Orthodox economics builds its exclusivist privileging of the mathematical formalist approach on the implicit understanding that the social world is such as to allow capture by axiomatic logic, with no fundamental uncertainty as to the truth-value of the axioms. The widely held view that this is the best scientific approach underpins the methodological monism of the orthodoxy. Within heterodox economics, on the other hand, there is a plurality of (pluralist) methodologies, with different schools of thought typically employing a particular range of methods (neo-Austrians focusing on case studies, institutionalists on long time-trends, and so on).

Warren Samuels provided the foundation for modern thinking on pluralism by emphasising epistemological reasons for these differing versions of knowledge, which in turn have (ontological) foundations in perspectives that differ as a result of differing experience (Davis 2012). Heterodox economics understands the subject matter as an open, evolving, complex system that cannot be captured by deterministic relationships and where knowledge is fundamentally uncertain (Lawson 1997). This being the case, there is no basis for demonstrating any one approach to be the 'true' approach, meaning that a plurality of possibilities can be defended. Accordingly, different heterodox approaches have built on different open-system ontologies and corresponding epistemologies and methodologies. To advocate a plurality of methodologies (drawing on different ontologies) is to engage in *methodological pluralism*.

Other possibilities are methodological monism and methodological dualism. Monism can be defined as advocacy of one sole approach, as with orthodoxy, while dualism can be defined as advocacy of one approach relative to a specified other. Dualism means assigning two categories that have fixed meaning and are all-encompassing and mutually exclusive, a characteristic of the closed-system orthodox approach (Dow 1990). But within the open-system approach of heterodox economics, identifying two categories is not dualistic in the same sense: they may be provisional and permeable, and apply to only one of multiple strands of reasoning. For example, variables are classified as endogenous or exogenous for any formal modelling, but this does not normally extend to the overall structure of argument of which any model can only be a part. We discuss below how far either monism or dualism can be said to characterise a heterodox approach.

Taking methodological pluralism forward

Methodological pluralism is the most common heterodox usage of the term 'pluralism' and is evident in the expression of pluralism on the part of organisations such as the Association for Heterodox Economics. Yet, debates over the characterisation of economics and the future path for heterodoxy sometimes still confuse the levels at which pluralism applies. In particular, does orthodox economics *now* embrace methodological pluralism, or still just theoretical pluralism?

There is no doubt that orthodox economics has evolved, most notably in its recourse to new types of evidence (such as survey and experimental evidence). Indeed, the shift from pure theory to applied (see e.g. Backhouse and Cherrier 2014) has gone to such lengths that much of orthodox economics looks more like applied statistics. But I would argue that, for all this fragmentation, any theoretical reference in applied work and even efforts to change theory still derive from the traditional approach with its emphasis on methodological individualism, mathematical formalism and logical positivism (Dow 2008). Some developments, such as behavioural economics, aim to modify the core of traditional orthodox theory and use novel methods. But that core remains the benchmark and the privileging of formal mathematics (the requirement for theory to be fully expressed in mathematical models) remains. Cedrini and Fontana (2017) argue that the growing specialisation within orthodox economics may create a more congenial climate, which might accommodate heterodox economics with its apparently fragmented landscape. But I would still argue that orthodox economics is not methodologically pluralist.

It has been noted that, while heterodox economists have been so closely associated with methodological pluralism, it has been seen by some instead as monist. However, since this advocacy of heterodox economics is almost always expressed in counterpoint to the orthodoxy, I would argue that this position is not monist, but accords better at least with dualism. Further, both apparent monism and dualism within heterodoxy involve a form of methodological pluralism in that they recognise otherness. Orthodox economists do not justify their approach relative to heterodox economics because adopting an alternative approach to the orthodoxy by definition disqualifies the alternative as economics. At the very least, heterodox economists have to recognise orthodoxy (which they are compelled to do for sociological and political reasons) in order to argue for an alternative.

This recognition of otherness is central to the epistemology that underpins methodological pluralism. Indeed, the willingness to engage in discussion of difference (at different levels) is a key characteristic of pluralism (Chick 2019: 241–2). Further, it is precisely because of the lack of demonstrable truth that vigorous justification is necessary. Pluralism and debate go hand in hand. But, from an explicitly pluralist perspective, for that debate to be effective there needs to be engagement and understanding of what underpins different approaches.

Pluralists may adopt a dualistic approach, in the sense of focusing on advocacy of one heterodox approach as the alternative to orthodoxy, for strategic reasons (see e.g. Kvangraven and Alves 2019). But the apparent dichotomy between this kind of persuasive justification and 'anything goes' is in fact a reflection of an orthodox form of dualism, whereby there is no middle ground between truth and lack-of-truth, and where classifications are all-encompassing and mutually exclusive, with fixed meaning. Rather, from a pluralist perspective, plurality of approaches, *including orthodoxy*, can be seen as occupying a spectrum where boundaries are provisional and permeable (Mearman 2005).

A focus on the distinction between the closed-systems approach of orthodoxy and the open-systems approach of heterodoxy might nevertheless be seen as dualism at the epistemological level. But, while a closed-systems approach is indeed unified, an open-systems approach allows for a plurality of methodological approaches depending on the particular combination of closures and openings adopted (Chick and Dow 2005). Thus the different heterodox schools of thought can be identified with their particular ontologies and methodologies. Further, far from 'anything goes', the logistics of knowledge production mean that the scope for schools of thought is limited, to what I have called 'structured pluralism' (Dow 2004b).

There has been some pushback from various quarters against continuing to think in terms of schools of thought. But it is important that (in line with open-systems theorising) specifications of schools of thought are not fixed, closed categories. Rather they are provisional, permeable groupings (see further Mearman 2012). This extends to orthodox economics, which also has what Victoria Chick (2019: 245) calls 'ragged edges'. Just as labelling heterodoxy relative to orthodoxy promotes clarity, even as an imperfect shorthand (see e.g. Stilwell 2016), so does labelling schools of thought. Indeed efforts to provide materials for students exploring beyond orthodoxy have performed a great service by tabulating summary characteristics of different schools of thought (see e.g. Dimmelmeier *et al.* 2017).

The onus is on the pluralist economist to explain their ontology and epistemology when justifying their approach to representatives of other schools of thought. As Bigo and Negru (2008) argue, such reflexive pluralism promotes the kind of understanding required for constructive interaction. Further, while they see this as a route towards reducing fragmentation in knowledge production, awareness of difference of approach ensures that any integration is coherent. Without reflexive pluralism there is a danger of ontological or epistemological inconsistency, for example, combining theory grounded in uncertainty as epistemologically core with theory which presumes no uncertainty; or combining model-uncertainty models with models which assume rational choice based on full information. Open-system theorising, involving multiple chains of reasoning employing different methods, often involves a very different kind of inconsistency: simplifying (not fictional) assumptions in one chain which are relaxed in another (Dow 1990).

Conclusion

So, what is implied for the most effective path for heterodox economics to follow in pursuing its pluralist agenda? Is it to appear to adopt a monist, or even dualist, strategy to counter orthodox monism (see Jackson 2018)? The danger of suppressing fundamental differences at the ontological and epistemological levels is that misunderstanding is perpetuated. It feeds into the monist orthodox refusal to address, never mind justify, their methodological stance. The argument developed here supports a forceful advocacy of methodological pluralism, explaining what it means (aware of the monist 'other'). It also supports explicit explanation of the ontology and epistemology underpinning theory when in debate with members of alternative schools of thought. The purpose of greater mutual understanding of foundations is not to set up barriers but to facilitate more effective communication, which in turn could lead to innovative cross-fertilisation of ideas.

Should pluralism extend to include the orthodoxy, given the range of asymmetries of power as well as epistemology? Mearman (2011) persuasively argues, on pluralist grounds, for inclusion of orthodoxy rather than rejection. But otherwise pluralists might readily accept that there is a range of paths that can take heterodox economics forward (Dow 2000). These paths might well be applied by heterodox economists according to their relative strengths and interests. A focus on shared principles could indeed be one of the plurality of paths; so could attempting to communicate with those orthodox economists displaying dissatisfaction but unaware of what heterodox economics offers; so could focusing on promoting cross-fertilisations between schools of thought, and so on. For many, of course, focusing on developing theory and policy within a school of thought is the primary activity and can have important persuasive impact, particularly in policy circles. But for the foundations of this activity, and thus the meaning of theory and policy arising from it, to be evident, there needs to be the methodological awareness which allows for meaningful discussion and debate. It is this that underpins the current push for pluralism and is ultimately the key to progress in the discipline.

Notes

1 Comments from Andrew Mearman are gratefully acknowledged.
2 See, for example, Cedrini and Fontana (2017) for an analysis of the recent literature on pluralism in orthodox economics, including different understandings of the term.
3 See the exchange between Dow (2004a) and Lawson (2004) for a flavor of the debate.
4 This is not to deny that there has been evolution in recent years in the types of evidence used to test formal results.

References

Backhouse, R.E. and B. Cherrier (2014). Becoming Applied: The Transformation of Economics after 1970, *Center for the History of Political Economy Working Paper Series*, No. 2014–15.

Bigo, V. and I. Negru (2008). From Fragmentation to Ontologically Reflexive Pluralism, *Journal of Philosophical Economics*, 1 (2): 127–50.

Cedrini, M. and M. Fontana (2017). Just another Niche in the Wall? How Specialization is Changing the Face of Mainstream Economics. *Cambridge Journal of Economics*, 42 (2): 427–51.

Chick, V. (2019). Interview, in A. Mearman, S. Berger and D. Guizzo (eds.), *What is Heterodox Economics? Conversations with Leading Economists*. London: Routledge, pp. 232–51.

Chick, V. and S.C. Dow (2005). The Meaning of Open Systems, *Journal of Economic Methodology*, 12 (3): 363–81. Reprinted in S.C. Dow, *Foundations for New Economic Thinking*. London: Palgrave Macmillan, 2012, pp. 178–96.

Davis, J.B. (2006). The Turn in Economics: Neoclassical Dominance to Mainstream Pluralism? *Journal of Institutional Economics*, 2 (1): 1–20.

Davis, J.B. (2012). Samuels on Methodological Pluralism in Economics, in J. Biddle and R. Emmett (eds.), *Research in the History of Economic Thought and Methodology: A Research Annual*, 30 (1): 121–36.

Dimmelmeier, A., F. Heussner, A. Pürckhauer and J. Urban (2017). Making the Incommensurable Comparable: A Comparative Approach to Pluralist Economics Education, *European Journal of Economics and Economic Policies: Intervention*, 14 (2): 250–66.

Dow, S.C. (1990). Beyond Dualism, *Cambridge Journal of Economics*, 14 (2): 143–58. Reprinted in S.C. Dow, *Foundations for New Economic Thinking*. London: Palgrave Macmillan, 2012, pp. 52–71.

Dow, S.C. (1997). Methodological Pluralism and Pluralism of Method, in A. Salanti and E. Screpanti (eds.), *Pluralism in Economics: Theory, History and Methodology*. Cheltenham: Edward Elgar, pp. 89–99.

Dow, S.C. (2000). Prospects for the Progress of Heterodox Economics, *Journal of the History of Economic Thought*, 22 (2): 157–70.

Dow, S.C. (2004a). Reorienting Economics: Some Epistemological Issues, *Journal of Economic Methodology*, 11 (3): 307–12.

Dow, S.C. (2004b). Structured Pluralism, *Journal of Economic Methodology*, 11 (3): 275–90.

Dow, S.C. (2008). Plurality in Orthodox and Heterodox Economics, *Journal of Philosophical Economics*, 1 (2): 73–96.

Garnett, R.F. (2006). Paradigms and Pluralism in Heterodox Economics, *Review of Political Economy*, 18 (Fall): 521–46.

Jackson, W.A. (2018). Strategic Pluralism and Monism in Heterodox Economics, *Review of Radical Political Economics*, 50 (2): 237–51.

Kvangraven, I. and C. Alves (2019). Heterodox Economics as a Positive Project: Revisiting the Debate, *ESRC GPID Research Network Working Paper* 19.

Lawson, T. (1997). *Economics and Reality*. London: Routledge.

Lawson, T. (2004). Reorienting Economics: On Heterodox Economics, Themata and the Use of Mathematics in Economics, *Journal of Economic Methodology*, 11 (3): 329–40.

Lawson, T. (2017). What is Wrong with Modern Economics, and Why Does it Stay Wrong? *Journal of Australian Political Economy*, 80: 26–42.

McCloskey, D.N. (1983). The Rhetoric of Economics, *Journal of Economic Literature*, 31 (2): 434–61.

Mearman, A. (2005). Sheila Dow's Concept of Dualism: Clarification, Criticism and Development, *Cambridge Journal of Economics*, 29 (4): 619–34.

Mearman, A. (2011). Pluralism, Heterodoxy, and the Rhetoric of Distinction, *Review of Radical Political Economics*, 43 (4): 552–61.

Mearman, A. (2012). 'Heterodox Economics' and the Problems of Classification, *Journal of Economic Methodology*, 19 (4): 407–24.

Mearman, A., S. Berger and D. Guizzo (2019). Concluding Thoughts, in A. Mearman, S. Berger and D. Guizzo (eds.), *What is Heterodox Economics? Conversations with Leading Economists*. London: Routledge, pp. 286–92.

Stilwell, F. (2016). Heterodox Economics or Political Economy?, *World Economics Association Newsletter*, 6 (1): 2–6. www.worldeconomicsassociation.org/files/Issue6-1.pdf.

16 Improving pluralism in economics education

Jack Reardon

Introduction

More than 150 years ago Henry George lamented that

> discovery upon discovery, and invention after invention, have neither lessened the toil of those who need most respite, nor brought plenty to the poor … all the dull, deadening pain, all the keen maddening anguish, that to the great masses of men [sic] are involved in the 'hard times' afflict the world today.
>
> (George 1879 [1948], pp. 5–6)

Alas, we are still battling the problems of the poor, anguish and the hard times, which presents a perennial challenge to economics, but in a different context where,

> technology is fundamentally changing how we produce and consume resources and how we provision. No longer is the world neatly divided into consumer and producer, buyer and seller, markets and commons; but each is morphing into something quite different, requiring a new lens and a new vision to understand our changing world … giving us fruitful pause (but certainly not long-lasting) to reconceptualize the firm, the industry, the role of government, and how we adequately provision for all.
>
> (Reardon 2018, p. 425)

And, as if this isn't enough, we are also battling climate change which 'is threatening to dwarf all the other issues [to] become the *only* issue' (Flannery 2005, p. 8; emphasis in original). These formidable and interrelated problems are creating pervasive and ubiquitous uncertainty, and especially for students: is our world changing? what will the environment be like when I graduate, when my kids are born, when I reach retirement? Will technology automate me out of a job?

Many students enroll in economics courses in order to understand their economy and how environmental changes are fast impacting it, to hopefully gain some confidence in the future. Instead they are baffled and frustrated by this 'technical and rarified discipline, of questionable relevance and limited practical use, a branch of applied mathematics where the aim is not to explain real processes and outcomes' (Hodgson 1999, pp. 6 and 9). Joe Earle, Cahal Moran, and Zach Ward-Perkins, lament in more detail,

> Having graduated now we are all keenly aware that our economics education has not equipped us with the knowledge or skills to justify any authority we [have been given]. In fact, we were so frustrated with how little our education was helping us understand the world that midyear through our second year at university we began a campaign to reform economics education.
>
> (Earle et al. 2017, p. 2)

After graduation they wrote the much-read book, whose title is self-explanatory: *The Econocracy: The Perils of Leaving Economics to the Experts* (2017).

This frustration has spawned a global, student-led movement to rethink and reconceptualize economics.[1] Central to this movement is the dissatisfaction with only one proffered approach, as if the one could explain everything; and the concomitant demand that economics must become pluralist:

> Too often the lectures leave no place for reflection. Out of all the approaches to economic questions that exist, generally only one is presented to us, [which] is supposed to explain everything by means of a purely axiomatic process, as if this were THE economic truth. We do not accept this dogmatism. We want a pluralism of approaches, adapted to the complexity of the objects and the uncertainty surrounding most of the big questions in economics…
>
> (Post-Autistic Economics Network 2000; emphasis in original)

And from the student organization, Rethinking Economics (2014),

> We need to recognize the plurality within economics … There is no recognition of the variety of schools of thought within economics, across history or across the world. Academic integrity requires that alternative economic theories be introduced to students, alongside those currently taught.

Although in the past, similar calls for pluralism were made and subsequently petered out, today the clarion call for pluralism has become entrenched in the public mind and embedded in curriculum reform. It has become vibrantly strong, 'we have reached a critical bifurcation point: economics will become pluralist and will never again be the same …' (Reardon 2017a, p. 12) There is no turning back. Pluralism is here to stay, for those of us interested in implementing pluralism, we have made a lot of progress, and a pluralist economics is inevitable. Nonetheless, we cannot rest on our laurels,

> [w]ithout doubt progress has been made, most notably in the form of the rethinking economics organization and its various local chapters. They and others are building up an impressive bank of materials for pluralist education ... But the pluralist community is much stronger now in my view, even if it has to operate in the shadow of the mainstream. Further, it may require a new generation of economists to affect change, so the student movement is the most helpful development.
>
> (Roundtable 2015, p. 291)

So, if pluralism is strongly demanded by our main customers and it works and is here to stay, then all we have to do is implement/increase it! Simple, right? Unfortunately, no. There is a host of difficulties and unanswered questions that the first section of this chapter will highlight and discuss. Then, the second section will discuss specific ways to encourage pluralism in the curriculum. The third section concludes.

Pluralism fundamentals

In 2009, I wrote over-optimistically that, since the case for pluralism has been persuasively made, all that is left to do is discuss its implementation (Reardon 2009). I was naively wrong. Yes, the case has been made, but not everyone has listened; and since the Great Recession of 2007–2009, a stiff and formidable resistance has blossomed (Reardon 2012). But the clarion call for pluralism continues.

Defining pluralism

But what exactly is pluralism? It is a complex word, like freedom, democracy, and sustainability, meaning different things to different people. In 2015, I conducted a 'roundtable on pluralism,' at the *International Journal of Pluralism and Economics Education* with guests ranging from renowned experts to beginning students, to get their take on a host of issues relating to pluralism, beginning with a definition. Perhaps I should not have been surprised that, given the multifaceted, faceted, and multilayered nature of pluralism, we should readily agree to a definition. While we disagreed over the basic wording, we essentially agreed that pluralism means a willingness to recognize and even listen to and dialogue with alternative views. The key to pluralism is recognizing that multiple meanings and interpretations exist, and multiple interpretations of reality are possible. Pluralism does not imply agreeing with alternatives or even identifying with them, only recognizing them as legitimate alternatives. The opposite of pluralism is monism, suggesting a dogmatic insistence on only one correct view; one correct interpretation.

Complicating matters is that pluralism exists on several levels:[2] (1) *theoretical*—multiple theories exist to explain phenomena; (2) *epistemological*—multiple types of knowledge; (3) *ontological*—multiple ways of knowing about the economy; (4) *methodological*—no single set of criteria that economists can use to decide which is the best theory; (5) *pluralism of method*—multiple ways of doing economics; and (6) *pedagogical*—multiple ways of teaching economics.

It is perfectly conceivable that economics could be pluralist in method, for example, but pedagogically monist, so it is important to explicitly clarify which level when discussing whether economics is pluralist. While it is important to fully discuss each level, as well as the shifting boundaries, the brevity of this chapter forces sole attention on education.[3] For me this is fine, since 'education is our most important function as human beings: it is an investment in ourselves, future generations, and the planet' (Reardon 2009, p. 267); and it is 'the most vital of all resources' (Schumacher 1973 [1989], p. 84). In addition, the demand for pedagogical pluralism is the foundational criticism of the student-led Rethinking Economics.

Pluralist or pluralism?

Another interesting finding from our Roundtable was that pluralism represents a modus operandi, a willingness to engage and to listen and to dialogue, and not necessarily a fulcrum of knowledge of the discipline's myriad views and schools of thought,

> the answer to the question whether heterodox economics is consistent with pluralism is not about the recognition of pluralism, but the attitude toward various alternatives. To be a pluralist is consistent with representing one particular school of thought, while being open, tolerant, and knowledgeable about others.
>
> (Roundtable 2015, p. 287)

To rephrase: if a person was complimented as being pluralist how would you fill in the next sentence: She is ___? To be pluralist should one become expert in every school of thought, exhibiting an encyclopedic knowledge, or is it enough to be adept in the ability to listen and dialogue? This is not exactly a binary, either/or choice; but, at least from my perspective, the emphasis should be on the former, but not excluding the latter. We need both, but perhaps not always in the same individual. With the former we need a different set of skills that have heretofore been largely ignored in economics education: listening, dialoging, compromising, and engaging. But these are precisely the skills needed to function effectively in a democracy,

> [t]he kinds of skills and qualities needed by citizens for a broad democracy to function effectively are learned, not innate and must be practised to be mastered. They include listening, compromise, the ability to critically evaluate verbal and numerical argument, and developing independent judgement. They can only come through practical experience of being

> involved in participatory democratic institutions. In this sense, moving towards a system of broad democracy is a process of learning by doing.
> (Earle et al. 2017, p. 152)

These skills can be effectuated and actively learned, as we discuss in the next section.

Anything goes?

If pluralism means listening, and at least recognizing, different views, does this mean that all views are legitimate, or are some views off limits? Pluralists, at least in Economics, have reached a consensus that pluralism is not 'anything goes,' but rather some views are legitimate and others clearly not. It is difficult not to dispute this logic, and to accept the opposite is to not impose boundaries on the discipline and to forfeit its status as a science; yet, at the same time, it is not clear how gray and fuzzy the line of demarcation is, and who determines which views are illegitimate. Who is the arbiter and what standards are to be used? Does this imply a tyranny for the majority? Does this mean that anything goes for opposing illegitimate views? And what about new and untried views? Is there a natural proclivity to parry or impugn them before they are even fully exposed? As pluralism advances, we must find a way to clarify and deal with this important issue.

Is pluralism beneficial? Arguments for and against

Despite the recent clarion call for pluralism, and its rightful place in the arduous task of reconceptualizing economics, unfortunately

> [n]ot everyone views pluralism as desirable. The concept is foreign to most orthodox economists, who, if they ever considered it all, might well assume that the concept sounds dubious and antithetical to the idea of economics as a rigorous science. Even amongst heterodox economists, the concept is controversial, with some arguing that it is neither intellectually warranted, nor of practical use to the heterodox agenda.
> (Thornton 2017, p. 35)

And, furthermore, some argue that too much ambiguity, controversy, and complexity might prematurely confuse student and teacher, which 'risks undermining the entire venture … with too many qualifications and alternatives [so that] teachers and their students may abandon economics entirely out of frustration born of confusion and uncertainty' (Siegfried and Meszaros 1997, p. 249).

Nonsense. The economy is complex, and the myriad interpretations and views of it are, not surprisingly, equally complex. If we are to teach the actual economy and not some idealized, fictitious version, then we have to teach about its messiness and complexity, which might confuse. At the same time, it is disingenuous and unethical to insist on only one way of doing economics. A good pluralist teacher does not have to be armed with every bit of knowledge about every school in economics; rather, it is often enough to inspire the student to learn, listen, inquire, dialogue, and explore.

Pertaining to the beneficial aspects of pluralism a lot has been written, but given brevity of space, the best I can do is bullet-point key arguments:[4]

- Pluralism ensures vitality and innovation since, 'in ideas, as in nature, variety is the evolutionary fuel. When pluralism and variety disappear, innovation and progress may slow to a halt ... Pluralism is necessary for innovation and scientific advance' (Hodgson 1999, p. 13; emphasis in original deleted).
- Not only is pluralism consistent with a democracy of ideas and a democratic society, but democratic interaction can lead to a 'transformative dialogue,' which can help move economics forward (Söderbaum and Brown 2011).
- Pluralism is useful because,

  > no paradigm or theoretical perspective can claim universal applicability, i.e., usefulness for all kinds of problems. Each paradigm or theoretical perspective may have something to offer and preference for one theoretical perspective over another is ... partly a matter of ideology.
  > (Söderbaum 2008, pp. 9–10)

- The quintessence 'of pluralism is to be intellectually open' (Thornton 2017, p. 2).
- Pluralism comports with the ideals of a liberal arts education; it opens one's eyes, forces one to be intellectually honest, and instills 'empathy, dialogue, humility, and understanding ... public policy benefits from a healthy pluralist debate. Pluralism enables student choice, monism constrains and disables' (Reardon 2009, p. 267). If we want educated citizens who understand the complexity of our economy, warts and all, we need pluralism.

Any evidence of pluralism's efficacy?

A universal, unequivocal study testing for pluralism does not exist, and perhaps it is quixotic to expect one. Complicating matters is not knowing what particular efficacy we are testing. Skills in listening and dialoging? Mastery of a stock of knowledge? Or willingness to learn the discipline of economics in a novel way? Most empirical studies are anecdotal and support the latter, finding that pedagogical pluralism enables the learning of key economic ideas and concepts, for both student and teacher. At least from my perch as editor of the International Journal of Pluralism and Economics Education (IJPEE) editor, I have not seen or heard of any evidence, empirical or anecdotal, that impugns the theoretical benefits of pluralism.

And what about assessment?

This promises to become an important issue, with preliminary efforts currently underway to assess pluralism. If pluralism, supported by anecdotal evidence is efficacious, how can we assess if our students have become pluralist? The late Fred Lee urged heterodox economists to grab the assessment bull by the horns, so to speak:

> But what is really necessary to do is for heterodox economists to challenge the research assessment exercises, subject benchmark statements, and the mainstream ranking of journals and departments through, perhaps, developing their own methods of research assessments and rankings of journals and departments.
>
> (Lee 2009, p. 206)

Likewise, we urge pluralists to do the same, to at least conceptualize this issue, so that we are not left in the cold.

Ostensibly simple but, in reality, much more difficult, and obfuscated by the contemporary effort to assess economics knowledge, which has largely been usurped by the hegemony of neoclassical economics. And, at what level do we assess: the university, the department, the student, or the professor. In the old thinking it was easy. Professors impart knowledge and students absorb, so assessment must test the knowledge that has been imparted and absorbed. But pluralism recognizes that knowledge and education are changing so that, rather than imparting knowledge, we teach students how to think. And what aspect of pluralism do we assess: the ability to listen and dialogue? Or knowledge of competing ideologies?

A problem that I have with economics assessment, at least as it is today, is that it assumes that knowledge is self-contained within well-demarcated and non-changing silos, with little crossover or interaction, so in effect we are testing the skills of yesteryear, rather than the skills needed for today. We need broad-based thinkers, who are knowledgeable about alternative views and theories, and willing to engage with those who think differently. And unfortunately, as often happens, students (and teachers) study and prepare for the test which means studying and assimilating yesterday's needed skills rather than today's. As we implement the UN 17 Sustainable Development Goals as an urgently needed recipe for sustainable living, who would you prefer: an economist dogmatically schooled in neoclassical economics, with no knowledge of its diversity, or a social scientist, well aware of the diversity of thought, and well skilled in the craft of listening and dialogue?

Pluralism: Disciplinary, Multi-Disciplinary, Interdisciplinary, or Trans-Disciplinary?

This for me is a most interesting and perplexing question, and one that I am asked frequently. Perhaps if asked a generation ago I would have said, disciplinary; period. Indeed, economics is fractured with its many tribes carrying on as if the others do not exist, each with its separate history, methodologies, conferences, publications, etc. Economics as a discipline does not speak with a unified voice; and only rarely are students taught about the discipline's multiple schools of thought. This must change,

> [e]conomics education needs to be radically reconceptualized, recognizing the diversity of human thought, and the complexity of human and ecological existence. It must welcome and actively cooperate with other social sciences. We must educate our students, not proselytize them. The traditional curriculum of introductory, micro/macro theory, statistics/econometrics, and upper division courses is too narrow [exacerbated by teaching from only one viewpoint] reinforcing insularity and instilling a false sense of security that only the economic way of thinking is needed [and worse: only one type of economic thinking].
>
> (Reardon 2017b, p. 328, thesis #90)

At the bare minimum, students must be exposed to the multiple schools of thought within economics. Gone are the days when only economics could ostensibly offer solutions for the problems of our generation, which are not solely economic, sociological, or political. In order to fully conceptualize our problems, and to effectuate workable solutions, we need the active cooperation of multiple perspectives spanning several disciplines. We need a new, pluralist education.

Within the discipline it should not be expected that each teacher master the intricacies of each school of thought; this is a recipe for madness for both student and teacher. Rather, it is the department's responsibility to ensure that we are graduating students of economics rather than students of neoclassical economics. Easier said than done, given that many neoclassical economists aren't cognizant of other schools within economics.

Given the urgency of climate change, disciplinary pluralism, however, is just a starting point; we must actively engage in all venues of pluralism[5] (not just pedagogical): *Disciplinary*—cooperation within the discipline; *Multi-Disciplinary*—cooperation between different disciplines; *Interdisciplinary*—an integration of the cooperating theories; and *Trans-Disciplinary*—whereby the theory of one discipline is combined with the empirical evidence of another, effectively forming a new discipline.

How to improve pluralism

Ostensibly simple, this section nevertheless raises several difficulties. For starters: If we are asked to improve, does this mean that pluralism is teleological, that is, after arduous improvements, will we reach a perfected ideal form, satisfying all? A nirvana, if you will? No, of course not. Our working definition of pluralism must be directly tied to the underlying conditions of our economy. Alfred Marshall wrote, in his best-selling *Principles of Economics*, that 'economic conditions are constantly changing, and each generation looks at its own problems in its own way' (1890 [1946], p. v). As conditions change, so must the definition and outreach of pluralism. As Earle et al. (2017) noted earlier, today we need a new set of skills, especially if we are to solve our problems democratically. And, given today's urgency of climate change, we need social scientists who can work well together; thus, pluralism must recognize and encourage the ability to listen and dialogue, and the existence of alternative viewpoints.

A defining feature of the new economy is the existence of platforms that are superseding the markets, which used to characterize the Old Economy. Pluralism is a platform, and as more people use it, the more positive externalities are generated for all. Unfortunately, not all economists are cognizant of the need for pluralism, especially those exclusively trained in neoclassical economics, whose training blinds them to the possibility of other viewpoints. This explains why pluralism has been resisted and why it has not been snowballing on its own. And this is why, in order to implement pluralism, we reconceptualize economics education, to which we now turn.

Radically reconceptualize economics education

A preponderant lesson learned in my 13 years as IJPEE editor is that no simple ready-made recipe to implement pluralism exists. Instead, there are multiple angles, or entry points if you will, none of which is preponderant, and all must be used. More specifically, all pluralism stakeholders must be recognized: the public, alumni, businesses, the economics profession, students, and teachers. And various entry points acknowledged: the department, the university, the national level, assessors, the discipline of economics (along with its various tribes), the overall curriculum in economics, individual teachers, and students. Brevity necessitates only a brief overview here.

If we are to reconceptualize economics so that it is once again useful in solving our problems we have to radically reform the curriculum from top to bottom. An immediate and frequent objection is the opportunity cost: if I teach this, I have to jettison this, which we must teach if students are to learn economics. Two comments. First, there is a lot of repetition in neoclassical pedagogy with upper division courses repeating and reinforcing what was learned in earlier courses (which to me smacks of proselytization),

> the essence of what is taught in most applied field courses is the same regardless of the specific questions and institutional context of the subject matter covered in the course. Economists teach the basic principles of economics—opportunity cost, marginal analysis, the role of prices as signals, incentives, specialization, unintended consequences—regardless of the name of the course to which they are assigned. The ideas are the same whether the applied field course focuses on factor markets or product markets.
>
> (Siegfried 2009, p. 219)

Needless to say, this statement is remarkable for its complete ignorance of competing schools of thought in economics and their pedagogical focus!

And, second, there is lot of deadwood in the economics curriculum, and if this means 'scrapping theories because they no longer work, or because underlying conditions have changed, so be it—this is how the discipline progresses' (Reardon 2017b, p. 328, thesis #89). I know of no other discipline that insists on teaching deadwood. But, of course, changing an existing curriculum to make it more pluralist,

> is a complicated process similar to that of changing institutions in general: the path is full of lock-ins, of interests of specific groups and individuals, of information asymmetry, strategic behavior, of power, and the like. The issue of how the economics curriculum should be designed and who decides on changing the curriculum is a matter of academic power.
>
> (Groenewegen 2007, p. 14)

Thus the necessity for multiple entry points recognizing all stakeholders. Easier said than done!

If economics is to become pluralist whereby our students are aware of alternative views, and can effectively listen and dialogue then, during the first year of the curriculum, students should not take any economics courses. Instead, given the emphasis on listening and dialogue, abetted by climate change, a prerequisite course for the economics major is 'listening and dialogue.' But given a paucity of economists who have been educated in pluralism, our instructors must come from outside the discipline—perhaps even team-teaching. Nothing wrong with this.

Additional courses to be taken as prerequisites for the economics major during the first year include: world literature, history of capitalism, and quantum physics. Briefly, the rationale for each:

- *World Literature*—There is no better primer on the diversity of the human condition than fiction. Properly taught, fiction can explain the myriad forms of behavior and human predicaments as good as, or even better than, any individual academic discipline.
- *History of Capitalism*—It is essential for economics majors to understand how the present system of capitalism has evolved, the role of government, and how people respond to contemporary problems by constructing appropriate institutions. There is nothing natural or inevitable about capitalism or any economic system.
- *Quantum Physics*—not only are many of the accoutrements of today's economy, such as the CD, laser, computer, MRIs, and traffic lights, the result of the intellectual achievements of quantum physics, but no better example exists of the scientific willingness to test and experiment, and the openness to reform theory if necessary, than quantum physics.

Is this a quixotic attempt at haphazard reform? No, not at all. Such courses should be part of a university curriculum, and the university must impart today's students with the skills necessary to actively participate in a democracy. The difference here is that for the economics major these courses must be taken as prerequisites. This will prepare students for the inevitable economics course that isn't pluralist in any form, with the material presented dogmatically. It also recognizes the student as a stakeholder in improving pluralism without undue burden.[6]

Improving pluralism: Sooner or later?

An oft-asked question is: given that we accept the need for pluralism and that we have decided to implement it, should this be done at the beginning of the economics curriculum or in later courses? I feel this is an artificially constructed either/or dilemma; instead, the curriculum should be pluralist and infused with the necessary skills from the beginning. To wait until later in the curriculum runs the risk of students either becoming ossified in their views or dropping out of economics altogether. Offering prerequisites in the first year renders this question moot, since the student is equipped to recognize alternative views.

Whose responsibility is it to teach alternative views?

The department's. Each economics department must take ownership for its graduates. While the urgency of climate change dictates immediate focus on developing listening and dialoguing skills, this does not mean that we ignore the other strand of developing pluralism, that of imparting and developing knowledge of alternative views. Every department should offer in the second year of study a required course on alternative economic views. If the department lacks the required personnel to teach such a course, then it must hire someone. To insist that every teacher crash-learn every school of thought so that every course is taught from every perspective is a recipe for madness for both teacher and student. Collectively, it becomes the responsibility of the department to impart the requisite knowledge, given, of course, that it has endorsed pluralism as a curriculum objective.

What can the individual teacher do?

What about the situation where no changes have been made in the curriculum, no prerequisites have been offered, and the rest of one's department is peopled by neoclassicals, blissfully unaware of alternative viewpoints, and thus even the need for pedagogical pluralism? Unfortunately, such a situation is not atypical, at least here in the US. What can the individual teacher do? Although certainly not ideal, it isn't as constricting as it ostensibly appears. Most of us have had teachers that have positively influenced us, setting us on a path that we might not have obtained otherwise. I wrote my first book on pluralism with exactly this type of teacher in mind, offering specific suggestions for courses at all levels ranging from principles, intermediate micro/macro to upper division courses such as international economics, monetary economics, and labor economics (Reardon 2009). And, in addition, at the IJPEE we have published dozens of specific articles containing both a 'hands-on' and a 'how-to' for teaching just about every course from a pluralist perspective. So, for the individual teacher interested in making a difference, despite a constricting environment, there is a plethora of resources.

Active learning

Among all schools of economics, there has been an active movement away from the traditional chalk and talk lecture to more active learning, which includes hands-on activities and learning by doing. While not 100 percent guaranteed, such an approach is much more amenable to pluralism than the traditional chalk and talk. This is because the material forces invite different approaches and different points of view. Many aspects of active learning require conversing and dialoguing with the public, which, if efficacious, must be done non-dogmatically.

Learning and teaching the UN 17 Sustainable Development Goals

In September 2015 the UN promulgated its 17 Sustainable Development Goals (SDGs), an urgent recipe for living sustainably and saving the planet. This is a game changer, not just for economics and how we provision as a society, but also for economics education. Taken together the SDGs,

> underscore the point that sustainability involves a lot more than concern with the environment. [They use the words] all, inclusive, and urgent; and the active verbs: end, ensure, achieve, promote, reduce, conserve, revitalize. This is the language of the SDGs, this is the language of urgency …
> (Reardon et al., 2018, p. 18)

And this should be the language of economics, but it isn't. Neoclassical economics was founded during the mid/late nineteenth century 'when economists thought, wrote, and prescribed as if nature did not exist' (McNeil, 2000, p. 335). If its founders were living today, they would embrace climate change as an opportunity to radically change the trajectory of economics, perhaps even moving away from the staid deductive track launched by David Ricardo. Instead the disciples have steadfastly clung to the original tenets as dogma.

My colleagues and I published a book that serves both as a primer for the general public and as a textbook for economics students on a new economics to comport with the 17 UN SDGs (Reardon et al. 2018). Instead of the usual chapters in the usual order found in every neoclassical textbook, we offer chapters on power, ethics, sustainability, resources and the environment, poverty, justice, empowerment, work, economic democracy, cooperatives, trade; along with more familiar topics (albeit with a sustainability twist) firms, markets, money, consumption, investment, growth, and recessions.

It is absolutely impossible to discuss sustainability from one perspective. It is absolutely impossible to discuss sustainability without discussing justice, ethics, and power. And it is absolutely impossible to discuss justice and power without developing the skills to listen and dialogue. It simply cannot be done. Start teaching the UN 17 SDGs, and pluralism with its myriad benefits becomes inevitable. This is why it is a game changer.

Resuscitating courses in the history of economic thought

It is not coincidental that the call for pluralism has also coincided with the call for the resuscitation of courses in the history of economic thought. They were jettisoned from the economics curriculum partly because it was believed by some that economics develops teleologically and what was best in earlier theories has been embodied in the new; and today's economics is better than what we had in the past, obviating the need to study the development of thought.

But economics is not teleological. Earlier arguments that failed to win public favor often did not do so due to inferior content; rather, quite likely the vested interests preferred one view over another, while often sweeping the other under the rug, so to speak. But as we try to understand our changing world, it is beneficial to peruse earlier arguments not only for intellectual content, but also to learn how earlier economists conceptualized existing problems and the world around them.[7] This reinforces the need for pluralism with its requisite skills of listening, dialoguing, and actively participating:

> Meeting essential needs requires not only a new era of economic growth for nations in which the majority are poor, but an assurance that those poor get their fair share of the resources required to sustain that growth. Such equity would be aided by political systems that secure effective citizen participation in decision-making and by greater democracy in international decision-making.
>
> (WCED 1987, p. 16)

Recognize and welcome a pluralism of gender and identity

Earle et al. (2017) lamented that 'the academic discipline of economics is so unrepresentative of wider society that it cannot hope to understand or engage with many parts of the population' (p. 161). The profession's discrimination is widely known in terms of hiring, tenure, promotion, journal publications, journal editorships, etc. Unfortunately, the problem runs deep, stretching back to the inception of modern economics when the discipline was neatly demarcated into the real economy where men wrote books and debated policy intended for male policymakers and male readers, while women were relegated to the domestic economy and charged with raising the family. Given the ubiquity of the dominating power structure, many women felt powerless to protest, but perhaps not surprisingly, many women fought back, protesting, writing tracts and offering policy suggestions to anyone who would listen. It is encouraging to read their work,[8] which should be incorporated into the broader economics curriculum, and especially in upper division courses on labor, gender, and the environment. How can the discipline of economics hope to become pluralist when it has jettisoned from its curriculum, the pioneering work of eighteenth- and nineteenth-century female writers?

In addition, economics (especially neoclassical economics) has long discriminated against those on the margin; and at least the economics that I am familiar with has never been outwardly friendly toward non-binary people. Identity for many is not a binary either/or; instead, for some, it is shifting, amorphous, and even elusive. While recent developments are encouraging (i.e., the formation of the American Economic Association's LGBTQ network) all of economics needs to do more to inclusively recognize and care about the pluralism of identities. Doing so naturally paves the way and opens the front door for pluralism in general, at all levels. A discipline cannot be pluralist if it refuses to recognize the work of non-binary economists (both today and from the past), and if it refuses to welcome and embrace everyone into the discipline of economics.

Renaming economics political economy

Language, and especially the words we use to describe/define an entity, determines how we relate to it. For example, labeling air and water pollution an externality led to the neoclassical theory of the firm devoid of environmental considerations. During the eighteenth century and most of the nineteenth century economics was known as political economy, and as the nineteenth century progressed, an effort was made to constrict the definition of political economy to something empirically verifiable with a concomitant effort to shorten the label (and hence constrict) to economics.

Given the current emphasis that economics is fundamentally about provisioning rather than a means–end game of allocating resources (the most important of which—ideas—is not scarce at all) and that endeavoring to provision is, by definition, multi-disciplinary, many are demanding a widespread return to the older eighteenth-century term *political economy* since,

> … one cannot understand contemporary societies very well unless politics, economics, psychology, and the other social science disciplines are all brought together to study the complexities of modern life. Another way of describing the political economy approach, then, is to say that it is interdisciplinary.
>
> (Bowles et al., 2005, p. 51; emphasis in original)

Frank Stilwell adds that,

> this interdisciplinary character of political economy is one of its strengths. Real world-phenomena do not fit neatly into boxes labelled economic, social, political or cultural. These categories have been constructed for academic convenience, and the disciplinary divisions—between economics, sociology, and political science, for example—can impede a full understanding.
>
> (Stillwell 2012, p. 3)

The label *political economy* embraces pluralism, while opening the door for multi- and interdisciplinary collaboration, and pluralism at each of the different venues. It is quaint to urge our students to think like economists—and neoclassical economists to boot—(Siegfried 2009) when we should be thinking like political economists (qua social scientists) and citizens of the world.

Changing our label becomes easier for the political economists to either split away from neoclassicals and/or join another department or form their own, if need be. Anecdotal evidence suggests this might be best for all, especially improving the education overall for the students (Stillwell 2011; Lavoie 2015).

Conclusion

If we are to solve the pressing and interconnected problems of our generation, and especially climate change, we need economics, but not as it currently is – a divided, hegemonic, and dogmatic discipline—but one that recognizes pluralism and diversity in all its wonderful manifestations. While this chapter offered suggestions on to how to improve pluralism, they are not meant to be implemented piecemeal, rather as a collective whole, although easier said than done.

Notes

1 For an interesting and expanded discussion see Thornton (2017, pp. 69–87).
2 For an expanded discussion see Thornton 2017, pp. 34–48; and Dow (2007). The description of each level is taken from Thornton 2017, pp. 37–38.
3 For a historical discussion of pluralism see Negru (2009); and for an interesting dissection of pluralism see Negru (2010); and Heise (2017).
4 For further discussion see Garnett and Reardon (2012).
5 For an expanded discussion and illustration, see Lemstra (2007); the definition of each pluralism was taken from Lemstra (2007, pp. 146–148.
6 Hill and Myatt hope 'to help stoke the fires of revolution' (2010, p. 2) from below by peppering their text with '71 Questions for Your Professor.' That this book had to be written speaks volumes about what is wrong with the economics profession;

unfortunately, there are several others that are just as critical; see Reardon et al. (2018, p. 13, note #6) for a listing.

7 See Deane et al. (2019) for interesting suggestions to make the history of economic thought pluralist.

8 For a wonderful book which gateways this prolific literature see Madden and Dimand (2019). As the book notes on its title page: 'The marginalization of women in economics has a history as long as the discipline itself.' This must change.

References

Bowles, S., Edwards, R., and Roosevelt, F. (2005) *Understanding Capitalism: Competition, Command, and Change*, New York: Oxford University Press.

Deane, K., Waeyenberge, E., and Maxwell, R. (2019) 'Recharting the History of Economic Thought: Approaches to and Student Experiences of the Introduction of Pluralist Teaching in an Undergraduate Economics Curriculum,' *International Journal of Pluralism and Economics Education*, Vol. 10, No. 2, pp. 137–154.

Dow, S. (2007) 'Pluralism in Economics,' in J. Groenewegen (Ed.), *Teaching Pluralism in Economics*, Cheltenham: Edward Elgar, pp. 22–39.

Earle, J., Moran, C., and Ward-Perkins, Z. (2017) *The Econocracy: The Perils of Leaving Economics to the Experts*, Manchester: The University of Manchester Press.

Flannery, T. (2005) *The Weather Makers*, New York: Atlantic Monthly Press.

Garnett, R. and Reardon, J. (2012) 'Pluralism in Economics Education,' in G. Hoyt and K. McGoldrick (Eds.), *International Handbook on Teaching and Learning Economics*, Cheltenham: Edward Elgar, pp. 242–249.

George, H. (1879 [1948]) *Progress and Poverty*, New York: Robert Schalkenbach Foundation.

Groenewegen, J. (2007) 'On Pluralism and Interdisciplinarity in Economics,' in J. Groenewegen (Ed.), *Teaching Pluralism in Economics*, Cheltenham: Edward Elgar, pp. 1–21.

Heise, A. (2017) 'Defining Economic Pluralism: Ethical Norm or Scientific Imperative?' *International Journal of Pluralism and Economics Education*, Vol. 8, No. 1, pp. 18–41.

Hill, R. and Myatt, T. (2010) *The Economics Anti-Textbook: A Critical Thinker's Guide to Microeconomics*, London: Zed Books.

Hodgson, G.M. (1999) *Evolution and Institutions: On Evolutionary Economics and the Evolution of Economics*, Cheltenham: Edward Elgar.

Lavoie, M. (2015) 'Should Heterodox Economics Be Taught In or Outside of Economics Departments?' *International Journal of Pluralism and Economics Education*, Vol. 6, No. 2, pp. 134–150.

Lee, F. (2009) *A History of Heterodox Economics: Challenging the Mainstream in the Twentieth Century*, London: Routledge.

Lemstra, W. (2007) 'A Practitioner's Perspective on Interdisciplinarity in Education: The MBT Case,' in J. Groenewegen (Ed.), *Teaching Pluralism in Economics*, Cheltenham: Edward Elgar, pp. 140–154.

Madden, K. and Dimand, R. (Eds.) (2019) *The Routledge Handbook of the History of Women's Economic Thought*, London: Routledge.

Marshall, A. (1890 [1946]) *Principles of Economics*, London: Macmillan.

McNeil, J.R. (2000) *Something New Under the Sun: An Environmental History of the Twentieth Century World*, New York: W.W. Norton and Company.

Negru, I. (2009) 'Reflections on Pluralism in Economics,' *International Journal of Pluralism and Economics Education*, Vol. I, Nos 1/2. pp. 7–21.

Negru, I. (2010) 'Plurality to Pluralism in Economics Pedagogy: The Role of Critical Thinking,' *International Journal of Pluralism and Economics Education*, Vol. I, No. 3, pp. 185–193.

Post-Autistic Economics Network (2000) 'Open Letter from Economics Students to Professors and Others Responsible for the Teaching of this Discipline.' Available at: www.paecon.ndet?PAEtexts/a-epetition.htm.

Reardon, J. (Ed.) (2009) *The Handbook of Pluralist Economics Education*, London: Routledge.

Reardon, J. (2012) 'A Radical Reformation of Economics Education: Educating Real World Economists,' *Real-World Economics Review*, No. 62, 15 December, pp. 2–19. Available at: www.paecon.net/PAEReview/issue62/Reardon62.pdf.

Reardon, J. (2017a) 'Editorial: When Will Economics Become Pluralist?' *International Journal of Pluralism and Economics Education*, Vol. 8, No. 1, pp. 7–13.

Reardon, J. (2017b) 'Why Economics Needs its Own Reformation: 95 Theses,' *International Journal of Pluralism and Economics Education*, Vol. 8, No. 4, pp. 319–329.

Reardon, J. (2018) 'Book Review: Free to Choose Medicine,' by Bartley J. Madden *International Journal of Pluralism and Economics Education*, Vol. 9, No. 4, pp. 425–428.

Reardon, J., Madi, M., and Cato, M. (2018) *Introducing a New Economics: Pluralist, Sustainable, Progressive*, London: Pluto Press.

Rethinking Economics (2014) www.rethinkeconomics.org/#!our-vision/colf.

Roundtable: Dialogue on Pluralism (2015) *International Journal of Pluralism and Economics Education*, Vol. 6, No. 3, pp. 272–308.

Schumacher, E.F. (1973 [1989]) *Small is Beautiful—Economics as if People Mattered*, New York: Harper Perennial.

Siegfried, J. (2009) 'Really Thinking Like an Economist,' in D. Colander and K. McGoldrick (Eds.), *Educating Economists: The Teagel Discussion on Re-evaluating the Undergraduate Economics Major*, Cheltenham: Edward Elgar, pp. 215–233.

Siegfried, J. and Meszaros, B. (1997) 'National Voluntary Content Standards for Pre-College Economics Education,' *American Economic Review*, Vol. 87, No. 2, pp. 247–253.

Söderbaum, P. (2008) *Understanding Sustainability in Economics: Towards Pluralism in Economics*, London: Earthscan.

Söderbaum, P. and Brown, J. (2011) 'Pluralism and Democracy in Political Economics,' *International Journal of Pluralism and Economics Education*, Vol. 2, No. 3, pp. 240–243.

Stillwell, F. (2011) 'Teaching a Pluralist Course in Economics: The University of Sydney Experience,' *International Journal of Pluralism and Economics Education*, Vol. 2, No. 1, pp. 39–56.

Stillwell, F. (2012) *Political Economy: The Contest of Economic Ideas*, Oxford: University of Oxford Press.

Thornton, T. (2017) *From Economics to Political Economy: The Problems, Promises and Solutions of Pluralist Economics*, London: Routledge.

WCED (World Commission on Environment and Development) (1987) *Our Common Future*, Oxford: Oxford University Press.

Postscript

Victoria Chick

It is symptomatic of the distortion of present-day economics that some approaches to the subject are defined in opposition to the approach which, because of its dominant position, we call mainstream or orthodoxy (the current approaches that count as orthodoxy were not always in that position, and may or may not remain so). The perception of the majority of economists – sometimes even the heterodox – is that we are united only by our opposition to mainstream economics, and to call ourselves heterodox reinforces that perception. But at least we acknowledge the existence of the orthodox alternative, whereas the mainstream does not acknowledge us as economists at all: we are beyond the pale – a pale they have erected around their approach and which they use to avoid any contamination by non-mainstream approaches.

In a recent post on the Social Europe blog,[1] Jayati Ghosh wrote of the dangers of such isolation. She cited the example of Tasmania, which had a rich set of tools and technologies some 12,000 years ago until it was cut off from mainland Australia by the melting of the polar ice cap. After that it not only stopped developing but also lost many of the advances it had already achieved. This was her model of the regressed pool of knowledge of the present-day mainstream.[2]

At the time of founding the Association for Heterodox Economics (AHE) 20 years ago, heterodox economists were in a rather similar state: the different schools of thought carried out their own research programmes without much interchange. The AHE was founded to improve dialogue between heterodox schools of thought. The pioneering work of Sheila Dow (1985, 1996)[3] and others on the methodological foundations of the different schools of thought revealed that more than simple dialogue could be achieved. Having realised that the opposition to orthodoxy was founded on methodological differences, we were now in a position to work to establish common methodological ground and, on the basis of that work, foster collaborative work to arrive at new insights.

This progression is mirrored in the discussions of pluralism. Early discussions were about approaching a subject from more than one point of view – the dialogue phase. They have moved on to what Ioana Negru has called 'pluralism by integration'[4] – incorporating insights from more than one school of thought, based on compatible methodology. This is quite new, and in its infancy, but there are explorations of this approach in this volume. I doubt that, without the forum provided by the AHE, heterodoxy would have come this far by now.

The problem with earlier attempts at synthesis – or indeed the resolution of differences – was that the methodological foundations of the relevant theories were not explored: the argument was entirely at the level of theory. This gave rise to the monster of the Neoclassical synthesis, which mixed a Keynesian demand story with neoclassical aggregate supply theory, the latter being able to generate unemployment only with an assumption (not, as with Keynes, an empirical observation) of sticky wages. The call for choice-theoretic microfoundations to Keynesian macroeconomics is another case in point. Both these constructions paste together a theory which demands certainty with one based on uncertainty – mutually exclusive categories.

The mainstream has little time for methodology. (Mind you, if I had built theories based on perfect certainty into the infinite future, I too would try to hide the fact.) One way to get around the difficulty of knowing the future – a fairly obvious impossibility – is to abolish time in your theories. The timeless world is one where the mainstream feels comfortable but the heterodox do not. We know that economies are evolving systems, where institutions and the behaviours they help to shape are changing all the time. The timeless method of statics may serve in physics – after all, atoms have been doing the same thing for aeons: but human beings think and innovate. That is the course of unpredictability; it is also the source of progress – or, in the case of the Global Financial Crisis, disaster. It means that all theories are context-dependent, even though we might not recognise the fact. That, in turn, leads to a concern with the history of economic thought, where the structure of the economy being discussed is rarely made explicit in the original texts, but which shapes the thinking of the economist trying to explain its workings. Hence the strong interest shared by the heterodox in the history of economic thought – another area with which the mainstream has little truck. While the mainstream looks for 'universal laws', as in their model subject, physics, the heterodox search out the circumstances and structures that existed at the time the theories were being formulated.[5]

There are many more similarities, but these are, I think, the main ones. Their only link to a rejection of orthodoxy is that orthodoxy does not think these issues are interesting and we think they are. There is plenty of work to be done by a comparatively small band of like-minded people if we are to forge an economics that more closely corresponds to the problems we face than the profession's accepted wisdom. The AHE is here to keep the dialogue flowing, keeping us on our theoretical mettle and preventing the dangers of isolation that have contributed to the present uselessness of much mainstream theory. And if the mainstream were to ever show an inclination to open up, we will talk to them too.

Notes

1 Jayati Ghosh (2019) *Social Europe*, 22 October. Available at www.socialeurope.eu/our-shrinking-economic-toolkits (accessed 22 October 2018).
2 Her source for the material relating to Tasmania is J. Henrich (2015) *The Secret of our Success*, Princeton, NJ: Princeton University Press.
3 S. C. Dow (1985) *Macroeconomic Thought: A Methodological Approach*, Oxford: Blackwell; (1996) *The Methodology of Macroeconomic Thought*, Cheltenham: Edward Elgar.
4 Ioana Negru (2018) Is CORE a pluralist economics curriculum? *WEA Blog*, 28 May (but listed as 31 May in the index). Available at https://weapedagogy.wordpress.com/2018/05/28/is-core-a-pluralist-economics-curriculum/. Unfortunately, Samuel Bowles and Wendy Carlin (2018) How to fix university economics courses, *Financial Times*, 16 February. Available at www.ft.com/content/bfd5ac14-fa11-11e7-9bfc-052cbba03425How (accessed 28 October 2019), use the same term to mean something quite different: essentially cherry-picking 'insights' and bringing them together without considering whether their methodological backgrounds and/or worldviews are compatible – an undesirable approach in my view.
5 A beautiful example of this approach is K. Niebyl (1946) *Studies in Classical Theories of Money*, New York: Columbia University Press.

Index

Note: Page numbers in *italics* indicate figures and in **bold** indicate tables on the corresponding pages.

abstract labour 101, 102
active learning 293
additive utility 111
agency 53–54
airports, public ownership of 201–204
Allen, F. 163
allocations mechanisms 43
'American dream' 50
American Economic Association 41
archaeology 38–39, 45
Ardzooni, L. 124
Aristotle 92
Arndt, H. W. 177
Arrow and Sen 40, 41
Association for Heterodox Economics (AHE) 1, 161, 275, 277, 299–300; macroeconomics and 166–167
Association of Heterodox Economists Conference 262
atomism 35
austerity policies 117
Austrian School of Economics 41, 42, 101, 111, 124
autonomous thinking 53–54
Ayres, C. 124

Barba, A. 152
Barry, J. 43
Beck, U. 35–37, 43
Bentham, J. 111
Berle, A. A. 124
Bernanke, B. 149–150
Bertrand, J. 17
Bhaskar, R. 65
Bigo, V. 279
Big Push investment strategy 171
Böhm-Bawerk, E. 111, 112
Bonbright, J. C. 124
Bowles, S. 295
Brancaccio, E. 153
Brexit 34, 48
Buhalis, D. 219

Cabezas, A. 215
Calvin, J. 50–51
Cambridge Journal 262
Cambridge Journal of Economics 27
Cantrell, P. 263
Capital 67–69, 79, 101–107
Capital and Class 262
Capital in the 21st Century 141
capitalism 48–49; autonomous thinking in 53–54; decline of Enlightenment critical thinking in economic science and 51–54; demand in 72–73; from Enlightenment to today 49–51; finance in 50–51, 122–123; mercantilist 50
'Capitalism. Competition, Conflict, Crises' 32
cardinal utility 111
Caribbean, the *see* tourism, Caribbean
Carney, M. 150
Cedrini, M. 278
center-periphery 171
central banking 141–142, 165, 259, 266–267; inequality and 147–150
chartalism 117
Chicago School 124
Chick, V. 279
China 91
Circuit Theorists 71–72, 73
Citizen's Income 89

Clarivate's Web of Science 233–234
Clark, J. M. 124
climate emergency *see* Green Economics
Coase, R. 30
Cobb, J. B. 44
Cobham, A. 147
cognitive dissonance 53
Colander, D. 160
Collected Scientific Papers 19
colonial rule in the Caribbean 210–211, 215–216, 217, 224
Commons, J. R. 44, 124, 125; on social value 131; Theory of Reasonable Value and of Negotiational Psychology 126
competition: false identification of perfect competition with real-life 21–22; perfect stagnation vs. dynamic 22–23, 28
Comte, A. 36
Constancio, V. 267
Cooper, B. 263
Cooper, P. 73–78
Copeland, M. A. 124
Courvisanos, J. 263
credit creation and rationing 122–123
critical realism (CR) 66
critical social science 37
critical thinking 48–49; decline of, in economic science 51–54
Cronin, B. 231–234
crowding out effect 117
cruise tourism 216–217
cultural assassination and tourism 217–218
cultural relativism 131–133
Currency School 51, 79
Currie, M. 20
Curtis, A. 52

Daly, H. E. 44
Dark Mountain Project 53
Deakin, S. 44
Debreu, G. 19–20, 21
deflation 120–122
degree of monopoly 74
demand management 44
demiregularities 66
democratic planning 130–133
Denis, A. 263
dependency theory 211–213
Detter, D. 192
Dewey, J. 124
dialectical processes 54–56
Dimmelmeier, A. 263
discursive rules 38–39
Disequlibrium Foundations of Equilibrium Economics 23–24
Dobb, M. 262
dopamine 53
dualism 277, 278
Dugger, W. M. 129
dynamic competition 22–23
Dynamic Stochastic General Equilibrium (DSGE) models 148
dynamics vs. statics: false identification of 'perfect competition' with real-life competition and 21–22; Franklin M. Fisher on 23–25; future for heterodox economics and 31–32; Goodwin and Schumpeter on 27–28; Hodgson and Cambridge as heterodox citadel and 25–26; Hodgson and Lawson on economics and ideology and 29–31; introduction to 13–14; mathematical-logical exercise and 19–20; Pasinetti on Keynes' unaccomplished revolution and 26–27; perfect stagnation vs. dynamic competition and 22–23; Robinson and Kaldor on Keynes and 28–29; role of general equilibrium in shaping economic policy and 20–21; scientific and vulgar economics and 14–19

Earl, P. 261
Earle, J. 283, 285–286, 290, 294
ecological economics 44
Econocracy: The Perils of Leaving Economics to the Experts, The 283
Economica 119
Economic Commission for Latin America and the Caribbean (ECLAC) 175, 186, 211
economics: allocation mechanisms in 43; archaeology and genealogy of 38–39, 45; decline of Enlightenment critical thinking in 51–54; diversity in 92–93; ecological 44; formation of inclusive 57–59; Green New Deal 34, 41–44; hidden history of 39–41; institutional 124–127; laissez-faire 39–40; neoliberal 123, 212; as part of governance 37–38; renamed political economy 295–296; silo mentality in 88, 89, 90; social power and history

of 37–39; steady state 118–119; vulgar 14–19, 53; *see also* Green Economics; neoclassical economics
economics education: improving pluralism in 289–296; introduction to 282–284; pluralism fundamentals in 284–289
'Economics and Ideology' 13
Economics of Welfare 28
Eggertsson, G. 163
ego 128
Elements 20
Elizabeth II, Queen 90
Elsevier 233–234
Ely, R. T. 124
Employer of Last Resort (ELR) policy 79
endogenous money 6, 117
environmentalism 5, 7
epistemological pluralism 284
Epstein, G. 154
Espinosa, P. 87
Essays in Persuasion 118

Fay, B. 36–37
fear 53
Feuerbach, M. 55
finance, capitalist 50–51, 122–123
Fisher, F. M. 23–25
Fisher, I. 16, 17, 18
Foley, D. 77
Fölster, S. 192
Fontan, C. 142
Fontana, G. 153
Fontana, M. 278
Foster, J. F. 124
Foucault, M. 34, 37–39, 45, 52, 56
Freeman, A. 68, 102, 103
Freud, S. 127–128
Friedman, M. 166
Fugger, J. 51
Furtado, C. 171, 172, 176, 177, 185

Gala, P. 181
Galbraith, J. K. 44, 124
genealogy 39
General Agreement on Tariffs and Trade (GATT) 212
general equilibrium theory 20–21
General Theory (GT) 26, 27–29
General Theory of Employment, Interest and Money 120, 123, 151
George, H. 195, 282
Ghosh, J. 299
Gibbs, W. 18
Gini coefficient 144–147, *145–146*
Global Financial Crisis, 2007–2008 90, 141, 150, 160–161, 166–167; problems with neoclassical economics and 162–163
globalization 52, 224
global value chains (GVC): conclusions on 186–187; industry as protagonist and 172–177; introduction to 171–172; new center and periphery division in context of 177–186, *178*, *180*, *182*, **183**
governance 37–38
governmentality 38
Gowreesunkar, V. 222
Green Economics: destructive economic theory, education and policies and 89–90; eruption of protest and 90–92; heterodoxy joining 96; introduction to 87–89; knowledge economy and 93–94; precondition of diversity in 92–93; suggestions for economists, politicians, and individuals 94–96
Green movement 44
Green New Deal 34, 41–44, 89
Groenewegen, J. 291
Guerrien, B. 21

Haavelmo, T. 26, 29
Hahn, F. 23
Haila, A. 194–195
Haldane, A. G. 150
Hamilton, W. H. 124, 125
Hartmann, D. 181
Hausmann, R. 179
Haveli, J. 71
Hayek, F. A. 22, 41, 57
Hegel, G. W. F. 49, 57; concept of master/slave 58; dialectic of 54–56
Heinemann, V. 88
Heinrich, M. 102
heterodox economics 1–3, 24–25; Cambridge as citadel of 25–26; explaining economic imbalances from perspective of 3–8; future of 31–32; Green Economics joining with 96; mainstream economists' view of 66–67; methodology of 63–67; open-system approach of 278–279; pluralism and 66, 275–280; policy action and 6–8

Heterodox Journal Quality Score (HJQS) 231–233; compared to new bibliometrics 235–236; conclusions on 241–242; recent developments in bibliometric ranking of journals and 233–234; results of **236–240**, 236–241, **243–258**
Hicks 13, 20
Hidalgo, C. A. 179
Hirsch, F. 124
Hirschman, A. 124, 171, 173, 174
History of Economic Analysis 27
Hobbes, T. 54
Hodgson, G. 13–14, 21, 24, 27, 131; on Cambridge as heterodox citadel 25–26; on economics and ideology 29–31
Hong Kong *see* public ownership in Hong Kong and Singapore
housing, public ownership in 197–199
human trafficking 93
Hymer, S. 224

ideology 29–31
imbalances, economic: conclusions on addressing 133–134; implications for economic and social issues 128–133; institutional economics and 124–127; macroeconomic 116–119; psychoanalytic perspective on 127–128; stagflation 119–123
inclusive economics 57–59
income inequality *see* inequality
industrialization 172–177
inequality: definition of 142–143; mainstream, central banker's and 147–150; post-Keynesians and 151–152; trends and facts of 143–147, *144–145*
inflation 119–122
Ingrao, B. 20
Instinct of Workmanship and the State of the Industrial Arts, The 125–126
Institute for New Economic Thinking (INET) 90
institutional economics 124–127; psychological contributions of 125–127
Institutional Economics, Its Place in Political Economy 126
institutionalism 5, 7
Institutional Practices: introduction to 259–260; pluralism and pedagogy and 260–264; three claims based on 265–267
instrumental value 131–133
Inter-American Development Bank 211
interest rates 152–156, *155–156*
International Journal of Pluralism and Economics Education (IJPEE) 284, 287, 290
International Journal of Political Economy 262
International Monetary Fund 211
International Review of Applied Economics 262
Israel, G. 20
'Is there a Future for Heterodox Economics?' 13

James, C. L. R. 224
James, W. 124
Jevons, W. S. 40, 42
Jevons Paradox 42
Journal of Post Keynesian Economics 262
Juniper, J. 263

Kaldor, N. 28–29, 31, 32
Kalecki, M. 41, 71–76, 151, 173–175, 177, 181
Kant, I. 55, 57
Kapp, K. W. 43
Keen, S. 166
Kennet, M. 88
Keynes and the Cambridge Keynesians: A "Revolution in Economics" to be accomplished 25
Keynesianism/Keynes, J. M. 41, 52, 300; on critical thinking 53–54; demand principle 174; differences between Goodwin and 27–28; on inflation and deflation 121; Robinson and Kaldor on 28–29; stagflation and 119–122; on steady state 118–119; theoretical approach of 69; unaccomplished revolution of 26–27, 29; wage and price flexibility and 122–123; *see also* post-Keynesianism
Kliman, A. 68, 102–104
knowledge economy 93–94
Korstanje, M. 222
Krugman, P. 160–161, 163
Kuhn, T. S. 38–39, 52, 64, 262; on crisis and scientific revolution 65
Kumhof, M. 148

labour, individual and social amounts of 104–105, **105**
labour-time 77–78
Lagrange 17
laissez-faire 39–40, 120–121
Lakatos, I. 65, 262
land, public ownership of 193–197
Lavoie, M. 154
Lawson, T. 13–14, 65, 66; on economics and ideology 29–31; on surprise element 66
Le Châtelier principle 18
Lee, F. 66–67, 288
Lee, F. S. 231–234
Lee, K. Y. 196, 198
legal institutionalism 44
leisure classes 53
Lerner, A. P. 70
Leviathan concept 54–55
Lipsey-Lancaster theorem 20
liquidity preference 28
List, F. 171
Locke, J. 49
Lubin, I. 124

macroeconomics 259–260; and the AHE 166–167; as contested area 259; imbalances in 116–119; imperfections in 4–6; orthodox principles for first-year course in 264–265; pluralism and 259–268
Magacho, G. 181
mainstream economists and inequality 147–150
maladministration 43
Manchester Post-Crash Society 90
Mandeville, B. 50
Mannheim, K. 7
Marginalist school 14–15
market failure 20
market management 44
Marshall, A. 31, 39, 41, 52, 68, 289–290
Martyn, R. 260–261
'Marx, Marshall and Keynes' 28
Marxists/Marx 5, 6, 7, 52, 63; compatibility between Kalecki, MMT, and 73–76; contending interpretations of 101–104; on critical thinking 49; critique of labour theory of value 40; dialectic of 54–56; economic theory of 68–69; on essence of man as communal 57–58; exploration of capitalism by 67–68; on language of economics 51; learning from post-Keynesians 78–79; on materialism 55–56; Monetary Expression of Labour-Time (MELT) 76–78; on profit as capitalist's motive 21; on 'Realabstraktionen' 32; on relationship between production and sales prices 108–109; Resource-based Theory (RBT) and 101–107; Silesian Weavers uprising of 1844 and 56; Temporal Single System Interpretation (TSSI) 72–73, 76, 78, 101–107; transformation of production values into production prices by 105–107, **106**; value theory of 19–20, 76–78, 102; vulgar economics and 14, 53
master/slave concept 58
materialism 55–56
McCloskey, D. N. 276
McGlone, T. 103–104
Mead, G. H. 124
Means, G. C. 124
Mearman, A. 263, 280
Mecanique Analytique 17
Menger, C. 111
mental labor 54
methodological pluralism 277–279, 285
microeconomic imperfections 3–4
Milberg, W. 184
Miles, D. 149
Mirowski, P. 14–19
Mitchell, D. 263
Mitchell, W. 41, 124, 125
mixed economies 116, 117
Modern Macroeconomics 92
Modern Monetary Theory (MMT) 63, 67, 70–76, 78–79, 117, 260, 264
modes of domination 52
Mohun, S. 103
Molloy, J. C. 100, 112
Monetary Expression of Labour-Time (MELT) 76–78
monetary policy, post-Keynesian 152–156, *155–156*
monism 277
monocultures of the mind 88
monopolies 75–76
Moon, B. K. 88
Moore, B. J. 153
Moran, C. 283
'More Heat Than Light: Economics as Social Physics, Physics as Nature's Economics' 14

Morgenstern, O. 22–23
Moseley, F. 69, 73
Myrdal, G. 39, 124

Nagatani, K. 102
Nakajima, M. 149, 150
narratives of power 56
naturalism 35
need or right allocation mechanism 43
Negru, I. 279, 299–300
Nelsen, A. 94
neoclassical economics 39–40, 48, 121–122, 124, 160–161; central banking and 147–150; destructive policies and 89–90; heterodox alternative to 65; methodology in 63; problems with 161–166
neo-Keynesian models 5
neoliberalism 123, 212
neo-Marxism 5
New Consensus Macroeconomics (NCM) 66
new institutional economics (NIE) 124
New Interpretation 102
New York Times 160
nominalism 35
non-truth 49
Nurkse, R. 173–174

objectivity 35
Oedipus complex 128, 129
Ogburn, W. 124
old institutional economics (OIE) 124, 129
ontological pluralism 284–285
ordinal utility 40
orthodox economics 2–3, 24–25; Austrian School and 41; closed-system approach of 278–279; destructive acts justified with 87–88, 89–90; evolution of 277–278; explaining economic imbalances from perspective of 3–8; macroeconomic principles for first-year course 264–265; methodology of 63–67; normative power of 20; understanding of the social world in 276; utility maximisation in 21–22
Orwell, G. 91

Palma ratio 147
Pareto, V. 14, 16–18, 40
Paris COP21 climate conference 95
Pasinetti, L. L. 25, 26–27
Pasinetti index 153, *155*, *156*
Pattullo, P. 213–214
Paul Samuelson and the Stability of General Equilibrium 24
pedagogical pluralism 285
Peirce, C. S. 124
Perez, M. 103
perfect competition 21–22, 28, 89–90
perfect stagnation 22–23, 28
phenomenalism 35
Phillips, A. W. 119
Phillips Curve 119–122
Pigou, A. C. 39, 42
Piketty, T. 141, 142, 147
Pitts, F. H. 102
Pivetti, M. 152
planning: democratic 130–133; economic 129–130
Plato 92
pluralism 2, 6–8, 53, 87, 259–260, 299–300; arguments for and against 286–287; assessment of 288; defined 276–277, 284–285; as disciplinary, multi-disciplinary, interdisciplinary, or trans-disciplinary 288–289; epistemological 284; evidence of efficacy of 287; fundamentals of 284–289; Green Economics and 92–93, 94–95; Hegel/Marx dialectic and 54–56; heterodox economics and 66, 275–280; how to improve 289–296; improved in economics education 282–296; Institutional Practices and 259–268; limits in 286; macroeconomics and 259–268; of method 285; methodological 277–279, 285; ontological 284–285; pedagogy and 260–264, 285; pluralist vs. 285–286; theoretical 276, 284
pluralist methodology 276
Polanyi, K. 124
Polanyi, M. 124
policy action 6–8
political economy 295–296
politics of truth 38
Poon, A. 222
Popper, K. 64
positivism 35, 36, 166
post-Keynesianism 5, 6, 7, 63, 67; compatibility between Marx, MMT, and 73–76; inequality and 151–152; interest rates and monetary policy in 152–156, *155–156*; investment/savings

model in 69, 71–72; learning from Marxists 78–79; Modern Monetary Theory (MMT) and 63, 67, 70–76, 78–79; sectoral balances approach in 70; *see also* Keynesianism/ Keynes, J. M.
post-truth 48
Potts, N. 103
power 37–39; narratives of 56
Pragmatism 124
Pratten, S. 67
Prebisch, R. 171, 173, 175, 177, 185
Prescott, J. 203
price allocation mechanism 43
price and wage flexibility 122–123
Principles of Economics 289–290
private property 49–50
private sector economy 116–117, 221–222
Production of Commodities by Means of Commodities 262
profit 76, 101, 116, 123–124
'protestant work-ethic' 50
protests 34, 35, 90–92
psychoanalytic perspective 127–128
psychological contributions of institutional economics 125–127
public companies 199–200
public ownership in Hong Kong and Singapore: of airports 201–204; fairness of 192–193; in housing 197–199; introduction to 191–192; of land 193–197; lessons from Singapore and Hong Kong 204–205; public companies and 199–200; of railways 200–201

railways, public ownership of 200–201
Ramey, E. 263
Ranciere, R. 148
Rank, O. 127
rate of exploitation 75–76
rational consumer 2
rationing 43
Reardon, J. 289
reasonable value 130–131
Recherches 17
rentiers 154–155
Resource-based Theory (RBT): addressing unresolved question within 107–108, **108**; contenting interpretations of Marx and 101–104; further discussion on 111–112; introduction to 100–101; method for measuring effect of firm-specific and market factors and 109–111, **111**; relationship between production and sales prices in 108–109; TSSI and 101–107
Rethinking Economics 90, 275, 283, 285
Review of Political Economy 262
Review of Radical Political Economics 262
Ricardo, D. 39–40, 51, 68, 195, 262
Rifkin, J. 94
Risk Society 35–37, 41, 44
Robbins, L. 41, 42
Robinson, J. 26, 28–29, 32, 40, 50, 52
Rocha, I. 181
Rochon, L.-P. 152
Rodrik, D. 179
Romer, P. 161, 165–166
Rosenstein-Rodan, P. 171, 173
Rothbard, M. 51
Rousseau, J.-J. 57

Samuels, W. J. 131, 277
Samuelson, P. 13, 18–19, 24; revealed preference approach of 40
Samuelsonian Economics and the Twenty-First Century 24
Say's Law 73
Schumpeter, J. 27–28
science 35–37; best practice in 64; crisis and revolutions in 65; demiregularities in 66; Theory-Ladenness in 64
scientificity 2–3, 19
scientific rationality 36
scientific theory 64
Scopus 233–234
Sealy, W. 216
Seccareccia, M. 154, 155
sectoral balances approach 70
Seiferling, M. 199
Sen, A. 212
Séraphin, H. 222
Setterfield, M. 152
Shaik, A. 14, 32
Sharot, T. 53
Shaw, G. B. 26
Siegfried, J. 290
Silesian Weavers uprising of 1844 56
silo mentality 88, 89, 90
Sim, I. 200
Simultaneous Dual System Interpretation (SDSI) 102

Simultaneous Single System Interpretation (SSSI) 102
simultaneous valuation 102–103
Singapore *see* public ownership in Hong Kong and Singapore
Smith, A. 50, 51, 89, 195
Smith, M. J. 35
socialism 56
social physics 14–19
social power 37–39
social security system, China 91
social value 130–131
Society of Heterodox Economists 262
Sraffa, P. 69, 152, 262
stagflation 119–123
stagnation, perfect 22–23, 28
statics *see* dynamics vs. statics
steady state economies 118–119
Steedman, I. 20, 68
Stewart, W. 124
Stiglitz, J. 147, 162–163
Stilwell, F. 296
structural factors in mixed economies 117–118
structural transformations 116–119
Sumner, A. 147
superego 118, 128, 129
surplus-value 73, 74–75
Survey of Consumer Finances 149

Taouil, R. 71
Tareq, S. 199
Tavares, M. C. 185–186
taxation, Pigouvian 42
Taylor, J. B. 153
Taylor, F. 41
Temporal Single System Interpretation (TSSI) 72–73, 76, 78; method for measuring effect of firm-specific and market factors and 110–111, **111**; Resource-based Theory (RBT) and 101–107; transformation of production values into production prices under 104–107, **105**, **106**
Thatcher, M. 191
theoretical pluralism 276, 284
Théorie Mathématique de la Richesse Sociale 17
Theory-Ladenness 64
Theory of Instincts 125–126
Theory of Reasonable Value and of Negotiational Psychology 126
'Theory of Value: An Axiomatic Analysis, The' 19–20
Thornton, T. 286
Toms, S. 101
Tool, M. R. 130, 131
tourism, Caribbean: academic institutions and civic society and 223; all-inclusive hotels in 214–216; conclusions on 223–224; cruise 216–217; cultural assassination and 217–218; dependency theory and 211–213; destination marketing companies and 222–223; exclusion, polarization, marginalization in 216; government policy and 220–221; historical background of 210–211; introduction to 209–210; nature and impact of transnational hotels in 213–214; private sector and 221–222; recommendations for 219–223; tour operators and wholesalers and 218–219
transcendental realism 65
Truman, H. 211
Trump, D. 48
Tugan-Baranowsky, M. 102
Tymoigne, E. 266

under-labouring 78
Union of Radical Political Economists 262
United Nations Development Agency 211
United Nations Framework Convention on Climate Change (UNFCCC) 87, 91
universal laws 35
usury 50–51
utility maximisation 21–22, 63

Value-Form Interpretation 102
value theory 19–20, 76–78, 102
Veblen, T. 40, 44, 53, 124–125; Theory of Instincts 125–126
Veneziani, R. 103
voluntary constraints and fiscal policy 266
vulgar economics 14–19, 53

wages 77–78, 120; full employment and flexibility in price and 122–123
Wagner, A. 116
Walras, L. 13, 14, 16, 17, 20
Ward-Perkins, Z. 283

Washington Consensus 193
Webb, D. 195
Winkler, D. 184
World Bank 211, 212
World Economics Association 275
Wray, L. R. 76
Wrenn, M. 52

Yellen, J. 141
Young Scholars Initiative (YSI) 90